Great
Economic
Debate

CY GONICK

The Great Economic Debate

Failed Economics and
a Future for Canada

James Lorimer & Company, Publishers
Toronto, 1987

Copyright © 1987 by James Lorimer & Company, Publishers

All rights reserved. No part of this book may be reproduced or transmitted in any form or by any means, electronic, or mechanical, including photocopying, or by any information storage or retrieval system, without permission in writing from the publisher.

Design: Brant Cowie/Artplus.
Figure illustrations: Dave Hunter.
Cover photographs of Marx, Galbraith and Friedman reproduced courtesy of Canpress Photo Service.
Author photo: Sooters Photographers, Winnipeg, Man.

Canadian Cataloguing in Publication Data

Gonick, Cy, 1936-

   The Great Economic Debate

   ISBN 0-88862-702-5(bound). - ISBN 0-88862-701-7(pbk.)
1. Canada - Economic conditions - 1971- * I. Title.
HC115.G65 1986   330.971   C84-098203-8

James Lorimer & Company, Publishers
Egerton Ryerson Building
35 Britain Street
Toronto, Ontario M5A 1R7

Printed and bound in Canada
5 4 3 2 1   87 88 89 90 91

To
Alice and Jesse Vorst
Friends for all seasons

Contents

Acknowledgements ix

Introduction xi

Part I: Contested Terrain 1

1 Ways of Seeing 3
2 Economic Theory and Ideology 19
3 Orthodoxy and Its Reformers 44

Part II: The Rise and Fall of Keynesianism 71

4 Keynes' Vision 73
5 Was There a Keynesian Revolution? 85

Part III: The New Right 103

6 Monetarism and Supply-Side Economics 105
7 The New Right: Theory and Practice 126

Part IV: The Post-Keynesian Response 143

8 The New State Interventionists 145
9 Incomes Policy: Theory and Practice 168
10 Industrial Policy 189
11 Industrial Democracy 209

Part V: Radical Political Economy 229

12 Income and Class 231
13 Where Do Profits Come From? 244
14 Business and the State 275
15 The Economic Roller Coaster 301

Part VI: The Economic Crisis 315

16 From Depression to Prosperity and Back 316
17 The Road to Recovery? 345

Afterword: Another Way Forward 381

Notes 389

Index 410

Acknowledgements

I would like to thank my friend and colleague Jesse Vorst who read through an early draft of several chapters; Marg Derry for her fabulous contribution on the word processor; Ted Mumford for his excellent editorial guidance; Linda Biesenthal who helped whip the manuscript into readable shape; my students who sat through my lectures on these subjects these past few years; the Industrial Relations Research Unit, University of Warwick, for offering me the use of its facilities in the fall of 1984 when I first began researching this book; and Arzina Burney for her help and encouragement.

Introduction

It is now eleven years since I wrote *Inflation or Depression: An Analysis of the Continuing Crisis of the Canadian Economy*. Jim Lorimer, on the receiving end of the chapters I was submitting, was becoming increasingly anxious. At one point he called me long-distance. "Do you realize this book will be over 400 pages? Are you sure this crisis will last because if it doesn't I'll never sell enough copies to cover my costs!"

It was a perfectly sensible concern. Back then it was not generally recognized that the recession of that year (1975), severe though it was, was merely one symptom of a massive economic convulsion that would take years to unfold. *Inflation or Depression* charted the early years of the crisis. It was still not at all clear how governments would respond. The language of liberalism, so predominant over the previous quarter century, had become virtually invisible. Keynesianism, the reigning economic doctrine, was in obvious trouble but the theoretical foundation for a sharp turn to the Right was barely in place.

In ten short years we have seen a remarkable counter-revolution of ideas and policy. The New Right has seized the ideological terrain, defining the issues, setting the agenda for change. Though dominant at the moment, it by no means has the field to itself. The crisis in the economy is matched by a crisis in economics. In fact, the crisis has given rise to a great economic debate. What caused this crisis? What new economic arrangements are required for recovery and renewal?

This book's structure mirrors this great economic debate. Alternative theoretical conceptions are presented on their own terms and are then subjected to a critique. I draw upon these as I proceed and end with my own analysis, which derives from the rejuvenated tradition of radical political economy.

Since ideology has played such a key role in the crisis and indeed in all history, Part I of *The Great Economic Debate* is concerned with how ideologies work and how they are lodged in economic analysis and economic policy. How does ideology blinker or enhance our understanding of reality? And how does economic reality in turn affect ideologies? These questions are explored through the classical economic theory of Adam Smith and the reformers who followed him and through current issues like free trade and deregulation.

Part II outlines the forgotten vision of John Maynard Keynes and the distortion of his economics as it was translated into Keynesianism in the Cold War years of postwar prosperity. Examining its policy application in this period, chapter 5 shows that the Canadian government's commitment to full employment has always been more rhetorical than real. Finally, the demise of Keynesianism is explored, in particular its inherent inability to maintain prosperity in times of declining profitability.

Part III outlines the rise of New Right economics in the form of monetarism and supply-side economics. It dissects the theoretical foundations of this neo-conservatism and examines their post-1975 application in Canadian economic policy.

Part IV looks at the revival of post-Keynesian economic thought in the late 1970s as an interventionist route out of the economic crisis. The genesis of its alternative — incomes policy, industrial policy, industrial democracy — is outlined, and each one of these major planks in the post-Keynesianism platform is scrutinized from the point of theory and Canadian and European practice.

Part V offers a radical political economy approach to understanding how our economy works, focusing on the generation of profit, the origins of economic crisis, the relationship between business and the state and the co-ordination of the global economy. It draws upon the economics of Marx and neo-Marxist analysis.

Part VI uses this theory to trace the route and chart the course of current crisis. It then examines the restructuring process now underway, assessing its chances for inducing economic recovery and concluding with an examination of the risks for economic and political stability produced by the restructuring process itself.

In the afterword I sketch a few ideas of an alternative economic arrangement and its political implications, all of which warrant fuller elaboration.

Cy Gonick

PART I
CONTESTED TERRAIN

1 | Ways of Seeing

Ideologies give us ways of seeing the world and understanding how it works; ways of ordering our perceptions of what our roles should be as members of a family, as citizens of a state, as employers or employees in an enterprise; ways of deciding what is good, just and fair. They tell us what is eternal and what changeable, shaping our expectations, hopes, fears and ambitions. We recycle ideologies and their underlying moral, social, political and economic assumptions from one generation to the next, adjusting them to fit changing circumstances. They find their way into political, social and economic tracts, novels, dramas, poetry and political programs. They gain popularity under certain circumstances and lose it in others.

Tory Talk

Reigning ideologies expose themselves through the language of political discourse. In the decades following the Second World War, the speeches of most politicians were replete with references to the goals of full employment, greater equality and income security. Liberals and social democrats had taken control of the language of political discourse. They created a nearly universal consensus around these goals; debates mainly revolved around the best means to achieve them. Even those who opposed this philosophical direction had to organize their dissent around these key ideas and the words used to clothe them.[1]

At the moment the whole country is talking Tory, talking about "tightening our belts," "living within our means," "becoming internationally competitive," "building business confidence."

The federal deficit has replaced full employment as the number one concern of government. Successive finance ministers are criticized, not because they haven't done enough to reduce unemployment, but because they haven't done enough to reduce the deficit. The Liberals support cuts; New Democrats hold their tongues so that no one can accuse them of "being irresponsible."

If corporation executives want deep cuts in government spending and a thorough deregulation of their own activities, others are heard to mouth the same demands. They have incorporated the dominant ideology as their own. At least some of the unemployed blame their predicament on too much "government interference." At least some of the victims of cut-backs — school teachers, health workers, film makers, broadcasters, technicians, et al. — have accepted their plight as inevitable. They blame themselves. "It's the deficit you know. We have simply been living beyond our means," they are heard to say.

One implication of the declaration "we must become internationally competitive" is that we accept the verdict that Canada's main activity will remain production for export. But another is that the Japanese and Taiwanese do everything cheaper than we do. The next link in the argument is that Canadian workers must accept lower wages ("belt tightening"), learn to work harder, more flexibly and co-operatively. Our economic survival depends on it.

There are other possible solutions — but they don't fit the new thinking. Canada could meet the Japanese competition by keeping Datsuns, Hondas and Tercels out of the country, unless they're manufactured here. But that's "protectionism," and protectionism is bad.

In Tory talk, capitalists are risk-takers — "the creative people," Finance Minister Michael Wilson has called them. They are the supply side of the economy and everything possible must be done to induce them to invest their earnings — such as reducing their taxes, deregulating their operations and privatizing whatever public assets they might wish to own. The trick is to reduce the risk for capital while raising the penalties for labour — or, as John Kenneth Galbraith said in mocking the even-handed majesty of Reaganomics, "The poor need the incentives of lower benefits while the rich require the incentive of lower taxes."[2]

Conflicting Ideologies

While certain ideologies dominate, they never have the field all to themselves. An example of the contest of ideas can be seen in the following stylized statements on the subject of wages and productivity in the Post Office. First, the then President of the Treasury Board, Donald Johnston:

> This government is not opposed to postal workers getting higher wages. Of course they want to earn more money, and they can do so through higher productivity. The union must discard its antagonistic attitude to management and join with management in developing more efficient and productive work practices. Labour unions must recognize that greater efficiencies bring a bigger pie for all to share, not just more cigars for the boss. The taxpayer

is already subsidizing the Post Office to the tune of some ten dollars per taxpayer. It seems unreasonable that these already heavily burdened taxpayers should be asked to fork over more money, when postal workers could earn extra money by improving their productivity.

Next the President of the Canadian Union of Postal Workers, J.C. Parrot:

> If it's good enough for civil servants to be awarded 25 per cent (over two years), if it's good enough for politicians to give themselves 20 per cent, and if it's good enough for doctors to get 15 per cent, the postal workers deserve 12 per cent with no strings. It is not our function to co-operate with management to raise productivity. We are not and will never become an arm of management. We are not opposed to improving efficiency in the operations of Canada Post. But we do not accept efficiency measures that adversely affect the jobs and working conditions of our members. By "improving productivity" management means forcing workers to work harder, take fewer breaks, ignore health hazards, work nights and evenings, and generally place themselves at the mercy of management decisions. Besides, for workers increased productivity often means working themselves out of a job. The Post Office objectives are not the same as workers' objectives — to protect jobs, to ensure the rights to decent working conditions, a fair share of the nation's wealth, respect from supervisors, and work design that is interesting and permits us to develop our talents.

Both Johnston and Parrot set out to define, each in his own way and for his own particular audience, how wages and wage demands operate in our society. The premise behind Donald Johnston's statement is that in a properly functioning economy higher wages come out of extra productivity, which increases the overall revenues available for meeting the costs of the enterprise. Workers should not be concerned with their relative position in society. They should advance their position by enlarging the pie, not by taking a larger slice of the existing pie. The statement makes sense if we accept the primacy of productivity and profitability, and the assumption that wage increases must not undermine these business goals. The premise behind J.C. Parrot's statement, on the other hand, is that workers deserve as much as they can get, because it is the tendency of capitalist enterprises (publicly owned ones as much as those in private hands) to pay workers as little as the bosses can get away with; moreover, wealth ought to be shifted from those who already have too much to those who have too little.

For Donald Johnston the demand for higher wages connects with the need to raise productivity; therefore, management and labour have a common interest in co-operating. For J.C. Parrot, postal workers' demands connect with the view that workers must fight all the way to extract the desired wage from their employers, irrespective of productivity, that where working conditions and jobs are at risk, unions cannot avoid taking an antagonistic position.

Nor are these ideologies unrelated to the positions these men occupy in society. J.C. Parrot is a postal worker and a prominent leader of a powerful union, the Canadian Union of Postal Workers (CUPW), which fights for the interest of those who work in the Post Office. He is also a union militant and a socialist. Given his position and interest in society there is good reason why he should think about wage demands and productivity in the way he does. Similarly for Donald Johnston. His philosophy on the absolute necessity for high profits and tying wages to productivity is fairly predictable, given his experience as a corporation lawyer and his position in government.

Ideology and Class

All "bosses" do not think alike — at least on each and every issue. Ideologies do not always correspond to class interest. There are many workers and many union leaders who do not share J.C. Parrot's militant position. Some take what may be termed the business point of view: unions are too powerful; strikes are bad; the economy is in bad shape because government spending is too high, because wages are out of line with productivity, and because too many people are taking advantage of the welfare state; restraint is the answer to what ails the economy.

From a working-class perspective, it might be argued that working people should think of a capitalist economy as something which exploits them for profit. Some workers do see things this way; others do some of the time. They experience the conflict in concrete ways: in the low wages they are paid, in the inhumane way they are treated, in the boring jobs they are required to do, in their powerlessness to do much about it.

When specific issues are at stake, the vast majority can readily identify their "class interest" but relatively few can find a language to generalize this experience. Leaving their own concrete but narrow experience, they do not have their own conceptual tools of analysis and many wind up making generalizations that are little different from the ideology of the dominant class, the so-called Establishment. Their families, schools and unions have not provided them with an alternative way of thinking about things.[3]

Before looking at the question of whether ideological differences reflect class differences, we need to deal with a more fundamental question. Are class divisions disappearing?

According to John Porter's *Vertical Mosaic*, Canadians have a classless image of their society.[4] White-collar and blue-collar workers live in the same neighbourhoods, wear the same clothes, drive the same cars, send their children to the same schools. They think alike, often along traditional and conservative lines. If anything, professionals and employers tend to be more liberal in their social and economic attitudes than ordinary workers. In any case, for all practical purposes the working class is indistinguishable from its surroundings. We are all part of the middle class now.

There is another side to this debate, however. The vast majority of Canadians (nearly 90 per cent) are not capable of generating their own economic activity. They do not have the wherewithal to set up their own business. They depend on employers for opportunities to work. By this measure, therefore, the vast majority of Canadians are members of the working class, broadly conceived. This was not always the case. At the turn of the century, nearly half of gainfully occupied Canadians were self-employed. As late as 1951 one in four was still either an employer or self-employed.

But the division of society into the working class and the capitalist class is obviously far too simple. For one thing, while most Canadians earn a living by selling their labour for a wage or salary, the job slots they occupy vary enormously. To take just one obvious indicator: incomes range from the $800,000-$1 million salary of the president of a large corporation to the $8,000-$10,000 wage earned by a chambermaid. Locating all "capitalists" in a single category also goes against commonsense. What does the chairman of the board of Canadian Pacific have in common with the owner of the corner grocery store?

Sociologists grappling with this problem have constructed a variety of solutions. Following the American sociologist Erik Olin Wright, we can first identify the three poles that anchor the class structure.[5] At one pole are workers who have little or no control over their own work, let alone the machinery they work with, the products they produce and the profits they help generate. This is the traditional proletariat. They may work in offices, stores, restaurants, hospitals or factories but the work they perform is routine and basically manual.

At the second pole are the bourgeoisie, the executives of large corporations who exercise ultimate control over all aspects of capitalist production, capital investment, production and the organization of work. Included among them is the top layer of management who are usually large shareholders and often presidents, vice-presidents, treasurers and division heads on the boards of directors. They set goals, select key personnel, approve recommendations and exercise financial control. The fact that they are on the same payroll as production workers and office clerks hardly locates them in the working class.

A third pole consists of the petty bourgeoisie, owners of small business who employ themselves but no others. These include farmers, fishermen and hunters as well as the storekeeper and a variety of self-employed professionals and semi-professionals.

Between these poles are the individuals who occupy what Wright has called "contradictory class locations." They have features of both, one foot in the bourgeoisie and one foot in the proletariat. A first group in this category contains semi-autonomous workers who are able and required to exercise some degree of control over how they do their work and at least some control over what they produce. Examples are teachers, librarians, nurses, scientists, professors, specialized secretaries, along with craft workers such as machinists, computer programmers. A second such location is occupied by middle- and lower-level managers, who supervise other people's work or are in command of some piece of the production apparatus but who do not enjoy overall control of production or investment. A third contradictory location includes small employers whose enterprise is small enough to require the owner's labour, as well as management.

Following Wright, we can picture the Canadian class structure in the following diagram. This provides a rough-and-ready picture, which could easily be refined by differentiating male and female, public-sector workers, multinationals and state functionaries within these categories. But it is sufficient to establish the main class divisions, and it allows us to address the question of whether class location has a significant influence on ideology.

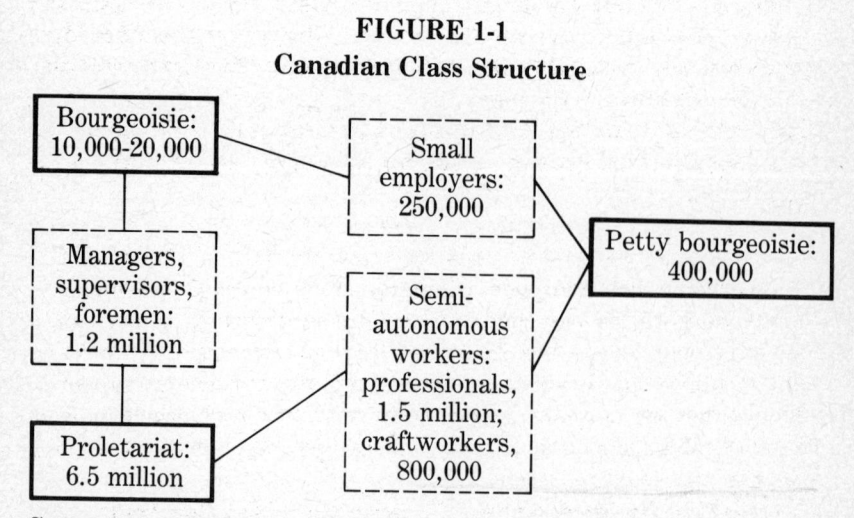

FIGURE 1-1
Canadian Class Structure

Bourgeoisie: 10,000-20,000

Small employers: 250,000

Managers, supervisors, foremen: 1.2 million

Semi-autonomous workers: professionals, 1.5 million; craftworkers, 800,000

Petty bourgeoisie: 400,000

Proletariat: 6.5 million

Source of estimates: *Census of Canada*, *The Labour Force* (Statistics Canada); Carl Cuneo, "Transition in Canada's Class Structure 1901-81," unpublished.

Utilizing Wright's categories, Professor William Johnston and Michael Ornstein surveyed the attitudes towards working-class rights, social-welfare issues, redistribution of income and distribution of power.[6] In response to the statement "During a strike, management should be prohibited by law from hiring workers to take the place of strikers," 26 per cent of the bourgeois respondents (including small employers), 45 per cent of the petty bourgeoisie and 68 per cent of the working class agree or strongly agree with the statement. The corresponding percentages for the "contradictory class locations," containing managers-supervisors and semi-autonomous workers, are 50 per cent and 54 per cent. Interestingly, as the level of education increases within any social class, the respondents show a declining degree of support for working-class interests. While these results do not demonstrate complete class polarization, they contradict the popular wisdom that class location does not count in how we view things. Tests run by the authors also show that the class position we occupy is a far better guide to our ideas than is our income, occupation or education.

The second set of statements on social-welfare issues asks what degree of public effort should be devoted to health and medical care, building public housing, protecting the rights of native people and eliminating discrimination against women. More than half the working-class respondents (52 per cent) believe that more or much more public effort should be put into health and medical care, compared to 36 per cent of the bourgeoisie and 33 per cent of the petty bourgeoisie. The corresponding results for managers-supervisors and semi-autonomous workers are 20 per cent and 43 per cent. Results for the other statements are not so striking but still undermine notions of middle-class benevolence towards the poor and minority groups. They also indicate that, contrary to hard-hat stereotypes, support for social-welfare measures runs far greater within the working class than among the middle class.

Concerning the distribution of income, 69 per cent of working-class respondents agree with the statement that there is too much of a difference between rich and poor, compared to 59 per cent of semi-autonomous workers, 54 per cent of managers-supervisors, 50 per cent of the petty bourgeoisie and 32 per cent of the bourgeoisie. While 54 per cent of university graduates agreed with the statement, support is much higher (67 per cent) among those without a high-school diploma. These results again demonstrate that less privileged groups are more likely to support egalitarian policies.

Regarding the distribution of power, the belief that trade unions have too much power is highest among the bourgeoisie and petty bourgeoisie and lowest within the working class. On the other hand, there is no apparent connection between class location and opinion on the power of large corporations. While most workers recognize unions as organizations that defend their collective interest, they fail to connect their own powerlessness with the concentration of economic power in the giant corporations. This benign — or at least ambivalent — attitude of Canadian workers towards big business is an important source of stability for Canadian capitalism.

What can we conclude from this survey? First, class location significantly shapes the position we hold on social, economic and political affairs. Second, while the working class is consistently on the Left on all major issues, it has a limited and incomplete analysis of how power works in our society. Third, at present the working-class vision of a better future is reformist rather than revolutionary. It looks to the possibility of a more equal distribution of income and improved social services within the existing economic system, rather than to any need for a fundamental alteration of economic and political structure.

Establishing Consent

While ideas differ, there appears to be sufficient agreement to permit society to carry on. We are given three alternative explanations of how popular consent is achieved:

- Society holds together because the majority of people share a common value system. An extension of this argument is that since labour depends on capital and vice versa, common interests of these two groups outweigh conflicting class interests. Workers accept the business point of view because they recognize that it is to their own advantage that business prospers. Capitalists accept the welfare state because it is in their interest to have a healthy, well-educated and contented labour force.
- There is a plurality of views and interests, often in conflict with one another — but a common view does emerge through the democratic process. Providing there is freedom of opinion and expression, that elections are governed by the principle of one person one vote, that opportunity exists to join or create a political organization and that proper rules of debate are followed at all times, people will abide by the decisions arrived at, even if these run counter to their interests.
- A third explanation is that the dominant classes control the production and circulation of ideas. Their ideas are everywhere — in the press, books, magazines, the electronic media, textbooks, in public debate — defining the issues and the possible solutions. With this monopoly, they can ensure that the subordinated classes share the

ideological frame of reference of the dominant class. This third explanation was first put forward by Marx and Engels.

The problem with these three explanations is, not that they are wrong, but that they are incomplete and leave out important dimensions.

A Commonly Held Value System?

First it is important to distinguish between different types of consent and the extent to which consent is achieved. It isn't necessarily the case that workers consent to their subordinate place in society. Their attitude is more likely one of a pragmatic acceptance. The very fact that workers have to labour to live itself constitutes a permanent pressure towards accepting their situation. This is the coercion of everyday life. As Charles Lindblom writes, the authority of the market can be as coercive as that of the state.

> Everyone does what he wishes. But a person whose style of life and family livelihood have for years been built around a particular job, occupation, or location finds a command backed by a threat to fire him indistinguishable in many consequences from a command backed by the police and the courts.[7]

Miners, for example, often do not press for better safety regulations or even for the enforcement of existing legislation. This reluctance is due, not to their acceptance of exclusive managerial rights in the mines or to their deference towards the owners, but to simple fear for their jobs if the companies were forced to bear the high costs of providing a safe working environment. It is not their acceptance of private enterprise and the profit system that governs their behaviour, but the real constraints it imposes, the risks to their livelihood.

More generally, we fall into line, accept things as they are. We can hardly think of any alternatives — and even when we do, we seem to be lacking the power to change things. We resign ourselves to a subordinate position because we can't imagine any other workable and feasible arrangement, and we end up seeking individual solutions to social problems. Alternatively, we defer to the people who have always run things: they're "up there" because they are the most capable people in society and we're down here because we lack their knowledge, talent and judgment.

However individuals approach their situation — by positive consent, pragmatic acceptance, deference or resignation — ideology works to interpret their roles in society. If citizens come to believe that those who rise to the top of the economic world are society's most capable individuals, that government is best entrusted to those with business backgrounds, that private enterprise is efficient and public enterprise inherently inefficient, that everyone with ability has an equal opportunity to succeed, that in a private-enterprise economy most people get what they deserve — then citizens are effectively turned into allies of business. It is a matter of persuading them that their own goals and aspirations can best be realized by protecting the existing economic arrangements and that a radically altered world would violate their own values and their own commonsense understanding of human nature, of how the world functions best.

There is something to the Marxist notion that consent is not merely spontaneously produced. Bias in the social order is indeed mobilized by powerful forces in society. Consensus is at least partially engineered. Business employs considerable resources to persuade citizens to associate private enterprise with political democracy. The extent of its success may be measured by the relative absence of debate on the grand issues which typify the business consensus: the private-enterprise system itself, the legitimacy of profits, a high degree of corporate autonomy, maintaining the existing distribution of income and wealth, and restricting union rights to those areas consistent with profitability. The socialist idea is made to appear foreign (literally and figuratively) and is all but ruled out of polite conversation. The area of legitimate public debate and the agenda of government is then confined to measures that will make the existing system work better.[8]

All ideas, once they become dominant, appear to be the only rational and valid ones. For example, it is taken for granted that the normal yardstick of investment is profit, not the creation of jobs or socially useful products. Similarly, it is taken for granted that the living standards of the propertyless should be set primarily by the terms on which they sell their labour, not in terms of their needs. Economic questions today are debated on the assumption that the mixed economy will continue, with a dominant private sector and a somewhat diminishing public sector. Total nationalization or even nationalization of "the commanding heights" would be considered by most everyone as impractical, unreasonable and extremist. Most everybody accepts that capital must grow and profits be maintained to keep the economy moving and people in jobs. The debate is set in terms of the right balance between private and public interests within the mixed economy, and how best to secure economic growth within a profit-oriented system.

Corporate political persuasion asks citizens to do nothing, not even stir themselves, but simply to continue to believe what they have been taught to believe since childhood. The school is plainly an important transmitter of political conservatism, particularly to the working class. Schools cultivate a consistently benevolent view of established authority. National heroes in our texts are always political leaders and economic entrepreneurs. The working class is simply absent from most accounts. For example, students would gather from textbook accounts of the building of the CPR that the track was actually laid by John A. Macdonald, William Van Horne and George Stephens.

The structure and everyday practice of the workplace is rehearsed in the classroom: external rewards, competition for grades, ranking and evaluation, stratification. More directly, the different levels of education prepare workers for different levels within the structure of production. The lower levels of education emphasize learning by rote and severely limit and channel the activities of students — which parallels the lowest levels in the hierarchy of enterprises that require repetition and rule-following. Community colleges allow more breadth for individual activity and less overall supervision — which parallels craft positions and lower- and middle-management positions that require dependability and the capacity to operate without direct and continuous supervision. Universities tend to foster social relations that conform more to the higher levels of the economic hierarchy. As students pass through one type of behavioural regulation they either are allowed to progress to the next or are channeled into the corresponding level in the job hierarchy.[9]

Similarly, there is a tendency for families to reproduce in their offspring a consciousness tailored to the character of the work world. Most frequently this involves parents preparing them for economic positions roughly comparable to their own. Studies have shown that working-class parents tend to emphasize obedience, neatness and honesty in raising their children — precisely the traits of rule-following and deference to authority required for successful performance at the lower end of the job hierarchy. High-status families are found to emphasize curiosity, self-control, creativity and independence — traits that correspond to successful job performance at high levels.

The sexual division of labour is also reproduced in the family. Even families that treat boys and girls equally in important respects cannot avoid sex-role typing when the father is only marginally involved in household labour and child-rearing. This sex-typing facilitates the submission of the next generation of women to an inferior status in the wage-labour system and lends an aura of inevitability to conventional domestic relations.[10]

Clearly the media of mass communication carry a heavy freight of business ideology. This is no surprise — if for no other reason than that almost all the print and broadcasting media are the private property of giant corporate enterprises. Proprietors usually do not choose to exercise direct influence on their newspapers, radio and television stations, but the people they put in charge share the assumptions and outlook of the world of business and government, and the writers and broadcasters quickly learn to censor their own material.

While some newspapers are more critical than others of certain business and government practices, all of them are fervently for the mixed private-enterprise economy and against any radical alternative to it. Some newspapers are more virulently opposed to militant trade unionism than others, but all of them are against it. Some are more ardent crusaders in the Cold War than others, but none of them fails to give full support to the basic contours of American foreign policy. Some newspapers support the Conservatives, others support the Liberals, but only one or two dailies have ever supported the New Democratic Party, not to speak of anything further to the Left.[11]

In contrast to thought control in Communist regimes, our dissidents, while greatly out-talked in the media, are not totally silenced. The broadcast media, for example, give at least token opportunity to social critics and to dissident voices. But it is sufficient to render unorthodox opinion marginal for thought control to be effective.

Contrary to the lip-service paid to liberal pluralism, there is an extreme imbalance of forces in the ideological sphere. What Canadians do and do not read tells us something about the lop-sided competition of ideas. Canada is without the mass circulation of dissident publications and newspapers, like those published in France and Italy. The circulation of all our Left journals and periodicals combined is less than 100,000, compared to the tens of millions of copies sold everyday of the Toronto *Star*, *Globe and Mail*, *Time*, *Reader's Digest* and *Maclean's*.

We have the appearance of a social consensus founded upon a common value system. But what we find is that, in addition to a formidable legal structure, an enormous investment of material and ideological resources has gone into the fabrication of this consensus.

The Democratic Linchpin

Widespread belief in the democratic equality of all citizens — and in the state representing the general interest — is a linchpin in securing consent of the masses. And it is not mere illusion. Voting, the resolution of legal disputes, the political process really do work in the way the ideology describes. What is illusory about this ideology is, not that it represents things falsely, but that it leaves out what stands behind these processes. It tells us how voting, the market and the law work. It doesn't tell us about the class foundation of these practices.

Rich and poor may be treated equally in the eyes of the law. But they are not equal in a wider sense. The law imposes a kind of fictional equality on a world where society is deeply divided into unequal classes. Anatole France put the point well: "Rich and poor alike are forbidden to sleep under the bridges of the Seine."

Similarly, we are all free to speak our minds. But in our society the main instruments for the circulation of ideas and opinions are the mass media, which are not indifferent to the message being conveyed. All

Ways of Seeing   15

of us are free to acquire a newspaper, radio or television station but, unlike Lord Thomson, few of us have the cash.

And while we are all free to join a political party or form a new one, unless we own a large corporation we must fund our political activities from our own incomes and we must volunteer our own time and energy. We do not have the sales revenue and the paid professional staff that can be thrown into political campaigns at no personal cost.

Liberal democratic ideology presents society as if classes with unequal powers do not exist. It is as individuals that we appear before the law, express opinions, act as buyers and sellers, vote as citizens. As individuals we seem to compete on a free and equal basis. Class structure with its unequal relations is left out of the account, and capitalism as an economic structure and as a system of power relations disappears from view.

The state then appears, not as an institution maintaining and regulating a particular economic system with built-in inequalities and exploitative relations, but as one arbitrating and co-ordinating the equal and competing concerns of all individual citizens. It appears to reflect the general interest of the nation over and above the interest of any one group or class.

This view is buttressed by nationalistic ideologies which replace class conflict with international antagonisms. Margaret Thatcher was bound for electoral defeat before the Falklands dispute. By diverting attention to a few square miles of windswept rock out in the Atlantic she managed to rally the nation around the flag and divert its attention away from economic failure and bitter class division at home. By successfully invading Grenada and eliminating the threat this nation of 200,000 posed to the U.S., Americans were told they could sit tall in the saddle once again. Ideologies of the common interest or national unity create national identities rather than class identities. "Them" and "us" become defined in terms of nations rather than classes.

The Marxist Juggernaut

The third (Marxist) explanation for popular consent has some merit, as we have seen, but it is also incomplete. It is also overly simplistic. Marx himself grossly underestimated the life expectancy of capitalist democracy. He thought of democracy as temporary and spasmodic, impossible as the normal form of capitalist society.[12] The combination of private ownership of the means of production and political democracy, he estimated, would generate an unresolvable contradiction: through the democratic franchise, the working class and the poor would demand improvements in their well-being that capitalists could not deliver, without ultimately jeopardizing their ability to function. Since capitalists would never give up power voluntarily, they would attempt to rule by force and under these circumstances would have to be overthrown by force.

Taking their cue from Marx, some of his followers insisted that if socialism did not take hold the twentieth century belonged to barbarism. The rise of fascism in Europe was seen as a terrible confirmation of Marx's prediction. But, except in the less developed parts of the capitalist world system, dictatorship turned out to be an aberration. We know now that capitalism can survive for long periods under democratic rule — even in the face of economic crises.

Marxists have not done very well in explaining how capitalism persists. An exception is the Italian Communist Antonio Gramsci, who highlighted the role of ideology in maintaining what he called the hegemony of the dominant classes. But he rejected the view that this domination was due solely to capitalist control over media, schools and other parts of the ideological apparatus. The implication of this analysis is that ruling ideas are simply implanted in workers' empty heads, that there is a conspiracy to trick workers into accepting things as they are.

Gramsci insisted that for an ideology to work, Marxism included, its explanations of everyday events and relationships cannot fly in the face of people's lived experiences. It must be validated continually by daily life. Thus for capitalist ideology to work in shoring up support for the status quo it must bear some resemblance to life as people actually experience it. And of course people *are* able and do exercise their preferences in both the marketplace and the polling booth. They *are* treated (more or less) equally before the law. Through their unions workers *do* negotiate wage increases and improvements in their working conditions. Through political representation they *do* gain new social services and some degree of income security.

But democracy's authority has bounds. The limits on Parliament stem from the fact that it doesn't make the final decisions on how the economy is run — it merely reacts to corporate decisions. The limits on trade unions stem from their dependence on the financial success of the enterprise as well as from the fact that they don't own and therefore cannot control the capital.

Looking at it the other way around, business is in a dominant position in a capitalist society precisely because its investments are necessary to supply the material needs of everybody else. Since profit is a necessary condition for investment, the actions of both government and trade unions are necessarily tied to the capitalists' performance. If the capitalist fails to earn sufficient profit to warrant new investment, production falls and employment, wages, consumption and taxes fall. "Capitalists are thus in a unique position in a capitalist system: ... they appear as bearers of universal interests ... while interests of all other groups appear as particularistic and hence inimical to future developments."[13]

While this puts them in a commanding position, unless they are prepared to rule by force, the interests of other groups must to some degree also be satisfied. This is where democracy (Parliament and trade unionism) comes to the fore. It's the mechanism through which distributional conflict is organized and temporarily resolved. It provides opportunities for amending outcomes that would otherwise be determined by market forces and arbitrary authority.

The opportunities are real enough, but they're also limited, for in the final analysis no matter how extensive the amendments, the dominant position of the employer on the shop floor and in the boardroom remains intact. Workers' benefits have to be tailored to the primary need of maintaining profitability.

In prosperous times, consent is more easily obtained — if only because concessions are more easily won. The rich may be getting richer but at least the poor aren't getting any poorer. But in hard times concessions go the other way and long-won gains can be lost.

Owners justify eliminating jobs and cutting back on wages by appealing to their need to repair corporate balance sheets. Governments use the language of incentives to justify new tax breaks for the rich and fiscal responsibility to justify phasing down social-services expenditures and income-support programs. But the language sometimes fails to work. The Mulroney government was forced to introduce a minimum tax on the rich to counter the image of unfairness produced by capital-gains exemptions. And it was forced to cancel plans to reduce pension indexation.

Consent to the existing social order is always tentative, and it's permanently conditional: "there exist material limits beyond which it will not be granted, and beyond these limits there may be crisis."[14]

Competing Ideologies

This account of ideology is still incomplete. There are always competing ideologies which also arise from within lived experiences. Workers can and do express the view that their jobs ought not to be sacrificed or their skills diluted because profit makes them redundant. They resist being treated like commodities, their worth determined by the law of supply and demand.

Working-class resistance finds its expression in collectivist ideologies. Because these arise from everyday experience, they cannot be totally suppressed, controlled or diverted. Collectivism possesses its own ethic, because effective collective action requires unity among workers. But just as consent, or at least acceptance, must be won — not imposed — by the capitalist class, unity among workers must be won rather than imposed.

So-called proletarian ideology need not be socialist. It may be and most often is reformist — set in terms of gains that can be won within the existing economic order. Nevertheless, there is an affinity between working-class existence and socialism. It lies in the fact that socialism is a projection of a future society that embodies all the central elements of working-class ideology — collectivism, solidarity, class consciousness. Socialism affirms that it should not be left to the market to decide human worth.

Workers are not reformist or revolutionary by nature. In the deep social and economic crisis following the First World War, workers in many countries were radicalized: they altered their ideological identification. The same thing occurred in the Great Depression. In the rising prosperity of the 1950s, the emerging welfare state had the effect of integrating the working class into the status quo. Reformist ideologies made the most sense. In the context of the present economic crisis, it is likely that these ideological commitments will come unglued, at least for some. Radical ideologies of the extreme Right and the extreme Left were bound to re-emerge.

2 Economic Theory and Ideology

Where ideology makes sense of society, theory explains how society works. Theorists possess an expertise in being able to give a coherent and systematic explanation of events. But in doing so, they draw on the same stock of knowledge, opinions and ideas available to everybody else. And their experience, like everybody else's, derives from definite social relations. Theorists belong to a certain order, they have a place in it, they benefit or lose from it. They see their future bound up in its success or failure. Intellectuals cannot escape from their social environments if only because the problems that reach them are usually socially determined — as is the degree of acceptance of their conclusions. As members of university departments, for instance, they do not have to be told which lines of theoretical and empirical research are most likely to be rewarded with tenure and promotion.

Although social scientists generally insist that their theories are not value laden, according to Karl Popper, a theorist's views come from "the very place which he inhabits, his social habitat. The social habitat of the thinker determines a whole system of opinions and theories which appear to him as unquestionably true or self-evident.... That is why he is not even aware of having made any assumptions at all!"[1]

Among social scientists, economists are the most insistent about the value-free nature of their enquiry. But not all are so convinced. In his encyclopedic study, *History of Economic Analysis*, Joseph Schumpeter describes constructing a theory as being similar to painting a picture or drawing a map of economic reality. Ideology "enters the ground floor" of this process. "Analytic work begins with material provided by our vision of things, and this vision is ideological almost by definition." To underline his point, Schumpeter adds that in our pictures of economic reality, "the way in which we see things can hardly be distinguished from the way in which we wish to see them."[2]

It would be difficult to discover a political slogan or program that does not have its theoretical counterpoint. This is as true for the Keynesian demand for full employment and Marx's cry "Workers of the world unite!" as it is for the slogans and programs of neo-conservatism. Political statements and economic remedies — such as "we must encourage greater profit to improve efficiency and create jobs," "we must control wages to defeat inflation, cut public expenditures, reduce the tax burden, and dampen expectations" — are all supported by elaborate and complex theories that give them a solid doctrinal base.

Theory can legitimate reform and revolution as well as the status quo. In fact, much economic theory is reformist in character, identifying and attacking facets of the system that require alteration. Removing the most glaring deficiencies gives both a system and a theory greater resilience.

We can observe at least four lines of defence against changing the status quo in a fundamental way. The first line of defence is simply to acknowledge positive features of an existing order — affluence, freedom — while ignoring negative features — poverty, exploitation, sexual and racial oppression. If negative features are admitted, as a second line of defence grounds are found to justify them — the poor are lazy, the wealthy are productive, and they both deserve what they get. Or demonstrations are provided to show that some negatives are necessary to achieve other positives, the "zero-sum society" approach — economic growth requires incentives and incentives produce inequalities. A third line of defence is to assert that injustices derive inevitably from human nature, that a just society is impossible because of the constitution of the human condition. Our system may have some serious problems, but others that violate human nature have problems that are far worse. A final defence is that undesirable features can be removed by gradually reforming some aspect of the existing order. Excesses and abuses can be expunged without having to alter the basic fundamentals.

We will meet these different lines of defence in the next chapter and throughout the book. A sample of some economic theory at this point will reveal the economist's "vision of things," the hidden assumptions that yield some rather bizarre conclusions.

Looking at Work and Pay

According to orthodox economic theory, people have the choice of entering the job market as either employer or employee. Workers selling their labour power can shop around for the best offer. They are free to decline the terms of employment if the preferred wage is not fair recompense for the tasks assigned to them. They can also withhold their labour power for a period, using the time to invest in themselves and build up their "human capital" to improve their competitive position and increase their market value. The fact that some individuals take on one means of livelihood and some take on another is largely a matter of personal choice. "The [resulting] distribution of income," according to Harry Johnson, "is determined by individual choice."[3]

The wage established between worker and employer is likely less than the worker would like to receive and more than the employer would like to pay — just as the price established between buyer and seller is likely too high for the consumer and too low for the producer. It is a compromise, and if one side or the other manoeuvres itself into too favourable a position and exploits its advantage, the state is there to step in to right the balance.

What is left out of this picture is that by the time worker and employer meet to conduct this transaction, history has long deprived the worker of the capacity to exercise freedom. Once ownership of the major means of production is confined to a tiny class of owners, the fundamental basis of the relationship is set. Although not physically coerced to work — as in slavery and feudalism — very few workers have the choice of whether or not to work as wage labourers. Workers are workers because they do not possess the means to work on their own account. Membership in the propertyless class confines their freedom to choose those means of livelihood that do not require possession of land or capital. At best they can choose between employers. How cheaply workers sell their labour depends on the bundle of economic goods they bring to the labour market.

Employers face far less urgency in concluding a bargain with their employees; they can hold out longer or move their business. They have the option of becoming wage earners, if that's more profitable, and easier access to other occupations. Workers, by contrast, can hardly cross over and become employers, save in the rarest of circumstances. All this leaves workers dependent on employers to a far greater degree and in a more significant sense than employers are on them, which is bound to have a fundamental influence on the wage contract.

Looking At Profit

If anything, the fate of profits in orthodox economic theory is even more confusing than the fate of wages. In standard textbooks on the principles of economics, for instance, profit makes its first appearance in the theory of the firm. Given plant size and technology, firms simply choose the level of output that maximizes the difference between cost and revenue. This constitutes profit. Providing the profit is positive, owners will stay in operation. If it is negative they will take their capital elsewhere. If the firm makes a profit other capitalists will be attracted to the same industry, and the added presence of their supply will drive down the price of the commodity and push up the cost of production on sales as they increase the demand for factor inputs. No sooner do profits appear than they disappear with the number of firms in the industry regulated by competition so as to leave zero profits in the typical firm.

Students will then learn from these textbooks that the profits that have evaporated are really abnormal profits. Even in their absence, owners of firms still receive normal profit which is considered part of their average cost of production. In other words, "normal" profit is viewed as being a cost of production. It is the price of owners' capital. Owners pay themselves a reward for advancing to their own firms capital that could otherwise have been hired out to other capitalists. It is therefore looked upon as their "opportunity cost" and is equivalent to the return they would have received had they hired the capital out to some other capitalist.

The justification of this price for capital (normal profit) is that capital, like labour, is productive. Both labour and capital are factors of production. The hiring of both incurs a cost and both receive a reward commensurate with their relative contributions to output.

One further refinement is necessary to make the treatment of capital symmetrical with that of labour. According to theory, workers receive a wage as payment equivalent to their contribution to production, but also as compensation equivalent to their estimate of the unpleasantness (or "disutility") of the work assigned to them. Nobody can argue that owners of capital suffer by hiring out their capital. But according to economic texts, when they abstain from consuming all of their income they also may be said to be undergoing a psychological deprivation. By using a portion of their income for capital investment, they are to that degree forced to delay the pleasure of consumption. Profit is therefore a reward for delaying consumption on the one hand and a payment in accordance with its productive potential on the other.

The symmetry is now complete. Both labour and capital are essential to production. Both are compensated according to their respective contribution to production. Both experience a sacrifice when they offer themselves for hire — leisure in the case of labour, current consumption in the case of capital.

Finally students will learn that in some industries "super-profits" (profits over and above those that can be justified by productivity and abstinence) can occur and do not disappear through competitive pressures. Because of certain monopoly power exercised through patents, control of essential inputs and consumer loyalty built up through massive advertising, large profits do not attract rival firms into these industries. There are high "barriers to entry." By virtue of their monopoly power, firms can force consumers to pay a price above the competitive price or they can force suppliers (including labour) to accept a price (wage) below the competitive level. "Super-profits" are condemned as both unjustified in terms of productivity and sacrifice and unnecessary to induce supply.

In such cases the solutions advanced include breaking up such firms, forcing the owners to sell off some plants, imposing fines when there is evidence of collusion between firms to hold up prices, or regulating prices through government agencies.

Treating profit as a reward for the productivity of capital confuses capital as means of production — raw materials, equipment or machinery and plant — with capital as property right and as legal entitlement. Such a view grants owners the productivity of things they own. On the one hand, capital as real goods produces commodities; it does not yield profit. On the other hand, capital as legal entitlement cannot produce commodities; it can only yield profits. As the celebrated economic dissident Joan Robinson put it, "owning capital is not [in itself] a productive activity."[4] To the extent that capitalists undertake supervisory and administrative duties, they are of course paid a managerial salary. After such salaries are paid there is still a surplus which can only be a reward for ownership. The problem is to explain the existence of profit as a consequence of ownership per se.

As for the argument that capitalists must get a reward for abstinence or waiting, it has not been shown that waiting for a reward causes discomfort, unless pangs of hunger are being suffered in the interval. Implicit in the notion of abstinence is the view that the ultimate purpose of all economic activity is consumption. The worker engages in economic activity with no other purpose than that of securing consumer goods and services, but to universalize this behaviour to all classes is to ignore what being a capitalist is all about. It is not a matter of simple greed; it is a question of the constraints the system places on capitalists. Consumption is for them no substitute for investment. To suggest otherwise is to ascribe to capitalists a freedom no less illusory than the freedom given to workers in choosing between work and leisure. The more they choose to use income on luxury living, the less likely it is that they will survive as capitalists.

The situation of capitalists is akin to that of hockey players. On the ice hockey players must play according to the rules of the game, which means helping their team score more goals than the opposition. Their motivation for playing is as irrelevant as their behaviour off the ice. To the extent that they are successful, they will advance up the ranks of professional hockey and enjoy the benefits of increased salaries and bonuses. When they begin to slow down they ride the bench or are sent back to the minors, in both cases suffering the loss of prestige and reward.

Capitalists must also play according to the rules of the game, a game in which their success is unambiguously measured in terms of their ability to make a profit. Whatever their personal values or motivation, they are driven to profit maximization because profit is the ultimate criterion of success and the key to survival in a capitalist economy. The freedom of capitalists to choose between consumption and accumulation is clearly constrained within the limits set by competition. Unless capitalists continuously renew their machinery and methods of production on an ever larger scale, their competitors will steal the markets through cost advantage.

So much for the orthodox explanation of the role of labour and capital and their respective rewards. The following discussion examines its wavering treatment of unemployment and its centuries-long advocacy of free trade.

What Ever Happened to Full Employment?

According to early orthodox economic theory, unemployment was not possible or, more precisely, it could not persist for long in a self-regulating economy. The appearance of unemployment was seen as a sure sign that wages were too high. But like all sellers of a commodity unable to find buyers at prevailing prices, workers were bound to offer their services for less. With competition among workers bidding down wages, each and every seller would eventually find a buyer. If this new equilibrium was not established rather quickly, it was presumed to be because trade unions were trying to end competition among workers for jobs.

Observing the mass unemployment of the 1930s, British economist John Maynard Keynes set out to show that the presumed self-correcting mechanism was absent as it applied to the labour market. He also absolved trade unions of all responsibility for unemployment. For Keynes and his followers, full employment could be established and maintained only through continuous state intervention in the economy.

But what did these economists mean by full employment? "More vacant jobs than unemployed men," an early definition,[5] was found to be unacceptably ambitious. It was amended to take account of workers in the process of switching jobs. In North America 97 per cent employment was taken by economists to approximate a state of full employment. It was assumed that about 3 per cent of the labour force was always in flux, quitting present jobs and searching for better ones. In Europe a smaller margin of 1 per cent was commonly allowed for.

In the event, these targets were seldom realized as other priorities took precedent over full employment. One was price stability. When

British economist A. W. Phillips thought he had observed a relationship between low levels of unemployment and high levels of inflation, the public woke up to the new world of "trade-offs." Government could stimulate the economy so as to achieve something close to full employment, but only at the expense of creating wage inflation.

The economic policy implications were clear. Government had a "menu of choices." It could have full employment with high inflation or stable prices with high unemployment, or some combination of the two. A combination of an "acceptable" rate of unemployment and an "acceptable" rate of inflation was the preferred choice that was to emerge. It was government's task to "fine-tune" the economy with a monetary and fiscal policy to achieve the desired trade-off. In Canada the 3 per cent definition was officially abandoned in 1972 when the Economic Council of Canada advised the government that a rate of 4.5 per cent was all that was obtainable if raging inflation was to be avoided.

Stripped to its essentials, the trade-off theory turns out to be a warmed-over version of the earlier blame-the-victim yarn. It tells us that, since unionized workers are responsible for inflation, it is they who force governments to slow down the economy, and it is they who must take the blame for the resulting unemployment.

Economists who subjected Phillips' theory to rigorous empirical tests in a number of national settings could find no stable relationship between wages, prices and unemployment. In fact, as the 1960s wore on, price levels and unemployment rates were rising simultaneously. With unemployment in the mid-1970s at 8 per cent and inflation at 10 per cent and soaring, the trade-off theory was blown away.

This finally made room for Milton Friedman's "natural rate of unemployment," a concept he first aired in his 1967 presidential address to the American Economic Association. Whatever government does to stimulate the economy, Friedman argued, unemployment always falls back to a critical rate. Should the government be prepared to trade-off some inflation for more jobs, any new jobs that it creates would soon vanish. Only inflation persists. Worse still, the more government tries to beat down unemployment the more it will succeed in accelerating inflation.

In policy terms, the conclusions are already obvious. There is no trade-off and there are only two choices on the menu: an unemployment rate high enough to lead to a stable or declining rate of inflation, or a lower rate that leads to ever-accelerating inflation.

The natural rate of employment is usually defined as that rate of unemployment consistent with stable prices or, more precisely, with "a steady non-accelerating inflation." It's the unemployment that still exists after the supply of labour has been brought into line with employers' demand for labour as a result of fluctuating real wages. The theory alleges that some among the unemployed prefer to stay that way; rather than accepting available jobs at prevailing wages, they choose welfare and unemployment insurance. Their unemployment is therefore voluntary.

What determines the natural rate? Mainly demographics and the extent of government largesse. On the one hand, the natural rate rises with every government-induced work disincentive such as unemployment insurance and welfare benefits. On the other hand, it rises alongside the increase in the population with a "weak attachment" to the world of work, such as women and youth. Both can often afford to have irregular work patterns because they have a preference for leisure (youth) or because they're only secondary or tertiary wage earners (women).

Aside from the fact that nobody has yet found a way to measure the natural rate of unemployment — by fiddling with numbers we can make it just about any level we wish — the ultimate question it poses is whether price stability is to be exalted above all other goals. This strand of orthodoxy appears to be saying that any unemployment that exists with price inflation is no net loss to society.

To shore up this argument, economists have gone to great lengths to show that unemployment is not what it used to be. In bygone years, so the argument goes, unemployment was a legitimate social concern. But it no longer brings unrelieved hardships, since we now have unemployment insurance and welfare. Moreover, in two- and three-wage-earner families, the unemployment of any one of them is cushioned by the regular incomes of the others. This is why sharp distinctions are commonly drawn these days between male and female unemployment; unemployment among heads of families versus non-family heads; and unemployment between youth and the "core" age group. Increasingly, only unemployment among the core is coming to count as real unemployment.

Subtracting jobless youth brings the current unemployment rate down from more than 10 per cent to less than 8 per cent. One more subtraction, unemployment among married women, brings it down further to barely 6 per cent. Using such arithmetical exercises makes unemployment evaporate. In fact, it turns out to be no great problem after all.

It took the financial press no time at all to appreciate the strategic value of the new concept. For example, the September 1976 issue of *Fortune* magazine warned that "when the unemployment rate is pushed below its natural levels by over-expansive monetary and fiscal policies ... wages are bid up to much higher levels .... Unemployment must remain at much higher levels than conventional political rhetoric demands." Maintaining unemployment at a permanently high level is vital, the article goes on to argue, because it improves the effectiveness of any additional unemployment in holding down wages. If unemployment were allowed to fall, "we would lose some of this benefit." It's not difficult to figure out who the "we" is who would lose some of the benefit when unemployment falls.

The natural-rate concept is by now almost universally accepted within the economics profession. It's become as much a part of the economist's daily jargon as "supply and demand." It amounts to a return to the old belief that in a market economy full employment, or something fairly close to it, will be automatically established. If unemployment appears and persists it must be due to trade union actions or government intervention — or by voluntary choice. If government feels that the natural rate of unemployment is too high, its duty is clear: weaken trade unions and reduce unemployment insurance and all other programs that slow workers' response to market forces.

The Free Trade Hobbyhorse

To paraphrase American author Robert Kuttner, "in the firmament of economists' ideological convictions, no star burns brighter than free trade."[6] While the Canadian economy was founded on the basis of state protectionism, this policy has always been a favourite target of economic theory. Now it appears that the economist has finally prevailed: Prime Minister Mulroney has made free trade a cornerstone of his economic policy.

No doubt the economist sees this radical departure as a prime example of the victory of economic wisdom over economic illiteracy. But the true meaning behind the conversion lies elsewhere. One of the paradoxical consequences of nearly a century of high protectionism has been the invasion of Canada by a swarm of American corporations. With the influx of American capital has come a growing continentalization of Canadian trade.[7] The concept of a free-trade arrangement with the U.S. has waxed and waned over the years. The idea gathered strength following the Second World War as the Canadian economy was being molded into a northern extension of the American. It was not the cleverness or persistence of the economist that turned the tide, but the growing dependence of Canadian business on U.S. capital, U.S. technology, machinery and markets on the one hand, and the current threat of U.S. protectionist forces on the other.

Free-trade orthodoxy has its roots in classical economic theory. Adam Smith devoted hundreds of pages in his *Wealth of Nations* to an attack on the mercantilist policy of building economic strength by barring the imports of manufactured goods while subsidizing exports. His pleas for free trade and against "picking winners" (as it would now be called) were key elements in his argument against all state regulations. Smith saw a multitude of virtues in free trade — the tonic of competition, broader consumer choice and the efficiencies that come with specialization.

Two generations later David Ricardo refined the argument. Each country should do what it does best and trade the excess. Even if one country is more efficient than its trading partners at everything, it still makes sense for it to specialize in those products at which its superiority is greatest while importing those products where its relative superiority is least. This is the law of comparative advantage: if someone happens to be a superior writer *and* a superior typist, a popular economic textbook explains, it is more efficient to hire a typist and spend more time writing.

Ricardo illustrated his original argument with the example of Britain producing textiles, Portugal producing wine, and the two countries exchanging their products to mutual advantage. Historians, however, point out that Portugal's concentration on wine arose, not through natural causes, but through a treaty imposed on Portugal by Britain in 1703.

One economic historian, noting the advantages that Britain gained from producing higher value-added manufactured products, and the tragic destruction of the textile industry in India by British colonial power, writes:

> It is fortunate for England that no Indian Ricardo arose to convince the English people that, according to the law of comparative costs, it would be advantageous for them to turn into shepherds and to import from India all the textiles that were needed.[8]

Few economists outside Britain and North America, and even fewer governments, were ever won over to the free-trade dogma. Frederick List, a German economist writing in the middle of the nineteenth century, argued that Britain's enthusiasm for free trade came only after Britain had achieved a dominant position in manufacturing. And the dominant position was gained not by free competition, but by forcing British products on colonial populations and keeping other producers out of British markets.

> It is a very common, clever device [List argued] that when anyone has attained the summit of greatness he kicks away the ladder by which he has climbed up in order to deprive the others of the means of climbing up after him.[9]

There are three fundamental problems with the orthodox free-trade argument. First, it describes a static world. It denies the possibility that competitive advantage can be created. It's also bad history. It denies the reality that competitive advantage has been created. Japan's system of controls over foreign investment, sheltered domestic markets, research subsidies and capital grants is an unequivocal violation of free-trade norms. But it has helped to establish Japan as a technological powerhouse.

Second, the argument assumes that products would be exchanged in competitive markets. It does not foresee the possibility that the firms trading products would be under the same ownership and that the prices would be artificially set to maximize the profit of the parent company. Yet this describes the situation in Canada where most trade is conducted between firms that are part of the same ownership structure. The arrangement is a clear departure from the classical notion of competitive market forces and throws the entire theoretical basis of the free-trade argument into question.

Third, its optimal results presume that the economy is operating at full employment and full capacity. But today's global economy is not unlike that of the 1930s with all countries suffering from both high unemployment and excess capacity. Fifty-three years ago when Keynes wrestled with free-trade orthodoxy in the context of the Great Depression, he wrote:

> I was brought up, like most Englishmen, to respect free trade not only as an economic doctrine which a rational and instructed person could not doubt, but almost as a moral law. I regarded ordinary departures from it as being at the same time an imbecility and an outrage .... It is astonishing what a bundle of absolute habiliments one's mind drags around even after the centre of consciousness has been shifted.[10]

In this heretical essay, titled "National Self-sufficiency," Keynes observed that since "most modern processes of mass production can be performed in most countries and climates with almost equal efficiency ... national self-sufficiency, though it costs something, may be a luxury we can afford." While not to be considered an ideal in itself, it helped to establish "an environment in which other ideals can be safely and conveniently pursued." The other ideals he had in mind, of course, were full employment and maximum production at decent wages.[11]

A contemporary, Lionel Robbins, ridiculed Keynes' proposal as "petty devices of economic nationalism" but, just as Keynes had foreseen, most basic industrial products can be produced almost anywhere — but by workers paid vastly different wages. In an era of mobile capital and portable technology, free trade creates intense competitive pressures to lower labour costs, and the location of comparative advantage can turn on which labour force will work for the lowest wages. In this environment free-trade logic counsels that, in the face of new, "revealed" foreign comparative advantage, all we can do is lower our wages and raise the rewards to capital.

It is little wonder then that the battle against free trade in Canada is being led by the trade-union movement and its political allies. As the federal New Democratic Party warns:

> The requirements of free trade between the two nations would mean a number of concessions from Canada. For example, if our tax rates were higher than those levied on corporations in the U.S., we would be pressured to cut them in order not to penalize companies operating in Canada; where our environmental safeguards were more stringent we would be pressured to lower them to prevent Canadian producers from operating at a competitive disadvantage; where our wages were higher, as they are in some industries and regions compared to those in the southern U.S., we would be under pressure to cut them.

The alternative to free trade advanced by economic nationalists, a return to protectionism combined with massive subsidies to industry, is hardly more palatable. A third option, along the lines sketched by Keynes, is begining to evolve.

Economic Theory and Economic Policy

Economists fight ferociously to defend their theories and to demolish and rout their rivals. Their investment in one theory or another is more than a merely intellectual one — although it is clearly that, if only because they have devoted many years of their life in mastering a set of techniques and solving a set of "puzzles" within a particular paradigm. But it is also an ideological investment because every theory and the policy prescriptions that flow from it are laden with values that have a deep meaning for their exponents. They express, in theoretical and policy terms, the ideological sentiments that have been nurtured through a lifetime and that appear commonsensical to their practitioners. Rival theories violate their sense of the way society works and should work.

One well-known economist, Robert Heilbroner, goes so far as to say that "every social scientist approaches his task with a wish, conscious or unconscious, to demonstrate the workability or unworkability of the social system he is investigating." It is not a matter of indifference to the orthodox or the radical economist, Heilbroner adds, "whether the data fits the hypothesis he is testing. Each struggles mightily to explain away, to minimize, or reject results that go counter to his initial beliefs."[12]

But what is the role of theory in influencing events? John Maynard Keynes, for one, believed it was crucial. In a famous passage in the *General Theory*, he gave us the classic statement exalting the role of ideas as the prime mover of events:

> The ideas of economists and political philosophers, both when they are right and when they are wrong, are more powerful than is commonly understood. Indeed the world is ruled by little else. Practical men, who believe themselves to be quite exempt from any intellectual influences, are usually the slave of some defunct economist. Madmen in authority, who hear voices in the air, are distilling their frenzy from some academic scribbler of a few years back. I am sure that the power of vested interests is vastly exaggerated compared with the gradual encroachment of ideas.[13]

These sentiments are by no means unique to John Maynard Keynes. Economists generally believe that their economic theories and advice inform government policy — and that policy in turn determines economic performance. Poor performance is invariably blamed on economic incompetence and erroneous advice: "If only the Minister of Finance (Governor of the Bank of Canada) gave up on those monetarists (Keynesians) and switched to our economics." No wonder economists take themselves so seriously. If they could only get the ear of policy makers and convert them to their theoretical persuasion, then policy can be changed, inflation (economic decline) halted and prosperity recovered. The theory of the state that underlies this way of thinking is astoundingly naive.

In conventional economic policy models, the state is treated as a competent and benevolent actor that pursues economic policies in the public interest. Powerful interest groups are rarely recognized. At best the theory presumes a pluralistic society of competing interest groups with the state shoring up the weakest ones and overriding the stronger ones, acting as the honest broker that presses on in the public interest.

This is a highly simplistic view of the way the world of practical affairs works. It assumes total autonomy for government, that it functions without external constraints, and that it is the only and, in any case, certainly the most important actor in economic affairs.

To illustrate the problem with such a conception, suppose that the government, or at least its most powerful officials, become converted to a post-Keynesian strategy that included developing a consensus around income-sharing and contractual-planning agreements, whereby government would subsidize certain corporate investment projects on condition that employers fulfill specified obligations to workers, environmental concerns and so forth. This is not impossible to conceive, but to make it happen would require many more difficult changes than are involved in the conversion of the policy-makers — which is not to underestimate the difficulty of that exercise. It would require major reforms of a whole set of institutions — for example, trade-union practices, management practices, disclosure laws. The conversion of policy-makers would be a fairly minor component of such a process.

Because government acts so publicly, it's seen to occupy centre stage. Less visible, but far more central to the process are the positions occupied by the actors off-stage, particularly labour and capital. This is not to deny all relevance of the ideas of policy-makers or how these are formed. It is only to make the obvious — but in some academic circles, the neglected — point that economic policy is not just constrained by the ideology or competence of policy-makers.

There are other problems. One is the definition of the objectives of economic policy. At the end of the Second World War, economists declared that full employment was the number one objective of government. Policy-makers had other concerns. Thus in its Full Employment Bill of 1946 the American Congress declared its policy to be one of fostering and promoting "free competitive enterprise" within which "there will be offered useful employment opportunities." The Canadian state ruled out "the expansion of government enterprise to provide ... additional employment." On the contrary, the White Paper on Employment and Incomes said government would make "every effort to create ... favourable conditions within which the initiative, experience and resourcefulness of private business could contribute to the expansion of business and employment."

It would seem that the means — private enterprise — comes before the officially declared goal — full employment. More precisely, in the minds of policy-makers full employment was clearly conditional: full employment, yes, but only to the extent that it could be achieved within the norms of the private-enterprise economy. Taking prevailing institutional arrangements like the property system as given, the economic theorist is blind to the constraints these pose to the implementation of economic policy objectives.

A curious omission in most accounts is discussion of why the state presumably acts in the interest of the community in general. It pursues full employment and a more just distribution of income simply because these are in the public interest. On the face of it this appears to be inconsistent with other postulates of economic theory, namely that individuals are motivated in the self-interested fashion depicted two hundred years ago by Adam Smith. Somehow these self-interested individuals, once they are elected to public office, are motivated by the public interest.

Adam Smith had a more sophisticated view:

Civil government, so far as it is instituted for the security of property, is

Economic Theory and Ideology 33

in reality instituted for the defense of the rich against the poor, or of those who have some property against those who have none at all.[14]

Smith also observed that the political arena is populated by "that insidious and crafty animal, vulgarly called a statesman or politician" whose decisions are bound to be dominated by "the clamorous importunity of partial interest" rather than by an "extensive view of the general good."[15] It was partly for this reason that Smith urged economic affairs be organized to avoid the political arena.

Unbelievable as it may seem, relatively few economists since Adam Smith have developed a coherent theory of government behaviour. All that economic orthodoxy has provided are the simplistic and inconsistent assumptions already reviewed. To give them their due, the neoconservatives have at least come up with a cohesive theory about what government does. Avoiding the inconsistencies of the conventional model, they assume that all actors, whether in the private sector or the public sector, are motivated by simple self-interest. In particular, the theory analyzes the likely outcome if voters, politicians and civil servants act to fulfill their own interests.

Voters, for example, are presumed to cast their ballots for the politician or party most likely to yield the greatest benefit to individual voters.[16] Politicians competing for votes support policies and back expenditures that will lead to their own re-election. Government bureaucrats serve their particular interests — power, prestige, reputation, salary or the perquisites of office — by attempting to increase the size and importance of the departments they run.

The predicted outcome of this combination of self-interested behaviour is a public sector whose size is bloated far beyond what can be justified in the name of public interest. Voters underestimate the cost of publicly provided goods because the cost of increasing the supply of money, the size of the public debt and indirect taxes is not well perceived by them. Having underestimated the price of public goods, they demand more of them ("fiscal illusion") — a result that perfectly suits both politicians and bureaucrats. It enables politicians to compete more effectively for patronage and bureaucrats to enlarge their budgets.

The logical solution is to constrain politicians and bureaucrats by imposing a legislated limit on the size of public expenditures. Most commonly recommended is a law that forces governments to balance their budgets so that taxes completely cover public expenditures. The Gramm-Rudman Bill, passed by the American Congress towards the end of 1985, exemplifies this strategy. It commits the American government to reduce the annual federal deficit from $212 billion in 1985 to zero in 1991.

Ignoring the fact that such a reform places the democratic process in a constitutional strait-jacket, the entire analysis is far less logical than its proponents would have us believe. In the first place, voting is irrational from a strictly economic point of view. There is the cost of the time it takes to vote which must be weighed against the influence one vote will have on the outcome of the election. Since the expected value of one vote is very small, in terms of our own self-interest we probably shouldn't bother. The fact that people do vote must therefore be explained by mainly non-economic factors: the democratic values we wish to uphold, identification with class or party, a sense of civic duty. In the second place, "fiscal illusion," where the cost of publicly provided goods and services are underestimated, is myopic behaviour and not particularly rational for a self-interested voter. In any case, it's unproven and if it exists at all its size may not be large.

The Marxist theory of state policy is directly concerned, not with individual behaviour and choice, but with the behaviour of various classes in society. More precisely, individual behaviour is seen as being conditioned by class location. Specifically, the Marxists have capital and labour confronting each other as aggregated groups of individuals. These "social categories have an existence that is independent of and must be analysed prior to individual behaviour."[17] And unlike the conventional economic model, Marxism assumes that power and influence are not equally distributed. In particular, the capitalist class is presumed to have a privileged position when it comes to state policy. This is a far cry from the view of the state as the honest broker acting in the common interest.

There is something intuitively real about the Marxist approach. As non-Marxist Charles Lindblom has written, "in any free enterprise system, a large category of major decisions is turned over to businessmen .... They are taken off the agenda of government. Business then becomes a kind of public official and exercises what, on a broad view of their role, are public functions."[18] These decisions include what is to be produced; how the labour force is allocated to different occupations, workplaces and tasks; who is to manage economic enterprises; where economic activity is to be located, the technology to be used in production, the quality of goods and services, the introduction of new products, how much of society's resources is to be consumed and how much invested — in short, all aspects of production and distribution.

Because the supply of goods and services, jobs, incomes, prices, growth, the standard of living and economic security of everyone all rest in the hands of businessmen, governments cannot be indifferent to how well they perform. At the very least, their tenure in office largely depends on the outcome. Since in an economy based on the law of private property governments cannot command business to perform, they must induce the required performance. These inducements will consist of whatever benefits businessmen require and demand — income, wealth, deference, prestige, influence, authority. In a word, governments of whatever stripe accept the responsibility to do what is necessary to assure profits high enough to induce businessmen to sustain output and employment.

What does this mean in practice? When businesses demand tax concessions to encourage investment, their demands are always seriously considered — and usually granted. If a corporation argues that obeying new pollution regulations requires prohibitive expenditures, the regulations will more often than not be suspended or delayed. If corporation executives say their industries need help for research and development, it will be provided. If a corporation asks for prohibitions on union organizing as a condition for locating in a particular province, at least some governments will attempt to oblige. When in the name of efficiency corporations speak out against restrictive anti-combines legislation that bars certain kinds of monopoly-creating mergers, the legislation will almost certainly be rewritten or shelved. When corporation executives request an opportunity to speak with government officials, including cabinet ministers and the prime minister, they will be accommodated.

All of this is familiar enough. So also is government's tendency to fill advisory committees, royal commissions and regulatory agencies with representatives of the corporate establishment. Undeniably, governments grant business a privileged position. It's important to add that they do not have to be bribed, duped or pressured to do so. Nor do they have to be uncritical admirers of business. It is sufficient that they accept private enterprise and profit-making as the foundation-stone of the economy — and they understand that to make a private-enterprise economy work government leaders must defer to the requirements of business leaders.

While the position that policy formulation represents the interests of the dominant class is more persuasive than the Keynesian position that it implements theories, it is also too simple and incomplete. For one reason, the dominant class is not homogeneous. It is fragmented into a variety of subgroups — financial/industrial, resource/manufacturing, big business/small business, domestic capital/foreign capital, western/eastern, etc. While these subgroups can all agree on some major questions of policy — the primacy of private enterprise, for instance — their interests are not always compatible. Though policy-making obviously involves a process of compromise around competing interests, which of the subgroups is accorded priority by policy-makers and why is not self-evident. It has to be discovered.[19]

For another reason, though businessmen get a great deal, they don't get everything they want. And there are plenty of occasions when popular pressure forces government to introduce measures that businessmen bitterly oppose. How does Marxism explain this?

In many Marxist accounts all power rests with the capitalist class and little if any power is left to the working class. By this accounting no explanation emerges for the very real gains won by the working class over this century, nor for variations of state policy which reflect, at least in part, the shifting balance of class forces as it is experienced within and between countries. Nor is it possible to see how such a powerless working class could ever mobilize its strength to make a revolution, the presumed goal of all Marxists.

Some recent Marxist accounts explain working-class gains as concessions meted out by the state to legitimize itself and the social order in the eyes of the public — ostensibly part of the process of building consent. Thus, while in the last instance, the state must look to the interest of capital, the basis of its political mandate is its commitment to such goals as justice, equality, individual rights and full employment. Just as the economic system and the interests of the dominant economic class impose constraints on policy, the necessity to maintain legitimacy and sustain consent in a liberal democracy also imposes constraints on policy-makers. The one can no more be ignored than the other. It is a delicate operation of state-craft. It involves establishing what those limits are at any moment in time while containing any threats to dominant interests.[20]

This goes part of the way in meeting the foregoing objections but it raises more questions than it answers: what determines the "limits" in particular circumstances; why are the limits on reform imposed by American capitalists so much more severe than the limits imposed by Swedish capitalism, for example. And the triumphs and successes of the working class are still downgraded. Despite concessions coming through the class struggle, nothing fundamental changes. On the contrary, by legitimizing the social order, each concession is seen to somehow strengthen the capitalist class.

These are complex matters for which we do not have all the answers. But there is yet one final point about the relationship between theory and policy that arises from the Marxist account. If economic policy reflects the needs of the dominant economic class at a given time, there is still the question of what those needs are and what they are perceived to be. For example, it could be argued that the policy of extreme monetary restraint and high interest rates that prevailed in the late 1970s and early 1980s was in the interest of business since the policy was demanded by various business organizations. But such an argument leaves unanswered why these business organizations should perceive a policy of high interest rates and rapid disinflation to be in their interests when it plainly created havoc for many firms. Obviously there is an explanation that makes sense of it, but it is not self-evident. The connection between theory and policy has to be discovered.

Case Study: The Macdonald Report

In its composition, premises and policy recommendations, the long-awaited report of the Royal Commission on the Economic Union illustrates the principles introduced in this and the previous chapter.[21]

The commission was established in 1982 under the chairmanship of Donald S. Macdonald to report on "the appropriate national goals and policies for economic development." Twelve other commissioners were appointed including a mix of industrialists, former politicians and senior civil servants, economists and a labour representative. While commissioners travelled around the country hearing briefs, a staff of researchers undertook a raft of studies to support the final recommendations.

What emerged is a report chock-full of the buzz-words of neo-conservative economics: liberty, efficiency, incentives, productivity, excellence, competitiveness, flexibility, dynamic adjustment, deregulation, free trade, etc. The commission heard from groups representing native peoples, women, farmers, workers, the unemployed, youth, the poor. But its final report took no notice of their concerns and rejected all their suggested reforms. In a barely disguised way it reproduced the corporate viewpoint and provided a good illustration of Marx's dictum: "the ideas of the ruling class are in every epoch the ruling ideas."

Of the 300 academics selected to undertake research, all but a few, and those mostly in disciplines other than economics, spoke in the voice and language of neo-conservatism. Not a single researcher was directed to investigate and pursue suggestions recommended by the democratic movements appearing before the commission.

According to the report's opening statement on the state and economy:

> Free markets, like democratic states, are crucial institutional arrangements, not only for the achievement of economic goals, but also for their contribution to human freedom and dignity. Both logic and history confirm that political democracy and individual freedom are sustained by a significant degree of autonomy in a private economic sector, and that they are incompatible with an economy in which such autonomy is non-existent.
> ...The primary political contribution of markets is that they locate essential decision-making processes concerning production and consumption in private hands, within a framework which ... provides a broad "accountability" ... to the consumer.... Secondly, markets generate the economic product from which the state can extract resources for the pursuit of its varied objectives. Thirdly, markets contribute to political freedom .... [They] decentralize and diffuse power. Opposition parties and free markets are integrally linked, one to another in democratic societies.

The chain of ideas is clear — political freedom is linked to economic freedom and economic freedom, efficiency and accountability in turn are linked to the free market. If producers make goods that don't sell they lose their profits and are forced out of business. The consumer is king. The "invisible hand" directs resources to their most efficient use. Anything that unduly restricts the free operation of the market — like government regulations — is bad because it restricts freedom and reduces efficiency. It's in the private sphere that society's wealth is produced. It should be protected from excessive interference, for unless it prospers the entire edifice of the economy may be threatened, including the ability of the state to provide public goods. The supply of goods and services via the market must take precedence over its redistribution via the state. It is presumed that the free market disperses economic power widely so that no individuals or groups can dominate the economic or political spheres.

A market economy need not shut out other forces entirely. As the statement goes on to say:

> the vertical power of management within firms and industries is balanced by unions, is subject to legislation affecting safety in the work-place and is generally constrained by an emerging category of worker rights which controls the exercise of employer discretion. [Moreover,] contemporary employer self-interest acts as an important internal constraint on management power. Higher productivity requires a harmonious relationship in the workplaces, creating a tendency to share power between management and the workers.

Finally, market outcomes can be modified by citizens exercising their democratic rights. "They use the State to impose criteria of equity.... The result is the welfare state ... which subordinates market results and our status as actors in the economy, to citizenship concerns and community values."

Here we have the pluralistic interpretation of democratic capitalism with a coalition of groups whose divergent interests are harmonized by a benevolent state acting on behalf of the community-at-large. And wherever management, under pressure from shareholders, pays insufficient heed to employee needs and claims of employees, the employees form unions to meet management on equal terms. The resulting compromise achieved through free collective bargaining is a harmonization of interests and a sharing of power in the workplace that parallels what occurs through the welfare state in society at large.

The commission claims not to wish to see this mixed economy/welfare state dismembered. A crisis has emerged, however, because of "a number of market-distorting, growth-suppressing policies which redistribute income ... reduce economic efficiency and inhibit flexibility."

The source of the problem is that "multiple constituencies [have become] habituated to the benefits and protections they receive from the State ... [which are then] viewed as entitlements or social rights."

The solution is to "significantly increase our reliance on market forces." To counter "rigidities" in the labour market, a "major overhaul" of unemployment insurance and social security is recommended. To force greater efficiency upon producers, a "fundamental realignment of industrial policy" is urged. In particular, "our proposals ... to enter into a free-trade arrangement with the United States reflect our general preference for market forces over State intervention in the economy, from which growth will follow."

Its treatment of unemployment, unquestionably the number one concern expressed in briefs put to the commission, is illuminating. Not surprisingly, the report accepts as its definition of unemployment the natural rate or, as it prefers to call it, the "non-accelerating inflation rate of unemployment" (NAIRU). According to "this critically important concept," more than half of the 1.5 million unemployed are out of work because they take weeks if not months searching for the perfect job, or because the availability and magnitude of unemployment insurance encourages them to quit their job and avoid a serious search for another until their benefits run out, or because the expectation of high wages attracts large numbers of women into the labour force who really comprise secondary wage-earners. Similarly, laid-off workers who accepted employment with a firm known to be subject to frequent layoffs should hardly be counted as unemployed. Their unemployment is surely voluntary, the report tells us, since they "knew the risk at the time of accepting employment."

Adding up all this "voluntary" unemployment, the natural rate is estimated at 6.5 to 8 per cent of the labour force. By this accounting, only about 2 to 4 per cent of the labour force has been involuntarily unemployed over the past several years. This problem would disappear too if it were not for government regulations that reduce the employers' demand for labour: minimum wages; product, environmental and safety standards; barriers to interprovincial and international trade and to foreign investment. In short, the economic crisis is entirely government-induced.

The report comes very close to agreeing with J.B. Say's 150-year-old law that, if left to itself, supply creates its own demand. On the fiftieth anniversary of the publication of John Maynard Keynes' *General Theory*, a work that thoroughly demolished Say's law, this in itself is a remarkable feat. Indeed the report completely disassociates itself from the mildly reform-minded Keynesian economics that has reigned supreme since the Second World War. Dismissing it as both "unrealistic" and unnecessary, the authors will have nothing to do with fine-tuning the demand side of the economy. All that is required of government is to free businesses from the layers of impediments they have inherited from previous governments.

The commission's policy agenda follows fairly consistently: abolish all barriers to free trade and foreign investment, as well as marketing boards and subsidies and bailouts to failing enterprises; privatize government-owned enterprise; link welfare provisions more directly to work incentives; link wages more directly to profits; freeze the minimum wage or get rid of it altogether; drastically reduce eligibility and magnitude of unemployment insurance.

The only sign of government meddling was a proposal for the imposition of incomes policy (i.e., wage controls) wherever recovery threatens to pass into inflation and a proposal for the removal of the right to strike (compulsory arbitration) in the public sector. What we have here, in short, is a return to the laws of the jungle and the survival of the fittest — unless or until the fittest turn out to be organized labour.

The commission was particularly keen to attack the disincentives to work allegedly created by the unemployment insurance and welfare systems. It recommends reducing the U.I.C. benefit rate, shortening the benefit period and raising the qualification period. By making unemployment less attractive a significant minority of perennial abusers will be thrown back into the active labour force. To help them adjust, the commission recommends a transitional adjustment assistance program for people who have exhausted their U.I.C. benefits and are willing to relocate or undertake training to improve their employability.

What trained economists apparently cannot see is that there are 50,000 to 100,000 job vacancies on any one day — compared to 1.5 million or so people seeking jobs. Punishing the unemployed will not create more jobs, nor will training programs. Many of those removed from the rolls of U.I.C. will end up on the welfare rolls. The governing party may well find the shift politically useful. While the federal government is generally held responsible for rising unemployment, galloping welfare can more easily be blamed on the deviant character and habits of the poor. Besides, the provincial and municipal governments pay a rising portion of the welfare bill.

To further reduce "rigidities" in the labour market, the commission calls for what it describes as a "radical" and "wholesale" shake-up of the welfare state. Family allowance, child exemptions and tax credits, guaranteed income supplements for the elderly are to be replaced by a "universal income security program" (UISP). The goal, according to the authors, is not to reduce the welfare contributions of the state. After comparing Canada's outlay with other countries, they could hardly say otherwise. Rather, the stated object is to redirect existing expenditures away from middle- and upper-income earners — not to the poor, significantly, but to the working poor. Above all, the program is designed to attract the unemployed employables back into the work force.

In one of its options, each adult would be given a guaranteed $2,750 a year and each child $750. A family of four would receive $7,000. If it had no other source of income, it would still be eligible for provincial and municipal welfare. The utterly destitute family would then get a grand combined total of $12,000, about the same as in the current scheme of things.

The main beneficiaries are the working poor, people earning the minimum wage or thereabouts and taking home a $8,000-$12,000 pay cheque. Deducting what they now receive from family allowance, child exemptions and tax credits, etc., from their UISP, their net gain would be $4,000-$5,000 a year. The overall consequence of the new program, then, is to make work at the lower end of the labour market more attractive. In effect, it subsidizes low-wage employers and incidentally improves their chances in the international competition game.

Not surprisingly the source of the subsidy is mainly the average wage-earning family. Families earning a combined gross income of $40,000, for example, would each contribute from $1,000 to $1,500. That's the difference between what they now receive from family allowance, etc., and what they would get from UISP. The way the commission researchers have worked it out, a $100,000 family would lose less — about $1,000.

The most affluent 25 per cent have relatively little to lose from abandoning the existing universal welfare-state structure. The benefits are an inconsequential portion of their income, adding up to only 1-2 per cent. Moreover, through any one of a number of tax loopholes, they can easily recover the $1,000 the UISP will cost them. The main losers would be the bulk of Canadians in the middle who already bear the brunt of government taxes. Now they are also targeted to lose benefits which today constitute up to 15 per cent of their net income. And they are much less likely to find ways of foisting their $1,000 plus contribution on to others. In effect, they are being asked to give up some of their income so that some employers needn't pay a living wage.

The purpose of this program is obviously not to alleviate poverty but to link social assistance to the market. In the report's own words: "We must emphasize ... that our reform package would never make it more financially advantageous to avoid work than to participate in the labour force as some income-security programs and some combinations of UI and social assistance may do today."

When the workers' movement demanded the welfare state years back, their goal was to weaken market despotism, to create a system of income entitlements that would deliberately reduce "work incentives." The idea was that workers should no longer be compelled to offer their services to any employer at any price. This is the feature of the welfare state that the commission seeks to expunge.

But free trade is the cornerstone of the entire report. Although the other recommendations can be evaluated on their own merits, to the report's authors all are linked to the trade proposal.

According to the report, in the old days of rapid growth and expanding international trade, Canada could afford the distortions and inefficiencies built into our overprotected and overregulated economy. In the new world of slow growth and rising international competition they can no longer be condoned. The whiff of competition introduced by free trade with the U.S. (and eventually the world) would immediately enforce higher productivity on Canadian firms. Weaker (smaller) ones would go under; stronger (larger) ones would survive. While some industries might disappear, others would restructure and expand.

Free trade may be the single most important policy issue of our generation, not only because it will increase our trade and investment dependency on the U.S., but because it is bound to touch nearly every thread of the social and cultural fabric of the country.

This is the case because in one way or another most of the social programs we have created and most of the labour and environmental standards we have legislated affect the cost structures of Canadian business. Some, like Medicare, lower their labour costs. American business says these programs give Canadian firms an unfair cost advantage. There are at least a few dozen similar examples of what are known as "non-tariff barriers." In a free-trade deal, some of them would have to go.

But there are also examples, like our minimum-wage laws, our health-safety legislation and some of our taxes, that place Canadian firms at a cost disadvantage. A free-trade agreement would put into place a dynamic such that after a few years Canadian business would be pleading this case to the government: "If you want us to compete on equal terms with the Americans give us their tax structure, their labour legislation and their pollution standards."

However it's realized, in anticipation of an agreement, negotiated during the talks or as a consequence of market pressures following the agreement, tax and social policy harmonization is a virtual certainty. Even the Macdonald Report concedes that "closer trade relations will increase the force of U.S. political influence at both levels of Canadian government." The alternative, as the authors see it, is far worse: "a *status quo* trade policy might lead very quickly, over the next few years, to calls for a planned economy." In any case, the decision is seen as the only way Canada can avoid the protective wall the U.S. is about to construct.

The logic is clear: we can't escape the international competitive game;

we must gain free access to a large market; the only one now available to us is the American market; to compete with American firms, market forces must be freed to shed unproductive enterprises and their workers; governments must abandon some cost-creating regulations; various social and regional equalization programs that American businesses see as unfairly subsidizing Canadians must be revised; and with money squeezed from U.I.C., the losers must be helped to adjust to the winds of change.

The authors of the royal commission report were likely aware that there are too many obstacles in the way of a speedy implementation of their program. The program itself is advanced in a fairly cautious manner. There is no question that what they have in mind is a radical rearrangement of social practices, a peeling away of the protective cover painstakingly built up to shield people from the market's system of punishment and reward. But to have argued for it without softening their language would have been too risky. They might have thoroughly antagonized some commissioners and lost all credibility with the public. Instead, they contented themselves with developing a theoretical framework, setting a policy agenda for the next decade and recommending some initial changes to set the process in motion.

Above all else, the Macdonald Report is an exercise in manufacturing consent. At the time it was established Canada was in a major recession after nearly a decade of high inflation and mass unemployment. Ruling circles knew that to survive the crisis intact, the private-enterprise economy had to be restructured. But what kind of restructuring would it choose? Free trade, deregulation and privatization had always been the favoured policy of certain elements of the Canadian business community, particularly big business and the multinationals. In the midst of the decade-long economic crisis with Keynesian policy in disrepute, they pressed their point. New governments were elected and civil servants and banking officials who were more sympathetic to neo-conservative policies were put in place. These policies received theoretical support by a new generation of New Right economists.

A major obstacle still in the way of rearranging the economy in light of this reborn vision of capitalist society was a public opinion yet committed to the ideology of welfare statism and regulation. The Macdonald Commission offered the "new" economists the unprecedented opportunity of addressing a national audience of Canadians to win them over to the economics of neo-conservatism.

3 | Orthodoxy and its Reformers

Never a monolithic discipline, economics has always had an orthodox stream and a radical stream. This division is not as neat as it sounds. For one thing, the specific contents of orthodoxy and radicalism shift from one generation to another as the economy throws up new problems to be analyzed and resolved. For a second, there has always been more than one variant of orthodoxy and of radicalism. The existence of so many contending schools of thought has produced a persistent tension within economics, a tension that mirrors within the sphere of ideas a persistent conflict in the real world between economic classes and groups.

Thomas Kuhn has suggested one way of understanding the rise and fall of dominant theoretical constructions in the physical sciences. With some important amendments, his interpretations can be useful in sorting out the development of economics, and its present drift and conflicts. In his *The Structure of Scientific Revolution*, Kuhn writes that throughout the history of science there are periods in each scientific domain when a theory emerges that constitutes what he calls a "dominant paradigm," a universally recognized scientific achievement that defines the problem and the manner of their solutions to a "community of practitioners." "To a great extent," he writes, "these are the only problems that the community will admit as scientific or encourage its members to undertake. Other problems, including many that had previously been standard, are rejected as metaphysical, as the concern of other disciplines, or sometimes as too problematical to be worth the time."[1]

The dominant paradigm reigns for considerable periods with its self-defined scope and limitations. Once these limitations are reached theory construction is ended and practitioners engage in "puzzle-solving" around the main problems. Socially important problems that are not reducible to the puzzle form are ignored "because they cannot be stated in terms of the conceptual and instrumental tools the paradigm supplies."[2] New theoretical advances await the emergence of an alternative conceptual framework on which a new theory will be based. The new theory will displace the old one in a scientific revolution and will itself then constitute the dominant paradigm.

Orthodoxy and its Reformers 45

For the social sciences, Kuhn's "dominant paradigm" has to be amended to take account of three factors. First, as we have already seen, theories are not isolated constructs. Theories become dominant because of their legitimating power. They confirm the status quo, even if this involves reforming existing social and economic arrangements to make them more acceptable to subordinate classes. When things are going well, they act as celebrations of the status quo and serve as legitimators of power and those who wield it. Immutable laws are propounded which "prove" on scientific grounds that the system is just, or reformable so that it can become just, and in any case necessary and predestined to go on forever. When things are not going well, the guardians of the theory attribute the malfunctioning of the system to violations of the sacred theoretical maxims.

Second, theories are finally displaced, not through rational argumentation — although this is its outward form — but through changes in material circumstances that make the underlying constructs demonstrably false. Unlike the struggles in the physical sciences, those between the practitioners of the social sciences mirror struggles within and between social classes. They are one dimension of broader struggles set off by rapidly changing circumstances.

Third, alternative and conceptually different explanations do not wait on the rejection of dominant paradigms. They have their own prehistories which may only await rediscovery and reformulation.

A case in point is the rise of Keynesianism. It became the overwhelmingly dominant school of thought in the thirty years following the Second World War because the earlier brand of orthodox economic thought had no acceptable answers to the Great Depression.

Whatever its actual practice, government policy was largely enunciated in terms of the Keynesian goals of economic stability and full employment. And whatever the merits of the claim, Keynesian economics took much of the credit for the long prosperity following the war, helping to legitimize the "managed" capitalist economy. When explosive inflation, massive and growing unemployment and chilling world indebtedness burst open the postwar prosperity bubble, Keynesianism itself fell into rapid disrepute. In the mid-1970s, many economists and business commentators blamed the economic crisis on erroneous government policy, which to them meant Keynesian economic policy. New doctrines like monetarism and supply-side economics and post-Keynesian economics began to surface and captured the attention of government policy-makers. Each of them is a reconstruction and amendment of theories developed in an earlier historical context. As well, a dissident generation of political economists rediscovered Marx and reformulated his theories which too have become an integral part of the Great Economic Debate of the 1980s.

Orthodox Fundamentals

The place to begin an examination of economic theory is the tenets of orthodoxy which link present thinking to the past.

Fundamental to orthodoxy is the view that what is produced, how and for whom is determined by individual preferences, technology and personal endowments. Consumers exercise their sovereignty in the market and determine what is produced. Technology prescribes how goods are made, transported and exchanged. Individual talents, skills and material wealth decide to whom society's output of goods are distributed. The economy cannot be changed without changing these foundation stones.

But they cannot be changed easily, and certainly not without violating what is regarded by orthodoxy as "human nature" and "natural liberty." Disturbing the income distribution, which depends directly on the initial endowments (abilities and wealth), would destroy incentives, given orthodoxy's assumption that all human effort is closely related to material reward. Technology is a datum given by science and history. Ignoring or by-passing individual preferences as expressed on the market violates the orthodox notion of freedom and likewise disturbs incentives.

Taking technology, endowments and preferences as given, an economy will produce a combination of goods and services at prices and quantities which reflect the maximization of consumer satisfaction and profit. The only way to obtain different results, a different combination of products at different prices or a different distribution of income is to impose a different set of preferences on individuals or alter the constraints which govern their decisions.

But to do so violates the basic principle of natural liberty. In a free society nobody is forced to make a sale. If individuals do sell, they must think themselves better off for doing so. The most natural method of organizing a society is therefore to let each individual make whatever exchanges he/she wishes to. Feudalism restricted the free exchange of labour. According to orthodox theory, socialism destroys the free exchange of capital and substitutes the preference of planners for the preference of consumers, thereby restricting the freedom of individuals. Socialism is unnatural, illiberal and inefficient. On the other hand, capitalism, in which all possible exchanges are allowed, is the economic system that nurtures individual freedom; it alone is in harmony with human nature.

There are two key institutions in orthodox theory — free and fully competitive markets for all commodities and private ownership of productive resources. Left to itself the free market provides an efficient mechanism for co-ordinating individual decisions so as to maximize the social good. The pursuit of self-interest ensures that resources flow to areas and products where they would be most profitably used while meeting people's wants as expressed through the market. At the same time it ensures that new techniques are adopted to lower the cost of production.

This benevolent result is enforced by competition which also protects the consumer from rapacious producers and workers from oppressive employers. The existence of large numbers of competing firms providing a wide choice for both consumer and workers ensures that neither will be exploited in the marketplace. Providing there are no obstacles to the mobility of capital and labour and to the movement of prices, the market also establishes prices so that all commodities produced will find a buyer — at a price — and everyone who wishes to work will find a job — at some wage or another.

At the heart of orthodox economic theory is the laissez-faire state. The marketplace offers unparalleled opportunities and freedom for individuals to choose how to make use of their talents, how to satisfy their wants, how to live the way they choose. State intervention intrudes on this sphere of liberty. It hands over arbitrary power to politicians and bureaucrats acting in the national interest, but in practice interfering with individual liberties and reducing the scope of the market. The role of the state needs to be confined to enforcing contracts, protecting property and maintaining a stable medium of exchange.

The Unknown Adam Smith

The blueprint for laissez-faire and free trade was first drawn in Adam Smith's *Wealth of Nations*, a massive intellectual assault on all forms of state interference in both the domestic and the international economy. Adam Smith shook up nineteenth-century thought as much as Marx rattled twentieth-century thought. His legacy is at least as enduring as Marx's — and as much based on convenient simplification and distortion.

The original absent-minded professor — it was said that he brewed himself a beverage of bread and butter and pronounced it the worst cup of tea he had ever tasted — Smith is recognized as the patron saint of industrial capitalism. But like all great thinkers, he is full of paradox and contradiction.

Adam Smith celebrated the individual in the free market who, intending only his own security and his own gain, is "led by an invisible hand to promote events which were not part of his original intention," the well-being of society. At the same time, he was not unaware of the great perils confronting competitive markets: "People of the same trade seldom meet together even for merriment and diversion, but the conversation ends in a conspiracy against the public or is some contrivance to raise prices...."[3] He went so far as to say that any proposal of a new law or regulation that comes from "this order" must be examined "with the most suspicious attention. It comes from an order of men ... who have generally an intent to deceive and even to oppress the public."[4]

Government, however, was an even greater threat than the private abuses of monopoly power. Smith's bias against the government of his day was based on the correct assessment that when it intervened it was precisely to charter monopolies and to impose regulations and tariffs for the purpose of protecting already existing enterprises. Remove the presence of government — "the great spendthrifts in the society"[5] — he argued, and the private abuses of monopoly power are bound to be eliminated by the competitive pressures that are always at work in a free-market system.

As his famous pin-factory illustration shows, Smith celebrated the division of labour as the key to increased productivity and wealth. At the same time, however, he also saw that it would cause moral decay and alienation. "The man whose whole life is spent in performing a few simple operations ... generally loses the habit of such [mental] exertion, and generally becomes as stupid and ignorant as it is possible for a human creature to become."[6] Unlike Marx, who looked forward to an end of the "idiocy" of country life and to a sharpening of the wits of the working class on the anvil of history, Smith predicted a growth in the idiocy of city life and a reduction of the working class to a condition in which the labourer is "incapable either of comprehending [society's] interest or of understanding its connection with his own."[7] Presumably he thought that more income outweighed, or at least compensated for, these hidden injuries.

Smith had no doubt that labour and capital were in constant conflict. Nor did he suffer from any illusion as to which had the upper hand.

> It is not difficult to foresee which of the two parties must, upon all ordinary occasions, have the advantage .... In all such disputes the masters can hold out much longer. A landlord, a farmer, a master manufacturer, or merchant, though they did not employ a single workman, could generally live a year or two upon the stock which they have already acquired. Many workmen could not subsist a week ... without employment. In the long run the workman may be as necessary to his master as his master is to him, but the necessity is not so immediate.[8]

Unlike many of his nineteenth- and twentieth-century followers, who have persisted in seeing the buying and the selling of labour services as merely a voluntary exchange, Smith himself understood it as a one-sided power relationship: "Masters are always and everywhere in a sort of tacit but constant ... combination not to raise wages of labour above their actual rate .... We seldom hear of this combination," he noted, "because it is the usual, and one might say, the natural state of things .... They are always conducted in the utmost silence and secrecy." But when workers resist this combination "by a contrary defensive combination ... or combine to raise the price of their labour because of the high price of provisions or the great profit which their masters make by their work, ... they are always abundantly heard of ...." They are, Smith wrote, "desperate and act with the folly of an extravagance of desperate men who must either starve or frighten their masters into an immediate compliance with their demands. The masters upon these occasions are just as clamorous ... and never cease to call aloud for the assistance of the civil magistrate and the rigorous execution of those laws which have been enacted with so much severity against the combinations of servants, labourers and journeymen."[9]

Smith offers no solution to this display of unequal power except to plead that "they who feed, clothe and lodge the whole body of the people should have such a share of the produce of their own labour as to be themselves tolerably well fed, clothed and lodged." Clearly government was not the answer, for, as we have already seen, Smith suffered no illusions about the role of the state. It is an "indispensable" instrument to protect "the rich against the poor, the property owners as against those who owned nothing at all."[10] This is not Marx, but Adam Smith to the same effect.

The "Father of Capitalism" even regarded the acquisitive itch with much disdain:

> The poor man's son, whom heaven in its anger has visited with ambition, when he begins to look around him, admires the conditions of the rich. He finds the cottage of his father too small for his accommodation, and fancies he should be lodged more at ease in a palace .... He is enchanted with the distant idea of the felicity [that money can buy]. Accordingly, the smitten fool devotes his life to arduous labour, ruins his health and his peace of mind, and accumulates a fortune, only to discover at the end that wealth and greatness are mere trinkets of frivolous utility ..., enormous machines contrived to produce a few trifling conveniences to the body ..., immense fabrics which it requires the labour of a life to raise, which threaten every moment to overwhelm the person who dwells in them.[11]

He went on to say, however, that this itch for riches serves a positive, even essential function. Without the itch workers would neither perform society's arduous tasks nor acquiesce to their subordinate status in life. It derives from a sense of awe for those who have gained riches, assuming that they must be deserving as well as wealthy.

While Adam Smith's great work is viewed as a paean to free enterprise, it is in fact a highly qualified tribute. However mind-numbing, unfair and self-illusory the new capitalism might be, these drawbacks were defended as the inevitable costs of economic progress. Meanwhile all of his reservations were ignored by the rising capitalist class in favour of his single most enduring point: let the market alone.

Economics of the Rich

In the heyday of industrial capitalism Smith's concerns were largely ignored by his successors. The plight of the poor was dismissed by resorting to Malthus' "law" of population, which blamed the poor for their desperate circumstances. A high-wage policy and government welfare measures only serve to make workers lazy. Poor people might be kept alive by charity, but since they would then propagate, such charity was only cruelty in disguise. According to Reverend Malthus, society was caught in a hopeless trap in which the human reproductive urge would inevitably shove humanity to the brink of the precipice of existence. No wonder the hapless utopian, William Godwin, target of Malthus' *Essay on the Principle of Population*, complained that his nemesis had succeeded in converting friends of progress into reactionaries.

Malthus gave little consideration to the positive benefits that trade unions might bring the poor. In his opinion there was little likelihood of their ever amounting to much. Economists of the next generation were not so complacent. In 1830 Nassau Senior warned about the threat of an arrogant labouring class resorting to strikes, violence and combinations that would threaten the foundation not only of wealth but of society itself. Senior declared war against trade unions, a war that economists, with few exceptions, have been fighting ever since.

The central problem, Senior noted, was that under pressure of "labour combinations" wages would be set to reflect the needs of the working family instead of the value of an individual's labour as determined by the free market.

> In the natural state [the relation between the capitalist and the employee is] a voluntary association .... But the instant the labour is paid, not according to his value, but his wants, he ceases to be a free man. He acquires the indolence, the improvidence, the rapacity, and the malignity, but not the subordination of a slave .... The present tide may not complete the inundation, but ... a breach has been made in the sea-wall, and with every succeeding eruption [the waters] will swell higher and spread more widely ... till rent, tithes, profit and capital are all eaten up.[12]

Senior was concerned that socialism, because it posited that inequality could be remedied, was naturally attractive to the poor and uneducated. "They grossly miscalculate the number and value of the prizes in the lottery of life, they think that they have drawn little better than blanks, and believe those who tell them that if all the high lots were abolished everybody might have a hundred-pound prize."

"As long as this is the political economy of the poor," he went on to say, there seems to be only three ways of governing — one is to exclude the vast majority from political life. "This is our English policy." A second is the existence among them of a "blind devotion to the laws and customs of the country." A third is to "rely on military power" — the only way open to France.[13]

Here it is worthwhile quoting in full a passage in which Senior lays out the task of economic theory as that of dispelling the fatal illusions of the economics of the poor:

> Men, whose reasoning faculties are either uncultivated, or perverted by their feelings or their imagination, see the great power of the State, and do not perceive its limits. They see that it disposes of great resources, and do not perceive how easily these resources may be not only exhausted but dried up. They are struck by the contrast between great superfluity and great indigence, between lives shortened by indolence and lives shortened by toil, by wealth squandered unproductively while cultivable lands lie waste and labourers ask in vain for employment. When excited by such a spectacle, what is more natural than to propose laws, by which the toil which appears to them excessive shall be forbidden, by which the government shall provide the strong with employment and the weak with relief; and obtain the necessary funds, partly from the superfluity of the rich, and partly by taking possession of the productive instruments which their present owners are too idle or too timid to turn to the best advantage? It requires a long train of reasoning to show that the capital on which the miracles of civilisation depend is the slow and painful creation of the ... enterprise of the few, and of the industry of the many, and is destroyed, or driven away, or prevented from arising, by any causes which diminish or render insecure the profits of the capitalist, or deaden the activity of the labourer; and that the State, by relieving idleness, improvidence, or misconduct from the punishment, and depriving abstinence and foresight of the reward which have been provided for them by nature, may indeed destroy wealth, but most certainly will aggravate poverty.[14]

In explaining England's relative peace and prosperity to a French correspondent, Senior declared: "it is the triumph of theory. We are governed by philosophers and political economists" who "by birth, manners and education belong to the class which is supposed to have the most to lose by disorder."[15] This was his understanding of why the viewpoint of the economist happens to coincide, not with what he had termed the economics of the poor, but with the economics of the rich.

Nature's Own Cure

Late nineteenth-century economists observed financial panics and cycles, but they were regarded as fleeting incidents in a rapidly growing, exuberant economy. Depressions were seen as temporary phenomena, an unavoidable part of capitalist growth to be borne in stoic silence. Left to themselves, depressions played a positive role in clearing the way for rapid recovery. They weeded out antiquated and inefficient modes of production; they killed off unsound investment projects fostered by the preceding boom; and they broke the back of labour militancy.

The idea that nature has its own cure meant that the old orthodoxy opposed all forms of government intervention. What producers need is lots of money — and therefore low taxes — and freedom from crippling rules and regulations. Unleash the producers and demand will take care of itself.

This harkens back to J.B. Say's famous law: "Supply creates its own demand." In a letter to Malthus, Say wrote, "whenever there is a glut, a superabundance of several sorts of merchandise, it is because other articles are not produced in sufficient quantities to be exchanged for [them]." But this shortage can only arise from causes outside the workings of the economy, "a political or natural convulsion, or the avarice or ignorance of authority."[16]

In short, if the system is allowed to work freely, production will generate income which, when spent, will be just sufficient to purchase the resulting output. Unemployment and idle capacity can be automatically eliminated by an increase in production (supply). Government policy need only be concerned to remove the barriers to such an increase. If gluts do occur it must be because capitalists have been discouraged from investing their savings by high taxes, unstable currencies, government regulation or trade-union intransigence.

Fiscal activism of government was particularly opposed because of another tenet of orthodoxy — that there is only a certain amount of savings at any moment available to finance private investment. The more government borrows and spends, the less is available for industry. The cure for unemployment was wage reductions ("sound economics"), while the cure for a rising government deficit was lowering government expenditures ("sound finance").

Running through the early orthodox accounts of the Great Depression and its failure to produce a recovery was the view that the interventionist trend of government and the rise of trade unionism thwarted the automatic adjusting mechanisms. Private and state-sponsored monopolies, price-fixing agreements, tariffs, state-sponsored producers' agreements and marketing boards and all types of government regulations seriously impaired the normal operation of the system, making it respond sluggishly to changes in market conditions.

These arrangements, so it was argued, tended to shield those sectors of the economy most in need of economic change. They had the effect of perpetuating excess capacity, obsolescence and poor management. "We eschew the sharp purge," wrote economist Lionel Robbins[17] in the midst of the Great Depression. "We prefer the lingering disease ...." "What we face is not merely the working of capitalism," complained Joseph Schumpeter, "but a capitalism which nations are determined not to allow to function."[18]

But the real villains in the old economic textbook were the trade unions. The natural forces of the economy always guaranteed full employment, they insisted. When some unemployment occurred it would be quickly eliminated by a fall in wages. By holding up wages irrespective of the state of the labour market, the trade unions must take full responsibility for unemployment.

These arguments notwithstanding, the economics profession fully expected that the recovery, as slow and gradual as it was, would finally take off and that the economy would resume its previous exuberant growth. It was the sudden and steep decline of 1937-38 that shattered this confidence. The recovery had just begun to make a real dent on unemployment when the depression struck again. Only then did Keynes's *General Theory of Employment, Interest and Money*, first published in 1936, begin to make its impact; for the 1937-38 recession revealed once and for all the bankruptcy of the dominant paradigm. And for the very first time the possibility was frankly faced that economic breakdowns not only were built into the system but were also not self-correcting.

The Social Democracy of John Stuart Mill

Orthodoxy produced its own liberal and reform-minded critics. Preeminent among them was John Stuart Mill whose *Principles of Political Economy* may be regarded as the first primer on social democracy.

Famous for his intellectual feats — he read Plato at age seven, mastered geometry, algebra and differential calculus, and wrote a history of Rome between the ages of eight and twelve — Mill had made a complete survey of all there was to be known in political economy at age thirteen. Thirty years later (1848) came his *Principles of Political Economics*. Seven editions were published before he died in 1873, each with significant amendments.

The most significant addition was the celebrated chapter "Probable Future of the Labouring Classes" inserted in the third (1852) edition.

As he noted in his autobiography, the interim period saw him studying the socialist writers, those whom Marx later called the utopian socialists. Collaborating with him was his wife, Harriet Taylor, who was largely responsible for the new chapter, and it was apparently she who convinced him of the distinction that should be drawn between the laws of production, which were deemed natural laws, and the laws of distribution, which depended on human will and hence could be modified. This distinction, it turned out, was to be Mill's most enduring contribution to economics.

"The laws and conditions of the production of wealth partake of the character of physical truths. There is nothing optional or arbitrary in them," Mill declared, "It is not so with the Distribution of Wealth. That is a matter of human institution only. The things once there, mankind, individually or collectively, can do with them as they like.... The rules by which it is determined are what the opinions and feelings of the ruling portion of the community make them." And the rules can vary from age to age and from country to country. So if society did not like the natural outcome of the free market it could tax or subsidize them, redistribute or expropriate them.[19]

While Mill attached no limits on the extent to which "human institutions" could redistribute the results of the laws of production, both conservatives and Marxists were quick to point out that the two spheres are not as separate and independent as he would have liked. A 100 per cent tax on profits, for example, would quickly bring on an investment strike that would grind production to a sudden halt.

Yet within limits there obviously is room to manoeuvre, at least some of the time. Mill established an agenda of reform. A believer in the possibility of changing social behaviour, he thought the working class could be educated to understand their Malthusian peril. With the pressure of population on wages removed, he argued that with the active intervention of the state, the lot of the working class could be dramatically improved. Thus while "laissez-faire ... should be the general practice," departures from it were acceptable if "required by some great good."[20]

He recommended several departures. Among them was a tax on inherited wealth. "The social arrangements of modern Europe," he wrote, "commenced from distribution of property which was the result, not of just partition, or aquisition by industry, but of conquest and violence."[21] While he was prepared to leave these past arrangements undisturbed, he gave no credence to current claimants. Why should they have income from the exertion and savings of others?

He also recommended a tax on gains from rising land values. This restriction on the right of property is justified not only because the gain is unearned, but also because "the community has too much at stake in the proper cultivation of the land ... to leave these things to the discretion of a class of persons called landlords."[22]

In addition to these tax reforms, Mill advocated laws to protect the rights of working people to form unions; to prevent the abuse of working children; to limit the length of the working day; and to introduce universal public education, a minimum subsistence for all those unable to work, and regulation or public ownership of monopolies.

His entire reform program rested on three basic arguments. First, "no rational person will maintain it to be abstractedly just that a small minority of mankind should be born to the enjoyment of all the external advantages which life can give, without earning them by any merit or acquiring them by any exertion of their own, while the immense majority are condemned from their birth to a life of never-ending, never-intermitting toil, requitted by a bare, and in general a precarious, subsistence."[23]

Second, "capital, strictly speaking, has no productive power." It only serves to set the production power of labour in motion. Yet owners of capital extort "a heavy tribute for the use of capital by their employees."[24] The prevailing system serves to "guarantee" to the owning classes "the fruits of the labour and abstinence of others."[25] Contrary to Senior, abstinence (from consuming their profits) is not the peculiar prerogative of the capitalist class. "Those who receive the least, labour and abstain the most."[26]

Third, the poor cannot be left alone to judge what would best promote their interests. They need the state to intervene on their behalf because they are powerless and unknowledgeable. On matters affecting them "the foundation of the *laissez-faire* principle breaks down entirely"[27] for it presumes that individuals are always the best judge of their welfare.

The upshot of Mill's pronouncements is the interventionist state.

> It is not admissible that the protection of persons and that of property are the sole purposes of government. The ends of government are as comprehensible as those of social unions. They consist of all the good and all the immunity from evil of which the existence of government can be made either directly or indirectly to bestow.[28]

Mill proclaimed himself to be a socialist, but he maintained that "however valuable [it is] as an ideal and even as a prophecy ... [it] is not available as a present resource .... For a long time to come the principle of individual property will be in possession of the field."[29] His reforms were therefore aimed not at subverting the system but at improving it. This they would accomplish by bringing about a gradual "change of character ... in the uncultivated herd who now compose the labouring masses, and in the immense majority of their employers." In the process, both classes would learn to "labour and combine ... for public and social purpose and not, as hitherto, solely for narrowly interested ones."[30] In effect, Mill ends up defending capitalist economic arrangments until people learn, through the process of reform, to behave in the public good.

Orthodoxy Reformed

John Maynard Keynes was to carry the mantle of reform and interventionism into the twentieth century. But in the meantime, somewhat more cautiously than Mill, others began to find room for some government action within a somewhat liberalized version of economic orthodoxy. State intervention was justified, it was argued, because the free-market system can achieve the optimal results only if many highly unrealistic conditions are present — such as perfect competition in the markets for goods and services, and labour and capital; perfect mobility of human and physical resources (between users and over spaces); and perfect information on all alternatives available to buyers and sellers. Where these conditions do not obtain, market outcomes are not nearly as favourable as promised and in fact often require government action to offset resulting inequities, misallocations and distortions.

A further reason for scepticism about the free market was raised by John Kenneth Galbraith. In his famous *Affluent Society*, the noted Canadian-born writer rejected orthodoxy's assumption that individuals are the authors of their own demands for consumer goods. Consumer tastes, he wrote, are shaped by advertising, packaging and frequent style changes. In challenging the doctrine of consumer sovereignty he concluded that, since the corporate sector, not the sovereign consumer, is responsible for production priorities, individual preferences need not be held so sacrosanct. In particular, the massive effort devoted to the sales effort inevitably produces a bias in favour of private consumption and a bias against collective consumption. The result is "private affluence" on the one hand and "public squalor" on the other. To correct the imbalance, Galbraith called for greater state expenditures on social services and public infrastructures.

More troubling still, not all consumer preferences are registered in the market. Unequal distribution of income means that some people have more say in the market than others. In this way the pattern of output that results from the market mechanism does not reflect all priorities and needs. If everything was supplied according to market criteria alone, many individuals would lack some of life's necessities.

Even if it were possible to remove all of these "imperfections," many economists admit that the market mechanism could still not act as the sole organizing principle in a modern economy. At least four types of commodities require some other mechanism. First are the so-called public goods, such as national defence, police services, street lighting and roads, which once provided to one individual are necessarily available to all others. Those who don't pay the price in purchasing them cannot be excluded from consuming them. But if a price cannot be universally charged, no profit can be made and there is no incentive for private firms to undertake their production. There is no alternative to state provision because only the state can force all to pay through the tax system.

Second are commodities which generate "externalities" or spill-over effects, such as the noxious by-products of certain industries, like smoke, noise or pollutants, that impose costs on the rest of the community but do not enter into industry costs and are therefore not reflected in the market price. The prime example of externalities is the private automobile. There are the costs of providing and maintaining roads and traffic controls (although these may be covered by gasoline taxes), health-care, police and court costs arising from accidents, the costs of air, noise and visual pollution, and not least is the incalculable cost of the gradual spoiling of our physical environment. It may be difficult to give exact quantitative significance to all of these hidden costs, but unless people are required to consider them, the choices they make are based on misinformation. In this instance, the price a person pays for an automobile is probably a small fraction of the full social costs incurred in its operation.

Third are alternative goods and services that could be made available with society's resources and skills but that do not emerge from the market because they are not profitable. For instance, for a sum that is a small part of the total social costs to the nation for maintaining private cars, it would be possible to provide a comfortable, efficient and frequent public transport service. Only if such a service were available and car buyers charged a price that covered the full cost of driving their own car could we expect a rational choice between public and private transit.

Fourth are services that could be provided by the market but that are generally provided by the government, largely because society assumes that coming from the state these services will be better and cheaper. Available private-health insurance schemes in the U.S., for example, are notoriously inadequate and limited in coverage, yet the U.S. spends a higher proportion of its GNP on health care than any other rich industrial country. Canada devotes 10 per cent less for better care. Similarly, automobile insurance rates average 15-20 per cent less in provinces with public automobile insurance plans than those that rely on private enterprise.

Absence of the necessary conditions for ideal results and deficiencies of the market mechanism have obvious implications for state intervention. Influenced by Galbraith and several other economists of a liberal persuasion, orthodoxy has amended its position to argue that, while the market system operates reasonably effectively in general, there are areas where state intervention improves the allocation of resources and better ensures their full employment. This is obviously the case for public goods where, as even Adam Smith recognized, there is no alternative to state provision. Regarding commodities that generate externalities, there is general agreement that prices should be adjusted through taxes and subsidies to more closely reflect social costs rather than only private costs and benefits.

While market and private provision are not replaced, the arithmetic is altered to produce better signals within the market system. In instances where external benefits arise, some economists are prepared to go beyond subsidization. They argue that to encourage consumption, these commodities should be provided by the state either free of charge or at subsidized prices. Most orthodox economists accept the need for state intervention to make markets more competitive, to improve resource mobility, to improve information flows and to regulate total spending through fiscal and monetary policy. Again, the point is, not to replace the market system, but to nudge it towards the conditions that would allow it to operate in the ideal manner.

Over the years, these criticisms and solutions have laid the foundation for a modified version of traditional orthodoxy — which in turn has provided the theoretical basis for what is popularly known as the mixed economy. These revisions of orthodoxy include a wide range of liberal to social-democratic variants which determine the precise content and terms of the public-private mix. In the twenty-five or so years of prosperity following the Second World War, a broad consensus among economists developed around what was called "the neo-classical synthesis" and much of the debate within economics occurred within the boundaries of this consensus.

Limits of Reform

By making individual firms more fully responsible for the social losses caused by their activities, social legislation and regulations have had some effect in reducing the magnitude of the social cost of production. Similarly, the welfare state has certainly moderated some of the worst outcomes of the system. Yet because social legislation and regulations leave the private-enterprise economy intact, influencing market behaviour and market outcomes at the margin, the overall impact is limited.

Marxists, for example, draw attention to the limited space within which the welfare state is condemned to operate. In the first place, welfare rates can never be allowed to provide a livable income, for as they approach the pay scales at the low end of the labour market they damage employers' chance of attracting a labour force to fill dead-end jobs. In the second place, the leveling effect introduced by progressive tax structures and universal social services is quickly nullified by market forces. Because the rich have near full control of the levers that determine their incomes, they can easily recapture their shares, which means that redistribution is mainly horizontal, within the working class, rather than between classes. The ultimate constraint, Marxists like to point out, is not insufficient will-power on the part of reluctant governments to do more, but the structure and the requirements of the economic system itself.

Beyond the Marxists lies another critical tradition that tends to be quite pessimistic about the possibilities for change within the existing structures of capitalism. Among the most prominent sceptics are environmentalists and those who have delved into the hidden and not-so-hidden injuries of the workplace. For example, aluminum has largely replaced steel and lumber as a construction material because it's far more efficient. But it requires about 15 times more fuel energy to produce than steel and about 150 times more fuel energy than lumber. The tendency to displace power-thrifty goods with power-consumptive ones is heavily borne by the environment.

Detergents, yielding a profit of 50 per cent on sales, have replaced soap, which yields only 30 per cent. To obtain the raw material for detergents, petroleum is distilled in an energy-consuming process; the burned fuel pollutes the air. To obtain the cleaning agent the purified raw material is subjected to a series of chemical reactions involving chlorine. This creates still more air pollution, as the total energy used to produce the active agent is three times what's needed to produce oil for soap. To produce the needed chlorine, mercury is used and released in the environment as another pollutant. Phosphate additives cause still further environmental damage.

Another example is the use of nitrogen fertilizer in agriculture. Between 1950 and 1970 its annual use in the U.S. rose by over 600 per cent, and the result was a 75 per cent increase in yields per acre. But the social costs have also mounted. The increased use of chemical fertilizers as well as pesticides and herbicides which has made the farmer more efficient per acre has polluted rivers and has caused a serious depletion of top soil.

Traditional economic theory treats these social costs as a minor and exceptional disturbance rather than an everyday feature emerging from competitive pressures in the market economy. The economist's solution is to impose a tax that covers these hidden costs. The producer pays the cost of pollution control or pays a fee for the benefit of using the environment as a dumping ground. The added cost is passed along to the consumer in a price increase, or where the tax is paid the revenue can be used by government to protect and restore the environment.

Setting aside the cost of licensing, taxing and monitoring such a complex program and the possibility that the damage is irreparable, the problem with this solution is that it is detached from economic realities. To improve its profits each firm searches for ways of cutting costs. Once one firm discovers a new cost-cutting material or process, other firms jeopardize their existence if they don't follow suit. In the words of Barry Commoner, from whose work these examples have been culled:

> The general proposition that emerges from these considerations is that environmental pollution is connected to the economics of the private enterprise system in two ways. First, pollution tends to become intensified by the displacement of older productive techniques by new, ecologically faulty, but more profitable technologies. Thus, in these cases, pollution is an unintended concomitant of the natural drive of the economic system to introduce new technologies that increase productivity. Second, the costs of environmental degradation are chiefly borne not by the producer, but by society as a whole, in the form of "externalities." A business enterprise that pollutes the environment is therefore being subsidized by society; to this extent, the enterprise, though free, is not wholly private.[31]

Polluting firms can be taxed or required to introduce proper controls, but such measures would nullify most if not all the prior pecuniary gains. They would add millions of dollars to costs of production without adding to the value of the output of saleable goods. The extra costs could be pushed onto the consumer, but this might jeopardize sales. And wage earners faced with higher prices would demand higher wages. The neat solution of the economist is rarely available.

Similar problems attend the treatment of labour. The costs of maintaining a worker in working-order and raising a new generation of workers are overhead costs that have, in private-enterprise economies, been converted into mere variable costs for employers. Except insofar as workers can exact wages to cover these expenses, they are no obligation of industry.

The conversion of these overhead costs into variable costs arises from the fact that in a capitalist labour market labourers as free individuals are not subject to private-ownership rights. They sell a service, they get a wage. Any extra costs incurred by workers are entirely their responsibility. This becomes particularly obvious after workers are laid off: the cost of the lay-off is zero to the employer because the entire overhead costs are borne by the workers and their families. In some instances it is also borne by local businesses in lost sales and by the community in the form of a lower tax base and higher unemployment relief. These omissions are not miscalculations by the employer: they are inherent in the capitalist wage system.

Typical employers will be similarly reluctant to consider as part of their costs any impairment to the physical and mental capacities of their work force. Their willingness to do so will be the greater the easier they find it to replace "worn-out," injured or diseased workers with new ones, and the more competitive pressures require them to raise productivity and reduce costs.

Economic theory dismisses this as a problem since it presumes that when workers hire on and accept a risky job they do so voluntarily, obtaining a wage premium that reflects the risk factor. The theory assumes full employment, perfect labour mobility and perfect knowledge — conditions which never exist in the real world. To the extent that unemployment is high and workers are tied down to particular locations and employments, they are compelled to accept whatever jobs are available at whatever the known risks. But more often than not the risk factors are not known. With six million chemical compounds in existence, and another 6,000 being introduced each week, this should come as no surprise. While *only* 33,000 chemicals are commonly used in industry, most of these have never been tested for carcinogenicity. Moreover, employers themselves have little incentive to inform themselves, let alone their employees, of the disease potential of these chemicals.

Management has a well-known tendency to deny the existence of health hazards and to attribute work injuries to worker carelessness and apathy. The asbestos case is particularly enlightening. Studies on the hazards of asbestos were available as early as the 1930s, and further studies completed in the 1960s demonstrated beyond a doubt that asbestos is a dangerous material. The Beaudry Commission, established in 1975 to examine the asbestos problem, disclosed that even at that late date asbestos companies deliberately kept "available information about the dangerous effects of exposure to asbestos dust away from the workers and the unions."[32]

It's estimated that on a typical eight-hour work day, 4,000 workers are injured on the job and that more than a million cases of occupational disease, injuries and fatalities are reported to provincial workers' compensation boards annually.[33] Moreover, some experts believe that many off-the-job problems begin in the workplace. According to Bob Sass, former associate deputy minister of labour for the Government of Saskatchewan:

> I have come to believe that all features of social life for workers are drawn into the problem of the workplace, while the workplace is the first cause of the social problems of the work force.... Hence, the conflict or the adverse effect of these stressors — whether they be wage payment systems, speed-up, piece-rate ... produce the social conflicts or adverse feeling outside of work, rather than in production. So it is that one's inability to love, read a book, or do housework, sleeping longer hours, general unhappiness, having extra-marital affairs, marital breakdowns, increased tiredness or irritableness, etc., becomes totally separate or disconnected from work. These are matters which are studied separate from work-time. Consequently, the literature suggests that these breakdowns last show up at work, *because all is sacrificed by the worker in order to maintain the employment relationship*. Work *is* the first cause of the social disease which is now believed to be of epidemic proportion, although it last shows up in the workplace.[34]

Generally employers do not bare the burden of the medical and social damage they inflict on and off the work site. The attitude is perfectly described in *Industrial Accident Prevention*, the classic text of H.W. Heinrichs, a safety superintendent of a major insurance company who defined an accident as "an unplanned interruption of the work process."[35] Aside from the premiums they pay to workers' compensation which amounts to less than one-hundredth of their total payroll, total expenditure devoted to improving the safety of the workplace is negligible.

Since the probability of being inspected is so small and fines so miniscule, government regulations have a minimal effect. Manitoba, for instance, has twenty inspectors in the field to monitor 42,000 work sites. The average business can expect an inspection once every seventeen years, and the average fine is less than $100 per offence and rarely exceeds $1,000.

A safe work environment is usually more costly than an unsafe one. Eliminating unsafe or untested chemicals as well as unsafe equipment and work processes is expensive, as is the installation of design engineering to eliminate the effects of toxic chemicals, an improved preventative maintenance and monitoring program, and a slowing down of the pace of work. The increased productivity associated with these efforts rarely, if ever, measures up to the extra dollar costs involved.

Business cannot usually maximize both profits and health and safety. It faces a contradiction between health and safety concerns and production and profit priorities. Nor does it have much freedom to trade off costs, production and profit for health and safety. In an economy based on competition there is often little room for investments and practices that yield no profit and in fact lower profit. It's less a question of personal morality than of commercial survival.

As long ago as 1950, a much ignored economist, K. William Kapp, declared that "capitalism must be regarded as an economy of unpaid costs.[36] At the conclusion of his brilliant *Social Costs of Private Enterprise*, Kapp writes:

> As soon as one passes beyond the traditional abstractions of cost-price analysis and begins to consider the omitted truth of social costs, it becomes clear once more that the alleged beneficial orderliness of the competitive process is all but a myth. For, if entrepreneurial costs do not measure the total costs of production, the competitive cost-price calculus is not merely meaningless but nothing more than an institutionalized cover under which it is possible for private enterprise to shift part of the costs to the shoulders of others and to practice a form of large-scale spoliation which transcends everything the early socialists had in mind when they spoke of the exploitation of man by man.[37]

According to Kapp, economic orthodoxy, both in its traditional and amended versions, omits serious treatment of social costs because of its assumption that the economic sphere can be separated from the people it affects. It is this implicit assumption that explains the acceptance of business expenditures as an adequate measure of total costs of production, and prices and private returns as relevant standards for measuring the economic benefits.

In urging a "new science of political economy," Kapp calls for a broadening of the scope of economic analysis, an end to the departmentalization of the social sciences, for a mode of analysis that integrates "social, economic and political reality."[38] Kapp is no Marxist but the only mode of analysis that comes even close to fulfilling the requirements he sets forth is the one provided by Marx a century ago.

Marx versus Orthodoxy

It has been said of Karl Marx that no thinker has been buried and revived more often and with such passion than has "the dark fellow from Trier." One writer has gone so far as to say that the entire edifice of neo-classical economics amounts to nothing more than "the undignified farce of sharp-shooting with toy Austrian popguns from behind a non-existing methodological wall."[39]

Born in Germany in 1818, Marx embarked on a career of journalism after receiving a doctorate in philosophy. But his journalism was a little too radical and having been expelled from most European states he arrived in England in 1849. There he made the most sustained and comprehensive attack that any economic system has ever had to endure.

Marx's target was capitalism, whose functioning had formed the basis of classical political economy. He trod closely in the footsteps of his predecessors.

What was important about the tradition and why it stood in stark contrast with the rising body of what Marx called "vulgar economy" — predecessor to neo-classical orthodoxy — is that it examined all economic questions as by-products of the class relations of society. His economic mentor David Ricardo defined "the principle problem of Political Economy" as the laws which regulate how "the produce of the earth ... is divided among three classes of the community, namely the proprietor of the land, the owner of the stock of capital necessary for its cultivation, and the labourers by whose industry it is cultivated."[40] But classical political economy, Marx argued, was blind to historical context, it failed to see capitalism in historical prospective.

What does Marxism offer as an alternative mode of analysis? If we examine any human society at any point in time, Marx said, we can identify a complicated network of beliefs, attitudes, behaviour, morals and institutions. But the dominant force which in each instance shapes human affairs is the need to establish the material conditions for physical survival. In every society, that requires labour effort and tools of production. What distinguishes one society from another is the particular manner in which this is accomplished, its "mode of production."

Two separate but interrelated components comprise any mode of production. First are the "forces of production," specific inputs to the productive process — the quality and quantity of labour, equipment, raw materials and level of technology. Second is each society's unique "relation of production," the social or class dynamics between various groups in society defined in terms of ownership of and control over the forces of production.

Labour is essential to human survival. But in most environments, at least those that progress materially, not all the working hours are required for basic survival. Beyond this "necessary labour" time is "surplus labour" time which can be harnessed for a variety of purposes. Since surplus time and surplus goods are critical in shaping the future, it is the relations under which surplus is produced, the purpose to which the surplus is used and to whose benefit it accrues that are the basic tools of Marxian analysis.

To receive the fruits of surplus labour — labour beyond that required for basic survival — without giving anything in return is Marx's definition of exploitation. To occupy such a position is to occupy a position of power. It enables members of the dominant class to consume without producing, or at least to consume far in excess of anything they produce. Control over the surplus gives the dominant class substantial control to shape the economic future, deciding how the surplus will be used, what new structures and what new products will be built, what new techniques will be developed, etc. It gives the dominant class substantial social and political power, providing material resources for political and cultural activity. In short, control over the economic surplus gives the dominant class the capacity to shape the direction of social change and the content of life inside and outside the workplace.

Under slavery and serfdom, labour and the means of production are brought together by command and coercion. The surplus is extracted from the producers in the process of production and used primarily to support the lifestyles of the masters and lords, who built monuments to honour themselves, hired jesters to entertain them, servants to wait upon them and armies to protect them.

Under capitalism, labour and the means of production are brought together through the labour contract under which the workers, in exchange for a wage payment, give up all rights of ownership to the products they produce. A surplus is extracted when capitalists pocket the difference between what they pay workers and the value of things workers produce. In this model "surplus value" becomes the source of capitalist profits. Unlike previous modes of production and distinctly superior to them, capitalism uses the surplus not only to support the lifestyle of the capitalist class, but also to increase the productive capacity of the economy.

For Marx, class is the key concept in describing the relations of production. The *Communist Manifesto* opens with the words "the history of all hitherto existing society is the history of class struggles." Society has always been split into the classes who control the means of production and those who do not. Under capitalism each day involves the struggle between capital and labour at the point of production — capitalists aiming to extract as much productivity as they can from workers; workers resisting, first, to ensure that they receive in wages and other benefits a higher proportion of the value they produce, and second, to win more control over the workplace by limiting the arbitrary power of the employer. In capitalist economies, labour is necessarily treated as a commodity, a factor of production, rather than as people with distinctive needs and aspirations.

Where orthodox theory's starting point is always the individual, Marxist theory holds that the individual exists within a class and that class position molds ideology and behaviour, and sets limits on income and choice. To start with the individual is to start at the wrong end of the chain of causation.

While orthodox economic thought has minutely analyzed market exchanges where the law of supply and demand reigns supreme, Marx entered the "hidden abode of production" which is the location of class struggle. At the surface level of market relations free choice is the order of the day. By the time workers and employers meet to conduct their labour-for-wage transaction, most workers have already been deprived of the capacity to exercise freedom. With the ownership of the major means of production confined to a small class of owners, they do not have the option of working for themselves. They must sell their labour power on whatever terms and under whatever conditions they can negotiate, individually or collectively.

The inequality of power between labour and capital is ultimately founded on the ability of those who own and control the means of production to admit or exclude those who depend on wage employment for a livelihood. Owners also operate within constraints. They must turn a profit in competition against rival firms. But they have a variety of options not easily available to most workers. They can relocate to more profitable areas, introduce new technology and new products or they can go out of business and hire themselves out as salaried managers.

Marxian economics argues that inequality and coercion, structured into class relationships and the distribution of property rights, are invisible to orthodoxy (in both its "left" and "right" varieties), because it takes for granted the existing system of ownership and the rights that go with property. By focusing on the individual making choices, orthodoxy loses sight of the fact that the range of choices available are systematically determined by the class location of the chooser.

Inevitability of Change

Like the neo-conservatives, Marxists find postwar welfare capitalism a contradictory phenomenon. But whereas the neo-conservatives see the solution in winding down the welfare state and reverting to a market economy unfettered by government regulation and management, Marxists look beyond capitalism for a lasting solution to its ills. And they believe, following Marx himself, that capitalism is no more eternal than feudalism was.

What causes one mode of production to be superseded by another? Economic and social systems evolve within their own framework until contradictions are generated which so frustrate further economic advancement that upheaval becomes inevitable. At some point the new forces of production and rising classes associated with it conflict with the vested interests of the ruling class. As the new mode of production develops alongside the old it challenges the fundamental principles upon which the existing society is based. At some point, usually in concert with other subordinate classes, the rising new class takes over state power to realign political and legal structures with the new mode of production.

According to Marxist analysis, this is precisely the process by which feudalism was replaced by capitalism. In order to advance, the rising new class of urban-based merchants and manufacturers required the abolition of all legal restrictions on the ownership of land and all restrictions on the mobility and use of labour and capital. Through the liberal revolutions of the seventeenth and eighteenth centuries, they seized political power from the nobility and passed laws, regulations, tax structures and tariffs appropriate for a national economy based on individual mobility, free contract and impersonal market allocations of work and rewards.

Just like slavery and feudalism before it, capitalism, Marx believed, was doomed to self-destruction because of its internal contradictions. Marx's critique of capitalism celebrated its singular achievement: for the first time in history a productive capacity had been created which could potentially provide for everyone's basic needs. In the *Communist Manifesto*, Marx wrote: "the bourgeoisie was the first to show us what human activity is capable of achieving. It has executed works more marvelous than the building of Egyptian pyramids, Roman aqueducts, and Gothic cathedrals; it has carried out expeditions surpassing by far the tribal migrations and the Crusades." Capitalism created the productive potential to permit, for the first time, a universal freedom. That is its great contribution. But within its framework, this potential can never be realized. Freedom and creativity must continue to be restricted to a privileged few. That is its fundamental and historical failure. Marx set himself the task of showing why and how the capitalist economy will ultimately collapse and be replaced by socialism.

While the basic problem of all previous societies was scarcity, the problem of capitalism is its tendency to overproduce. Goaded by relentless competition that generates unceasing innovation and technological change, the forces of production thereby undergo continuous expansion. Their capacity to produce is almost limitless. But commodities must be produced and sold at a profit, for capitalist production has no other purpose.

Whatever the immediate cause that triggers it, when capital ceases to be able to extract sufficient "surplus value," an economic slump ensues marked by overproduction, unemployment and poverty. Underused machinery and unemployed people co-exist with unfilled human needs because it is not profitable to use the resources and it is not profitable to fulfill the needs.

Paralleling Marx's economic critique is his moral condemnation of capitalism as a social system. His concern was not only the widening gap between rich and poor. Even if it were possible to jack up wages to an extremely high level, this "would only be an improvement of slaves and would acquire neither for the worker nor for labour its essential human destiny and dignity." Whatever the wage level, all the control remains with the owners.

> Within the capitalist system all methods of raising the social productiveness of labour are brought about at the cost of the individual labourer; all means for the development of production transform themselves into means of domination over, and exploitation of, the producers; they mutilate the labourer into a fragment of a man, degrade him to the level of an appendage of a machine, destroy every remnant of charm in his work and turn it into a hated toil; they estrange from him the intellectual potentialities of the labour process in the same proportion as science is incorporated in it as an independent power; they distort the conditions under which he works, subject him during the labour process to a despotism the more hateful for its meanness.... It follows therefore that in proportion as capital accumulates, the lot of the labourer, *be his payment high or low*, must grow worse [emphasis in original].[41]

People have diminishing control over the tools they work with; they have less identity with the product they have made, except as an "object of worship"; they have become alienated from each other, as objects for manipulation; they become poorer as income fails to keep up with their growing "appetite for things."

> No eunuch flatters his tyrant more shamefully or seeks by more infamous means to stimulate his jaded appetite, in order to gain some favor, than does the eunuch of industry, the entrepreneur, in order to acquire a few silver coins .... The entrepreneur accedes to the most depraved fancies of his neighbour, plays the role of pander between him and his needs, and awakens unhealthy appetites in him, and watches for every weakness in order, later, to claim the remuneration for his labor of love.[42]

Given this savage critique, Marx quite clearly relished the prospect of capitalism's demise. And he demanded more of his followers than the study of the inner workings of the capitalist economy. "The philosophers hitherto have only interpreted the world," he wrote as a young man, "the thing, however, is to change it."

The working class and its struggles are positioned at the heart of social transformation. Indeed, it is one of the major tenets of Marxism that the working class is the primary agent for revolutionizing capitalist society. Revolution is not viewed as inevitable, but it is seen as one possible outcome of the contradictions and conflicts inherent in the capitalist economic system. The working class is regarded by Marxists as potentially *the* revolutionary class, not because it is the most oppressed group of people in society, but because it alone can bring capitalist production to a halt.

Whether the working class in alliance with other oppressed groups will develop a revolutionary consciousness and a revolutionary political organization is not a foregone conclusion. The expected clarification of proletarian attitudes has not in fact taken place. It is one of the dilemmas of contemporary Marxism that the working class in mature capitalist economies has recoiled from revolutionary politics and that socialist revolutions have been confined to underdeveloped capitalist countries, resulting in an "underdeveloped socialism."

In every way but the most crucial one, the years between the First World War and the Second World War appeared to confirm the Marxist scenario. The contradictions between the forces and relations of production brought the system to the point of collapse. Many Marxists predicted that the end of capitalism was close at hand as fierce conflicts arose between labour and capital. But there was no proletarian revolution and after the war capitalism rose like a phoenix from its ashes. Firmly in the grip of Stalinism, Marxists were content to repeat familiar formulations which were totally inadequate for analyzing the long wave of postwar prosperity. A discredited Marxism lost its audience in Western Europe and North America. Workers were too busy keeping up with the Joneses to bother about politics, let alone revolution. Academics were busily constructing theoretical models that looked upon worker militancy, student protest, indeed any form of protest, as some kind of deviation from the norm of political stability and social harmony.

It was not until the early 1970s that Marx was rediscovered. Since then Marxism has enjoyed a remarkable and unexpected renaissance, for several reasons.

First, mainstream economics failed to predict and cannot account for the appearance of inflation in the 1970s and "slumpflation" in the 1980s. Sophisticated government management was supposed to have made such economic crises extinct. With the world-wide reappearance of mass unemployment, with the welfare state under attack and government policy in disarray, the question of whether capitalism has a future is once again on the agenda.

Second, Marxism was finally freed from the heavy hand of Joseph Stalin. For over a quarter of a century it had been cast into handy formulas used to close off debate rather than engage it. Instead of being treated as a working hypothesis, it became a holy scripture —complete with catechism and inquisition — to fight off "renegades" and "deviationists." When Marx found his theories being used in a similar fashion in the 1870s, he felt forced to remark, "all I know is that I am not a 'Marxist'." Matters were not helped by the Cold War when Marxists were themselves regarded as heretics and hounded out of the arts and the universities.

It was the turbulent 1960s and the war in Vietnam that produced a new generation of Marxist scholars and activists. Not surprisingly, they have pushed Marxist thought into new fields — the family, sexuality, sports, film, education — matters of everyday life.

Marx left behind a comprehensive social science, an intellectual system without boundaries. No question of contemporary relevance is left outside the scope of his system of enquiry. Yet he was often wrong. His discussion of class, the state, the family, the transition to socialism, and the political and cultural spheres was fragmentary, deterministic and sometimes simplistic. He gave inadequate weight to such forces as nationalism and religion. Yet long after historical materialism had pronounced it dead and buried, religious revival, often fused with nationalism and sometimes with racism, is sweeping the world. In Latin America, the soldiers of Christ are in the forefront of the revolutionary march. And no socialist movement speaking in the name of Marx has come into power without relying on the force of nationalism.

In short, despite the thousands of pages of manuscripts and notes he produced, Marx left behind more questions than answers. For years his work has been treated as gospel, a closed and completed system. Now a new generation of Marxists is opening the system to scrutiny, and updating, revising and reconstructing it according to new experience, new realities and new knowledge. A great debate is flowering within Marxism — every bit as sweeping, vigorous and containing as much heat and rancour as current debates within orthodox social science.

In North America at least, Marxism remains a movement for intellectuals. It has gained currency in some sections of the woman's movement; and the tools of Marxist analysis are selectively drawn upon in Christian social action documents, such as the Canadian Catholic bishops' "Ethical Reflections on the Economic Crisis." But Marxism has barely penetrated the movements of the working class. Most disturbing for Marxists is that the collapse of the political centre has benefited the Right more than it has the Left. Marxists have as yet failed to develop a socialist vision and a socialist strategy that can command the attention and mobilize the energies of working-class activists. In the sphere of political action Marxism is as isolated as it was a decade or two ago. But in the intellectual sphere its standing has never been greater. Certainly nobody would have predicted a decade or so ago that Marxism would be a full participant in what historians will undoubtedly look back upon as the most profound debate of the last half of this century. But Marxists were the first to predict, announce and analyze the current world economic crisis while orthodox economists still remained unaware of it or denied its existence.

PART II The Rise and Fall of Keynesianism

4 | Keynes' Vision

John Maynard Keynes was born the same year — 1883 — that Marx died. Beyond that they shared little else — Marx had hoped to bury capitalism, Keynes is commonly regarded as its saviour. In the midst of the Great Depression, Keynes gave the capitalist democracies a program to fight both fascism and communism.

Like many others, Keynes was revolted by the sight of masses of unemployed going hungry and poorly clothed while warehouses and granaries were overflowing, and food and fibre were deliberately destroyed or allowed to rot in the fields. Unlike other economists, however, he was convinced that human misery was produced not by natural economic laws but by economic institutions. While conceding that capitalism's problems were generic, he thought they were partial and, more to the point, they could be remedied. The ultimate source of the problem was not material shortages but a "failure in the immaterial devices of the mind."[1] Correct thinking and correct policy could save the system. "It may be possible by a right analysis of the problem," he wrote, "to cure the disease while preserving efficiency and freedom."[2]

The regime Keynes envisioned was "liberal socialism ... a system where we can act as an organized community for economic purpose to promote social and economic justice, while respecting and protecting the individual — his freedom of choice, his faith, his mind and its expression, his enterprise and his property."[3]

It was as early as the 1920s that Keynes began his break from the orthodoxy of his day. It was a time, like today, when conventional remedies led to absurd outcomes. With unemployment rates averaging no less than 12 per cent, Britain was by then already in the midst of its great depression. Keynes' target was the "treasury view" which counseled thrift as the solution to stagnation and wage reduction as the solution to unemployment. Suspend public works and public spending, the experts argued (as they do today), and private investment will rise in response to the resulting decline in interest rates. "Simply suicidal," Keynes rebutted. Rallying to the support of Lloyd George's public-works scheme in the 1929 general election, he charged:

> It is not an accident that the Conservative Government has landed us in the mess where we find ourselves. It is the natural outcome of their philosophy:
> "You must not press on with telephones or electricity, because this will raise the rate of interest."
> "You must not hasten with roads or housing, because this will use up opportunities for employment which we may need in later years."
> "You must not try to employ every one, because this will cause inflation."
> "You must not invest, because how can you know that it will pay?"...
> They are slogans of depression and decay — the timidities and obstructions and stupidities of a sinking administrative vitality.
> Negation, Restriction, Inactivity — these are the Government's watchwords. Under their leadership we have been forced to button up our waistcoats and compress our lungs.
> There is no reason why we should not feel ourselves free to be bold, to be open, to experiment, to take action, to try the possibilities of things. And over against us, standing in the path, there is nothing but a few old gentlemen tightly buttoned up in their frock coats, who only need to be treated with a little friendly disrespect and bowled over like ninepins.[4]

Keynes Rebuts Orthodoxy

Here was a case of a policy — state interventionism — in search of a theory. Keynes finally provided that theory in his hastily written but brilliant *General Theory of Employment, Interest and Money*. In the preface, he confides that "the composition of this book has been for the author a long struggle of escape ... from habitual modes of thought and expression."[5]

One of the key elements of these habitual modes of thought, as we have already seen, is that trade unions cause unemployment, for if they did not hold up wages everybody would ultimately find work. Keynes broke with economic orthodoxy by accepting the presence and permanence of trade unions. They hold up wages, he acknowledged, but a general decline in wages would more likely produce more unemployment rather than less. Wage cuts might be a feasible remedy to save jobs in particular trades or companies, just as improved labour mobility and training could help remove frictional unemployment. But neither of these remedies could alleviate economy-wide involuntary unemployment. Having demonstrated that even an economy free of trade unions shows no tendency to full employment, Keynes went on to examine more powerful and systematic forces that determine the level of output and employment under given supply conditions.[6]

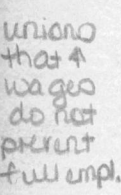

For Keynes the main force holding back total spending and causing unemployment was excessive saving. For previous generations of economists the act of saving was not only a virtue, it was the vital key to vigorous economic growth. In the nineteenth century with the opening up of territories, with major new technologies and innovations, like the railway, economists could easily assume unlimited growth and market potential. The only thing that could hold back economic progress was capital funding, thus the great importance attached to abstinence — the need for capitalists to be frugal. In the mature capitalist economy, Keynes wrote, with an abundant stock of capital in place and with massive amounts of savings being generated, the problem shifts from inadequate supply to inadequate demand.

Keynes radically demoted the merits of saving and abstinence. The Keynesian revolution was at least in part a revolution in ethics. Keynes described himself as an "immoralist," rejecting the Protestant ethic and the Puritan system of self-discipline. Keynes emphasized, not the piling up of money and achievements for the greater glory of God and national wealth, but rather the existential value of living in the present, for "in the long run," he wrote "we are all dead." His message was that the Age of Plenty was close at hand, the fruits of past abstinence could now be enjoyed — provided human affairs were run with greater intelligence.

Keynes stressed the problems that arise when some of the money earned in the course of production is saved. If these sums were borrowed and invested, the money would go to wages, profits and other incomes, and the level of output and employment would be maintained. This is what old orthodoxy assumed would always occur in an unfettered market economy. Marx had dismissed this theory as "childish babbling," but respectable economists paid no attention to Marx. It was the great merit of Keynes, a half century later, to work his way through the thicket of accumulated confusion towards a clear understanding that there is no reason to suppose that the amount of money kept off the market by the accumulation of profits and the savings of the rich would necessarily be counterbalanced by the willingness of corporations to invest in new plant and equipment. According to him, whether savings are in fact requited with investment depends on the fickle intentions and "animal spirits" of the business executive and financier.

In light of the Great Depression, Keynes saw the distinct possibility that economic stagnation was the natural tendency in mature capitalist economies. With consumption occupying a smaller proportion of output, thus generating increasing amounts of savings, and with the existing stock of capital being relatively abundant, thus reducing the likelihood of new investment being profitable, there would be a tendency for the economy to stabilize at a level of output below full employment. The slump in profit rates may become so severe at this point that a solution to stagnant investment through reductions in the rate of interest would simply not be available.

Keynes' Solution

Keynes advocated three far-reaching remedies.

The first dealt with state supervision of private investment. As he put it in a famous passage, "When the capital development of a country becomes the by-product of the activities of a casino, the job is likely to be ill done."[7] "In conditions of laissez-faire," he surmised, "the avoidance of wide fluctuations in employment may ... prove impossible without a far-reaching change in the psychology of investment markets such as there is no reason to expect. I conclude that the duty of ordering the current level of investment cannot be safely left in private hands."[8] Ultimately, "a somewhat comprehensive socialization of investment will prove the only means of securing an approximation to full employment."[9]

What he meant by this was never fully spelled out. In his 1926 essay "The End of Laissez-faire," he urged compulsory disclosure of information enabling society [to exercise] directive intelligence" over many of the inner intricacies of private business; central control over the supply of money; and "some coordinated act of intelligent judgement" to determine what portion of annual income should be saved and invested and what portion of domestic savings should be allowed to be invested abroad.[10]

Public works and capital projects, funded if necessary by government deficits, were one measure to combat an anticipated shortfall in private investment. Long before the Second World War proved his point, Keynes wrote: "Pyramid-building, earthquakes, even wars may serve to increase wealth [and employment] if the education of our statesmen on the principles of classical economics stands in the way of something better."[11]

In addition, and most importantly, private investment could be encouraged by a policy of permanently low interest rates. Against those who would attempt by pushing up interest rates to halt over-investment before it kills the boom and causes the economy to slide into depression, Keynes advocated lowering the rate of interest permanently to enable the boom to last. "The right remedy for the trade cycle," he admonished, "is not to be found in abolishing booms and thus keeping us in a semi-slump; but in abolishing slumps and thus keeping us in a quasi-boom."[12] Keynes estimated that within a twenty-five year period, this process would lead to the "conditions of a quasi-stationary community."[13]

Keynes' Vision   77

The state would have stimulated the growth of capital equipment to the point of saturation, where because of the abundance of capital there would be no new investment earning more than its replacement cost. The only income from property would then be temporary reward for risk-taking. Keynes had in mind a regime of permanent full employment with all goods selling at prices proportional to the labour embodied in them, and with gross prices just sufficient to pay labour and management costs, replacement costs and a small premium for risk-taking.[14]

Increasing consumption spending by various redistributional measures was, for Keynes, a secondary solution to the stagnation problem. But he was aware of the need for still a third measure — incomes control — for contrary to conventional accounts, Keynes did recognize that permanent full employment would generate inflation.

Indeed inflation was clearly built into his model. He noted that before full employment is reached, prices begin to increase because of rising costs associated with shortages of some commodities and production bottlenecks and because of increases in money wages due to the enhanced bargaining position of workers as unemployment declines. He believed that inflation, provided it exceeded the rise in wages, was in fact essential to the achievement of full employment. As already noted, he conceded the neo-classical position that in the short run growing employment could only be gained at the expense of real wages. In the long run of course, with increased productivity from technological change, employment and real wages can grow together.

Keynes distinguished this "semi-inflation" which occurs naturally in the course of rising output from "true inflation" which occurs when full employment has been achieved. As long as there is mass unemployment, increases in aggregate demand will increase output and jobs. As full employment is approached, it will increasingly affect prices. Beyond full employment true inflation takes over because there is no further scope for expanding production and employment.

Keynes' solution for true inflation was already rehearsed in 1925:

> Now there are two alternative ways of bringing about the reduction of money wages. One way is to apply economic pressure and to intensify unemployment by credit restriction until wages are *forced down*. This is a hateful and disastrous way, because of its unequal effects on the stronger and on the weaker groups, and because of the economic and social waste whilst it is in progress. The other way is to effect a uniform reduction of wages by *agreement*, on the understanding that this shall not mean in the long run any fall in average real wages.... Can we not agree, therefore, to have a uniform initial reduction of money wages throughout the whole range of employment, including government and municipal employment, of (say) 5 per cent, which reduction shall not hold good unless after an interval it has been compensated by a fall in the cost of living?[15]

Keynes went on to observe that trade-union leaders, when faced with such a proposal, would probably ask the prime minister "what he intended to do about money payments other than wages — rents, profits, and interest." Keynes allowed that he could not see how labour's objection could be met "except by the rough-and-ready expedient of levying an additional tax on all income other than from employment, which should continue until real wages had recovered to their previous level."

It was not until his wartime writings that Keynes returned to the question of inflation. In the context of war, he wrote, the fiscal problem is how to permit an increase of incomes by 15 to 20 per cent without any of this increase being spent on real consumption.[16] One answer is "nature's remedy": in the absence of positive government policy, simply allow "a rise of prices sufficient to divert real resources out of the pockets of the main body of consumers into the pockets of the entrepreneurs and thence to the treasury, partly in the shape of a higher yield from existing taxes, particularly Excess Profit tax, and partly in contributions to loans out of the increased savings and reserves of the entrepreneurs." While the resources taken from consumers are handed over to what Keynes here calls the "profiteers," the profiteers are in effect converted into tax collectors for the government.

Keynes was well aware that trade unions would not sit idly by and watch the erosion of living standards. He concluded that without some form of wage control "nature's remedy" would prove disastrous. The only thing that prevented a disaster in the First World War, he noted, was the time lag in adjusting wages to prices. Wages caught up with prices after one year. The act of spending these higher wages pushed prices up by the same amount so that the rate of inflation did not accelerate. But during the Second World War with "everybody, including trade unions, having become index-number conscious, wages will push prices with not so lame a foot. And this means that the old type laissez-faire inflation is no longer to be relied upon."[17]

This analysis led Keynes back to a program of wage controls which, to make them "socially just and politically acceptable," were to be administered along with government subsidies of essential goods and services. Before his death in 1946 Keynes did not have the opportunity to elaborate much further on his solutions to inflation but various articles, notes and correspondence indicate his direction.

In an article appearing in 1943 in *Economic Journal*, he refers to the view that "severe slumps and recurrent periods of unemployment have been hitherto the only effective means of holding [down] wages within a reasonable range. Whether this is so or not remains to be seen." A letter that same year has him asking: "How much otherwise avoidable unemployment do you propose to bring about in order to

Keynes' Vision 79

keep the Trade Unions in order? Do you think that it will be politically possible when they understand what you are up to? My own preliminary view is that other, more reasonable, less primitive measures must be found." In a second letter he writes: "Some people over here are accustomed to argue that the fear of unemployment and the recurrent experience of it are the only means by which, in practice, Trade Unions have been prevented from over doing their wage-rising pressure. I hope this is not true. But ... it is a *political* rather than an economic problem." About this passage, Lord Kahn, Keynes' literary executor, remarked, "Here can be seen the germs — but not more than the germs — of incomes policy, under which the rate increase in wages and prices is largely determined as a result of negotiations on a political plane."[18]

Keynes was advocating a very different kind of capitalism. In the context of the 1930s his solution was clearly seen — indeed, he himself put it forward — as an alternative to the necessity for socialism. By turning around Say's law — if demand is right, supply will look after itself — he undermined the socialist case for comprehensive central planning and public ownership. There is no need to choose between capital and labour. Keeping demand buoyant will underwrite both profits and employment. Adam Smith's invisible hand need not be abandoned, but merely guided by government controllers. The authoritarian state system, he wrote in the *General Theory* (he must have had Germany, Italy and the U.S.S.R. in mind), "seeks to solve the problem of unemployment at the expense of efficiency and freedom. It is certain that the world will not much longer tolerate the unemployment which ... is associated ... with present day capitalistic individualism. But it may be possible by a right analysis of the problem to cure the disease while preserving efficiency and freedom."[19]

(It may be noted that at the time Hitler's was the only New Deal that actually succeeded in eliminating unemployment. Roosevelt's certainly didn't. There were 15 million Americans out of work when he assumed office in March 1933; there were still 11 million unemployed in 1937 when the economy turned down again. Full recovery only arrived with rearmament and war. Sweden's New Deal is also a myth. Unemployment there dropped from 30 per cent in 1933 to 11 per cent in 1938, but mainly because of the revival of exports.)

What Keynes had done was to shift the focus of attention away from the labour market to the capital market. Whereas orthodoxy found the cause of unemployment to be excessive wages, Keynes saw the breakdown of the system in the contradiction between savers and investors. Under the guidance of a benevolent state that would take over responsibility for delivering both saving and investment in an economy that finally superseded (but did not replace) the profit motive, workers and industrialists would coexist in harmony. The ultimate benefit of his vision, Keynes thought, was that it would lead to a world free of war. A world of full employment would eliminate the economic causes of war.[20]

John Kenneth Galbraith described this as "the mandarin revolution," which neatly summarized Keynes' belief that public affairs could be managed by intelligent and disinterested public servants. He did not believe that either the capitalists or the "boorish proletariat" could or would lead the way to this higher form of organization. His own class position was clear: "Ought I to join the Labour Party? ... To begin with, it is a class party, and the class is not my class ... the class war will find me on the side of the educated bourgeoisie."[21]

The immediate problem of the capitalist economy, according to Keynes, was that it had no mechanism to ensure that total spending would be sufficient to provide employment for all those seeking work. In this he was very specific:

> It is not the ownership of the instruments of production which it is important for the State to assume. It need only put into place an apparatus that can regulate the total amount of spending on consumer and investment goods. When 9,000,000 men are employed out of 10,000,000 willing and able to work, there is no evidence that the labour of these 9,000,000 men is misdirected. The complaint against the present system is not that these 9,000,000 men ought to be employed on different tasks, but that tasks should be available for the remaining 1,000,000 men. It is in determining the volume, not the direction, of actual employment that the existing system has broken down.[22]

But like Adam Smith, "the father of capitalism," Keynes, its supposed saviour, found capitalism nearly as objectionable as Marx, its gravedigger. Keynes looked forward to the day when the accumulation of wealth was no longer of great social importance. When that time arrives, he declared in "Economic Possibilities for Our Grandchildren":

> We shall be able to rid ourselves of many of the pseudo-moral principles which have hag-ridden us for two hundred years, by which we have exalted some of the most distasteful of human qualities into the position of the highest virtues. We shall be able to afford to dare to assess the money-motive at its true value. The love of money *as a possession* — as distinguished from the love of money as a means to the enjoyments and realities of life — will be recognized for what it is, a somewhat disgusting morbidity, one of those semi-criminal, semi-pathological propensities which one hands over with a shudder to the specialists in mental disease. All kinds of social customs and economic practices, affecting the distribution of wealth and of economic rewards and penalties, which we now maintain at all costs, however distasteful and unjust they may be in themselves, because they are tremendously useful in promoting the accumulation of capital, we shall then be free, at last, to discard.[23]

Post-scarcity society was still a few generations away, he thought. But in the meantime, as a by-product of full-employment capitalism, society would have achieved at least one fundamental structural reform. It would be rid of the despised "rentier," that class of "functionless" financier who lived off the earnings of savings. Through a policy of capital saturation — twenty-five to thirty years of investment at the full-employment level — the old problem of capital scarcity could be conquered within a generation, and with it "the euthanasia of the cumulative oppressive power of the capitalist to exploit the scarcity value of capital."[24] A major source of unearned income would be all but eliminated and inequality would no longer be justified as the price that must be paid to obtain necessary capital.

In the final pages of the *General Theory* Keynes asked: "Is the fulfillment of these ideas a visionary hope? Have they insufficient roots in the motives which govern the evolution of political society? Are the interests which they thwart stronger and more obvious than those which they will save?" His own answer to this question is well known: "I am sure that the power of vested interest is vastly exaggerated compared with the gradual encroachment of ideas."

Keynes' ideas did indeed come to dominate the thinking of a generation. But they were not the thoughts set forth in the *General Theory*. It was to be a diluted and emasculated Keynes that would dominate "the ideas which civil servants and politicians and even agitators applied to current events."[25]

The Illusions of Mr. Keynes

For all its eloquence, Keynes' grand vision was a grand illusion. For one thing it assumed that wherever human actors, behaving according to the rules of the capitalism game, get themselves into a dilemma from which there is no escape, the state can descend from its Olympian heights to remedy the situation. But the state is not God. It is also one of the actors and, like the others, it too is subject to the capitalist rules of the game. Secondly, it ignores, even denies, the power of capital to defend its rights of ownership, its freedom to seek ever-expanding profits and its status as helmsman over the economy.

Some of the contradictions of full-employment capitalism were revealed by a then relatively obscure Polish-born economist, Michael Kalecki. In a 1943 article "Political Aspects of Full Employment," Kalecki listed three reasons why industrial leaders would oppose a regime of permanent full employment imposed by state regulations.

- Under a regime of laissez-faire, the level of economic activity depends greatly on the state of business confidence, and any policy that shakes this confidence must be avoided because it could lead to an economic crisis. The capitalist class thus acquires enormous political leverage, perhaps even veto power over state policy. Once government takes charge of the economy and achieves full employment by its own devices, capitalists lose this indirect control. Their position as helmsman of the economy is challenged.

- There is no business opposition to government activities that are clearly and positively associated with improving profits (protective tariffs, government subsidies and regulation of trade unions) or are outside the traditional sphere of private enterprise (highways, schools, hospitals). But the scope of public investment of this type is narrow and there is always the danger that government, in its search for employment-generating activities, might be tempted to invade the domain of private enterprise. Every accretion of state power is seen by capital as potentially encroaching on its prerogative as the dynamic and controlling agent of the economy.

- Should opposition on these grounds be overcome, which under popular pressure it well could, the maintenance of full employment would cause social and political changes that would produce grounds for even more powerful opposition from business leaders. "Under a regime of permanent full employment 'the sack' would cease to play its role as a disciplinary measure," Kalecki argues. "The social position of the boss would be undermined and the self-assurance and class consciousness of the working class would grow. Strikes for wage increases and improvements in conditions of work would create political tension ...." "Discipline in the factories" and "political stability are more appreciated by the business leaders than [even] profits. Their class instincts tell them that lasting full employment is unsound from their point of view and that unemployment is an integral part of the 'normal' capitalist system."[26]

A regime of permanent full employment is bound to permanently shift the balance of power between labour and capital in favour of labour. It increases workers' bargaining power over wages and enhances labour's ability to challenge capital on the shop floor. An insightful editorial appearing in the January 23, 1943, *London Times* warned of this danger:

> The first function of unemployment ... is that it maintains the authority of master over man. The master has normally been in a position to say: "If you don't want the job, there are plenty of others who do." When the man can say: "If you don't want to employ me, there are plenty of others who will," the situation is radically altered .... The absence of fear of unem-

ployment might ... have a disruptive effect upon factory discipline. Some troubles of this nature are being encountered today, but in wartime, the overall appeal of patriotism keeps them within bounds. In peace-time with full employment the worker would have no ... moral obligation to refrain from using his new-found freedom from fear to snatch every advantage that he can.[27]

There is another contradiction in Keynes' system. He concentrated on maintaining total spending at a level sufficiently high to clear the market in a fully employed economy, assuming that if the demand is there supply will take care of itself. His predecessors concentrated on the conditions that would induce capitalists to produce, assuming that if the supply is there demand will take care of itself. In fact, neither supply nor demand is automatic. Economic expansion in a capitalist economy only proceeds when both conditions are met. Capitalists will continue to invest and hire workers when they perceive that they can earn a profit in production *and* sell the commodities profitably.

Capitalism's problem is that the conditions for successfully achieving one part of the process can ultimately contradict the conditions for successfully achieving the other. For example, other things being equal, profit is served by keeping wages low. But low wages limit the size of markets. High wages create larger markets but unless accompanied by even higher productivity, they put the squeeze on profits. Capitalists would like the impossible situation of low wages for their own workers but high wages for the workers of all other employers. Similarly, high levels of government spending prop up demand, but to the extent that it crowds out private investment, it reduces the scope for profit-making.

When Keynes talked about saturating the capital market he ignored the basic law of capitalist production. Profit is the fuel of economic expansion in a private-enterprise economy. Saturating the supply of capital until it drastically reduces the rate of return grinds the system to a halt. Capitalism cannot endure, let alone thrive, as a "quasi-stationary community." Long before that moment approached, capitalists would conduct an investment strike designed to recreate conditions on the supply side that would make for higher profitability, conditions that would undoubtedly include lower wages produced by periods of prolonged unemployment, as well as lower taxes, privatization, deregulation and reduced social services.

Keynes' vision was flawed. While all theorists aim to make their theories as internally consistent as possible none is free of contradictions; the important question is how its practitioners seek to resolve them. In assessing a theory's social consequences, we need to know how it came to be used.

Keynes' grand vision of permanent full employment had little utility for ruling establishments. In the context of the early postwar era it was quickly dropped, and did not surface again for thirty years. But many of his technical innovations were eminently adoptable. Not surprisingly, his economics was twisted and contorted into a shape that suited the class that adopted them. The economists were an important part of the process, popularizing, revising and refining Keynes so that his theory fit the postwar reality. Instead of the profound structural changes advocated by Keynes, these economists produced what his colleague Joan Robinson has called a "bastardized" version of Keynesian theory, in which all that was required to maintain stability was the simple manipulation of a few aggregates, like the supply of money, the size of government budgets, deficits or surpluses.

5 | Was There a Keynesian Revolution?

As Michael Kalecki had anticipated, a Keynesian policy of permanent full employment proved unacceptable to business leaders. The arguments rehearsed by Kalecki surfaced during debates surrounding the full-employment acts introduced in most countries after the Second World War.

In the U.S., for example, the president of the National Association of Manufacturers then asserted that only three developments could bring prosperity to a halt: "mismanagement of the money and credit system; granting or perpetuation of special privileges; prevention of an adequate flow of capital into productive, job-making activities." Freely translated, the first point is a demand for sound money; the second for an amendment of the 1936 Wagner Act to better regulate trade unions, and the third for limits on the size of the federal deficit.[1]

In fact, the most typical attitude of business representatives was that if government really wanted full employment it would create a climate in which business could flourish. The U.S. Full Employment Bill, they charged, reflected "a lack of confidence in the American system of free enterprise." Assurance of the right to a job, they contended, would undermine the incentive to work. Professional economists lent their support to this position by injecting their opinion that "allowance of 5 to 6 per cent employment is essential for flexibility and freedom." Business leaders strongly preferred a dole over public works and full employment, which reflected their desire to keep workers in line. As well, unemployment insurance did not challenge the central position of business in the economic order, whereas full employment would.

The emasculation of the Murray Full Employment Bill and its re-emergence as the Employment Act illustrates the results of this opposition. The original bill called for a national budget which would "provide such volume of Federal investment and expenditure as may be needed ... to assure continuing full employment." As conceived by the sponsors of this bill, the president would present estimates of full-employment output on the one hand; anticipate private, state and local government expenditures on the other; and, finally, arrive at the amount of federal investment and expenditures needed to fill the gap between the two.

The government contribution was thus, even in the original bill, considered to be a residual, a far cry from the conception of Keynes. But the bill that was eventually passed in February 1946 was purged of fighting words like "full" — as in "full employment" — "guarantee" and "assure" — as in "assure or guarantee the existence of employment opportunities" — and "right" — as in the "right to employment." It reads:

> The Congress hereby declares that it is the continuing policy and responsibility of the Federal Government to ... foster and promote free competitive enterprise and the general welfare, conditions under which there will be afforded useful employment opportunities, including self-employment for those able, willing and seeking to work, and to promote maximum employment, production and purchasing power.

This surely represents the most nominal concession to Keynes. One wonders in retrospect what the excitement around the so-called Keynesian revolution was all about. Similar bills passed in Britain and Canada also avoided any clear-cut commitment to achieve and maintain full employment.

Britain's initial plans for a full-employment welfare state were drawn up under Winston Churchill's wartime coalition cabinet by William Beveridge. His first report, written in 1942, laid out a blueprint for the welfare state, which was adopted elsewhere, including in Canada. Two years later Beveridge issued his second report, *Full Employment in a Free Society*, which describes why full employment must be the centrepiece of social citizenship. It also elaborated precisely the means by which Keynes' permanent full employment could be achieved. Some months before Beveridge had issued his report, however, the British government brought out its White Paper on Employment Policy. Beveridge was scathing in his criticism of it:

> The Government in the White Paper treats private ownership of the means of production as fundamental; my Report treats it as a device to be judged by its results. The Government in the White Paper are conscious of the need for giving confidence to businessmen by monetary stability and budgetary equilibrium. They appear to be unconscious of the still greater need of giving confidence to the men and women of the country that there will be continuing demand for their services, so as to secure their co-operation, individually and collectively, in reasonable bargaining about wages, in working for the maximum of production without fear of unemployment in relaxing restrictions, formal and informal, on the full use of resources. This confidence will not be given by a promise to undertake public works whenever unemployment threatens to become serious. It will be given only when the steady expansion of demand ... has been ensured and when it is proved by experience that though technical progress may sometimes involve a change of jobs there are always more vacant jobs than idle men....[2]

Canada's White Paper on Employment and Income

Precisely the same arguments could be made against Canada's 1945 White Paper on Employment and Income, which committed the government to reduce unemployment, not to maintain full employment. Private enterprise was still seen as the engine of economic progress. Only when the private economy temporarily ran out of fuel was government to step in with its own solutions. It would make "every effort to create by all of its policies favourable conditions within which the initiative, experience and resourcefulness of private business could contribute to the expansion of business and employment."

Instead of announcing a national investment board to institute a somewhat comprehensive socialization or regulation of investment, the White Paper promised a somewhat comprehensive subsidization of private investment: tax concessions, loans, grants and other forms of assistance. Government excursion into investment would be confined to a ready shelf of public works to supplement private investment when heavy unemployment threatened. Subordinating public works to the whims of private investment is hardly what Keynes had in mind. William Beveridge condemned just this policy: "Public outlay should be looked upon as a weapon against gigantic social evils, not a gap-filling device to take up the slack of private outlay."[3]

Not suprisingly the Ottawa editor of *Saturday Night* magazine suggested that "the now famous White Paper may be regarded as a relatively conservative document...." In the words of a *Winnipeg Free Press* editorial (April 13, 1945):

> The report reveals, over and above all, the obvious determination of the government to get Canada back on its traditional course of free, competitive enterprise, guarded and policed by the government to prevent monopolistic practices on the one hand, and to guard against the creation of a regimented, socialist state on the other.

Instead of the old Gladstonian doctrine of "sound public finance," the White Paper declared that "the Government will be prepared, in periods when unemployment threatens, to incur the deficits and increases in the national debt. In periods of buoyant employment and income, budget plans will call for surpluses.... The Government's policy will be ... to maintain a proper balance in its budget over a period longer than a single year."

This is a policy of semi-sound finance, for in reality there is never full employment in an ordinary boom. Government surpluses in buoyant times must therefore be associated with something less than full employment. This is a far cry from Keynes. A Keynes budget would be balanced when everyone was employed, regardless of whether there was a surplus or deficit in the public accounts. It would be based on human resources rather than on financial resources.

The View From the Top

Contrary to conventional accounts of the period, Canadian business was never converted to Keynesian economics and the welfare state, as this sample of early postwar opinion indicates:

> If our economic process, our business life and jobs were to become socialized by a government of economic tinkerers and experimenters, fear and uncertainty would replace the public's spending plans.
> H.T. Hunter, President
> Maclean Publishing Co.

> We deceive ourselves and others if we accept and promulgate the idea that security can emanate effortlessly from Government, acting in the role of benevolent and bountiful provider.
> G.W. Spinney, President
> Bank of Montreal

> Politicians [must] cease their misleading propaganda, causing people to believe that post-war conditions will be free from want, free from fear, free from unemployment, free from depressions; that people will enjoy higher standards of living; that we shall have shorter working hours — which means less production at higher costs; that if we can finance war production we can finance peace production.
> C.H. Carlisle, President
> Dominion Bank

The *Financial Post*, reflecting the attitude of Canadian business, carried on a relentless campaign against full-employment economics and the welfare state. It inveighed against the "fine theories floating around Ottawa," intoxication with the magic phrase "full employment," and any form of state planning. Dominant themes of the corporate establishment included lower taxes and less government spending, balanced budgets, excessive wage demands, increased productivity, stable prices, deregulation of business and greater control over unions, in particular over the right to strike.

The new economics dominated the thinking of the postwar generation of Ottawa mandarins but it made little impression on corporate barons and only slightly more on cabinet ministers. A *Saturday Night* columnist wrote:

Keynesian Revolution?

I strongly suspect that the Cabinet lags a considerable way behind the social theories of the "bright young men" in Finance, in the Bank of Canada and in Reconstruction who have been acting as economic advisers. The Prime Minister goes "all the way" in respect to social insurance, but this is essentially a negative, not a dynamic, measure. I very much doubt whether Mackenzie King is a convert of Messrs. Beveridge, Keynes and Hansen as respects the use of public resources to create "effective demand" for full employment. Mr. Ilsley is an orthodox and even conservative Minister of Finance, with no great faith in "deficit financing" or other newfangled experiments on Government direction. Mr. St. Laurent sounds like a thoughtful man not wedded to orthodox policies. Mr. Howe is a man of direct action, who would probably favor giving the "private enterprisers" every chance to do their stuff....[4]

Evidence over the subsequent few decades suggests that cabinet ministers never did catch up to the "bright young men" and that the Ottawa mandarins finally adjusted to the corporate parameters of the Liberal state.

What Did Ottawa Do?

Mackenzie King and the Liberals, however, could not afford to turn a deaf ear to the new economics being espoused by their academically trained economic advisers. Though the White Paper was a concession to them, it would be a mistake to credit the Ottawa mandarins for whatever conversion came about. Throughout the latter half of the 1930s they had already been advocating a variety of social reforms, including unemployment insurance and extensive public works. And they had absolutely no effect on King; he stuck with orthodox views and opposed all proposals for social reform.[5]

Laundered versions of the events of this period place the Ottawa mandarins at centre stage (see, for example, Granatstein's *The Ottawa Men*), but it was not their theories or their clever arguments that turned King around. Much more persuasive were the returning soldiers expecting a better life; an agitated working class that demanded better wages, fewer working hours and recognition of their unions; and the sudden rise in the opinion polls of the dreaded socialists.

The socialist CCF passed both the Liberals and Tories in 1943 opinion polls and formed the official opposition in Ontario. Workers were flocking to unions and in 1943 one out of three trade unions went on strike, mainly for union recognition. A public opinion poll taken towards the end of 1943 showed that Canadians were more reform oriented than Americans and the British: 71 per cent opted for reform from prewar status quo.

In the midst of these results King was advised by Graham Towers, chairman of the Bank of Canada, to anticipate that postwar workers would far more "likely ... face unemployment ... with much greater resentment — to put it mildly — than what was displayed during the Depression Years. In the interest of peace, order and good government," Towers warned, Ottawa would have to "assume full responsibility" for the unemployment problem.⁶

It was in this context that King introduced unemployment insurance, family allowance and veterans' benefits and committed his government to maintaining "a high and stable level of employment and income" and to passing legislation compelling companies to recognize duly elected unions. Not all of these measures were opposed by business interests, which preferred family allowance to increasing wages during wartime (the family allowance was in fact sold to working people as a substitute for increased wages). As well, municipalities and provincial governments were urging the federal government to take over the health and welfare services they could not afford. Still, these were hard-won concessions gained by an embattled working class, buoyed by the confidence that accompanies full employment and full of expectations that could be put off no longer.

The wily King knew what was required of him, perhaps even as early as 1938 when a similar mobilization of popular forces caused him to note in his diary:

> In politics, one has to continually deal with situations as they are in the light of conditions as they develop from time to time. The world situation has headed ... countries ... more and more in the direction of the extension of State authority and enterprise, and I am afraid Canada will not be able to resist the pressure of the tide. The most we can do is to hope to go only sufficiently far with it as to prevent the power of Government passing to those who would go much farther, and holding the situation where it can be remedied most quickly in the future, should conditions improve.⁷

Conditions did improve, and when they did King set out to retrieve lost ground. The welfare state had barely been allowed to get out of the starting gate. Pensions remained restricted and niggardly. A promised comprehensive health system was put on the shelf, where it stayed for the next twenty years. And while forced to grant trade unions the recognition they sought, federal and provincial governments passed laws and instituted regulations that restricted labour's rights and freedom.

As for the government's commitment to maintain a high level of employment, it was rarely tested. A massive pent-up demand for goods and services, the baby boom, cheap materials, new technology, moderate wages, strong export markets, high levels of investment, and a stable international order, all combined to create a long wave of economic expansion. Increased levels of government expenditures on goods and services (from 10 per cent of gross national product in the 1920s to 15 per cent in the 1950s and early 1960s) raised domestic demand, but it was hardly the critical factor. As for the highly touted counter-cyclical demand management, it was almost nowhere in evidence. For example, when rapid growth came to a temporary halt between 1958 and 1962, producing unemployment rates as high as 7 per cent, government economic policy was more restrictive than expansionary. Other concerns took priority over unemployment.

Deficits alternated with surpluses but they were rarely the result of deliberate government policy. Recessions automatically caused deficits, mainly as a result of lower tax revenues and of increased expenditures on unemployment insurance and welfare benefits. Prosperity automatically created surpluses as tax revenues rose and unemployed insurance payments and welfare expenditures fell. The so-called automatic stabilizers effectively smoothed out the business cycle —they held up incomes and employment in times of recession and curbed inflation in the upswing. But because both recessions and inflationary tendencies were moderate, the stabilizers had relatively little work to do. Would they be able to hold off deep recessions and inflationary booms? The answer did not emerge until the 1970s and it turned out to be negative.

Government paid lip-service to the Keynesian doctrines of demand management but rarely practised it. Its ideological value far exceeded its practical value. It was on the supply side rather than on the demand side that government policy was oriented with its measures aimed at creating favourable conditions for capital accumulation. These included an immigration policy to secure cheap labour; a commercial policy to secure markets for Canadian resources; a defence policy to support the mining, armaments and airline industries; a tax policy to encourage foreign and domestic investment, exploration and research; an industrial-relations policy to secure labour peace; fire-sale privatization of most of the assets built by public funds during the war; and major expansion of state-provided or state-subsidized transportation, communication and hydro-electric facilities.

This represents no major departure from the traditional state policy that began with the subsidization of the C.P.R. and even earlier. In the nineteenth century it was called the National Policy; in the post-Second World War era it was called the Mixed Economy. Contrary to popular mythology, there never was a laissez-faire period in Canadian economic history. Big government had merely grown bigger.

Taking the Credit

Conventional presentations offer a different account. The overwhelming viewpoint is that active government demand management was a major success story through most of the postwar period and it only began to fail because it could not handle a series of unrelated supply shocks — mainly to do with food and fuel — introduced into the system in the 1970s. The following statement is typical: "Thus, in one of the great accomplishments of this century most western governments committed themselves to the Keynesianism strategy after the war, laying the basis for a politico-economic consensus which led to a quarter-century of political and economic stability."[8] This belief, however widespread, is not supported by any of the empirical investigations of the actual performance of fiscal policy.

H. Scott Gordon, for example, found that J.L. Ilsley, minister of finance in 1945-46, followed Keynesian principles of budgeting but misread the economic situation. D.C. Abbott (1947-54) abandoned this policy and pursued a Gladstonian balanced budget principle. Walter Harris (1955-57) returned briefly to Keynesian budgeting, only to modify his position prior to the 1957 election. D.M. Fleming (1957-62) at first pursued Keynesian budgeting, but eventually gave way to a Ricardian view, which regards unemployment as "due to a structural mismatching of the demand for labour and the supply of labour, and calls for efforts to realign these structures." Walter Gordon (1963-65) rejected Keynesian budgeting for a return to Gladstonian balanced-budget principles. It is not difficult to see how this modest commitment to Keynesian principles could result in a fiscal policy performance which according to Scott Gordon was adequate less than 30 per cent of the time.[9]

Economist Irwin Gillespie has neatly summarized the results of several studies on government performance.[10] While the studies he examined utilized various techniques to measure fiscal performance, Gillespie developed three general categories for assessing the results: adequate — fiscal policy headed in the right direction (restrictive or expansionary) and of approximately the correct magnitude; inadequate — policy moving in the right direction but of insufficient magnitude to achieve the stabilization objective; perverse — a destabilizing fiscal policy that is going in the wrong direction.

The most charitable assessments found that fiscal policy was adequate no more than two-fifths of the time, and inadequate or perverse three-fifths of the time. The least charitable assessment showed fiscal performance to be adequate only one-fifth of the time and perverse two-fifths of the time. As Gillespie notes, it is possible that the combined effect of both fiscal and monetary policy was stabilizing even though fiscal policy alone was inadequate or perverse. But as he points out, the evidence suggests that during the postwar period monetary policy was no more stabilizing than fiscal policy.

Why was government policy off base so often? It is possible that Canada's federal system gives Ottawa limited scope for an active fiscal policy. But Ottawa has almost total control over the tax side of the budget and it has shown substantial ability to introduce new programs on the expenditure side when the need for these programs was perceived by cabinet. Errors in forecasting can no doubt account for some of the problem. On the other hand, as Gillespie asks, is it conceivable that the undeniably capable officials in the Department of Finance could be wrong for most years over a thirty-year period?

Gillespie hits the nail on the head when he suggests that assessing government policy in terms of stabilizing incomes and employment yields dismal results because the goal of stabilization has in practice "not been the sole goal, or even the most important among several goals, or (possibly) even *one* of the goals, which the Federal government has actively attempted to achieve."[11]

There were at least seven other goals. Besides Keynesian fiscalism aimed at something like full employment, there is the traditional Gladstonian fiscalism aimed at sound finance and balanced budgets; a mercantile fiscalism aimed at balancing external accounts and protecting the value of the dollar; a monetarist fiscalism aimed at stable prices; a supply-side fiscalism aimed at stimulating private-sector investment; a welfare-state fiscalism aimed at legitimizing the social order; and a Kaleckian fiscalism aimed at achieving electoral majorities.

While there have been moments when these objectives were mutually consistent, this has not always or generally been the case. Which of these policies or policy combinations prevail at a particular time depends on the conjuncture of the relative strength of class forces and class factions, economic structures, political representations, ideological traditions and general economic conditions.

Keynesian full employment, for example, has always been the primary goal of organized labour and its political representatives. Countries with powerful working-class movements and social-democratic governments are much more likely to actively intervene to sustain something close to full employment. Where working-class movements are divided and weak, other goals are given priority when they clash with full employment.

These developments were anticipated by Michael Kalecki in 1943:

> In the slump, either under the pressure of the masses or even without it, public investment financed by borrowing will be undertaken to prevent large-scale unemployment. But if attempts are made to apply this method in order to maintain the high level of employment reached in the subsequent

boom a strong opposition of "business leaders" is likely to be encountered ... and they would probably find more than one economist to declare that the situation was manifestly unsound. The pressure of all these forces ... would most probably induce the government to return to the orthodox policy of cutting down the budget deficit. A slump would follow in which government spending policy would come again into its own.[12]

Kalecki gave the label "the political business cycle" to this regime in which "full employment would be reached only at the top of the boom, but slumps would be relatively mild and short lived."

Only one modification is necessary. By the mid-1970s it was clear that nothing like full employment would be attained even at the top of the boom. It was the boom that was "relatively mild and short lived" while the slumps had become severe and sustained.

Where was the revolution in economic policy? It represented little more than the fanciful thinking of economic scribblers. Having taken credit for the long wave of prosperity following the war, Keynesianism would be blamed for the long wave of stagflation that set in in the 1970s. Yet Keynesianism was about as irrelevant to the economic crisis of the 1970s as it had been for the prosperity of the 1950s and 1960s. Much more profound forces were at work (see chapter 16).

Bastardizing Keynes

As elsewhere, in Canada the vast majority of economists had swung over to the new economics early in the postwar era. In switching their allegiance from the old orthodoxy, however, virtually none went so far as to adopt Keynes' own vision of full-employment capitalism and all the institutional rearrangements that it entailed. Instead, it was the laundered American version of Keynes that they accepted.

Keynes' *General Theory* was compulsory reading for graduate students in the 1950s and 1960s. But our instructors advised us that we could safely skip over chapters representing what was perceived to be Keynes' incorrect view of the tendency towards permanent stagnation in mature capitalism. In his *Guide to Keynes*, Alvin Hanson told us that "the rentier euthanasia discussion is a kind of free wheeling detour by Keynes in his less responsible moments." The essential Keynes was provided in the chapters that dealt strictly with the short run. Here the Keynesian tools of the consumption function, the multiplier, among others, could be appropriated to yield prescriptions sufficient to treat temporary aberrations from full employment. This after all was the heyday of fine-tuning. Keynes' vision was exorcized from the textbooks. It was thus an emasculated Keynes that filtered down into the elementary and intermediate textbooks.

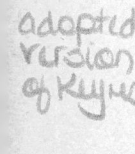

On the political and philosophical plane, economists were not interested in Keynes' concern with the top-heavy income distribution and shabby quality of life in capitalist society, in his call for the "euthanasia of the rentier" and "somewhat comprehensive socialization of investment." His vision of a "liberal socialism" was alien and repugnant to them. Caught up in the atmosphere of the Cold War, American economists converted Keynes' concern for higher aggregate demand and employment into a justification for armament spending and "brush-fire wars." Keynesianism was militarized. In Canada, Keynesianism was more often invoked in support of traditional goals of economic expansion.

On the technical plane, economists were instinctively uncomfortable with the untidy and imprecise economic model Keynes had bequeathed to them. For Keynes this imprecision and untidyness only reflected the capitalist economy itself and in particular the expectations based on "vague fears and hopes" that governed investment decisions. Keynes had chided his fellow economists for their "pretty, polite techniques which tries to deal with the present by abstracting from the fact that we know very little about the future." He insisted that "there is no scientific basis" in which to predict future events: "We simply do not know."[13]

Economic theorists were unable to cope with the element of uncertainty so crucial to Keynes' own thinking. Instead, they appropriated those parts of his analysis that could be recast in a mechanistic and prettified model with neat predictive powers — the very tendency in economics that Keynes himself had deplored. On this basis they built forecasting models designed to capture past relationships which are extrapolated into the future. In a stable environment such techniques can be a reliable guide to future events. But capitalism is a dynamic and inherently unstable system. Is it a wonder that the economists with all of their high-powered computers have proved to be so inept as long-run forecasters?

Contrary to the expectations of both Keynes and the Marxists, the capitalist world was not beset by a major slump following the Second World War. Nor did one appear over the next quarter-century. Some economists interpreted this to mean that the innate Keynesian tendencies were being offset by government action. But most of their colleagues interpreted it to mean that there was something wrong with Keynes' basic analysis of late capitalism.

They rejected his vision of capitalism as an inherently unharmonious system without an invisible hand ensuring a level of investment sufficient to absorb the savings generated at a full-employment level of output. They managed to provide "proofs" that his conclusion of sustained levels of high unemployment only held under special conditions of wage and price rigidities. In short order hundreds of models were produced, demonstrating that with different assumptions growth was possible without any serious departure from full employment. Under these circumstances incremental variations of the rate of interest and government budgets were a sufficient remedy for any temporary aberration from the golden path to prosperity and stability.

Whenever the economy showed signs of weakening (as savings exceeded investment) the Keynesian demand-management tool kit could readily be put into action: taxes would be reduced and/or government spending increased; a greater money supply would lower interest rates. Governments would spend their way to prosperity by enlarging their budgetary deficits and expanding the money supply to accommodate the increased spending. Once recovery was underway government could retreat. Should demand rise to a point where it exceeded what the economy was capable of producing at full employment, fiscal and monetary policy would go into reverse. Purchasing power would be removed from the economy by raising taxes and/or reducing government spending and contracting the supply of money. Credit would be made more expensive by raising the rate of interest.

The main point is that the budgetary exercise was seen as a means of balancing the economy. Government finances need not always be in balance. Deficits at one stage and surpluses at another create a financial rhythm that can smooth out the business cycle. This watered-down version of Keynesianism is what "planning" and "the managed economy" came to mean in North America.

Above all, the new Keynesian orthodoxy lent credence to the idea that economics might be coming of age as a science. Backed by sophisticated theories and quantifiable models, economics appeared to have developed a range of techniques to manage the economy. And other disciplines like sociology, psychology and political science were attempting to emulate economics with the hope that a science of society would eventually emerge.

To a generation for whom the chaos and misery of the Great Depression was still a living memory, the possibility that society could manage its affairs in an orderly and rational way seemed like a great advance from the days when they were left to chance and the vagaries of market forces. Comprehensive planning and a wholesale reorganization of society was not necessary. The underlying principle of the self-regulating market economy was not so much flawed as it was soiled. It was a matter of trimming out some of the instability and imbalances with judicious piecemeal intervention.

"Social engineering" was the favoured expression of the 1960s. Seen as the answer to both socialism and laissez-faire, it involved managing the demand side of the economy to ensure a high level of economic activity and employment, a safety net to guard against the hazards of the market economy, a progressive tax structure to even out inequalities and a bevy of regulations to protect the worker, the farmer, the consumer and the environment.

The new welfare state/managed economy cut the ground from under the socialists. Indeed, they quickly became its most avid supporter. As Britain's Anthony Crosland put it, "the planned full employment welfare state ... is a society of exceptional merit and quality by historical standards .... It would have seemed a paradise to many early socialist pioneers!"[14]

While for liberals, state intervention was justified because it made the market economy more stable and humane, for parliamentary socialists the world over, the new tools of state management offered the opportunity of gradually transforming capitalist society. Extensive state ownership and detailed economic planning were no longer necessary. Instead, the extension of social services and other collective amenities, the equalization of incomes through progressive taxation and the stabilization of income through demand management would lead society, one step at a time, towards the new Jerusalem. Like John Stuart Mill before them, the new welfare socialists took the productive system of capitalism for granted. They assumed that their desired changes in the distribution of income, an increased dosage of state regulation, and an expansion of social services were all compatible with private ownership and the profit system.

Trading Off Full Employment

As the fear of a return to depression conditions dissipated, economists came to see inflation as a problem that was at least equally as harmful as unemployment. In fact, with the establishment of unemployment insurance and the welfare state they decided that the economy could easily tolerate a fair amount of unemployment, and inflation took over as their major concern.

Economic theorists discussed two causes of inflation: demand-pull and cost-push. According to the first, the demand for goods and services exceeds what can be supplied: "too much money chasing too few goods." The result is higher prices and wages. The same volume of goods and services will be purchased at higher prices — in this way absorbing the excess demand. According to the second, inflation is produced by trade unions demanding wage increases that exceed the growth of productivity. If these are granted by businesses who in turn raise their prices accordingly, a general inflation will result.

Demand-pull and cost-push were combined in the so-called Phillips curve, which expressed a trade-off between inflation and unemployment. Economist A. Phillips thought he had discovered a statistical relationship between unemployment and inflation with higher unemployment associated with lower inflation and lower unemployment associated with higher inflation. When demand is high and unemployment low, Phillips explained, trade unions are able to bid up wages and employers are willing to pay, for under these conditions they can easily raise their prices; when unemployment is high, trade unions have less power and wages and prices rise more slowly. Society has to choose what mix of unemployment and inflation it prefers. Within mainstream economics of the 1960s this became the criterion for distinguishing between economists "of the left" and economists "of the right." The former argued for more inflation and less unemployment, the latter for less inflation and more unemployment.

But the Phillips curve had another dimension. Bastardized Keynesianism had been converted into a technique for causing unemployment and into a weapon to be used against worker militancy. Its message was anything but subtle: militant workers cause unemployment because their wage demands force government to take measures that increase unemployment.

This was a new version of the iron law of wages. Wage increases must be held to increases in productivity. When wages exceed productivity, labour costs rise, and inflation can be said to result from higher wages if they are not offset by falling profits. Under this assumption any attempt by workers to redistribute income between wages and profits comes to be labeled as inflationary.

As the situation worsened in the late 1960s and early 1970s, requiring more unemployment to lower inflation, the new economics again blamed it on the workers. Either trade unions were becoming excessively powerful or workers were becoming increasingly unemployable. The latter hypothesis provided the rationale for tampering with the official unemployment figures and produced the mysterious change in the definition of full employment — from 3 per cent in the 1950s and early 1960s to 5.5 per cent in the mid 1970s, 7 per cent in the late 1970s, and up to 8 per cent in the 1980s.

So long as inflation and unemployment were inversely related, the trade-off theory had some plausibility. It became increasingly untenable when unemployment and inflation began to rise simultaneously. When both went on rising at an accelerating pace, bastardized Keynesianism was in trouble.

The new economics was finally put to the test in the early 1970s when the favourable condition for long-term growth began to dissipate. But ballooning deficits produced, not prosperity, but inflation followed by stagflation (simultaneous stagnation and inflation). Mainstream economists admitted defeat. A decade earlier Paul Samuelson had declared, "Everywhere in the western world governments and central banks have shown they can win the battle of the slump." Now he sadly observed, "Whatever government does to handle the 'flation' part of our stagflation inevitably worsens the stagnation part of the problem ... likewise whatever government policy does to help the 'stag' part of stagflation will ineluctably worsen the inflation part of stagflation."[15]

End of the Keynesian Era

The heyday of the managed economy came in the early 1960s. A decade later it lay in tatters. The war in Vietnam, intractable poverty at home, continuing exploitation of the Third World, student rebellions, severe slumps combined with an inflationary explosion and followed by nearly a decade of stagflation spelled the end of the postwar consensus.

Optimistic theories of post-capitalism — of a smoothly evolving, affluent industrial order guided by the steadying hand of the state — began to appear entirely implausible. Pronouncements of the end of class warfare and the end of ideology seemed hopelessly premature. The new economics had failed to predict the economic crisis and could discover no solution for it. While the mixed economy was discredited and in disarray, capitalism was rediscovered in theory and in practice. Economists on the right, the neo-classical theorists of the unfettered free market, were ready to pounce, while those on the left were ready to rediscover Marxism.

Economists such as F. A. von Hayek and Milton Friedman had for many years warned against tinkering with the market. As early as 1944 Hayek had called state interventionism and the welfare state "the road to serfdom" and economic ruin. But in the heady days of postwar prosperity such ideas were not taken seriously except by a small circle. In the midst of the Keynesian disarray, the anti-collectivist doctrine of Hayek was rediscovered by a generation of economists untouched by the Great Depression, with little intellectual or emotional investment in the Keynesian Revolution. As Friedman put it, the collectivist trend which

> has now lasted three-quarters of a century in Britain, half a century in the United States ... is crumbling. Its intellectual basis has been eroded as experience has repeatedly contradicted expectations. Its supporters are on the defensive. They have no solutions to offer to present-day evils except more of the same. They can no longer assume enthusiasm among the young who now find the ideas of Adam Smith or Karl Marx far more exciting than Fabian socialism or New Deal liberalism.[16]

The old Keynesianism was dead, or certainly appeared to be. But the original faith in the ability of the capitalist state to bring order to human affairs still stirred in the minds of those who would convert neither to neo-conservatism nor to neo-Marxism. These post-Keynesians resurrected and elaborated upon Keynes' original prescriptions for fundamental reforms in the institutions of capitalist society, which had been watered down in the high tide of the neo-classical synthesis. Now they were reclaimed, reconstructed and recast to meet the economic crisis of the 1970s and 1980s.

These are the protagonists in the Great Economic Debate of the 1980s. We'll meet them again in the chapters ahead. But before turning to them, it will be worthwhile to retrace our steps.

In the aftermath of the Second World War, the Canadian state formally accepted responsibility for the functioning of the economy, committing itself to maintaining a high level of income and employment. The view that the economy could be left to develop automatically was consigned to the scrap-heap of economic shibboleths. If avoiding another depression required the state to give an extra boost to the private sector using deficit spending, it was small price to pay for economic stability.

But as the men came home from the front and the women were moved back into their kitchens, it soon became obvious that more than economic stability was required. Industrial stability was needed too. The new industrial unions had shown that they could disrupt the war effort; if they weren't regulated they would also disrupt the reconstruction. The quid pro quo for union regulation was union recognition. By the mid-1960s the same rights of collective bargaining were accorded to the rapidly expanding public-sector unions.

Demands for economic and industrial stability were followed by demands for social stability. An aroused labour movement was agitating for new kinds of security from the state — a minimum wage, unemployment insurance, publicly funded health care, improved welfare, pensions — some of which were supported by fiscally deprived municipal and provincial governments. To stop the hordes from stampeding to the CCF (predecessor to the NDP), the Liberals borrowed from the CCF program. They were buying more than loyalty to their party; they were also buying loyalty to the system. Universal and comprehensive social programs expressed the idea of one nation within market capitalism and class inequality. The welfare state looked like an eminently sensible way of tempering freedom with security, enterprise with stability and economic growth with social concern. It also seemed like a small price to pay.

Economic stability, industrial stability and social stability were accepted by the state as responsibilities it had to assume to make capitalism work under the circumstances prevailing in the mid-twentieth century. What resulted was a genuine reformation of classical capitalism, a blend of capitalism and modest collectivism that only tempered the market economy while leaving existing class structures intact. In short, liberalism became the order of the day because it answered the needs of the times.

In practice, conditions for economic growth were so favourable for the quarter-century following the war that the state was not required to actively intervene on the demand side to sustain prosperity. Instead, it pursued other goals which were, as often as not, destabilizing. Keynesianism was more important as an ideology legitimizing the role of the state in pursuing other objectives. In fact, state intervention on the supply side proved to be more significant than Keynesian demand stimulation.

Thus by the early 1950s, Canadian society had settled down to a period of industrial peace and gradual social gains. A modest dose of social democracy was accepted by all political parties. While the revolutionary Left lost its constituency, the socialists found a comfortable place within the postwar consensus. They were the true believers of the Keynesian Revolution, virtually equating the managed capitalist economy and welfare state with the good society. The only problem for them was that there was not enough social welfare. So-called responsible unionism triumphed over the less accommodating currents in the labour movement. The working class accepted the terms of what has been called the postwar settlement between capital and labour. Modest but regular increases in living standards, income and job security and increased provision of social services were the prices it exacted for coming to terms with corporate capitalism.

This climate found intellectual reflection in the works of Daniel Bell, Clark Kerr and others, who confidently proclaimed the "end of ideology," the advent of the "classless society" and the "withering away of the strike." The calamitous business cycle as well as the class war belonged to another age. In this "post-capitalist" era the social sciences were harnessed to manage the economy, eliminate poverty and ameliorate social strife. Business was no longer dominated by the greedy capitalist but by socially responsible corporate managers, products of the "managerial revolution" which had separated the control function from ownership. The old classical capitalism had been left far behind.

In retrospect the era of quiescence and stability was rather short-lived, based on what turned out to be a combination of temporary developments. A crisis of industrial and social conflict erupted in the mid-1960s, including the emergence of such traditional non-aggressive groups as public-sector employees and the poor who demanded not only higher wages and better jobs but also more social services. Wages and salaries previously had accounted for two-thirds of all income; by the early 1970s they stood at nearly three-quarters. Government expenditures on goods and services amounted to no more than 18 per cent of the gross national product until the mid-1960s, but claimed 24 per cent by the early 1970s — primarily because health care had by then been taken over by the government.

This spurt, which amounted to a second wave of welfare state legislation, was also stimulated by the rediscovery of poverty in North America. After Michael Harrington shocked the U.S. by demonstrating that about one in five Americans were still living in poverty (*The Other Americans*), similar studies elsewhere, including Canada, showed that the conditions of millions of people had been untouched by over a decade of unprecedented prosperity. They also revealed that, contrary to conventional wisdom, there was still a fundamental inequality in income distribution. The conclusion was obvious: the social services needed extending; minimum wages needed to be raised; unemployment insurance had to be broadened and made more generous. Race riots in America caused President Kennedy to declare the War on Poverty and President Johnson to institute the Great Society. Movements of the poor and mobilization of native people caused Prime Minister Trudeau to commence the Just Society.

This wage and social-wage militancy came at the worst possible time for the private sector. Faced with higher material costs and growing international competition, its profit margins tumbled. Passive Keynesianism — the automatic stabilizers — had been sufficient to bolster an already buoyant economy with healthy trade balances and a vigorous investment climate. Under the new circumstances massive government injections were required to boost and stimulate flagging private-investment spending. They managed to maintain employment and output levels as well as to finance the higher social wage, but only at the cost of unprecedented inflation. When double digit inflation turned into stagflation in the mid-1970s, the Keynesian era was over.

PART III | The New Right

6 | Monetarism and Supply-Side Economics

The theoretical shortcomings and the policy failures of Keynesian economics created fertile ground for a return to economic conservatism. Monetarism and supply-side economics draw upon certain common tenets of the old orthodoxy. They identify labour and in particular trade unions as a major cause of economic ills and call upon the state to strip them of their rights. They advocate a redistribution of income towards the rich, a much smaller role for the public sector and massive reductions in taxes, public expenditures and government regulation.

Beyond these points there are important differences among the neo-conservatives. Chief among them is whether inflation is best fought by slowing the economy down or speeding it up. This chapter surveys the theories of the New Right in its various guises and looks at how they have been applied in Canada.

Monetarism

Like the old orthodoxy, monetarism attaches a great deal of importance to market order and liberty. According to its godfather, Milton Friedman, liberty, or the freedom to choose, is perfectly achieved in the self-regulatory market. The key insight of Adam Smith's *Wealth of Nations*, Friedman likes to recite, is misleadingly simple: "If an exchange between two partners is voluntary it will not take place unless both believe they will benefit from it."[1]

"Adam Smith's flash of genius," Friedman writes, "was his recognition that the prices that emerged from voluntary transaction in a free market could coordinate the activity of millions of people, each seeking his own interests, in such a way as to make everybody better off." The price system (including wages) transmits the only information people need to know to guide their decisions as buyers and sellers of both goods and labour services. What commodities get produced, what price tags get put on them, and what prices the market sets on services,

106   The Great Economic Debate

including labour, are all ultimately determined by consumers looking to maximize the satisfaction they get from the dollars they spend.

Whatever interferes with the free market is an enemy of liberty and efficiency. Like Adam Smith, monetarists point their finger at government as the main enemy. According to them, taxation is a denial of voluntary contract. Government spending is inherently inefficient because it lies outside the competitive system. Public enterprise is an invasion of an area that should be reserved for private entrepreneurs. Trade unions are monopolistic suppliers of labour and deny workers the right to negotiate an individual contract. Inflation is a debasement of the currency and an involuntary tax on savers.

Free marketeers draw a distinction between equality of opportunity and equality of outcome. The first, where ability alone determines a person's opportunities, is consistent with liberty. Equality of outcome — everyone should finish the race at the same time — clearly conflicts with liberty and attempts to promote it have been a major source of bigger and bigger governments. Instead of socializing the means of production, so it is argued, the progressive income tax and the welfare state socialize the results of production. By destroying the incentive to follow its signals, such measures destroy the work of the price system. But in the end, the drive for equality must fail because it violates one of the most basic instincts of all human beings: "the uniform, constant and uninterrupted effort of every man to better his condition," according to Adam Smith.[2]

Welfare agencies siphon off private wealth in administrative expenditures and attractive pay scales that should be going to the poor. Worse still, all such programs put some people in a position to decide what is good for others. "The effect is to install in the one group a feeling of almost God-like power; in the other, a feeling of child-like dependency."[3]

Similarly, regulatory agencies produce a bureaucratic nightmare, strangling businesses in a maze of red tape. Instead of providing protection for consumers and workers, they benefit mainly the legion of bureaucrats hired to administer the regulations and special interest groups. Left to itself, market competition protects the consumer better than government mechanisms. Monopoly is an ever-present danger but it is best countered not by more regulation but by removing existing barriers to international trade. "Alternative sources of supply protect the consumer far more effectively than all the Ralph Naders of this world."[4]

Monetarists emphasize that a sound currency (stable prices) is essential to a properly functioning market order. Inflation places a premium on forecasting the inflation rate and coping with its consequences rather than on being efficient and competitive at producing and distributing "real" goods and services. But sound currency is threatened by democracy as governments are pressured by their electorate into promising more than they can deliver. In the words of one of Canada's leading monetarists, Thomas Courchene, the problem comes down to the fact that "the distribution of ballots in the political market is more equal than the distribution of 'dollar votes' in the market place." Government has been pressured "away from guaranteeing equality of opportunity and towards guaranteeing equality of result" precisely because the public has greater concern for protection and security than it has for individual liberty and efficiency.[5]

Business groups have also pressured governments to grant them protection from the results of free-market forces by imposing tariffs, quotas, licensing, marketing boards and other devices that reduce competition. The political repercussions are minimal because the resulting subsidies are hidden and the costs are widely dispersed across the consuming public. Yet free marketeers insist that the damage is incalculable. By sheltering firms from the discipline of the market, this type of intervention eliminates price competition, inhibits innovation, depresses economic growth, causes some firms to over-invest and tilts income distribution in favour of the regulated.

Canadian free marketeers are particularly adamant about the virtues of eliminating all barriers to international trade and moving towards free trade. Canada is highly dependent on trade, they argue, with an economy that is necessarily shaped by its comparative advantage in certain economic activities as revealed by market forces. Distorting these market forces by artificial trade barriers is bound to be costly and in the final analysis self-defeating. Canada must abide by the price signals of the market and adjust its wage rates, capital flows and public infrastructures accordingly.

The ideology is well summarized in a 1982 speech by Tory spokesman John Crosbie:

> I believe they [these principles] reflect fundamental values shared by the majority of Canadians — that reward should be the result of effort, not speculation; that excellence should be appreciated, not envied; that true social justice demands equality of opportunity, not an enforced equality of results; that there is no inalienable right to the good life — it must be earned individually and collectively; that we have a moral obligation to help those who need our assistance — not those who want a Good Samaritan state to underwrite their lifestyles.

Government Overload

The source of today's economic problem, monetarists argue, is the "political marketplace." Political parties compete for popular votes just as business markets compete for customers, except that the price tag which disciplines the consumer in the economic market is absent in the political market. In the past, the masses had been restrained in their demands by the Protestant work ethic, by hierarchy and deference and by appeals to patriotism. But these constraints prove to be transitional. Economic groups (read "trade unions") now use their "full market power" to gain excessive wages from employers while citizens use their electoral power to make excessive demands on government services. Excessive democracy and excessive equalitarianism are the ultimate problems: "the democratic idea that government should be responsible to the people creates the expectation that government should meet the needs and correct the evils affecting particular groups in society."[6]

The idea of social rights and entitlements and the notion that it is the government's responsibility to underwrite these is buttressed by the vested interests of the state bureaucracy. Far from being a benevolent servant of the public in the manner presumed by Keynes, the bureaucracy has become its own interest group. Since the status, salary and power of the bureaucrat grows with the size of the bureau, there is a built-in "law" of bureaucratic growth which hides behind the cloak of public interest. Once government programs are instituted, the mandarinate presses for their expansion and resists all efforts to dismantle them. In Friedman's graphic language:

> In the government sphere, as in the market, there seems to be an invisible hand, but it operates precisely the opposite direction from Adam Smith's: an individual who intends only to serve the public interest by fostering government intervention is "led by an invisible hand to promote" private interest, "which was no part of his intention."[7]

The result of all these forces is government overload: demands made on government far exceed its capacity to meet them. The economic expression of government overload is inflation, the political expression is more or less permanent frustration, the "ungovernability of democracies."

Democracy is damaging to liberty. It cannot be eliminated but it can and must be confined. Thus the monetarist goal is to curtail it by depoliticizing the economy. The evils of "unlimited democracy" can be minimized only by "limiting the power of government."[8] Friedman and the monetarists would strip the government of virtually all its current responsibilities, save law and order and defence and a few "public goods" like roads. As far as economic policy is concerned, the state should have none, except regulation of the money supply to guarantee stable currency.

The Quantity Theory

That competitive markets produce an optimum use of resources is one proposition underlying monetarism; the other is the old classical quantity theory of money. As the theory runs, the level of output is determined by the physical and human resources available and by the improvement in knowledge and capacity to use them. At best, output can only grow fairly slowly, perhaps by 5 per cent a year — the "natural rate of growth." The supply of modern forms of money, on the other hand — paper and bookkeeping entries in the accounts of the chartered banks — is subject to no physical limit. In order for prices to be stable there must be a balance between the quantity of goods and services produced and the quantity of money available to purchase them. With inflation, the supply of money is rising more rapidly than the supply of goods and services, which is what the monetarists mean when they say that "inflation is always and everywhere a monetary phenomenon." And government controls the supply of money — through its issuance of coins and dollar notes and its regulation of bank credit. So it is government that is always to blame for inflation. Why not the oil sheiks and OPEC? They had the power to impose a higher price for oil but not to create inflation. Higher oil prices would have been offset by declines in other prices had the government exerted firm control over the supply of money.

Providing it is financed by taxes or by borrowing from the public, increased government spending is not the source of the problem, since more spending by government is offset by less spending by the public. Inflation only occurs when higher government spending is financed by increasing the quantity of money in circulation. The usual way this is done is by selling government bonds to the Bank of Canada (the central bank) which pays for them either with freshly printed dollar bills or by entering a deposit on its books to the credit of the Canadian treasury. The treasury can then pay its bills with either the cash or a cheque drawn on its account with the Bank of Canada. When this new money is deposited in the chartered banks by its initial recipients, it serves as reserves for them which they can then loan out, thus increasing the quantity of money.

Crowding Out

For monetarists, then, inflation is closely associated with rising government deficits financed by an infusion of new money. A related phenomenon is the so-called crowding-out thesis, another revival of old orthodoxy. Once the economy reaches capacity, so the theory goes, the flow of savings will have also reached its maximum, making it progressively more difficult to finance higher budget deficits from funds borrowed from the public. Henceforth any further increase in the government's budget deficit can only be achieved at the expense of private investment. In effect, saving is shifted from private investment to public expenditures. In this instance, because there has been no net increase in total spending, there need be no inflationary impact, only the crowding out of private investment. Should the deficit be financed by the issue of new money, there is both inflation and crowding out. Here inflation is the mechanism by which government is able to transfer resources to its own account.

Underlying this hypothesis is the revival of an even earlier theory in classical economics which distinguishes between productive and unproductive sectors of the economy. The distinction is not between how useful the goods and services are but whether or not they produce profit. The real issue for monetarists is that most public-sector services are produced and distributed in accordance with criteria other than profitability. Extended too far, the public sphere reduces the funds available for profitable investment as well as reducing the sphere where production for profit is possible.

In contrast to Keynesians, monetarists insist that increases in the supply of money can never result in a permanent increase in output — only in prices — because, they argue, output is determined not by demand but by supply forces (the quantity of labour, capital, the skills of labour and management and technology). The competitive system ensures that potential output is always at its maximum, unless trade unions prevent competition in the labour market, or because people registered as unemployed are really exercising a voluntary choice.

Three policy goals follow. The first is that government must ensure that the growth of the money supply never exceeds the rate of output the economy is capable of producing. The second is that since competitive markets lead to an optimum use of resources and to the maximum desired output, the state must withdraw from regulating business and from providing services that are best left to the private sector. And in particular, borrowing to finance public expenditures must be drastically cut because it leads to increases in the stock of money and therefore to inflation. The third is that trade unions should be stripped of their power to control the supply of labour.

The "Natural Rate of Unemployment"

Monetarism gives central place to the operation of the labour market. People will sell their "productivity" if the price (wage) exceeds their "opportunity cost" in terms of leisure. Firms will buy this "productivity" providing the cost (wage) is no greater than the additional revenue that can be obtained in the sale of the final product. Only if workers are unwilling to, or prohibited from, accepting wages consistent with their productivity will they be unable to find jobs.

As the pattern of demand for and supply of goods and services constantly changes, different kinds of workers are required by different firms in different places. Imperfections of the labour market arise when job seekers and job vacancies are not matched, the margin Friedman calls the "natural rate of unemployment," a concept almost universally accepted by the economics profession.

The short-term unemployed are just between jobs, as the theory goes, and the long-term unemployed, if they are in a depressed area and refuse to move, are voluntarily unemployed. Then there are the young or women for whom work is "not essential," and who are therefore not really unemployed. This not only "proves" that there are very few really involuntarily unemployed people, but it also explains why: unemployment insurance and welfare rates are too high. As for unskilled workers, minimum wage laws force employers to discriminate against them. "Unless an employer is willing to add 90 cents in charity for the $2.00 that the unskilled person's services are worth, he will not be employed."[9]

As for unions, when they use their monopoly power to force up the price of their members' productivity they restrict the "sales" (that is, employment) in these industries and occupations, thereby swelling the supply of labour in other industries and occupations and pushing down their wages. "The gains that strong unions win for their members are primarily at the expense of other workers."[10] Universal unionization would not alter the situation either, for that would mean high wages for those with jobs and no jobs at all for the others.

If it's natural, unemployment cannot be lowered by artificial means. Further, neither unemployment nor output can be expanded by government stimulation, since the productive potential of an economy is set by "real factors," like the size and skills of the labour force, the quantity and productivity of capital equipment and the efficiency of management. Thus when governments attempt to push the rate of unemployment down below the natural rate by stimulating demand through an expanded supply of money, it does not achieve higher output or employment, only inflation. Once the economy has reached its natural capacity — which it will do without government stimulation — it has no more output to give. The increased supply of money will force higher prices on the existing supply of goods and services. It can raise output and the demand for labour temporarily but it can only bring forth a greater supply of labour by raising wages (since, according to monetarist account, everybody who wants to work at prevailing real wages has already found work). When this forces up prices these workers drop out, realizing that they have been tricked into believing that they would be receiving higher real wages. The natural rate of unemployment is then re-established.

But the process does not stop there, for as government intervenes again with another injection of extra spending power, everyone gets used to continuing inflation and it gets built into their expectations. As a consequence, the natural rate of unemployment gets re-established at continuously higher rates of inflation. The upshot is that governments have far less manoeuvrability than Keynesians have led them to believe. They cannot affect the level of unemployment and output in any permanent way — only the level of prices.

Unions are not the ultimate instigators of higher prices in the Friedman version. Unions merely force up wages in line with government-induced inflation. The more common view among monetarists is that trade unions push up the level of prices by excessive wage demands. What is their solution? Not wage and price control which involves another intrusion of government and which distorts relative wages and prices. On the other hand, a tight money policy that forces up interest rates to extremely high levels would inflict massive unemployment and business closures, a politically unpalatable measure. The final solution to the inflation question is of course to break the power of the unions.

In a letter to *The London Times* (June 13, 1980), Hayek urged that unions be stripped of their powers to resist market forces; otherwise they could cause a high level of unemployment and stagnation that would endanger the Conservatives' prospect of winning a further term of office. He proposed a national referendum on the abolition of all legal rights granted to trade unions since 1906.

In sum, according to monetarists, an economic crisis occurs in the form of massive inflation because state intervention interferes with the system's own "natural" economic order that produces a "natural" rate of growth and "natural" rate of unemployment. The economy prospered over a twenty-five-year period but that was despite, not because of, "the new economics." When governments attempted to counter declining natural rates of growth by accelerating their own credit-financed spending, they ultimately produced stagflation. Government efforts to achieve higher than natural rates of growth and lower than natural rates of unemployment can only succeed temporarily; the final outcome of state stimulation is always inflation.

The short-term monetarist solution is a drastic contraction of the supply of money and a sharp increase in the rate of interest. A strict monetarist regime restricts the supply of money and size of the government budget to induce a depression. By creating sufficient slack in the market it forces inefficient firms to shut down and the others to modernize and rationalize. Improved productivity and a more competitive environment brings the desired results in prices. Massive unemployment brings the desired results in wages. However painful the depression may be for businesses and workers, it is essential for any long-term recovery. One economist, Richard G. Stapleton, writing in the leading British monetarist journal *Economic Affairs*, put the point very clearly:

> Not only is a recession good for efficiency. It is probable that the deeper the recession, the better for the long-term health of the economy, especially after decades of slack management anaesthetised by inflationary full employment policies and menaced by increasingly assertive unions. The extreme example of the benefits of industrial destruction is the performance of Germany and Japan after the post-war chaos. Freed from out-of-date plant by allied air-forces and dismantling teams, Germany has shown the world the way to productivity and economic welfare.

Finally, a long recession has proved more effective than a short, sharp one; when firms could rely on an early reversal of previous credit squeezes, they avoided the painful rationalization process. No less desirable, a long depression compels public-sector firms and even government departments to examine their working practices.[11]

In effect, economic policy becomes the sole responsibility of the monetary authorities. Because they are not elected to office they are insulated from the pressure of public demands. The political authorities which determine fiscal (spending) policy must function within the parameters set by the central bank, a complete reversal of the conventional processes of parliamentary democracy.

A purely self-regulating market regime would then let the rate of growth of output be determined by the individual preference of savers and investors, let the composition of output be determined by consumer preferences, and the rate of unemployment by workers. So long as they are prepared to accept a wage low enough to make somebody want to employ them, and so long as trade unions do not prevent them from accepting such employment, no one need be without paid work.

A monetarist regime drastically curtails the size of the public sector. According to the theory, reducing the deficit transfers savings from the public sector which had been "crowding out" private investment.

By shifting income back to individuals via lower taxes, monetarism reasserts the principle of "consumer sovereignty" over the principle of "collectivism" and injects greater "dynamism" and "incentives" into the economy. By transferring nationalized industries and social services — like education, health and pensions back to private enterprise — it enlarges the scope of the profit system and thereby injects "financial discipline" into these sectors. By curtailing the rights of unions, eliminating minimum wage, unemployment insurance, family allowances and welfare benefits, it frees the capitalistic labour market. By eliminating tariffs and other barriers to international trade and finance, it forces firms to depend on their own efficiency for survival, ensures that countries concentrate their production in industries where they have a "comparative advantage," and achieves an optimally efficient division of labour and capital on a world scale.

A curious paradox of monetarism is that while its ideology claims to be against a strong interventionist state, the immediate impact of its policy actually strengthens the state. Monetarism drastically reduces the independence and autonomy of government departments and boards, nationalized industries, municipal governments and school boards in their spending and financial plans. Since more than 40 per cent of the gross domestic product is disbursed by government and its agencies, stricter centralized controls over this disbursement represents a significant sharpening of the state's economic power.

The Monetarist Agenda in Canada

By the mid-1970s monetarist principles and prescriptions had captured centre stage in Canada. The monetarist counter-revolution hit academia swiftly and completely. Monetarism has come to dominate the economic departments of nearly every major Canadian university. Keynesian textbooks of an earlier era were drastically revised or entirely replaced by other texts espousing the "new" doctrine. Monetarism provided a welcome theoretical basis for traditional business ideology.

Within the corporate community it is not surprising that the chartered banks are the most persistent and explicit carriers of the monetarist message. For example, in its 1982 report, "Resolving Canada's Economic Dilemma: An Analysis of the Problem and an Agenda for Action," the Bank of Montreal makes the case for deep cuts in government spending to bring down the deficit; for eliminating or modifying social security legislation that has added to business costs and has allegedly reduced incentives to work and save; and for phasing out government operations that compete with private enterprise and that are usually heavily subsidized.

Monetarism 115

The report further calls attention to labour policy, in particular minimum wage and labour regulation; food policy, particularly marketing boards that restrict production and hold up prices; regional disparity policy that provides incentives to locate industry in areas of "uneconomic activity"; trade policy that imposes tariffs and quota restrictions; foreign investment policy that scares off new foreign investment and discourages existing foreign investors; industrial policy that maintains inefficient industries; environmental policy that raises production costs; immigration policy that places "restrictions on the entry of skilled and semi-skilled labour"; research and development policy that subsidizes research which "in many cases can be imported more cheaply"; regulatory policy that reduces competition and supports high cost; public service salary and employment policy that provides excessive wages and salaries, pensions and security of tenure.

Besides academia and the corporate sector, top bureaucrats in economic portfolios of government were also swept along by the tide of monetarism. Nowhere was this in greater evidence than in the Bank of Canada.

In September 1975, Gerald Bouey, Governor of the Bank of Canada, announced before the annual meeting of the Canadian Chamber of Commerce in Saskatoon his conversion to the principles of what he called the "new monetarism." The inflationary explosion occurred, he argued, because central banks throughout the world attempted to counter the slow-down of the early 1970s by dramatically increasing the supply of money. Inflationary expectations caused wage and price spirals which central bankers accommodated by further increasing the money supply. Now the Bank of Canada would break the cycle of inflationary expectations by imposing strict controls over the supply of money. Henceforth long-term price stability would take precedence over concern with the level of unemployment in the short- to medium-term. The long-term prospects for employment would be disastrous unless inflation was defeated, once and for all. Instead of steering interest rates on a contracyclical direction, the Bank of Canada would focus on a target rate of growth of the money supply which would be set at a rate that would gradually lower the price level.

With a series of announced reductions in the growth rate of the money supply — so-called monetary targets — the Bank of Canada would convince Canadians that cost increases could not be passed on in the form of higher prices. While restricting the growth of money would contract output and employment, providing the Canadian public could be made to understand the implications of its policy, inflationary expectations could be unwound without sacrificing much in the way of employment and production.

Bouey doggedly followed this tight money policy over a seven-year

116   The Great Economic Debate

period. But gradualism failed to produce the expected results. Inflation continued to soar in the last half of the 1970s and bank officials were beginning to express doubts that gradual reductions of the money supply and modest increases in the interest rate were sufficient to "dampen inflationary expectations." Gradualism gave way to a more extreme form of monetarism. In the Bank of Canada's 1980 report, Bouey signalled that he would tighten the monetary screws to whatever extent was necessary to produce the desired results. But responsibility for the consequent damage, he warned, rested not with the Bank of Canada but with the Canadian people: "The influence of monetary policy will be felt throughout the economy but how the economy will respond will depend very much on the reactions of the various groups within it — governments, business and labour. Their reactions will determine how much economic stress and strain is involved in the reduction of inflation."

In practice, Canadian monetary policy shadowed the policy inflicted on Americans by the Federal Reserve Board in Washington. When the Reserve Board decided that more stringent controls were required, causing American interest rates to soar, Mr. Bouey, concerned about the depreciation of the Canadian dollar, followed suit. At the outset of the experiment, Bank of Canada officials had announced that the money supply was to be the sole target of their manipulation. Interest rates would be permitted to "float," as would the exchange rate. But when Canadian speculators sent their money south to reap the rewards of higher American interest rates, the exchange rate began to tumble. Fearing the impact of depreciation on Canadian price levels, the Bank of Canada began to pursue the twin course of monetary targeting and protecting the value of the Canadian dollar. In the final analysis, managing the exchange rate took precedence over strict monetary targeting. In 1982 Mr. Bouey was left to remark: "I very much hope that the United States will be able to conduct its affairs in a way that will bring about significantly lower and more stable interest rates in that country. Such development would give us somewhat more room for manoeuver in conducting our monetary policy."[12]

This combination of forces led to extraordinarily high interest rates; in 1981 they stood at well over 20 per cent. With an unemployment rate of 12.0 per cent, business bankruptcies that more than doubled between 1977 and 1983 and unused production capacities of 30 per cent or more, inflation was finally beaten to the ground. It fell from 12.5 per cent in 1981 to 5.8 per cent in 1983 and to around 4.5 per cent in 1984. Meanwhile, real wages per worker fell almost continuously from 1976 to 1984. The average employed worker had about a thousand dollars less purchasing power in 1984 than five years earlier.

In its effort, the Bank of Canada won the co-operation of government and forced the compliance of trade unions. First, the federal government deliberately held down its expenditures to the rate of increase in the gross national product so that government share of GNP has remained virtually unchanged since 1975, slightly more than one-fifth of the GNP. If interest payments on the national debt are removed, government spending as a percentage of the GNP actually fell slightly. (This was reversed in 1982, however, as a result of increased transfer payments induced by the depression.) While the size of the government deficit has soared since 1977, this has had far more to do with the effects of increased debt charges, stagnation and depression (slumping tax revenues and increased outlays on unemployment insurance and welfare) than with allegedly rampant government spending on goods and services.

Second, government made an effort to shift the composition of its spending away from social services in order to maintain programs that contribute to the growth of capital. By reducing the share of total expenditure going to social affairs (from 46.1 per cent in 1976-77 to 40.1 per cent in 1982-83), the federal government was able to maintain the relative size of its economic programs while at the same time paying the large increases in public debt charges caused by the growth of the size of deficit and the rate of interest on borrowed money. While the federal state did not dismantle the social service system, it stalled all further initiatives, partially de-indexed security payments, reduced its contribution to medicare and post-secondary education and, most importantly, restructured and redefined the purpose of social programs. Instead of meeting social needs, preventing poverty and redistributing income, the government's main objective has been subtly transformed to that of improving "the stock of human capital" and helping economic recovery — the "marketization" of social policy, as it's been called.[13]

Third, the federal government has "marketized" some of its other programs. Deregulation has been introduced into the airline industry. Some profitable lines have been eliminated from VIA Rail. The subsidization of transportation costs for western farms has been eliminated with the termination of the historic Crows Nest Pass agreement. Some public enterprises have been sold and several others are on the selling block.

Fourth, the government is pursuing free-trade arrangements with the U.S. Successive rounds of GATT (General Agreement On Tariffs and Trade) negotiations will bring the average rate of tariff protection down to between 9 and 10 per cent by 1987. The Liberal government began discussions with Washington to eliminate all trade barriers for a variety of specific industries, along the lines of the Auto Pact. The Tories are pursuing a North American free-trade zone.

Fifth, government regulation of new foreign investment was checked when the Liberals diluted the Foreign Investment Review Agency

(FIRA). The Tories upped the ante by replacing FIRA with Investment Canada whose mandate is to do everything possible to encourage foreign investment.

Finally, governments everywhere have begun to dismantle the system of collective bargaining, the centrepiece of the so-called postwar settlement between labour and capital. The right to strike has been entirely removed in a broadening list of "essential services." Governments have increasingly resorted to ordering striking workers back to work, something almost unheard of before 1970. The open shop is being forced back onto construction sites. The anti-inflation program of 1975 to 1978 limited negotiations to prescribed guidelines. The 1982 federal public-sector restraint program tore up agreements government itself had signed, applied fixed percentages to wage increases and entirely eliminated collective bargaining. Similar wage-restraint programs were introduced in nearly all provincial jurisdictions. While controls of any sort are clearly not part of the monetarist agenda, humbling trade unions certainly is. In the minds of at least some analysts, the 6-and-5 program is part of the government's "grand plan" to permanently remove the right to strike from federal employees.[14]

The monetarist agenda was set by Liberal governments. Its pursuit by the Tory administration therefore represents an acceleration, not a departure, from previous policy.

Supply-Side Economics

While the monetarists preach a policy of austerity and restraining demand, supply-side conservatives shift concern to increasing the total amount of goods and services that companies supply to the marketplace. At face value it is a far more attractive package: inflation can be reduced without increasing unemployment; tax rates can be reduced without increasing government deficit; economic growth can be restored without real sacrifice.

Supply-side economics revives the economics of J.B. Say. If the market is left alone, production will generate incomes (wages, profits, rent) that are sufficient to clear the market of all goods produced. If supply is cultivated, demand will take care of itself.

But it is the capitalists who make up the supply side. They are the source of savings that finance the investment that produces jobs and the growth of goods and services. To coax capitalists to save and invest they must be adequately rewarded. And nothing demoralizes capitalists more than the high marginal tax rates whose proceeds are used to finance the welfare state. Through its power to tax, government

Monetarism 119

introduced a "wedge" between what one gets for working and investing and what one is allowed to keep.

In a throw-back to Robert Malthus, the supply-siders argue that taking care of the poor saps the vitality of the capitalist elite and only serves to make the poor more hopeless as capitalists reduce their effort, their investment and their output. "Material progress," George Gilder tells us, "is ineluctably elitist: it makes the rich richer and increases their number, exalting the few extraordinary men who can produce wealth over the democratic masses who consume it.... Material progress, though democratically demanded, is procedurally undemocratic."[15]

Supply-siders have a fondness for quoting fourteenth-century Moslem philosopher Ibn Khaldun: "At the beginning of the dynasty, taxation yields a large revenue from small assessments. At the end of the dynasty taxation yields a small revenue from large assessments." In other words, tax increases so undermine incentives to produce that beyond a certain point further increases will depress the level of economic activity and the total amount of tax collections. But the reverse is also true. Incentive effects on the suppliers of capital are so potent that lower tax rates will actually increase tax collections, so efficiently will they stimulate investment and economic growth.

This is the point of the much-touted Laffer curve, the creation of supply-side guru Arthur Laffer. Laffer's claim, essentially just a more outlandish version of business folklore, was never accepted by most economists. But the supply-siders popularized the capital-supply worries of Wall Street and infused them with a democratic flavour: rewards to the rich unlock new prosperity for all. "Regressive taxes help the poor," Gilder writes.[16] Cutting the taxes of the rich will so stimulate business and pre-tax incomes of the rich, that they will wind up paying more in taxes, which will allow tax cuts for everybody else.

Supply-side economics is a throw-back to the musings of American robber baron Andrew Mellon: "The prosperity of the middle and lower classes depends on the good fortune and light taxes of the rich." Efforts to redistribute income are held to be ineffective. More particularly, it is the welfare state's coddling of the poor that keeps them from participating in the economy by sapping their incentive to work. "They have been turned into kennel dogs sitting on their haunches yapping for the next handout, not hunting dogs alert and lean of muscle foraging for food," says former president of General Motors, Charles Wilson, another favourite of the supply-siders.

According to the supply-siders, high taxes on the rich not only cause reduced output and unemployment, but also produce inflation. High taxes act as a brake on production, which causes inflation by reducing the supply of goods. More directly, taxes form a cost of production and like other costs are passed on as increased prices. Since it is the high cost of the welfare state that induces higher taxes, it is government with its proliferating services and inefficiencies that is the chief cause of inflation.[17]

This is where supply-siders part company with the monetarists. Government is their common enemy, but for supply-siders it is government taxes that cause inflation, not government-induced increases in the money supply. In fact, restricting the money supply to fight inflation can only serve "to dampen private-sector growth" which alone is "the best way to fight inflation."[18] Where monetarists are concerned to hold down aggregate demand by controlling the money supply, for supply-siders the only solution is "an unremitting cultivation of the supply of new goods."[19]

As for the monetarists, democracy is a key problem for the supply-siders. When "mass sentiment is allowed to dictate to the powerful ... the result is a failure of political authority ... and a tendency toward national decline."[20] A successful economy depends on the proliferation of the rich, unfettered by the government and protected from the masses who push misguided politicians into counter-productive redistributive schemes.

Supply-Side Economics in Canada

Supply-side economics has had a long run in Canada. Immediately after the Second World War, large numbers of workers paid no income tax at all, those who did paid only a small portion of their income in personal taxation, while the marginal rates on the highest income bracket exceeded 80 per cent and corporations supplied a very substantial part of overall government revenues. In the 1950s a fiscal counter-revolution began; it continued for two decades and dramatically accelerated after 1970.

In 1951, corporations contributed a slightly higher proportion of total government revenues than did individuals through personal taxes (28 per cent as against 24 per cent). By 1985-86 the corporate share, reduced by a wide range of special allowances and exemptions had fallen to 14.0 per cent while personal taxes had risen to 45 per cent. (Sales taxes and customs levies make up much of the other tax revenues.)

This development has taken place largely out of public view partly because evidence is often confined to footnotes in corporate financial reports. Officially, corporations pay tax at a rate of 46 per cent. In fact, their rates are often dramatically lower. In 1980 corporations were able to use various tax breaks to reduce their effective tax rates to an average of 23 per cent. In 1970, before the introduction of the most generous tax incentives, corporations paid tax at an average rate of 34 per cent.

Shell Canada is a good example. Its 1982 annual report pegs the company's income taxes at $152 million on pre-tax profits of $302 million. In a note, it calculates that this gives the company an effective income tax rate of 50.4 per cent — a hefty rate by any standards. But another note indicates that Shell deferred $199 million in taxes in 1982, which wiped out the tax bill and left Shell with a tax credit of $47 million.

Deferring taxes is one of the key ways the tax system allows corporations to reduce their tax burden. The government allows companies to deduct investments in plants, equipment, research, development and exploration from profits at an artificially fast rate, thereby reducing profit levels for taxation purposes. The difference between pre-tax profits and this reduced profit level is income that will not be taxed that year, or the next year, or the year after.

The word "deferred" is, in fact, misleading because in almost all cases the taxes are "deferred" indefinitely and the corporation holds on to the money indefinitely. As much is admitted in a paper prepared by the Department of Finance for the May 1985 budget: "While, strictly speaking, a fast write-off provides a tax deferral, such tax deferral can be valuable to a firm particularly if they are for long periods of time. As well, if the firm continues investing, the deferral can be indefinite and thus tantamount to complete exemption."[21] Yet according to accepted Canadian accounting principles, companies include these deferred taxes as though they had been paid when they calculate their tax rates.

As Ottawa has created more and more opportunities for corporations to defer taxes, the proportion of the total corporate tax bill deferred each year has grown. Not surprisingly, the vast majority of these benefits (82 per cent) has been enjoyed by a handful of firms (13 per cent of the 450,000 firms in Canada). In 1982 Imperial Oil paid $62 million in tax and deferred $322 million, bringing the company's total accumulated deferred taxes to $1.29 billion. In 1980 Bell Canada deferred taxes of $129 million, bringing its total accumulated deferred taxes to $1.2 billion. Stelco deferred $30 million, bringing its total deferred taxes to $390 million. MacMillan Bloedel deferred $55 million, bringing its total to $227 million. In 1982 Gulf Canada paid taxes of $67 million and deferred $106 million.[22]

Besides deferments, supply-side tax breaks include such items as exploration and development write-offs for oil, gas and mining companies and full deductions for equipment and buildings purchased for research and development. Tax incentives saved the corporate sector a total of $6.7 billion dollars in 1980.[23] Corporations were granted nearly a billion dollars more in tax incentives in the 1983 budget, and the

March 1985 changes in petroleum tax structures, dubbed "A Private Enterprise Energy Program" by *Investors Digest*, had relieved the industry of an estimated $2.2 billion tax bill by 1986.

Tax incentives reduced the nominal federal corporate tax rate of 36 per cent by one-half. But the more capital-incentive and larger firms, which are best able to take full advantage of fast capital write-offs and resource write-offs, have pared down their tax bills even more. Mining companies on average are taxed only 13.2 per cent, utilities 16.1 per cent and manufacturers 16.5 per cent.[24] Smaller, more labour-intensive firms benefit from various small business deductions but end up with a marginally higher rate. The service and retail trades, for example, pay about 20 per cent. Thus the decline in the share of total tax revenues paid by corporations has been due not only to the gradual drop in the nominal rate at which corporation taxes are taxed but more importantly to the sudden proliferation of tax loopholes or tax incentives as they are usually called.

With business paying a declining share of the tax bill, the general public has been forced to pick up most of the tab in the form of income taxes and sales tax. But the distribution of the tax burden within the general public has also undergone a dramatic shift.

Consistent with supply-side economics, the tax rate on the incomes of the rich has been gradually reduced over the years and especially since the early 1970s. In 1949 the highest marginal rate of tax was 84 per cent. In 1972 this rate was reduced to 65 per cent by then Finance Minister John Turner, and in 1981 it was cut again to barely over 50 per cent, only about double the rate paid by individuals in some of the lowest tax brackets. The marginal tax rate of a millionaire is 49.98 per cent compared with 24.99 per cent paid by an individual with $1,000 taxable income and with 36.75 per cent paid on a $21,000 to $28,000 taxable income.

These changes are in full accord with the theories of supply-side economics and were, in fact, justified by supply-side arguments. By allowing high-income earners to retain more of their incomes, it was said, they would have both the capacity and the incentive to invest more, which in the long run would stimulate economic growth and improve the incomes of everybody. Extreme versions of supply-side economics go even further, arguing that corporate tax should be abolished altogether and a flat tax imposed on all personal incomes.

The real tax spread is even narrower than these figures show because of the panoply of exemptions which allow the rich to pare down their taxable incomes. In 1981, for instance, people with incomes of more than $250,000 theoretically had a tax rate of 53 per cent on the part of their income that exceeded $250,000. But once they had claimed all deductions, they were actually left paying tax at an effective rate of 27.9 per cent, roughly the same as an individual earning between $35,000 and $40,000. As the Finance Department points out in its 1981 paper "Analysis of Federal Tax Expenditures for Individuals," "some high income individuals are extraordinarily successful in reducing their taxes."

Behind these large discrepancies lies the particular form of tax politics practised in Ottawa. Consistent with supply-side principles, the government has built in a variety of exemptions allegedly aimed at improving incentives for certain kinds of economic activity, a form of supply-side economics called "tax expenditures." Formally, it is defined as special provisions in the tax status which result in designated types of income being taxed at a lower rate than would otherwise be the case and in government foregoing tax revenues which would ordinarily be collected. In the words of the federal Finance Department:

> The Canadian tax system contains a number of provisions that give preferential treatment of certain groups of individuals or businesses in the form of tax exemptions, deductions, reduced tax rates, or tax credits. The purpose of these provisions is to grant a subsidy or incentive for those engaging in a specific activity or for those in certain special circumstances by lowering or deferring their tax liabilities.... Such tax forgiveness or postponement is equivalent to the government first collecting the sums involved by imposing tax on a more comprehensive base at uniform rates and then making a direct expenditure or loan in an amount equal to the revenue foregone due to the tax preferences. Such provisions have thus come to be called expenditures.[25]

Tax expenditures for individuals, like those for the corporate sector, also add up to billions. According to the federal government's own estimate, tax expenditures for individuals cost the federal treasury nearly $14 billion in 1979. Without them, Ottawa would have collected $30.8 billion in income tax compared to the $17 billion actually collected. Including corporate tax expenditures, federal tax revenues were shrunk by $26 billion, a sum equal to almost one-half of the total federal expenditures for that fiscal year and far in excess of the federal deficit. Six years later in 1985, Auditor-General Kenneth Dye estimated that tax-avoidance schemes cost the federal treasury between $35 and $50 billion annually — between 55 and 80 per cent of tax collections.

While not all tax expenditures granted to individuals benefit the rich, they managed to reap a very large proportion of the concessions. The study prepared for the Department of Finance for 1979 reveals just how lucrative expenditures can be. On average, individuals within $100,000 plus tax bracket received a benefit of $46,000 in reduced federal taxes compared to $10,000 for individuals in the $50,000-$100,000 range and $771 for those with incomes between $10,000-$15,000. In 1982, 235 superstars of tax avoidance paid no tax at all on incomes averaging $635,000, while 1,200 who earned $100,000 paid no taxes.

Tax expenditures emerged as a favoured instrument in the 1970s. The growth of anti-government sentiment encouraged this hidden welfare system. Unlike social services the cost of tax expenditures are not monitored with any care. Unlike direct subsidies which involve procedures for eligibility and some degree of control over how the subsidy is spent, tax incentives leave the initiative in the hands of the beneficiary and involve less governmental interference in management decisions.

Supply-side measures first accelerated while John Turner was minister of finance. Turner beat back a move to create income supplement programs for the working poor by introducing more than $2 billion in new tax breaks for the rich in his November 1974 budget. Two months later he told the cabinet that the $1 billion programs for the working poor could not be afforded because there was no money left to finance it.

Personal income tax expenditures increased by 50 per cent in 1974, 18 per cent in 1975 and 34 per cent in 1976. More than 30 per cent of personal income tax revenue was lost as tax expenditures in 1976, a sum more than 50 per cent higher than in 1973. Federal and provincial corporate tax expenditures amounted to 69 per cent of total corporate taxes collected in 1975 compared to 37 per cent in 1964.

They took another dramatic jump in the May 1985 budget when Finance Minister Michael Wilson introduced a new lifetime capital gains exemption of $500,000. This loophole will only benefit a minority but its gains will be very substantial, up to $125,000 of lifetime tax savings for high-income taxpayers. Altogether the capital gains exemption will have cost $1,250 billion in lost revenue by 1990-91. The gradual extension of RRSP contribution limits from $5,000 to $15,500 by 1990 grants the rich yet another hefty bonus. By 1990 the $80,000 earner will enjoy $2,500 more in tax savings from RRSP. (The $30,000 earner gains only $200.)

In a study prepared for the C.D. Howe Institute, Professor Irwin Gillespie wrote that "many Canadians appear to believe that the federal government has been acting like Robin Hood." His analysis of the 1970s demonstrates that, on the contrary, "more often than not the lowest-income families benefited least from the distributive effects of budgetary policy during the 1970s." In his 1974 budget, for instance, John Turner stressed that throughout his term as finance minister he had aimed "to protect those of our citizens burnt by inflation who are least able to protect themselves." Gillespie's calculations show that the average poor family gained $134 from Mr. Turner's 1973 budget compared to an average benefit of $1,823 for families in the highest-income group.

Changes introduced in the May 1985 budget had similar results.[26] A two-income couple with two children — the average poor family ($15,000) — will have lost $135 in 1986 compared to a loss of $208 for a middle-income family ($35,000). The rich family ($80,000), on the other hand, will have enjoyed a tax saving of $631. By 1990 the cumulative results of the new tax regime would show the poor family to have lost $1,879 over the five-year period, compared to a cumulative loss of $1,125 for the rich family with an income more than five times greater. The middle-income family will have suffered the largest loss — $3,452 — over the period. The cumulative results are even more unequal in the case of single-income families. While both the poor and middle-income families will have been forced to transfer substantial amounts of money to government over the five-year period ($2,422 and $4,216), rich families actually will come out ahead by a total of $5,662.

Responding to concerns that some high-income taxpayers were able to use tax shelters so effectively that they ended up paying little or no tax, the government introduced a new minimum 24 per cent tax. However, the scheme included a $44,000 exemption, about ten times the basic personal exemption allowed for ordinary taxpayers. As a consequence, lower-income taxpayers could end up paying a larger chunk of their income in tax than high-income individuals paying the minimum tax.

The shift of the tax burden onto the average Canadian taxpayer has led to a period of ideological windfall for laissez-faire economics. In reality, Canada's total taxes are near the bottom of the list of industrial countries. But the increasingly regressive distribution of taxes may have led ordinary taxpayers to conclude that a heavy tax burden has helped kill economic growth.

7 | The New Right: Theory and Practice

The 1980s have brought the New Right to power in Washington, London, Ottawa, Victoria and elsewhere. It has set the tone for political debate, defined the economic agenda and forced its opponents to debate the issues on its reactionary terms. This chapter focuses on the theory and practice of the New Right, especially on inflation, the focus of conservative prescriptions.

The Inflation Conundrum

The persistent inflation of the past thirty years is a new historical phenomenon. During the competitive phase of industrial capitalism, falling prices were the dominant trend as the many relatively small firms engaged in an industry were forced to compete by upgrading technology and machinery and passing the resulting lower costs on to the consumer. Wars and investment booms created waves of inflation, but these only punctuated long periods of declining prices. Periodic crises and mass unemployment checked rising wages by continually re-creating a balance of power in the labour market in favour of employers. They also eliminated the least efficient firms, raising the average productivity and lowering operating costs throughout the economy.

This trend changed dramatically during the phase of monopoly capitalism following the Second World War. Given the very favourable conditions that prevailed until the end of the 1960s, inflation was continuous but mild, averaging less than 3 per cent. This creeping inflation was considered a small price to pay for near full employment. The picture began to change in the late 1960s because of the Vietman war but continued long after the war had ended. By the 1970s, inflation was approaching double-digit proportions and in several countries exceeded 10 per cent (see Table 7:1).

Many theories have been proposed to account for inflation and its persistence for over a decade. The monetarists point to excesses in government spending and the money supply, conservatives generally to the increased power of trade unions and rising taxes. Other expla-

TABLE 7:1
Consumer Prices:
Percentage Changes from Previous Period

	Average 1961-70	1971-78	1979	1980	1981
U.S.	2.8	6.7	11.3	13.5	10.4
Japan	5.8	9.8	3.6	8.0	4.9
West Germany	2.7	5.2	4.1	5.5	5.9
France	4.0	9.0	10.8	13.6	13.4
U.K.	4.1	13.2	13.4	18.0	11.9
Italy	3.9	13.0	14.8	21.2	19.5
Canada	2.7	7.6	9.1	10.1	12.5
Total	3.2	8.0	9.3	12.2	10.0
Total OECD	3.3	8.5	9.8	12.9	10.6
OECD Europe	3.8	9.9	10.6	14.2	12.3

Source: OECD, *Economic Outlook*, December 1982.

nations — corporate power, arms spending, the OPEC oil shock — have been forwarded, but none is convincing.

When prices are rising it is always possible to point to some factor, such as the dramatic rise in world commodity prices, especially oil in 1973-74 and again in 1979. Another example is an increase in indirect taxes on liquor, cigarettes or gasoline, or a rise in the general sales tax.

There are four factors that contribute to the cost of producing goods and services: wages, profits, indirect taxes and prices of imported materials. When the general level of prices rises, one or some combination of these factors must be involved. This is a mere statement of fact, however, not a theory of causation.

Why did workers get big boosts in pay? How did companies come to take bigger profits? Why did governments raise indirect taxes? Why did the Arab sheiks raise oil prices and what conditions in the world market allowed them to do so successfully? In fact, what were the conditions that allowed any group to obtain more than before? An increase in any one of these "appropriations" may result in a once-and-for-all increase in prices, but not in continuously rising prices. What would cause a sustained price increase from any of these sources?

The Monopoly and Arms Race Arguments

Such arguments easily apply to the monopoly theory. An increase in the extent of monopoly could once and for all increase prices and hence profits, but could not by itself lead to continuously rising prices. Once the initial impact of increased monopolization is absorbed in higher prices, the inflation rate should fall back to its previous level. Moreover, increases in monopoly prices can cause a general increase in prices only if it is accompanied by an increase in the supply of money. Without more money in circulation, higher-priced monopoly goods would absorb a larger proportion of consumer dollars. With fewer dollars chasing other goods, their prices are bound to fall. In fact, their decline should just about match the increase in monopoly prices.

The average rate of inflation in the decade 1973 to 1983 was about 10 per cent. The average rate of inflation in the decade before was about 3 per cent. Did monopolization increase by a correspondingly large factor in the interim, or did monopolists suddenly become that much more greedy or powerful? An argument could just as easily be made for the reverse: the liberalization of the world economy produced more competition, at least for many products. Furthermore, inflation fell by half in 1982-83. Did the degree of monopolization decline over night by the same amount?

The problem with the monopoly theory of inflation is that it confuses condition with cause. Monopoly can be a condition that nurtures inflation. Without it, employers would not be able to pass along to consumers their increases in wage costs or imported fuel or taxes. But monopoly is not itself a cause of inflation.

The permanent-arms hypothesis for inflation is likewise impossible to sustain. Military expenditure declined in relative importance between 1955 and 1979, when defence spending as a proportion of the GNP fell from 7.1 to 6.2 per cent for all industrial countries in the West and continued to fall until the 1980s. The growing importance of state expenditures has been mainly due to rapid increases in the provision of collective services by the public sector and in the rising proportion of household expenditure financed by transfer payments.

The Monetarist Argument

According to monetarist theory, inflation is caused by excessive increases in the money supply by the central bank, probably acting under instructions from the government. Monetarists claim support for their theory by showing that in any country there is a fairly close correlation between the rate of increase in the quantity of money and in the level of prices. Inflation can only be brought under control, they argue, by determined government action to restrict increases in the money supply.

The criticism of the monopoly theory of inflation applies equally well to the monetarist argument. The expansion of the money supply is best viewed as a symptom rather than as the cause of inflation. For example, when firms pay for increased costs for labour, raw materials and machinery by taking out loans, they are credited with increased deposits by their banks. Since the volume of bank deposits is the main component of the money supply, the money supply thereby increases. When the government wishes to raise public spending without increasing taxes, the extra dollars must be financed by borrowing either from the public through the sale of bonds or from the banking system. The first course creates the distinct danger of competition for funds driving up the rate of interest, which is a sufficient inducement for the government to finance at least part of the deficit by borrowing from the banking system. Once again, the total volume of bank deposits rises and the money supply with it.

Far from indicating that an increase in the supply of money is the prime mover of the inflationary process, the evidence should be read the other way around. Increases in the price level caused by increases in costs or government expenditures call forth accommodating increases in the supply of money. Understanding the root causes of inflation requires an examination of the factors which push up costs and state expenditures and squeeze profits.

In other words, inflation has less to do with government policy than with the way the economy is organized. Inflation is closely related to the difficulties of maintaining profitability. When costs rise, companies normally attempt to protect their profits by raising their prices. And other groups, like unions and governments, will press for proportional increases to protect their spending power. Without easy access to credit, they would all lose their ability to protect themselves from higher costs. The reason for inflation is not that governments are weak or undisciplined spendthrifts, although they may in fact be all of these things, but that profitability and prosperity come to demand it.

Governments can break an inflationary spiral but only by squeezing credit so hard and raising interest rates so high that they bring the economy to a halt and force it into a depression. And they can keep it under control only by restoring competition, which means dismantling the large companies, public agencies and trade unions that dominate economic activity.

The feasibility of unscrambling the results of the last 200 years of capitalist development is not very great, to say the least. If only people would act as isolated individuals; if only workers would not organize into unions; if only businessmen would not seek to monopolize their markets; if only trade associations and marketing boards did not exist; if only the poor would refuse assistance; if only big businesses would not co-opt politicians. These are the "frictions" that monetarists say governments must overcome before their prescriptions will take effect. But these frictions are the real grit of contemporary corporate capitalism. If governments ever followed monetarists' advice to its logical conclusion, it would produce a degree of unemployment and bankruptcy and social tension capable of destroying the stability of the social order that monetarists and government officials want to preserve.

Monetarists have a problem with unlimited democracy; their solution is to simply limit the powers of government and release the forces of the market. But they also have a problem with social justice. Like nature itself, the market order knows neither justice nor injustice. Free individuals put up with the costs of the market order if they want its benefits. Social obligation, the idea of solidarity between self and community, has no place in the monetarist logic. But as one author has observed, "The fatalism implied in the view that submission to the 'spontaneous' market order is the best we can do — whatever it may bring in its wake — is at odds with the entire western spirit of activism and mastery of the environment."[1]

Conservative thinkers have assumed that economic freedom begets civil freedom, religious freedom, political freedom and social freedom, an assumption that is supported neither by history nor by logic. Are we a less free society today then we were in the latter half of the nineteenth century, the alleged heyday of competitive capitalism? Are the Swedes with their extensive welfare system less free than the Americans or the Japanese who are least afflicted by the welfare state? Are the dying and impoverished children found in the streets of Calcutta, where enterprise is unencumbered by regulations, more free than the highly regimented, better-fed children of Peking?

Chile is the one place in the world where monetarism was implemented to the letter. The whole operation was managed by ex-students of Milton Friedman, not surprisingly called "the Chicago boys." All state controls were abandoned — except strict regulation of the money supply. Government spending was slashed and welfare programs virtually abolished. The government watched with apparent satisfaction as the economy slumped and unemployment soared along with inflation. In time inflation was brought under control. No doubt this was partly due to the elimination of that other source of "labour market imperfection," trade unions. Strikes were prohibited, most unions dissolved; their leaders, the lucky ones, were jailed. Real wages sank, but with little apparent effect on the demand for labour. Unemployment remained high. Before inflation began to soar once again, F.A. von Hayek visited Chile and called it liberty. To be sure, the vision of Friedman, Hayek and others is not facism. It is economic liberty. But when political freedom does not follow economic freedom, and especially when it gets in the way of economic freedom, it must be corrected or, with regrets, eliminated altogether.[2]

Chinks in the Monetarist Armour

Monetarism's failure to produce results in anything like the short time-frame first promised (eighteen to twenty-four months of restraint) has produced two predictable responses. The first, championed by Hayek, is that since it takes several years and possibly decades before a gradualist policy makes a significant impact on inflation, "no democratic government can stay the course" of such a slow reduction of inflation. He recommends instead a crash course: "even 20 percent unemployment would probably be borne for six months if there existed confidence that it would be over at the end of such a period."[3] This is analagous to the argument posed by some during the Vietnam war that if "we nuked the gooks" the war would end immediately and the total losses would be far less than they would be if the war were conducted with "conventional" weapons.

A second response, championed by the rational expectations school, is analogous to the argument that if we could convince the North Vietnamese that we would drop the bomb we would never have to do so; if we could convince people that we are prepared, if necessary, to destroy the economy with such a tight monetary policy that the whole economy would collapse, then inflationary expectations would be so dramatically dampened that we would not have to destroy the economy after all. Producers would reduce their price hikes, workers their wage benefits, and banks their interest rates.

Nearly a decade of monetarism has produced substantial evidence that the core of the doctrine is suspect. While price increases are always associated with an increase in the money supply, there is no evidence that the line of causation runs from money to prices. Monetarists originally proposed that price changes followed changes in the primary supply with an eighteen-month to two-year lag. But looking at data for nine countries, Nicholas Kaldor has shown that in less than six out of twenty-seven cases is there any semblance of a two-year lag.[4]

A key misconception of monetarism is that the banking authorities have the power to control the supply of money. The Bank of Canada, for example, has often failed to keep M_1 (currency in circulation plus chequing accounts) within the targeted range and it ultimately was forced to confess to having lost track of M_1 altogether. But even if the Bank of Canada were able to control one monetary aggregate, a society that is constrained in its expenditures by any one means of payment soon evolves new money forms. Even if the monetary authorities were able to establish absolute control over the supply of money, they cannot control the number of times it is used. Rising velocity, by offsetting a reduction in the rate at which the supply of money is allowed to grow, can negate any impact that such restrictions on the money supply might have on prices.

There remains, despite these gaping holes in the theory, a large investment of faith and political judgment in monetarism. But what about its side effects?

- In order to achieve any noticeable impact on inflationary expectations, central banks have to raise interest rates far enough above current inflation rates to push real (inflation-adjusted) rates to record levels. Whereas real interest rates have traditionally been in the 2 to 3 per cent range and have almost never exceeded 3 per cent, in 1982-84 they climbed to 7 to 8 per cent (and over 10 per cent in the U.S.). Few firms can find new investment opportunities that will cover these rates and still turn a profit. Besides paralyzing new investment, such historically high interest rates have caused serious deterioration of corporate balance sheets, pushing tens of thousands of small and medium-sized companies into bankruptcy. The companies in worst trouble are those that contracted huge acquisition and expansion loans in the 1970s when real borrowing costs were negligible (less than 1 per cent for much of the decade). Even those monetarist stalwarts, the banks, cried "uncle." Bank of Montreal head W.D. Mullholland told the Canadian Club in 1982 that "policies being implemented in the name of monetarism are threatening the gradual destruction of the North American economy."
- While Keynes called on the state to make capital so abundant that interest would virtually disappear and with it the "euthanasia of the rentier," monetarists ask for the very opposite, calling on the state to deliberately act to make capital scarce. Monetarism's high interest-rate policy has resulted in a sizable transfer of wealth from industrial and commercial capital to finance capital. Producers are forced to pay premium sums to gain access to funds for operating expenses and investment.
- Interest and miscellaneous income accounted for only 3.2 per cent of Canada's national income in 1961. In 1982 lenders captured 8.6 per cent of the total. This amounted to almost $30 billion (second quarter) and compares to only $21 billion received as profits in the same year. This is the first time in the last forty years that interest payments have exceeded profits. In 1961, by comparison, profits accounted for 10 per cent of national income, more than three times

New Right   133

the figure that fell to interest. Ironically, monetarism has struck a blow against profits, the motor force of the capitalist economy.

- To the extent that wages respond only sluggishly to higher unemployment, the burden of monetarism again falls ironically upon profits. In this instance, a decrease in aggregate demand has a significant effect on wage demands only when a recession has become severe enough to threaten mass lay-offs for workers and bankruptcy for their employers. Control over wages is exerted only through a severe and damaging squeeze on firms.
- While severe economic contraction can drag down wages for a while at least, the damage it inflicts upon capital can be not only severe but long-lasting. Some firms may indeed have been made efficient and lean in the process of fighting for survival. Many inefficient firms may undoubtedly be eliminated in the process and their exit raises average productivity — just as shooting the wounded raises the average health of an army. The most likely survivors, however, are those that are least vulnerable to external shocks; past conservatism may be a greater protector than efficiency. In the meantime, sustained contraction can permanently destroy substantial segments of the economy's productive capacity.
- While the effectiveness of monetary restraint in reducing inflation is indirect and subject to long lags, its impact on costs is immediate. When interest rates are raised, the increases are built into a firm's cost structures, and in the short run at least, the upward pressure that high interest rates adds to the supply price more than offsets their dampening effect on demand. Moreover, by discouraging consumer and business borrowing, a high interest-rate policy forces firms to operate well below capacity levels, driving up per unit costs of output and raising prices still further.
- High interest rates also add to the size of the public debt — yet another irony of thwarted monetarist intentions.

In the neo-conservative tradition, monetarists insist that at current levels disability payments, social-security payments and unemployment insurance induce people not to work. Contrary to their belief, such a "moral hazard" — the term used to describe this behaviour — does not appear to exist. A cross-country comparison of the association between more extensive systems of income maintenance and labour force participation reveals no withdrawal of labour. For instance, Japan, which devotes 20 per cent less of its gross domestic product to income maintenance compared to Sweden, has a labour force participation rate less than half that of Sweden. In the period 1960-80, when Canada was increasing by 36 per cent the proportion of its Gross Domestic Product devoted to income maintenance, labour force participation rose 10 per cent, from 54.2 per cent to 64.0 per cent.[5] The fact of the matter is that many factors are responsible for changes in labour force participation. For instance, the significant rise in female labour force participation can be largely attributed to the declining income level of single-earner families.

Neo-conservatives cite several empirical investigations to prove another of their nostrums, namely, that increased payments to the unemployed cause unemployment. But if there is a causal relationship between these two variables, there are equally valid grounds for believing that it runs in the opposite direction, high unemployment creating pressure for improvements in unemployment insurance. Examining these econometric studies in his MA thesis, George Allen Harrison found that the selection of periods and other specifications biases their results upwards. When he changed the specification of their models, the results did not support the hypothesis that unemployment insurance benefits significantly affect measured rates of unemployment. Using an alternative model, he says, leads to "a strong rejection of the hypothesis." Harrison's discovery is a useful reminder that we should be wary of supporting policy prescriptions based on econometric studies that use simplistic models purporting to say something about human behaviour.[6]

The monetarist hypothesis that the government deficit crowds out private expenditures is related to the broader question of the unproductive sectors of the economy crowding out the productive sectors. Is there any validity to these claims? Looking at the crowding-out thesis in its narrowest meaning, there would be some plausibility to this proposition if the economy were operating at or close to full capacity such that the volume of public borrowing would absorb excessive amounts of available loanable funds, forcing up the rate of interest and thus crowding out the private sector. This was likely a factor at work in 1965-75 at the onset of the crisis. With the economy operating at well below full capacity this argument can no longer hold. There is evidently room for both private spenders and the government to increase their levels of expenditure.

Looking at the broader issue of productive versus unproductive sectors of the economy, the distinction obviously has some validity from a capitalistic viewpoint. Public expenditures are ultimately financed from the profit-making sphere of the economy. In an economy that is operating at full capacity they involve a diversion of funds that restricts the private sector. And if they result in anything like full employment they tip the balance between labour and capital in favour of labour, in the manner described by Michael Kalecki. In an economy operating at well below full capacity, deficit-financed public expenditures are helpful in maintaining demand, including demand for marketed goods and services. But even in this circumstance, by undermining the labour market, they can still create problems for the private sector.

Here it is useful to note that the conservative offensive against the public sector is aimed as much at reorienting as it is at reducing public expenditures. Besides social services the state provides services that, while not directly productive of profits, are vital in allowing the private sector to make profits. If the state did not shoulder the cost of providing such services as transportation, communication, research, hydro-electric power and manpower training, the prospects for profitable production would be greatly restricted. The objective is to redirect public expenditures away from social services that are a drain on private capital and that interfere with the labour market and towards programs that are closely linked to private wealth creation.

Supply-Side Syndrome

Since free-market supply-siders also attack the public sector, trade unions and all redistributional efforts, their solutions are subject to criticisms similar to those aimed at monetarists. But what about their proposition that massive cuts in the marginal tax rates would result in such an outpouring of private economic activity that inflationary pressures would be reduced and that tax revenues would actually rise.

The claim must be resolved by empirical facts and not solely by logic. And the available facts show that the claims are, at best, wild exaggeration. As admitted by Martin Feldstein, former chairman of Ronald Reagan's Council of Economic Advisors, the supply-side "revolution" which was spearheaded by the Reagan tax cuts has failed to reach its objectives.

> The experience since 1981 has not been kind to the claims of the new supply-side extremists that an across-the-board reduction in tax rates would spur unprecedented growth, reduce inflation painlessly, increase tax revenue, and stimulate a spectacular rise in personal savings. Each of those predictions has proven to be wrong.[7]

Do people work more when their after-tax wage rate increases, and if so, by how much? While there are no studies of labour supply that are not open to serious objections of one kind or another, none of the available studies shows a large positive response to reductions in marginal tax rates. The most optimistic recent American estimate shows that a 30 per cent reduction in tax rates would lead to only a 1.5 per cent increase in total hours worked. This is hardly the sort of massive response that is envisioned by supply-siders. The same negative conclusion follows from the fact that marginal tax rates there are not much different today than they were in the 1960s and are considerably lower than those in European countries whose pre-1983 productivity gains excited the envy of North American businessmen. This hardly suggests that high marginal tax rates on workers' incomes are a major factor in North America's poor economic performance.

Would a large drop in marginal tax rates increase productive effort enough to raise government revenue? Again the results of econometric studies do not support the Laffer-curve hypothesis. Recent research shows that the net change in tax revenue from a 30 per cent cut in tax rates on workers' wages is a revenue decline of about 20 per cent. In other words, the revenue feedback would be only one-third of the revenue loss.[8]

Estimating the effects of a reduction of marginal tax rates on savings and investment is difficult, but a study by the Federal Reserve Bank of New York concluded that "the presumption that a higher return to saving [resulting from a tax reduction] will spark a substantial increase in the amount of saving undertaken (or any increase at all) is not well founded." France and Germany have among the highest savings ratios as well as the highest tax burdens.

While supply-side analysis insists that there is no distinction between saving and investment — all saving will be invested — in a recent review of the literature, University of Toronto's Richard Bird discovered

> three rather disconcerting conclusions ... (1) we know amazingly little about the efficiency and effectiveness of investment incentives ... (2) what little we do know suggests that these incentives are neither efficient nor effective ... (3) the available research techniques are incapable of improving this sad state of affairs very much.[9]

Bird found that all existing studies agree that tax-incentive schemes affect the composition of investment — causing firms to alter their location, technology and timing of investment decisions — but they do not have much effect on the total amount of investment. These conclusions have been confirmed in a recent study prepared for the Department of Finance which "calls into question the ability ... of the tax system to override other determinants of investment ...."[10] It shows that industries benefiting most from federal tax incentives, such as manufacturing, forestry and construction, have not been investing at a higher rate than the industries that benefit least. Moreover, their record of employment growth has been decidedly worse. Industries showing the most employment growth, in particular the service sector, have benefited least from tax incentives. And tax incentives designed to increase investments may cause businesses to substitute capital for labour, thus reducing employment opportunities.

There is virtually no evidence to support the proposition that individuals work more because of higher after-tax returns. Sceptics are entitled to dismiss a doctrine which says, in essence, that the poor won't work because they have too much money and the rich won't work because they have too little. Nor is there any evidence that total saving in the economy has much to do with the rate of return on saving. Nor, finally, is there any guarantee that investment increases as a result of lower taxes on business income. Moreover, financial investment is clearly not necessarily productive investment. In periods of excess capacity the rich are prone to pour their savings in and out of commodity exchanges, tax-sheltered real estate, corporate mergers, gold and art objects, none of which adds one whit to productive investment and economic growth.

Even conceding, for the sake of argument, that greater inequality may be conducive to higher personal savings, there are many forms of collective saving, such as pension funds and national budget surpluses, that do not depend on income inequality. In Sweden, for example, the National Pension Fund has become the single most important form of savings, matching both household savings and corporate profits. "If you rely entirely on traditional private capital to solve the capital formation problem," says Anna Hedborg of the Swedish Trade Union Confederation, "you have to accept more inequality than we can possibly tolerate."[11] Socialization of savings is social democracy's answer to supply-side economics. As it turns out, the nations with the highest savings rate rely least on corporate earnings, whereas Canada, the U.S. and the U.K., with the lowest national savings rate in the OECD, are the most heavily dependent on corporate earnings for their savings.[12]

B.C.'s New Economic Reality

Canada's gift to the New Right is British Columbia.[13] Some months after its 1983 electoral victory, the cabinet of British Columbia's Social Credit government assembled at an Okanagan retreat to be briefed by Michael Walker of the Fraser Institute, a right-wing think-tank once regarded as part of the lunatic fringe of Canadian politics. A few weeks later, Premier Bill Bennett's government stunned the province with a budget and legislative package that was unique in Canadian history.

A few years before the infamous July 1983 budget, which incorporated much of the Fraser Institute's program, the institute devoted much of its energy to moving public opinion towards the ideas and prescriptions of the New Right. Its publications and broadcasts were all geared to preparing residents of British Columbia for what was deemed to be necessary cutbacks and deregulation.

These policy prescriptions were music to the ears of the giant corporations. Pressing for limitations on trade-union activity, for the elimination of minimum-wage laws and for the dismantling of various labour rights and protective mechanisms falls in line with corporate efforts to weaken the labour movement. Efforts to promote the idea that anti-discrimination and affirmative action laws are ineffectual help give corporations a free hand in their hiring practices. Advocating the deregulation of zoning, the elimination of anti-pollution legislation and other restrictions allow corporations an unrestrained hand in promoting big projects.

The Fraser Institute lists among its 320 members giant corporations including the country's top 8 financial institutions, top 8 insurance companies, 4 of the nation's 5 industrial corporations, Canada's 2 major newspaper chains as well as Maclean-Hunter and some of the giants of the broadcasting field. They pay the bills of the institute; grants from four Canadian foundations and seven U.S. foundations supplement their corporate support. While some of these organizations may not agree with everything director Michael Walker says, they evidently support the general direction of the institute's agenda for Canada — enough to supply it with a million dollar annual budget.

Bill Bennett obviously bought the institute's agenda for B.C. In February 1982, six months before the federal imposition of 6-and-5, the B.C. Socreds introduced their Compensative Stabilization Program to cap public-sector wage increases. They also chopped $56 million from school district budgets and eliminated 2,600 public service positions, 6 per cent of the total — mostly by attrition.

The 1983 budget, brought in at a time when provincial unemployment had reached 14 per cent, assaulted a number of programs without introducing any overall restraint. Spending was actually slated to rise by 12.3 per cent, mainly because of increased welfare, education and health costs that the government was not yet in a position to contain. The provisions contained in twenty-six bills nevertheless defined an agenda for the new economic reality that would fundamentally alter the political and social life of the province.

- Bill 2 proposed a dramatic expansion of managerial rights. It was an attempt by the employer — government — to gain through legislative power what it had been unable to achieve at the bargaining table. Questions related to the establishment and elimination of positions, assignment of duties, work scheduling and staff reductions were dropped from the bargaining process.
- Bill 3 committed government to reduce public-sector employment by 25 per cent over an eighteen-month period, signalling Socred intent to decrease the size of the government. It would have ended

employment security for all public-sector employees by giving government the power to "terminate employment ... without cause." This was later amended by listing conditions for termination: insufficient work; insufficient funds budgeted; change in organizational structure; discontinuation of a program, activity or service; or reduction in the level of an activity or service. These changes did nothing to reduce the scope of the government's arbitrary termination powers.
- Bill 5 abolished the "rentalsman" office and rent controls.
- Bill 6 deprived local school boards of their right to levy taxes on non-residential property and gave the minister of education control over the size of the budget for each local board. By depriving local school boards of their major source of revenue and stripping them of their power to spend their own money, this bill effectively ended the long-established principle of local decision-making in education.
- Bill 9 eliminated all regional planning by municipalities.
- Bill 11 extended public-sector wage controls indefinitely.
- Bill 20 eliminated local representation on college boards and gave the minister of education control over courses and budgets.
- Bill 26 removed minimum employment standards such as pregnancy leave and safety provisions from all collective agreements.
- Bill 27 repealed the Human Rights Code and abolished the Human Rights Branch and Commission. Gordon Fairweather, chairman of the Canadian Human Rights Commission, described the bill as "emblematic of a police state." After considerable outcry the bill was dropped, but it was brought back substantially unchanged in 1984. The Speech from the Throne gave the Socred rationale for this privatization of human rights: "British Columbia is entering a new era in human rights, where a greater emphasis will be placed on individual responsibility for eliminating discrimination."

While major public-sector unions were able to negotiate exemptions from Bill 3, subsequent legislation introduced in 1984 saw the removal of still more long-standing union rights. Bill 28 limited political protests involving job action, outlawed secondary picketing, empowered cabinet to designate as "economic development projects" projects in which strikes were outlawed, and limited unions' rights to discipline their members for violating union codes.

Having seized control over local and regional boards and centralized power, the government was in a position to institute the kind of restraint it promised but could not deliver in 1983. Besides cutting the civil-service payroll by 25 per cent (from 46,000 in 1982 to 35,000 in early 1984), 4,100 teaching positions were chopped between 1982 and 1984; the ministry of human resources fired over 1,000 of its full-time staff, eliminating or reducing several child-care programs. Besides cutting grants to community-based health clinics, over 3,000 hospital-staff positions were eliminated, hundreds of hospitals closed and a few thousand beds eliminated. In the income and maintenance program (Guaranteed Annual Income for Need), cut-backs included a freeze on welfare rates for all recipients and a reduction in rates for people under twenty-five years of age.

Under cover of restraint, the new-reality regime aims to fundamentally restructure public-sector power, activity and spending. Five strategies are involved:[14]

- The centralization of fiscal and administrative power in the cabinet and the corresponding suppression of alternative locally based arenas of decision-making. Public-sector wage controls is one example; another is the undermining of the autonomy of elected bodies such as schools, college boards and municipalities.
- The privatization of social services. Unemployed youth are forced to turn to their families for help; churches and voluntary agencies are expected to fill the void left by cut-backs in child and family services; nursing homes and psychiatric programs are turned over to individuals and corporations motivated by profit.
- The undermining of institutions that had provided a forum for appeal, redress or opposition to provincial government action. The clearest examples are in the fields of human rights, consumer affairs and tenant protection.
- The streamlining of government spending to make long-run reductions in the share allocated to health, education and social services. The money saved is slated for the promotion of private-sector economic development and for freezing, or in some instances reducing, business taxes. The 25 per cent civil-service staff reduction and cuts in ministerial expenditures, for example, freed up money to pay for B.C. Place, Expo 86, Northeast Coal, ski resorts and B.C. Rail.
- The deregulation of private-sector business activity, efforts to tilt the balance of power in industrial relations against labour, and the removal of legislative and administrative impediments to business activity and investments. Examples include termination of rent controls, major reductions in health and safety inspection, abolition of regional-planning functions, privatization of forest-management responsibilities and the assault on trade-union rights.

To date, the overall impact of the Social Credit's supply-side effort has been no more impressive than the ones concocted by Thatcher and Reagan. As of May 1984 B.C.'s unemployment rate stood at 15.6 per cent, the highest rate west of the Maritimes. With a stagnating domestic market, there are no signs of a strong investor response to the improved business climate promised by the new reforms. And in the meantime, the closing down of plants means that the stock of capital available for long-term growth will be lower than otherwise. Further, the cut-back in the financing of forest management and salmonid enhancement programs could reduce the volume of timber and fish available for harvesting.

All of this was brought about in the name of free enterprise and individual initiative. The irony is that there will be little scope for individual initiative or free enterprise in a society dominated by huge corporations backed by a government that seals itself off from popular influence.[15]

Conclusion

The experience of the Depression had receded from memory as a new generation of economists nurtured in affluence and security came onto the scene. There is little question that this generation, christened "the new economists" by *Newsweek*, have swung markedly to the Right. They rejected the Keynesian canons of the 1960s and attempted to reformulate macro-economic theory in a way consistent with traditional theories of individual behaviour and the workings of the market system. All of the problems of the economy were treated as symptoms produced by state actions which impeded the natural workings of the market. The economics of the New Right have given a mystique of credibility to a business community that sees cut-backs in government programs, reduced labour costs and less regulation as the principle economic cures. Large parts of the general public, burdened by high taxes and increasingly impatient with government's failure to secure jobs and stable prices, have also become convinced that restraint of government expenditure and deregulation are what is needed.

Since 1975 governments in Canada have swung over from a rhetorical belief in a comfortable Keynesianism to a position that accepts many of the promises and principles of both monetarism and supply-side economics. From monetarism comes the belief that the state can do little to stimulate economic recovery without producing inflation. Before a lasting recovery can occur, inflation must be finally conquered, holding down government spending and controlling the money supply — even if the immediate effect is to produce a severe economic downturn. From the supply-siders comes the belief that the state should provide tax incentives for the rich to encourage saving and tax incentives and deregulation for the business community to stimulate investment. One clear objective of government policies has been to humble Canadian workers and particularly their trade unions. Sustained unemployment is expected to make workers less forceful in pressing for higher wages; more inclined to grant concessions to employers; less concerned with cut-backs in health, education and social assistance.

Yet public provision of health services, education and the wide assortment of income-security programs and human and collective bargaining rights are the result of long political struggles in which the labour movement was prominent. Attempts to remove these carry risk for capital because of the political mobilizations that inevitably rise to defend them. It has never been clear whether business would stay the course of political and social instability and mass bankruptcies that accompany neo-conservative austerity, deregulation and privatization. Meanwhile, the brutal impact of beating down inflation by crashing the economy via monetarism and resorting to tax handouts for the rich and retrenchment for the poor as the path to recovery via supply-side economics has sparked a vigorous response among economists still committed to the Keynesian goal of full employment. These so-called post-Keynesians are true descendants of Keynes and his grand vision of a government-led permanent full-employment capitalism. We turn to them in the next chapter.

PART IV
The Post-Keynesian Response

8 | The New State Interventionists

When he died in 1946, Keynes left behind a hardy band of faithfuls who valiantly fought a losing war against those who, in Keynes' own name, distorted his analysis and narrowed his grand vision of a government-led full-employment capitalism. Led by Joan Robinson in Britain, the group was contemptuously dismissed as doctrinaire cranks mired in Depression economics. After bastardized Keynesianism fell into disrepute, and most of its practitioners had joined forces with the monetarists, Keynes' disciples reappeared on the main stage of the Great Economic Debate. Dubbed post-Keynesians in the U.S., they founded the *Journal of Post-Keynesian Economics*. In Britain, the banner was carried by the Cambridge Policy Institute. A new generation of economists including Robert Reich of Harvard, Lester Thurow of M.I.T., Kerry Schott of London, Paul Davidson of Rutgers, Robert Kuttner and many others built on the foundations laid by the likes of J.K. Galbraith, Joan Robinson, Michael Kalecki, Nicolas Kaldor, Roy Harrod and Sidney Weintraub.

This school of economic thought has no one coherent voice in Canada. It is generally espoused by groups — like left-leaning liberals, social democrats and trade unionists — that have traditionally argued for an active role for the state in economic life. Their arguments can be found in publications of the Science Council of Canada, Walter Gordon's Canadian Institute for Economic Policy, in the programs of the New Democratic Party and the Canadian Labour Congress and in the writings of economists Abraham Rotstein, Clarence Barber, John C.P. McCallum, John Cornwall, James Laxer, Bruce Wilkinson and Myron Gordon.

At the most general level, post-Keynesians believe that a resolution to the economic crisis of the 1980s requires not less but more state intervention. They deny that the economic and social forces that brought Big Government into being can be reversed. They call the free marketeers economic romantics who are blind to the realities of modern-day capitalism.

What are these realities? Increasing concentration and centralization of capital; growing dependence on massive state investment in research, energy, transportation, training and education; increasingly serious environmental threats arising from unregulated private enterprise; intensifying international rivalries in a new environment of rapid technological change; growing competition from state-assisted and state-owned enterprises in other advanced capitalist countries.

State interventionists insist that what is needed in the face of these realities is substantial state-planning and co-ordination of the process of capital accumulation; not necessarily more state ownership, but fairly direct involvement in determining the direction of future investment and in supervising the division of income between wages and profits.

As the state-interventionists argument goes, every major industry is so deeply involved with and dependent upon government that no sharp distinction can be drawn between private and public spheres. The personal daring and initiative so vital to social progress in a frontier economy no longer fits the reality of an increasingly complex economy where the free market has been supplemented by interlocking networks of subsidiaries, conglomerate headquarters and financial institutions, by big governments and big trade unions. Collaboration and collective adaptation are more important to a nation's well-being than private ambition and rugged individualism.

The clash between ideology and reality makes it doubly difficult to promote change among the three pillars of industrial societies: capital, labour and the state. Because they cannot admit to the intimacy of the relationship, governments are forced to respond to each industry's plea for assistance as if it were an exceptional case. The resulting hodge-podge of quotas, tax relief and bail-outs ends up maintaining the industrial status quo in an economic environment that is changing rapidly and demands swift adjustments.

According to the post-Keynesians, all groups in contemporary society are seeking to take more out of the economy than they put in. Corporations invest enormous energy and capital in lobbying for government hand-outs, in asset rearranging through mergers, in manipulating their balance sheets and in tax avoidance. Executives assign themselves exorbitant salaries, bonuses and share options while real returns to shareholders and workers stagnate. The economy gains no new capacity to produce from such nefarious practices and paper gains.

Workers cling to work rules and rigid job classifications and fight technological change in order to secure their jobs. And to increase their share of a frozen or shrinking national pie, unions demand wage increases in excess of productivity. When other unions do the same, wiping out their gains, the process starts all over again and ends up in an inflationary spiral. As corporate managers harden their position in the face of declining profit, they are apt to adopt hostile counter-strategies —

taking away previously won concessions; hiring consultants to bust up unions; moving factories to other locations. This produces a further deterioration of co-operation between labour and management. When every element in society engages in beggar-thy-neighbour tactics, argues Harvard's Robert Reich, "the end result is an industrial jungle that breeds cynicism towards any collective endeavour."[1]

The gospel of the self-regulating market treats the individual as the unit of account and focuses its analysis on how resources can best be allocated to satisfy consumer preference. Post-Keynesianism takes the nation as the unit of account and focuses its analysis on how resources can best be mobilized to maximize national output. More specifically, the nation is treated as a single enterprise competing with other similar enterprises in the world economy. In this national project, much attention is usually given to securing collaboration among the major classes and interests involved in industry. In the free-market tradition, the focus falls much more on competition.

Where it points to the market system as the instrument to achieve its objectives, post-Keynesians are more likely to stress the importance of state policy. Where the war cry of the free marketeers is "laissez-faire" and their slogans "individual liberty," "freedom," "fiscal responsibility" and "self-reliance," the equivalent for post-Keynesianism is "the mixed economy" with slogans of "social contract," "consultation," "planning" and "the national interest."

Arguments Against Free Marketeers

Attacking inflation by depressing the economy is seen as a nonsensical approach by post-Keynesians, who see the source of inflation, not as money-induced, government-inspired excessive demand, but as the excessive power wielded by certain of the key actors on the supply side, namely Big Business and Big Labour. Big Business is able to hold up prices even in the face of large-scale declines in the demand for their products. In fact, the large corporations are likely to raise their prices in response to a fall in demand as a way of preserving their total profit. Similarly, Big Labour is also impervious to the state of demand. Even in the face of large-scale unemployment, trade unions insist on large pay increases. Only a massive depression would force unions to accept a lower pay packet and companies to lower their prices.

In the view of post-Keynesians, governments followed the prescriptions of the monetarists and induced just such a depression, which eventually did bring inflation under control. "To find a comparable case of misguided virtue," writes Abraham Rotstein, "we would have to hark back to the medieval era when doctors practiced blood-letting for curing high fever."[2] Rotstein estimates that monetarist policy cost Canada $12 billion of lost output in 1982 and cost the government nearly $17 billion in lost revenue and additional transfer payments from 1976 to 1982.

What About the Deficit?

Post-Keynesians insist that the paralyzing concern over the growth and the size of the deficit is largely misplaced. They point out that our national debt of more than $100 billion would seem less abhorrent if we were reminded that it, like everything else, must be corrected for inflation. In nominal dollars, the federal deficit increased from $16.8 billion in 1947 to $150 billion in 1984. But measured in constant (1971) dollars, it only increased about 10 per cent. The only meaningful measure is to compare the magnitude of the debt to the economy as a whole. The greater the total output and income, the better the economy can cope with a given amount of debt. The following figure indicates that, by historical standards, current debt levels are not abnormal. The national debt of the 1980s as a per cent of GNP is less than it was anytime in the 1920s, 1930s, 1940s and most of the 1950s; it is barely a third of what it was in 1947.

These comparisons indicate that a large debt by itself need not hold back economic growth or bring the kind of disastrous results predicted by the neo-conservatives. It might be inflationary if we were already operating at full employment, and it might pose dire problems for many poor economies; but for economies with enormous resources and a greatly underused productive capacity and labour force, it does not pose a clear and present danger. A much larger postwar debt was clearly no obstacle to Canada's substantial growth only a few decades back.

Contrary to the impression given by the New Right, Canada's debt compares quite favourably with the debt of other other countries (see Table 8:1). Up to 1982 Canada had a better debt record than all major Western countries except the U.S. and France. It got out of line after 1982 only because the depression struck Canada more severely. As in the mini-depression of 1958-63, unemployment and falling profits reduced the tax base while increasing welfare and unemployment expenditures.

But there are three additional factors accounting for the massive deficits. On the one hand, governments, following monetarist prescriptions, have fought inflation with a tight monetary policy that has forced interest rates up to record levels. Higher interest rates, in turn, have become a growing burden on government finances. Interest payments

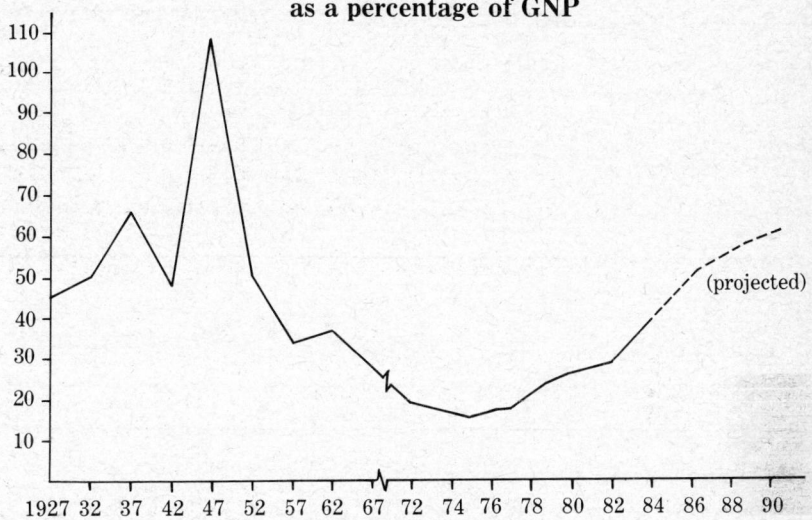

FIGURE 8-1
Govt. of Canada: Net Public Debt as a percentage of GNP

[Graph showing Net Public Debt as a percentage of GNP from 1927 to 1990, with values peaking around 1947 at over 100%, declining to a low around the mid-1970s, then rising again with projected values through 1990.]

Source: Macdonald Commission Report, Vol. 2, p.251.

TABLE 8:1
International Comparison of Government Budget Balances as Percentages of GNP, 1975-84

	Canada	U.S.	U.K.	France	Germany	Italy	Japan
Total Government Sector							
Average, 1967-74	0.9	−0.5	−0.9	0.5	−0.2	−6.3	0.9
1975	−2.5	−4.2	−4.9	−2.2	−5.8	−11.7	−2.8
1976	−1.7	−2.1	−5.0	−0.5	−3.6	−9.0	−3.8
1977	−2.4	−0.9	−3.4	−0.8	−2.4	−8.0	−3.7
1978	−3.2	0.0	−4.2	−1.9	−2.5	−9.7	−5.5
1979	−1.9	0.6	−3.1	−0.7	−2.7	−9.3	−4.8
1980	−2.1	−1.3	−3.2	−0.3	−3.1	−8.3	−4.2
1981	−1.2	−1.0	−2.0	−1.6	−4.0	−11.9	−3.9
Average 1975-81	−2.1	−1.3	−3.7	−1.1	−3.4	−9.7	−4.1
1982	−5.3	−3.8	−2.0	−2.9	−4.1	−12.1	−3.3
1983	−6.2	−4.1	−3.3	−3.4	−2.7	−11.8	−3.3
1984*	−6.0	−3.2	−3.1	−3.5	−1.7	−13.5	−2.2

Source: OECD, National Accounts of OECD Countries, 1962-80; Volume II OECD, Economic Outlook, December 1982; Statistics Canada, National Income and Expenditure Accounts, Cat. 13-001; Survey of Current Business, U.S. Government; and Department of Finance.

* OECD Forecasts

on the public debt increased six times between 1975 and 1984 (from $3.7 billion to $21.3 billion), absorbing a rising share of government budgets (from 10 per cent in 1975 to 20 per cent in 1984). The combination of an exploding debt and soaring interest rates has made the cost of servicing the debt the fastest rising component of government spending.

A recent study reveals that in 1983, if the economy had been operating at a level closer to full employment, with 7.5 per cent unemployment rather than 12 per cent, the federal deficit would have been nearly eliminated. Federal government revenues would have been up by $14 billion and expenditures would have been down by $4 billion. The combined total of $18 billion accounted for three-quarters of the 1983 deficit. If the economy had been operated at 6 per cent unemployment, there would have been budgeting surpluses at all levels of government. As the authors of the study point out:

> Federal and provincial governments in Canada have pursued a fiscal strategy similar to that in the early stages of the Great Depression of the 1930's. Then, as now, government fiscal policy was oriented towards stabilizing the depression induced fiscal deficit, rather than reducing the magnitude of the depression that was the root cause of the deficit.[3]

While a neo-conservative monetary policy has ironically increased the size of government expenditures required to service the debt, a neo-conservative fiscal policy has dramatically diminished a number of important sources of revenue. Since 1972, Canadian governments have created a variety of new tax exemptions and tax deferral programs in the mistaken belief that these would spur new corporate investment spending. By far, their more important effect has been to increase the size of the deficit.

A third reason for the growing deficit, one not always cited by the post-Keynesians, is the rapid build up of arms. Arms spending doubled between 1975 and 1981 and increased by nearly half again between 1981 and 1984. Next to interest payments on the public debt, it has been the fastest growing component of government expenditure.

According to the crowding-out argument, when savings are insufficient to finance both the deficit and capital investment, the deficit crowds out the supply of funds that would otherwise be used to finance new investments. This is simply not the case in Canada. With the Canadian savings rate among the highest in the world, there is no evidence of a shortage of saving; quite the opposite, there is a shortage of investors willing to expand their productive capacity and hire on workers. The deficit has never crowded out investment; rather it has provided an alternative outlet for savings that would otherwise have gone unused because of the absence of sufficient profitable opportunities acceptable to the investor class. Had the government been unwilling to incur a growing deficit, the economy would have been even more depressed than it has been.

Studies relating inflation to the size of government deficits show no apparent correlation (see Table 8:2). West Germany, for example, a country with a relatively low rate of inflation over the past few decades, ranks among the countries with the highest deficit. Canada and the U.S. have enjoyed relatively small deficits while suffering high inflation rates. Nor is there evidence of a causal relationship between the size of the deficit and the rate of interest. The causal relationship runs the other way: high rates of interest increase the size of the deficits. Most recently, interest rates have been coming down even while government borrowing has soared.

During the war years from 1941 to 1945, the government ran a deficit that was 22 per cent of GNP while holding down interest rates to less than 1 per cent of GNP. And this was a time when economic resources were being stretched to the limit. Thus far in the 1980s, the average annual deficit has only been 4.3 per cent of GNP and there has been plenty of slack (11 to 12 per cent of the labour force and 25 to 30 per cent of manufacturing capacity). Yet the average interest rate has been over 12 per cent on long-term government bonds.

Why the difference? Because during those war years private ownership of the banks and industry was not allowed to divert the war effort. Controls were imposed on prices, wages, profits, investment and credit; scarce consumer goods were rationed; a lid was placed on interest rates.

TABLE 8:2
Deficits and Inflation

	Change in surplus or deficit as a % of GDP 1960-63 to 1977-79	*Acceleration in average % change in consumer prices 1960-63 to 1977-79*
Japan	−7.9	−0.2
Italy	−6.7	12.1
Germany	−5.1	1.6
Denmark	−4.2	6.2
Sweden	−3.9	7.1
U.K.	−2.9	11.2
Austria	−2.4	1.6
Netherlands	−2.3	2.2
France	−2.0	6.6
Canada	−1.0	8.0
U.S.A.	−0.2	8.5

Source: OECD National Accounts.

All was not perfect but the experience showed that if necessary a huge deficit could be financed without requiring soaring interest rates.

Finally, post-Keynesians point out that government debt is like a kind of national banking operation that adds to the flow of income that government siphons into households and businesses. Contrary to the image of the debt as a vast burden borne on the backs of the citizenry, when the government borrows and spends funds it is creating income for those who receive its disbursements. As the debt gets repaid, about 90 per cent of the interest is paid to Canadian households and institutions. It is money owed to the citizens.

The new interventionists reject the free marketeers' approach, but they also reject Keynesian fine-tuning as too broad, too blunt and too much removed from the real processes of the economy. It is particularly unsuitable when applied to Canada's stunted economy. Should government resort solely to expansionary fiscal and monetary measures to stimulate recovery, given Canada's heavy dependence on imports, a large portion of the increased demand would be spent on imported goods. Unless Canada's trading parties follow a similar policy, exports would not increase to a similar extent. The result is negative trade balances, balance of payments problems and a falling currency. Should the currency be propped up by borrowing abroad, interest rates would rise, thereby choking off recovery. Should the currency be allowed to fall, the price of imported goods would rise, increasing inflation and setting off a wage-price spiral.

The state must develop other policy instruments to accompany Keynesian stabilizing tools. In particular, post-Keynesians argue that government must adopt an industrial strategy to restructure Canadian industry, an incomes policy to lessen conflict over income shares, and a social policy that is more closely geared to future economic requirements. Unless this course is followed, governments will continue to alternate between expansionary policies that result in higher and higher levels of inflation and policies of restraint that wring inflation out of the economy but only at the cost of higher and higher rates of unemployment. In the words of the Science Council of Canada:

> If Canada does not gain control over its own industrial and technological development and rebuild its industries, a rather unpleasant form of restructuring (i.e., deindustrialization) will be imposed upon it by virtue of excessive vulnerability to external conditions. This latter alternative will be far more costly in terms of the decline in our standard of living and employment opportunities than taking the initiative to make structural changes in the economy ourselves — changes designed for the maximum benefit for all Canadians.[4]

Many post-Keynesians concede that the introduction of such far-reaching reforms cannot proceed very far unless the antagonistic relationship between labour and capital is suspended or at least curbed. The burdens and benefits of rapid economic change fall unevenly. Older jobs are threatened, older industries are jeopardized, and many citizens are forced to hold down their consumption as money is transferred to the business sector to finance its restructuring. The idea of making do with less so that Big Business can have more is obviously a hard pill to swallow. Workers who doubt that the burdens and benefits of rapid adaptation will be shared equitably will resist change or resort to various forms of industrial sabotage. Unless new systems of consultation and participation are instituted, workers will never develop a sense of common cause with their firms or mutual obligation and responsibility for the national interest. And unions will be forced to rely on their usual weapons to protect their members' interests.

Citing West Germany, Austria, Sweden and Japan as examples, these post-Keynesians call for institutional innovations both at the level of the firm and in the economy at large. Workers and their unions must be invited to take part in decision-making — on the shop floor, in the firm and industry. And governments must find new political structures in which representatives of both labour and capital can participate in decisions dealing with investment, job-training and income-sharing.

Convinced that the dislocations and conflicts that inevitably arise in any recovery program will be aggravated and prolonged if the process is steered by the free market, post-Keynesians believe that the process can be hastened and the conflicts better managed if the restructuring is directly supervised by the state in elaborate forums with labour and business. The term "corporatism" or "tripartism" is commonly applied to such political structures.

By combining demand and supply management, post-Keynesians argue, there is no inherent economic obstacle to full employment and price stability. Providing an expansionary fiscal/monetary policy is matched with an industrial policy and an incomes policy, the goals of full employment, price stability and economic growth can all be met. The main obstacle is the political one of creating a zone of harmony between conflicting groups.

This is the vision of post-Keynesian economics and represents the progressive face of state interventionism.

Social Partnership

Post-Keynesians maintain that the theoretical relationships posited by the orthodoxy of the New Right have not materialized, not even in precisely those countries where, according to orthodox precepts, they should have emerged most sharply. Countries with the lowest rates of unemployment and the largest welfare states have often enjoyed the lowest rates of inflation. And almost invariably, they have been the most heavily unionized with the economic strength of the working class typically accompanied by political clout.

The results run contrary to orthodox expectations, so the argument goes, because economists of the New Right tend to ignore institutional arrangements and political representations. "Their professional training instructs them to pierce the institutional veil and look beyond institutions to rational 'optimizing' individuals. Social institutions are messy; they resist quantitative modelling. Most economists leave the study of institutions to lesser disciplines, like sociology."[5] Post-Keynesians insist that at least part of the differences in economic performance is explained by the different political arrangements that have emerged because of the diverse distributions of economic and political power.

Specifically, where working-class power is relatively strong, it has been more successful in soliciting a commitment to full employment on the part of government. Where the working class has developed an encompassing and centralized organization and acted in concert with a similarly organized business grouping under the mediation of social-democratic governments, the commitment to full employment has been sustained. In this context of a "social partnership ideology," where trade unions are assured of full employment, expanding social services and a quasi-official role in some aspects of economic policy, they have usually been willing to sacrifice short-term wage gains for longer-term political and class objectives. Where wages and prices have not been restrained in this way, expansionary policies cannot be sustained for long. Though a work force may not be sufficiently powerful to obtain or enforce social contracts, it is powerful enough to hold up wages (and prices). In this context, only extreme doses of government-induced recession can bring them back into line.[6]

In support of this thesis, post-Keynesians point to national rankings of the famous "misery index," the unemployment rate plus the rate of inflation. For the 1970s, of the seven nations with misery rates below 9 per cent, five can be considered corporatist — Austria, West Germany, Sweden, Norway and Holland. The other two, Switzerland and Japan, are regarded as special cases. The worst mix of high inflation and high unemployment is found in the U.S., Britain, Canada and Italy, where inflation was brought under control only by allowing unemployment rates to soar to 10 per cent or more.

The last four countries all experienced high increases in wages only to have them dissipated by high inflation and subsequent unemployment. In the other seven, workers accepted a drop in wages between 1964 and 1981, thereby holding down the rate of inflation. While they also experienced a modest fall in real wages, they were in most instances able to bargain for reduced taxes and substantial improvements in unemployment insurance and social services while at the same time holding down the rate of unemployment to less than 4 per cent.

Sweden's active labour-market policy is a mechanism highly favoured by post-Keynesians. Instead of expanding aggregate demand until the whole economy is heated up, the government intervenes selectively to soak up the unemployed. A national labour market board is mandated to co-ordinate job-training, relocation, placement and job creation. Local tripartite boards, made up of representatives of business, labour and local government, design local programs to allocate funds from the national board. During recessions, the boards use temporary public-service jobs, stockpiling of goods, early retirement, retraining, sabbaticals and investment subsidies to hold down unemployment. During boom periods they utilize retraining and relocation measures to reduce labour bottlenecks.

The Post-Keynesian Theory of Inflation

Underlying this interpretation of events is the post-Keynesian theory of inflation. Whereas monetarists insist that inflation is always and everywhere a monetary phenomenon ultimately caused by government over-stimulating the economy, post-Keynesians are just as adamant that excessive demand is not the source of the 1970s inflationary explosion.

Post-Keynesians see industry divided into two sectors: core industries, which are characterized by large-scale national and global enterprises using vast amounts of capital and modern technology; and peripheral industries, which are characterized by small-scale enterprises using much less capital and simpler technology and managerial organizations.

Competing with hundreds or thousands of rivals, peripheral enterprises have no control over their prices. When sales are brisk and they can barely keep up with demand, they take advantage of the situation to raise their prices. During recessions when customers are scarce, they fight to maintain their sales by dropping prices.

Giant corporations in core industries have far more control over their selling prices. They typically have substantial amounts of unused capacity so that output can usually be raised by simply adding more workers. Until full capacity is reached, a point which may never arise, these firms can meet an increase in demand by increasing output at the prevailing cost and price levels. In periods of recession, they protect their profit margins, holding up prices by restricting output. In all instances, for core industries, prices are largely insensitive to demand.

Workers employed in peripheral industries are mostly unorganized, have dead-end jobs, are poorly paid, and have little if any job security. On the other hand, workers employed in core industries are usually members of trade unions or associations and have job security, better pay and working conditions and some opportunity for promotion.

What triggers inflation is less important than the process that develops from it into a wage-price spiral. Inflation can be triggered by a sharp rise in oil prices, by a sharp rise in income taxes, by some group of workers trying to leap-frog over others, thus momentarily upsetting a long-accepted wage contour, or by a large wage increase in an industry which is matched by an equivalent rise in productivity but which sparks a similar wage increase in the public sector where productivity rises more slowly. Whatever triggers the original inflation, militant trade unions protect the real disposable income of their members and their relative position in the wage contour. And large corporations protect their profit margins by passing the resulting higher wages on to their consumers.

The upshot of this analysis is that in core industries, which overwhelmingly dominate the goods-producing sector of all modern economies, increases in demand have little impact on prices, while general increases in cost are almost instantly absorbed in higher prices. These increases can come in the form of higher interest rates, raw material prices, tax rates or wages. Most versions of this analysis concentrate on money wages in the organized sector of the labour force.

Emphasis on the labour sector arises first from the fact that wages, salaries and fringe benefits account for nearly 60 per cent of the market value of all goods and services sold. Second, the influence of wages on prices is seen to be even greater than this because core business firms set their prices by applying a fixed mark-up to their costs. According to the price-setting model produced by the late Sidney Weintraub, a founder of the *Journal of Post-Keynesian Economics*, prices are determined by three variables: wages, productivity and the mark-up of prices over unit labour costs. Since in Weintraub's estimation, mark-ups tend to be constant, prices are simply determined by the relationship between wages and productivity. It follows from this that inflation is caused by wage increases that exceed productivity gains.

Not surprisingly, many post-Keynesians point to trade unions as the real culprits. As one writer put it, to understand price levels from any economic principle is futile because this level depends "on what number trade union leaders pick out of the air when they make their wage claims."[7] With equal impunity to market forces, large corporations pass on the higher wages to consumers. It all comes down to the mood of trade union leaders and their jealousy of rival unions as they attempt to leap-frog over them in their wage claims, or the take-over of important union positions by left-wing leaders bent on conflict with employers.

But even where union demands have not played a major part in causing higher inflation rates and even though labour's real income may have declined, reducing the rate of increase of wages and salaries is still seen as the main solution to halting inflation. "The process by which wages and prices are set in our economy, a process that is decentralized in both time and space, means that the rate of increase of salaries and wages plays a key role in perpetuating inflation, once it is underway."[8]

Exceptionally high growth rates experienced in the postwar period permitted real income to double between 1948 and 1973. In the post-Keynesian view, steadily rising incomes gave rise to "a growing feeling of entitlement," a feeling that people are entitled to regular increases in their living standards. But by the early 1970s the conditions underlying this postwar prosperity had petered out. With no further reductions in trade barriers and with rates of productivity growth declining, people were having to accommodate themselves to a slower rate of increase in real incomes. This is a world-wide phenomenon, but in Canada it has been compounded by a failure to respond to this challenge by adjusting our industrial base.

Some post-Keynesian analysts emphasize that inflation was aggravated by "supply shocks," by sudden price increases in resource-based products and by the slowing down of the growth of the world economy. We may expect frequent recurrence of supply-shocks, they say, and a permanently reduced growth rate.

These post-Keynesians argue that inflation results when people resist this decline in real income growth and try to maintain their accustomed growth in living standards by demanding higher wages and salaries. Corporations pass these on and a wage-price spiral ensues. In the words of Robert Reich, "inflation is the monetary manifestation of an unacknowledged struggle over how to allocate the losses from economic decline."[9] While the strongest and best organized groups can to a point protect their claims, they win the struggle at the expense of the least organized and poorest segments of the population.

A perfectly competitive economy could adjust to supply shocks and slow-downs without producing inflation because prices and wages would be perfectly flexible. A reduction of output would force down wages and prices. An increase in the price of some goods would be exactly offset by falling prices of other goods. But this is the unreal world of monetarist theory, which has long been by-passed in the real world of Big Labour and Big Business.

Post-Keynesians in a Hurry

By the early 1950s, if not before, the CCF (predecessor to the NDP) had become fully converted to the mild reformism of Keynesianism. If the business cycle could be conquered, or at least tamed, and full employment secured by regulating private investment and the supply of money, what logical argument could be advanced for public ownership of industry and the banks?

In the depths of the Great Depression, CCFers had pledged that "a C.C.F. government would not rest content until it had eradicated capitalism." The Regina Manifesto argued that "when private profit is the main stimulus to economic effort, our society oscillates between periods of feverish prosperity in which the main benefits go to speculators and profiteers, and of catastrophic depressions in which the common man's normal state of insecurity and hardship is accentuated." It insisted that "these evils can be removed only in a planned and socialized economy in which our natural resources and the principle means of production and distribution are owned, controlled and operated by the people."

This was obviously a revolutionary program, but CCFers were not revolutionaries. The CCF always contained a small contingent of Marxists, but by far it was dominanted by Fabian socialists, who might best be called bureaucratic socialists. The Regina Manifesto is replete with boards of technical experts, the presumed agents of social change in the co-operative commonwealth — the same technocratic elite that Keynes entrusted with introducing his fiscal revolution. The Manifesto spoke of the "exploitation of one class by another" but the CCF remained wedded to a concept of politics confined to Parliament. It rejected any notion of class struggle and engaging in industrial action to challenge corporate rule. Unions were there to win better wages and working conditions; politics was the domain of the politicians. What would the capitalists be doing after the CCF announced its timetable for nationalization? The question was never asked.

What Keynes demonstrated in theory and the wartime experience appeared to demonstrate in practice — that the economy could be fully regulated by the imposition of state controls — caused the CCF to abandon its goal of eradicating capitalism and the profit system. By humanizing capitalism through the welfare state and removing the worst abuses of profit-making through the tax system, capitalism could be gradually transformed to the kind of society socialists aimed to build. Leaving production largely in private hands, the state could socialize distribution through a variety of techniques and thus go a long way towards the egalitarion goals of socialism. No sharp disruptions were necessary.

This conversion to a mild-mannered reformism was no doubt assisted by the pilloring of the party in the earliest days of the Cold War when CCFers were depicted by the media as wild-eyed Bolsheviks. By this time the Regina Manifesto had become a millstone around their necks. But the conversion also harkens back to the reform politics of pre-Depression days. The trade unionists, clergymen, teachers and farmers who coalesced to form the CCF had never thought of society in terms of a permanent contest between an exploiting and an exploited class; rather they saw a series of problems that could be solved by reason, compassion and social reforms within the framework of capitalism. It was the desperate conditions of the Great Depression that forced them to veer so sharply to the Left. In the context of postwar prosperity they easily returned to their original perspective.

Throughout the postwar period, it was the CCF and organized labour that emerged as the most consistent force pressing the state to stimulate the economy at the first sign of unemployment. While the old-line parties seemed prepared to sacrifice full employment when it conflicted with other priorities, the CCF/NDP and their union allies became a kind of watchman for the Keynesian state in Canada.

Consistent with Keynes' own call for a "more or less comprehensive socialization of investment," the CCF/NDP called for an investment board to regulate corporate investment and a development fund to mobilize and channel some of the funds of insurance, trusts and other financial institutions. With state control over investment secured, all that was necessary was to fill in the gaps of the welfare state and to redistribute income through a rigorous application of progressive taxation and regional equalization payments. Aside from the existing utilities, the role of public enterprise was confined to instances of private failure or to industries too risky or insufficiently profitable to attract private capital — public ownership if necessary but not necessarily public ownership.

In the public mind, the CCF/NDP became identified as the party of government spending which screamed for more whenever pensions, hospitalization, medicare, minimum wages and other measures were under consideration. While the other parties accepted the mixed economy, the CCF/NDP wanted it a little more mixed.

The radical 1960s gave rise to the so-called Waffle Movement which was an attempt to transform the NDP into a socialist party. Its manifesto, "for an Independent Socialist Canada," resembled the old Regina Manifesto in calling for widescale public ownership. But it focused primarily on U.S. economic and cultural domination and in particular on the economic and political costs of a branch-plant economy, arguing that socialism would not come to Canada until the hold of the multinational corporations was broken. It also differed from the Manifesto in calling for extra-parliamentary action: "The New Democratic Party must be seen as the parliamentary wing of a movement dedicated to fundamental social change. It must be radicalized from within and ... from without." The Waffle position was never able to garner the support of more than a quarter to a third of NDP members and through a process of expulsion the Waffle insurgence was crushed.

It was not until the late 1970s when the severity of the economic crisis became evident that the NDP and the labour movement affiliated with it seriously explored the structural problems of the economy and began developing an industrial policy. Using much the same post-Keynesian analysis as the Science Council and the Canadian Institute for Economic Policy, the NDP and the Canadian Labour Congress(CLC) adopted a strategy that relied much more on steering the economy through direct state intervention, including the establishment of new crown corporations in strategic sectors.

Back in the 1940s Prime Minister Louis St. Laurent aptly described CCFers as "Liberals in a hurry." By the 1970s their NDP successors had become "post-Keynesians in a hurry."

The NDP/CLC calls for a policy of fiscal expansionism and a made-in-Canada interest-rate policy that would fix the rate of interest one or two percentage points above the rate of inflation. It acknowledges that these policies are not sufficient: in the first place, given the import-prone character of the economy, fiscal expansionism would soon result in a large imbalance of payments deficit, leading to speculation against the Canadian dollar and pressure on the Bank of Canada to raise interest rates in support of the dollar; in the second place, a made-in-Canada interest rate would likely cause an outflow of Canadian dollars seeking higher interest premiums in the U.S. To counter these expected responses, the NDP/CLC advocates an industrial policy to build up Canadian manufacturing and an interest equalization tax that would tax away some of the benefits of investing abroad.

Both the CLC and particularly the NDP have elaborated a fairly detailed blueprint of their strategy. Most of the proposals listed below are drawn from NDP discussion papers, but they are very little different from the proposals that can be found in CLC policy documents.[10]

- To ensure that economic stimulus does not worsen the balance of payments and result in an export of jobs, the NDP advocates content legislation for offshore producers and production agreements with multinational manufacturing firms. They would aim at ensuring that their production in Canada would equal their sales in this country. For example, off-shore car producers would have to meet Canadian content regulations. Through temporary import restrictions, Auto Pact producers would get a breathing space to retool and redesign in exchange for job, investment, production and sourcing guarantees.

- The NDP advocates shifting away from tax expenditures to direct government grants so that transfers to corporations are made more visible to the public. Such grants, in turn, should be made conditional upon meeting public policies regarding investment and job location. "Just as private investors expect something in return for their money, the public has a right to benefit from its investment. Without some such returns public welfare for corporations must occur at the expense of public services...."
- As a means of improving job security, the NDP proposes a Lay-off and Redundancies Board which would be empowered to hold hearings in which employers would have to justify plant shut-downs and mass lay-offs. The Board would also be empowered to "veto lay-offs and/or seize assets when necessary."
- The NDP would impose a special job-training tax on employers which would be refunded provided employers fulfilled their quota of job-training or retraining.
- The mandate of the now defunct Foreign Investment and Review Agency should be strengthened to include periodic reviews of all large foreign firms to assess their performance.
- Contending that Canadian private-sector energy producers act no differently than foreign subsidiaries, the NDP would expand Petro-Canada by the purchase of Imperial Oil.
- To gain "a window" in the banking industry, an NDP government would nationalize one of the chartered banks.
- The NDP favours "a reassertion of the Canadian genius for public enterprise" and proposes to establish a dozen or so new crown corporations in strategic sectors to promote increased manufacturing. These include: "Enterprise Canada" to fund research and development by Canadian owned firms and in publicly owned corporations; "Auto Can" to undertake research, take equity position in existing Canadian-owned auto parts companies to provide them with the necessary capital for relocating and redesigning, enter into joint ventures projects with the major automobile companies, and negotiate long-term purchasing agreements with major international auto companies; a "Mine Machinery Corporation" that would take equity positions in privately owned firms, participate in joint ventures or act alone to replace the input of mining machinery with Canadian-made machinery; a "Crown Forest Products Corporation" that would enter into joint-venture projects with private-sector machinery companies, develop new technology and more end-use products to make fuller use of forest resources; a "Health Products Development Centre" to develop health products and new technology either independently or jointly with industry. Many of these particulars are drawn from the Ontario NDP which also proposes a "Nickel Insti-

tute" to investigate the replacement of imports of nickel-based products and an Ontario Crown Investments Corporation (similar to that established by the NDP in Saskatchewan) which would both act as a holding company of all public economic agencies and co-ordinate public-sector activity "within a comprehensive industrial strategy."

The NDP and CLC are in accord with the standard post-Keynesian analysis that Canada's economic problems are structural, stemming from the domination of foreign-based multinationals. On the other hand, it dismisses any suggestion that high wages are part of the problem: "For years Canadian wages were lower than those in the United States — but that advantage did not lead to a strong manufacturing base." It also disagrees with proposals to establish Canadian-owned multinationals: "the multinational corporation is a form of economic organization that works against the interest of a small country like Canada.... Even Canadian corporations which expand their international operations into a larger market often find it profitable to locate production, research and management in the area of that market."

We may refer to the standard model as liberal post-Keynesianism and the NDP/CLC model as social-democratic post-Keynesianism. They both envision greater state supervision of the restructuring process rather than leaving it entirely to market forces. The liberal solution involves the use of fiscal measures to alter the economic environment within which decisions are made. By means of these measures, the state would guide the private sector towards industrial renewal and "technological sovereignty" (see chapter 10). Because of its limited leverage over foreign subsidiaries and because foreign ownership is regarded as part of the problem and not part of the solution, the principle agent for this project is seen to be large-scale Canadian entrepeneurs. The social-democratic version emphasizes more extensive use of direct state intervention. This includes both regulation and planning agreements and a heavier dosage of "state enterprise capitalism" to provide "windows on the private sector." Instead of "eradicating capitalism," the goal is to steer capitalism towards "the public purpose."

Looking over official NDP documents, it is clear that James Laxer was wrong when in 1984 he chastised the NDP for being old-fashioned Keynesians, concerned only about the demand side of the economic recovery. In fact, its industrial policy proposals are as identical as they could be to his own. Yet Laxer's criticism in *Rethinking the Economy* is not without some validity; for while the NDP has developed a rather full set of supply-side proposals for restructuring the economy, they are rarely referred to on the hustings or in parliamentary debates. In the 1984 federal election, for example, except for references to a made-in-Canada interest rate, the imposition of a levy to finance worker training and some tax reforms, the economic policy presented by the NDP involved little more than fiscal stimulation to create jobs and preserve the welfare state.

It is unlikely that this electoral strategy is to be explained as simply the NDP's "instinctual" Keynesianism, as Laxer contends. More likely, it arises from an estimation by NDP leaders that today's political climate is inhospitable to a policy that emphasizes more government intervention. Whatever the case may be, at least on paper, a social-democratic industrial strategy is now part of the contested policy terrain.

The social-democratic position on incomes policy is much more tenuous. In the advanced industrial countries of western Europe, voluntary incomes policy has been invariably introduced by social-democratic governments through some form of corporatist framework and as part of a social contract. One of the main obstacles to a voluntary incomes policy in Canada has been the absence of a federal social-democratic government which is trusted by the labour movement.

Since the mid-1960s when incomes policy was first looked at in Canada as a possible solution to the inflation/unemployment trade-off syndrome, the Liberal Party has been the main advocate of some form of incomes policy. When in 1969 the newly formed Prices and Incomes Commission recommended voluntary guidelines as a solution to inflation, it was rejected by organized labour in favour of a two-year price freeze:

> We reject outright the idea that voluntary guidelines can cope effectively with the current inflation. This is a highly oversimplified approach to a very complicated problem .... For guidelines, or an incomes policy to be at all fair it would require all non-wage and salary forms of income, including profits, rents, interest, professional fees, unincorporated business income, speculation in real estate prices, and so on, to be effectively restrained. We do not believe that it is at all possible to bring many of these forms of income under a meaningful policy of voluntary restraint.[11]

The NDP responded by supporting an incomes policy providing it included controls of all non-wage and salary increases as well as prices.

Five years later the Canadian Labour Congress (CLC) refused to participate in the income control scheme being put forward by Finance Minister John Turner. The CLC felt that, while other forms of income were now formally included in the proposed plan, it was really designed to restrain only wages. In addition it did not include the compensation for low-wage earners requested by the congress in the form of tax credits, full-employment policies and a guarantee that tax incentives to corporations be tied to investment plans.

This conditional rejection was in fact a compromise between two opposing camps within the congress. One camp, including CLC President Joe Morris, was in full agreement with the necessity of restraint. The CLC's participation in a series of "consensus-building" meetings sponsored by Turner was based on this group's view.

> The CLC cooperated, at least in part, because of a belief that wage expectations among the rank-and-file were becoming unrealistic. Ultimately, according to this line of reasoning, the result of high settlements would be higher unemployment, especially in a country heavily dependent on international trade. A voluntary controls programme would thus provide external support for union leaders more moderate in their wage demands than their memberships.[12]

A second camp opposed voluntary wage restraint on any terms. Some public-sector unions believed that they would be the main targets of any wage-restraint program. Many unions opposed a voluntary incomes policy because it would reduce the autonomy of individual affiliates while shifting power to the CLC which would inevitably become involved in the administration of the program. In fact, centralization of power within the labour movement is what CCL officers had clearly in mind. Through tripartite structures, congress leaders would finally receive the recognition and status they had long been seeking as the voice of organized labour in Canada.

The mandatory Anti-Inflation Board (AIB) controls introduced in 1975 included precisely the same provisions offered on a voluntary basis and rejected a year earlier. Not surprisingly it was denounced by the CLC, which initiated a considerable campaign against it. The CLC position was undermined by the embarrassing fact that the three NDP provincial governments welcomed the program. But CLC officers likely undermined their own mobilization effort when they began a series of quiet meetings with the federal government centring around conditions for ending controls and around the shape of "post-controls society."

The imposition of controls, followed by Trudeau's "new society" musings (unless "people learned more self-discipline and restraint ... the Government will have to continue controlling in some way or other"), convinced CLC leaders that the days of arm's-length Keynesianism were over. A permanent income-control mechanism was inevitable, they concluded. The question for CLC leaders was whether labour should participate in a controls program or remain aloof. Their answer was contained in "Labour's Manifesto for Canada," presented to the 1976 congress convention. The Manifesto made four points.[13]

First, in order to cope with the problems of Canadian society, "some measure of private decision-making power has to be taken over by the government."

Second, the government knows it cannot take over direct management of the economy without the co-operation of organized labour and business.

Third, from labour, "the present government wants the kind of cooperation in which we willingly accept reductions in our wages." The congress rejects this "liberal corporatism": "Labour must not willingly enter into any arrangement where only half the income equation, i.e. wages, is to be determined .... To enter into a tripartite agreement under such adverse circumstances would indeed be using the union organization as an arm of both bosses and government to restrain the workers."

Fourth, in the "social corporatism" proposed in its stead — a system of tripartism in which labour would have an equal share in economic and social decision-making with business and government — the Manifesto repeated its requirement that an incomes policy encompass all non-wage forms of income. In a subsequent proposal, the CLC called for the establishment of a tripartite council of social and economic planning. The council would be given the responsibility for developing plans for an incomes policy and an industrial policy. Beneath it, a tripartite labour market board, responsible to Parliament through a minister, would be granted authority over manpower training and mobility, unemployment insurance and immigration as well as power to affect the timing and location of public and private investment.

In short, the CLC accepted the principle of an incomes policy but only on a "full-partnership" basis. Other forms of income would also have to be restrained if labour were to agree to restraining wages and salaries. As well, business must agree to give up exclusive control over pricing and investment. This is the price labour set for co-operation. As the Manifesto argued:

> Labour has always set the price at which it would "support the system." At the local or plant level labour, through collective bargaining, negotiates the price at which it agrees to support the plant enterprise. At the national level the price of labour's support has been legislative measures in the field of social security such as the universal right to education for all, pensions, unemployment insurance, old age security, family allowance and others. The price of labour's future support must be an equal share in the economic and social decision-making on a national basis with other partners — business and government.

It was obvious from the start that neither the state nor capital would accept these terms as the price for co-operation. And opposition forces within the labour movement continued to reject corporatism, whatever its stripe. Notwithstanding this opposition, CLC leaders held a series of meetings with government and business leaders to discuss a much watered-down consultative process with no decision-making power. This too was torpedoed when the government insisted that any consultative forum must include representatives of other groups besides labour and business.

As we shall see in a subsequent chapter, some collaborative ventures with much more limited mandates did eventually emerge. What is important about the whole exercise, however, is that major elements of organized labour including the leadership of the Canadian Labour Congress committed themselves to the kind of incomes policy and corporatist structures prevalent in many European countries.

That they were unable to duplicate the European experience or even an advisory consultative forum is to be explained, in the main, by their relative weakness compared to their European counterparts. Both government and business leaders concluded that the CLC is too decentralized and the Canadian labour movement altogether too fragmented and politically divided to administer wage restraint on a national scale.

As well, the labour movement together with the NDP has never exercised enough industrial and political power to require Canadian governments to sustain anything like full employment. Free to use massive unemployment to regulate wages, there was no necessity for incorporating the leaders of organized labour in state policy as has been the case in some European countries. A voluntary incomes policy requires conditions that in combination have thus far not obtained in Canada. Yet the persistent recurrence of the subject over the past decade reflects a realization shared by the leaders of organized labour that its day may yet come.

Conclusion

The role of the state in economic life lies at the core of the debate among the three rival theories we have examined thus far. The free marketeers, monetarist and supply-side, argue that the size of the state and its enhanced regulatory function cripple the operation of the private-enterprise economy. The welfare state, legislated labour standards, progressive taxes, state regulations and public ownership interfere with incentives and siphon off income and wealth that is best left in private hands. Monetarists add that government efforts to stabilize the macro-economy by means of fiscal and monetary policy are futile if they attempt to by-pass or over-reach limits imposed by the economy's "natural rate of growth" and "natural rate of unemployment."

Post-Keynesians argue to the contrary that the free-market approach is both futile and destructive. The minimal state has been antiquated by the structural demands of the contemporary capitalist world. Instead of adjusting to the imperatives of technological change and the new international division of labour, Big Business uses its leverage with the state to preserve the industrial status quo. And Big Business and Big Labour are locked together in an obsolete industrial-relations system that preserves self-destructive and sterile labour-management practices and sets off wage-price spirals. In this setting, the old fine-tuning, arm's-length economic management is insufficient. They insist that the state, in collaboration with representatives of labour and capital, must take a direct hand in restructuring industry, industrial relations as well as the welfare state. Social democracy offers a variation of this theme. The following chapters critically assess their analyses and solutions.

9 | Incomes Policy: Theory and Practice

Monetarism may not provide as efficient a solution to inflation as its disciples like to claim, but it finally works — if only by bringing the economy perilously close to the brink of collapse. By comparison, the post-Keynesian alternative appears increasingly more plausible on theoretical grounds and more progressive and humanitarian.

Yet, before the horrific experience of monetarism blunted some memories, the general consensus after years of experimenting with incomes policy in a variety of countries was that it didn't work very well either. In the standard work on the subject published in the 1970s, Ulman and Flanagan concluded that "the accumulation of experience in the countries studied in this account suggest that in none of the variations so far turned up has incomes policy succeeded in its fundamental objectives, as stated, of making full employment consistent with a reasonable degree of price stability."[1]

Post-Keynesians tend to view collaboration as a costless item. But they are anything but costless to corporations, which guard their autonomy as fiercely as their profits. In contrast to labour, the corporate sector already has easy access to government, and corporatist structures only institutionalize this relationship. But these structures also force corporation owners to deal with labour officials and, most importantly, to share information, shop floor control and perhaps even face demands for decision-making power over the disposition of profits. Corporate executives are usually quite willing to share perspectives in consultative forums, but they are most reluctant to share control. They will contemplate doing so only if wage moderation and industrial peace can be purchased at no other price.

In the wake of major working-class victories in the 1950s and 1960s, labour throughout much of Europe was conceded a place in decision-making bodies as part payment for wage moderation. In other words, when the balance of political power made it impossible to tame the working class by sustained unemployment, governments had little alternative but to achieve co-operation by offering a range of concessions (tax reductions, improved social services and extended bargaining rights) and integrating trade unions into tripartite state structures along with representatives of capital. But the major partners were seldom satisfied for very long with the compromises. When the results turned out to be harmful to workers, they grew restive, repudiated and often replaced their union leaders, and engaged in militant actions that torpedoed wage-restraint agreements. When, in exchange for wage restraint, unions demanded too much by way of investment control and profit-sharing, business tended to lose its interest in the consensus-building process.

Incomes Policy in Three Waves

European incomes policy and tripartism arrived in three fairly distinct waves in the postwar period. The first attempt occurred in the years immediately following the end of the Second World War. Notwithstanding the high levels of unemployment associated with shortage of equipment and materials, there was widespread agreement that reconstruction required wage restraint while price controls were being quickly dismantled. This phase came to an end when world-wide price inflation associated with the Korean war caused rank-and-file repudiation of union co-operation with continuing wage restraint.

The second phase occurred in the buoyant years of the 1950s and 1960s. This time unions agreed to voluntary wage restraint in return for a commitment by the state to maintain full employment. By the end of the 1960s most of these experiments had been abandoned or greatly de-emphasized. The most recent examination of the entire European experience concluded: "Although there were some instances of short-term restraint of increases in money wages, these periods of apparent effectiveness were often terminated by waves of wildcat strikes, wage explosions and severe disruptions in national systems of industrial relations. There was even less evidence of short-term price restraint, so in several countries the net effect of incomes policies was a reduction in real wages." Significantly, the authors of this study add that the breakdown was nearly universal, whatever "the degree of centralization of bargaining institutions, the degree of political support by the trade union movement, or the degree of compulsion used in the enforcement of the policy."[2]

For example, the Netherlands had produced an "international paragon of incomes policy"[3] for nearly two decades after the end of the war. The Foundation of Labour, a group representing labour, business and agriculture, negotiated general wage and price increases with the Board of Mediation, an independent agency of prominent academics and other professionals. The negotiations were guided by recommendations issued by the tripartite Social and Economic Council whose semi-annual reports were in turn based on economic forecasts produced by the independent Central Planning Bureau.

The system began to break down in the late 1950s when wages were held below the rate of inflation to correct a growing deficit in international trade. Union leaders came under strong criticism from the grass roots and some unions suffered losses in membership. While official strike figures were very low, there were a number of wild-cat strikes in the early 1960s. In 1966 a wild-cat strike led by construction workers touched off riots in Amsterdam. When the wage norm was ignored in the next round of collective bargaining, the Board of Mediation proceeded to reject agreements covering more than half a million employees. When the government issued a six-month wage freeze in 1970 it was met with "the most widespread exhibition of industrial and political action witnessed in post-war Netherlands."[4] A new government elected soon after was obliged to cancel the decree.

In Sweden it was to avoid a government-imposed policy that the Swedish Confederation of Trade Unions (LO) and the Swedish Employers' Confederation (SAF) initiated a system of centralized bargaining. The LO followed a "Solidaristic wage" policy of narrowing wage differences within occupations, industries and regions. Faced by perennial labour shortages, however, and to placate an increasingly restive work force, large corporations were forced to offer wages above the agreed-upon norms.

A rash of wild-cat strikes in 1969-70 ended this phase of Sweden's incomes policy. While most of the strikes were engineered by groups that considered themselves unfairly treated by the leveling nature of the agreements, there were a number of other triggering issues. One was a drop in real disposable income due to stagnant real wages and rising taxes. A second was rank-and-file dissatisfaction with a remote and authoritarian union bureaucracy that developed in the context of centralized bargaining.[5] A third was deteriorating working conditions produced by employer's efforts to control costs in the face of declining profits and growing international competition.

In Britain the election of a Labour government in 1964 was to herald "the end of the class war." A voluntary incomes policy was introduced with wage and price guidelines to be monitored by the tripartite National Board for Prices and Incomes. The program was barely in place, however, when it was abandoned in the face of severe pressure on sterling. The government instituted a twelve-month freeze on wages, prices and dividends to accompany a severely deflationary monetary and fiscal policy. The Trade Union Congress reluctantly endorsed the freeze, but its co-operation was repudiated by unofficial strikes and negative votes at union conferences. The explosion of wages and earnings in 1970 ended the experiment, and that same year the Labour government went down to defeat.

The breakdown of incomes policy in the latter half of the 1960s reflected its inability to suppress inflationary pressures arising from a buoyant economy with continuous full employment and labour shortages. Shifting the balance of market power away from labour would have required a devaluation or sustained deflationary policy. But at that time, "the political and economic costs of these alternatives were regarded as too high."[6] Because authorities failed to control prices, incomes policy amounted to little more than wage control. As the authors of the Brookings report concluded:

> Even unions with close ties to the incumbent political party ... need rewards for accepting restraint on money wages, and by design or implementation, first-generation policies failed to provide significant rewards for cooperation. In particular, the distributional implications of most of the policies were not advantageous to labor, and efforts by national union officials to cooperate with the incomes policy objectives of their governments eroded the institutional authority of the officials over the rank-and-file membership. In fact, cooperation by national union officials with government incomes policy objectives in several countries brought about reductions in real wage growth that were followed by grass-roots revolt, wildcat strikes, and the wage explosions of the late 1960's. In some countries a significant reaction against the centralized bargaining structure that had exercised wage restraint and explicit demands for decentralized negotiations in the future resulted.[7]

The third phase of incomes policy covers the period of the 1970s to the early 1980s. Increased worker militancy, reflected in a significant rise in strike activity and factory occupations, ended in wage explosions that spread through most of Europe in the early 1970s. Since manufacturers were blocked from fully passing increased labour costs to export prices, real wages outpaced labour productivity. Profits were squeezed and the distribution of incomes shifted towards labour. With falling rates of return dampening investment, policy makers began to think of incomes policy as an instrument to reduce real wages and shore up profit.

But a second round of wage explosions followed the sharp rise in the prices of oil, raw materials and food in 1973-74. With no comparable increase in the growth of labour productivity, profits were squeezed still further. With trade-union efforts to protect the real incomes of their members being frustrated by further rounds of price increases, the case was made for another try at an incomes policy.

In exchange for wage restraint, trade unions now demanded a new social contract: cuts in personal income tax, improved social services and a greater involvement in decision-making at the shop-floor, enterprise and national levels. Even at the best of times, business would not have embraced these demands. In the climate produced by the economic crisis, business countered with its own demands: less state regulation, less state expenditures and social services, less union interference with technological change — as well as lower wages. Under these circumstances, it is not surprising that the voluntary consensus that was temporarily re-established tended to break down yet again.

Britain was the site of the most absolute collapse. The social contract envisioned by the 1974-78 Labour government promised that in return for wage restraint the government would introduce statutory price controls; extensive income and wealth redistribution; a new industrial strategy including tripartite planning agreements to control private investment and extend public ownership; and "real moves" towards industrial democracy. While the trade unions delivered on their commitment — wage increases fell from 25.5 per cent in 1974-75 to 8.8 per cent in 1976-77 — the Labour government reneged on nearly all of its commitments. Price controls and food subsidies introduced in 1974 were weakened and phased out; public expenditures on social services were cut back; industrial democracy came to nothing as did the new industrial strategy. Bowing to pressures from British capital and the International Monetary Fund (IMF), the government's deflationary budgets contributed to a doubling of the unemployment rate from 2.6 per cent in 1974 to 5.5 per cent in 1976 and 1977.[8]

The social contract finally collapsed in the "winter of discontent" of 1978-79 when, with low-paid public-sector workers at the forefront, the number of people striking jumped from 1 to 4.5 million and the number of lost working days from 9.5 million to 29.5 million. With the social contract shattered, Margaret Thatcher's massive victory in May of 1979 came as no great surprise.

In their appraisal of five attempts at incomes policy stretching over about thirty years, Cambridge economists Roger Tarling and Frank Wilkinson wrote that their net effect was to produce lower real wages than would likely have been the case in the absence of controls. They added that profit margins are protected, if not enhanced, by the pricing rules inevitably introduced into the regulations. Price and dividend control, they argued, are of symbolic value only, designed to induce wage restraint under the guise of fairness. In the 1967-70 controls period, for example, it is estimated that, of 9 million price changes that occurred, only 345 were modified or rejected.

With minor amendments and one or two exceptions, Tarling and Wilkinson's assessment of the British experience can stand for the rest of Europe:

> Whether they have been introduced by a Labour Government as part of a package of economic and social measures agreed with the unions, or imposed

by a Conservative government in face of union opposition, the main effect of incomes policy has been to reduce wage increases relative to price increases.... Incomes policy, as part of an economic strategy, are used to lower real wages to productivity, as part of a total package aimed at attacking inflation, switching resources from consumption into exports and investments and switching incomes from workers towards the state (higher taxes), capitalists (higher profit) and foreign suppliers (more expensive imports).... The growing disillusionment of the working class with economic policies in general and incomes policies in particular is due to the fact that such policies have repeatedly succeeded in slowing down improvements in, or actually reducing, living standards...without ensuring that the fruits of this sacrifice are put to useful purposes.[9]

The collapse of Holland's third phase was nearly as complete as Britain's. In exchange for promises of wage constraint and as partial compensation for increased unemployment, the government promised and delivered dramatic increases in social expenditures. In relation to wages and salaries, social-security benefits rose from 32 per cent in 1970 to 46 per cent in 1978.[10] Minimum-wage increases and rent control were also part of the package. Owners in turn accepted subsidies as compensation for these concessions. Yet attempts to implement centrally bargained wage agreements broke down year after year. Neither employers nor workers accepted the restraints negotiated by their federations. On each occasion the government was forced to impose temporary wage freezes to obtain the desired result.[11]

In this restrictive collective-bargaining environment, unions turned to political bargaining for so-called "non-material" gains to compensate workers for the imposed wage restraints. They asked for joint industry committees to discuss plans for plant closures, investment and employment; an excess profits tax to be disbursed by unions to retiring workers; greater worker control of the shop floor; and a reduced work week. Too weak and divided to fight wage freezes, they were no more successful in winning these "non-material" demands. Employers were not prepared to share authority and profits with unions. Nor would they share the benefits of wage restraint by guaranteeing job security and/or the shorter work week.

Coming out of the strike waves of 1969-70, Swedish trade unions also exacted a much tougher bargain as its price for continued wage restraint. In addition to continued commitment to full employment from government, it demanded new worker rights at the point of production and union involvement in investment decisions at enterprise levels. When businesses refused to bargain away their authority, the LO used its political connections to achieve these goals through legislation.

In 1972 an act was passed entitling workers to appoint two members to the board of directors of corporations with a hundred or more employees.[12] In 1973 an amendment to the occupational safety and health legislation empowered union shop stewards to stop any work they regarded as dangerous until the issue had been resolved by government inspectors. The most far-reaching work-reform legislation came in 1976 when the Riksdag passed the Law on Co-determination in Working Life. It nullified the management-rights clause in union contracts by making it mandatory for employers to negotiate investment decisions on how work is organized and allocated; notify unions on technological change, lay-offs and plant closures and supply them with all relevant information required for negotiating these changes. Under this law unions are free to strike on these issues even while collective agreements are in force.

However reluctantly, owners accepted these innovations, but they fiercely fought against the Meidner plan which would have been the death of private enterprise in Sweden. The Meidner Plan, named for the research director of the Swedish Trade Union Confederation, was five years in the making before it finally surfaced in 1976. It was specifically designed to counter the concentration of industrial wealth, which had actually been increasing under social-democratic rule. According to the plan, 20 per cent of an enterprise's pre-tax profits were to be transferred into shareholding funds under the administration of directly elected worker representatives. With this capital assets base, it was calculated that wage-earner funds would grow sufficiently large to transfer majority ownership to workers in twenty to thirty years.[13]

In any event, even with wage restraint, Swedish capital was again feeling the pinch of the full-employment welfare state. Mainly because of a 40 per cent rise in social-security payments, labour costs in industry jumped by 25 per cent in 1975 and another 15 per cent in 1976. Occurring in the midst of the severe world-wide recession following the price explosion of a few years earlier, productivity gains could not come close to offsetting this acceleration of labour costs. Swedish business was particularly hampered with new subsidy programs for temporary employment and on-the-job training. Together with notification legislation for lay-offs and plant closures and other work-reform measures, it was hard put to restructure operations in response to increased competition for the declining world market.

The 1976 electoral defeat of the Social Democrats after forty years in office signalled a major retreat from "social consensus." While the new centre-right coalition government could not renege on all the new arrangements, it scrapped the Meidner plan, dragged out the implementation of the 1976 reforms and encouraged a much tougher employer stance in centralized bargaining. Real wages in manufacturing actually fell in 1977, 1978 and 1979. The process began to break down when, on Labour Day (May 1), 1980, 110,000 workers went on strike and

600,000 more were locked out by employers. Another wave of strikes and lock-outs erupted a year later. In the round of bargaining for 1983-84 central bargaining was abandoned altogether.

This breakdown occurred in spite of both the Social Democrats return to office and the acceptance of a much watered-down version of the Meidner plan, ensuring that majority control remained with corporate owners. Thus incomes policy appears to be in as much trouble in Sweden as elsewhere.

The sole exception is Austria where consensual arrangements have flourished since 1956. According to standard accounts the explanation for Austria's uniquely stable incomes-policy regime rests on four factors. The first is that, for some time at least, the visibility of price controls was far greater than elsewhere. Together with tax bargains and an unparalleled record of full employment, this has given union leaders protection against the kind of repudiation that occurred in other countries.

The second is the extreme centralization of the Austrian Trade Union Federation (OeGB), which shielded the leadership from the rank-and-file dissent and militancy which erupted everywhere else. John Windmuller has gone so far as to say of the OeGB that "it would be difficult to carry central authority over collective bargaining further without transgressing the limits acceptable in a democratic society."[14] Except for Israel, Austria is the only example where unions are not affiliates of labour federations but, rather, are arms of a labour centre that directly controls their internal structures and all their activities, and directly collects members' dues while retaining about 80 per cent of the funds. Moreover, shop stewards and works councillors, the only directly elected union representatives, are full-time union functionaries no longer accountable to the rank-and-file. Given this structure, "it is scarcely surprising that the industrial militancy [in the rest of Europe] passed Austria by."[15]

The third factor is that Austrian unions have not attempted to use collective bargaining to narrow wage differentials. Instead, they have relied on legislative measures to advance egalitarian objectives.

The fourth factor is that trade-union leadership was brought into the state apparatus to a degree unparalleled in other capitalist societies. OeGB leaders not only are appointed to the boards of nationalized companies and the Austrian National Bank, but have also occupied the position of minister of social administration since 1945.[16]

It is dubious at best whether these particular features of the Austrian experience are exportable. Moreover, the Austrians have been no more successful than anyone else in being able to escape the economic crisis as it worsened in the early 1980s. In any case, tripartite agencies which had already begun to stumble are to some degree being by-passed in the tough decisions around how to cope with the crisis. By the mid-1980s Austria too was moving to the political right.

West Germany is the other country whose "economic miracle" is credited to "social partnerships" and "social consensus." But economists who actually studied postwar West Germany have demystified the miracle. Tripartite arrangements were only formalized in 1967, when a new law called upon the government to initiate "concerted action" among unions, employer associations and public authorities. On the basis of an analysis by an independent council of economic experts, the three groups were to agree upon wage increases consistent with price stability and full employment. These wage guidelines were to form the basis for collective bargaining.

However much admired by foreigners in search of importable solutions, the role of concerted action in the West German economy has been grossly exaggerated, if for no other reason than "concerted-action meetings have been largely ceremonial and informational — too short, sometimes lasting less than a full day; too infrequent, held only two or three times a year; too unwieldy, sometimes attended by more than a hundred people; and too understaffed, having no permanent secretariat — to function as policy-making sessions."[17] Moreover, despite the efforts of union representatives to broaden discussions, the meetings were never allowed to stray beyond the question of wages. Under the guise of offering regular and substantial participation in the formulation of national economic policy, concerted action provided the government and the central bank with an effective forum to exert strong moral pressure on trade-union leaders to moderate their wage claims. By expanding co-determination to all large companies in 1976, the social democratic government attempted to rejuvenate interest in social consensus among a much disillusioned trade-union membership. But concerted action collapsed for good a year later.

West Germany's economic miracle of rapid growth, full employment and price stability can be fully accounted for by a combination of sustained tight money policy; a highly appreciated currency; an unparalleled tough employer class that answered strikes with co-ordinated nation-wide lock-outs "to drain union strike funds"; and trade-union loyalty to social democratic governments.[18] As a member of the German employers' association remarked on the success of Chancellor Schmidt's constant efforts to moderate trade-union demands in the 1970s: "There is no better capitalist chancellor than Schmidt. He handles the unions and leaves the rest to us."[19]

But with the Social Democrat government defeated and no longer able to restrain worker discontent, the stage was set for a massive industrial confrontation. With unemployment approaching 10 per cent, the metal-workers union struck the iron and steel industry for the first time in fifty years on the issue of work time. Following their old pattern of responding to strikes with a co-ordinated nation-wide lock-out, the employers won yet another round. But by now it was clear that West Germany's economic miracle had not survived the world economic crisis.

Lessons from Europe

What can we learn about the post-Keynesian incomes policy from this survey of the European experience?

- Implicit in the post-Keynesian analysis is the assumption that with proper management something close to permanent full employment is feasible. Traditional Keynesian fiscal and monetary policy, an industrial policy to steer investment, manpower policy to steer labour, and incomes policy to handle inflation comprise the four essential components of state machinery. These institutional reforms are the necessary and sufficient conditions for stable economic growth, full employment and price stability. We need only add the "Quality of Working Life" type schemes to secure labour co-operation and increased productivity to obtain the post-Keynesian vision of a new civilized capitalist order.

  Behind this entire edifice is Keynes' assumption that there are no inherent obstacles to steady growth that cannot be overcome by state actions based on "a correct analysis of the problem." The problem on the demand side is under-consumption on the one hand and distributional conflict on the other. On the supply side it consists of a faulty industrial structure and an obsolete style of industrial relations.
  But what if the capitalist economy is prone to periodic breakdown? And what if an economic crisis is necessary to clear away the obstacles to economic recovery? Then the state cannot eliminate the crisis; it can only supervise it. In the crisis context post-Keynesian remedies take on a complexion which is very different than the benign designs of their post-Keynesian authors.

- Post-Keynesian theorists argue that, since the origins of inflation are to be found in the competitive power struggle within and between different social groups and not in excessive aggregate demand, a policy designed to restrict aggregate demand cannot halt inflation. It only causes smaller output and unemployment which heightens the distributional conflict. An incomes policy, they suggest, would allow the state to achieve full employment while moderating wage claims and thus inflation.

Taken to its extreme, the post-Keynesian position is untenable. It is unreasonable to argue that the state of demand has no impact on wages and prices. Yet that is what a pure post-Keynesian position assumes and it is the key assumption behind the belief that we can have a full employment level of output *and* wage and price stability. There need be no trade-off between inflation and unemployment provided Keynesian demand management is combined with an incomes policy. But to deny that the rate of change of demand (if not the level) exerts an influence over labour and capital is mere dogma. While changes in wages do not clear the labour market, it has been widely observed that the labour sector bargains harder and for a more rapid rise in wages and fringe benefits when labour markets tighten. Employers, in turn, are reluctant to risk a strike when profits are high and are more willing to accept higher wage demands. At the other extreme, a sudden high level of unemployment in an industry with the threat of further redundancies or even bankruptcy weakens the willingness of workers to resist low-pay offers. As for firms, a low level of demand and excess capacity reduces the ability of the employer to raise prices and stiffens resistance to workers' demands. The idea that the rate of wages is determined by trade-union fiat and that Big Capital can always and does always pass higher wages on to the consumer is neither reasonable nor supportable.

The importance of this assumption may be gauged by examining what happens if it is dropped, for then it can no longer be argued that Keynesian demand management combined with an incomes policy could produce full employment and price stability. As it did in the 1960s, full employment would build up inflationary pressures that an incomes policy could not repress. More realistic post-Keynesians admit that an incomes policy does not dispense with the need for monetary-fiscal restraints, only that it allows for a less deflationary policy — monetarism with a human face.

- If all groups accept the existing distribution of income and if the introduction of an incomes policy does not change that distribution, then an incomes policy that sets quantitative guidelines could well prove effective — at least in the short-run. By removing inflationary expectations it would put an end to what has been called defensive inflationary behaviour, by means of which each group seeks to maintain its share of the national income.

But these assumptions are restrictive and unrealistic. If inflation is caused, at least in part, by behaviour emanating from a rejection of the existing distribution of income, or if the effect of incomes policy is to alter the distribution of income in favour of one of the parties, the theory loses its plausibility and the policy loses its coherence, and fails as an instrument of social consensus. Worse still, by raising disagreements over income shares to the political level, incomes policy may actually sharpen the conflict.

- Only widespread consensus about distribution or an army of enforcement inspectors can produce anything like adherence to a control regime for more than a brief period. To secure even minimum consent among workers, prices and other incomes have to be controlled. Dividend restraint is relatively painless except for small shareholders; so long as the economy is growing, large shareholders prefer to take their gains in the form of rising share prices. Restraint on prices and profits, however, involves heavy costs. High profits are essential to obtain greater output and productivity because profit is both the source and the incentive for investment. An effective program of price controls has been impossible because in part governments are notoriously reluctant to interfere with profits. Hence, incomes control boils down to wage controls with the hope that price increases will thereafter be moderated. Not surprisingly, under these circumstances consensus tends to break down and the only way the controls regime can be sustained is by government command.
- Experience has shown that sustained periods of full employment (with unemployment rates remaining below 3 or 4 per cent for several years in a row) always produce substantial increases in wages, a rise of labour's share in the national income and a squeeze on profits. The consequential decline in investment and deterioration in foreign competitiveness result in investment crises and balance of payments problems. Since voluntary wage restraint is often insufficient to restore economic order, and most often breaks down under conditions of sustained labour shortages, other measures are required. These have often involved (in the U.K. and the Netherlands, for example) a freeze on wages or some other drastic measure to halt the redistribution of income, to renew conditions for profitable investment and to recover balance of payments equilibrium.

Why is this the case? The claims of the foreign sector and, to some extent, those of the government act as a constraint on the total share of income available as profit and wages. Given the presumed primacy of profits, a deterioration in the terms of trade or an increase in government expenditure must, in the main, be deducted from the wages share. According to conflict theorists, inflation arises precisely because trade unions do not accept this fact of life. They strike to protect and advance the real disposable income of their members in the face of rising taxes and import costs, by shifting a part of the burden onto profits. Not surprisingly, the imposition of severe wage restraint, even when agreed to by union leaders, eventually produces an outbreak of labour militancy, usually destroying the social consensus around which incomes policy was originally established. This has been the repeated experience of countries like Belgium, the Netherlands, Great Britain and Sweden. In short, incomes policies tend to break down not long after they are really put to the test. Though they are often re-established, indicating their social utility, the stability and harmony attributed to such schemes are fragile and transitory.

- Unions are the first to bear the brunt of workers' dissatisfaction. Leaders who entered into these agreements are likely to be voted out of office. The same pattern tends to be repeated in general elections. No parliamentary government in the West that has introduced a compulsory wage freeze has been re-elected in the subsequent election.
- To the extent that incomes policy constrains price changes and freezes or erodes wage differentials, it paralyzes the primary allocating mechanism available in capitalist economies. After a point, the price and wage distortions produced by controls can bring the economy or key sectors of it to a virtual standstill. Where they cannot evade price controls altogether, large corporations are able to launch investment strikes that can create physical shortages severe enough to force governments to remove or relax the controls. And where they cannot evade inconveniencing wage controls, corporations find other ways of overcoming specific labour shortages. This usually involves paying wages that exceed the control norms (wage drift). The evasion of controls can become so widespread that the system ultimately disintegrates. Little wonder that an 1980 OECD study concluded that "few countries have managed to maintain an incomes policy for more than two or three years at a time."[20]
- When a controls regime is phased out, unless it has been accompanied by restrictive monetary and fiscal policies that create slack demand and a large pool of unemployment, wage-price explosions can dissipate whatever gains have been made in constraining wages and prices as the parties attempt to make up whatever sacrifices they have endured during the controls period.
- In periods of rapid growth, rising real wages can be accommodated, especially if incomes policy plays a role in moderating the wage claim and wage sacrifices are in fact translated into higher investment. But the problem of gaining a consensus is particularly acute during periods of stagnant output with companies facing declining and in some instances negative profits, heavy debt and severe cash flow problems. In such periods the state has little to offer the working

class. Anything extra it gives to labour must be subtracted from capital. But with profits being clearly squeezed, this could place the motor force of the system in jeopardy. Effective control over prices and profits under these circumstances would be suicidal for capital. During periods of crises there must be a shift in allocation the other way, from consumption to investment. Real wages must be sacrificed in favour of profits; state expenditures on social services must be cut back in favour of increased subsidies to industry. But with the state in effect nationalizing part of labour's income and transferring it to capitalists, consensus is not possible and whatever agreement had been forged in different times inevitably breaks down. As Ted Hanisch of the Norwegian Institute for Social Research observes, an incomes policy in conditions of economic stagnation "consumes working class solidarity without reproducing it."[21] It is then either imposed through state coercion, eliminating basic trade union freedoms, or abandoned. It is in any event an inherently unstable regime.

- Even so, while unions may agree to wage restraints in the interest of increasing business investment in new plant and equipment, they have no means of guaranteeing workers that their sacrifices will in fact be translated into greater investment. If returns to new capital investment are not sufficiently attractive, firms will decide to use surplus funds in other ways — investing abroad, paying off debts, engaging in takeover bids of other firms. Whereas some unions may choose to give up some present consumption for the promise of greater future consumption arising from an expanding economy, when investment stagnates "there is no sense in the workers maintaining cooperation any longer, and they will in all likelihood become more militant and press their maximum claims."[22]
- To sustain these arrangements under these circumstances, some labour organizations upped the ante by demanding some control over investment and shop-floor decisions through significant equity ownership and worker control. But this has proved to be an untenable basis for sustaining a social consensus. Even in Sweden where the corporate sector has learned to live with a massive welfare state, a half century of near continuous social democratic rule, and lower profit margins, such arrangements turned out to be totally unacceptable to capital. This merely demonstrates that whatever other compromises are worked out, the consensus must be contained within the parameters of the private-enterprise system.
- Many of the countries widely acclaimed for their smooth adjustment to the energy prices explosion — Austria, Belgium, Germany, the Netherlands — were assisted in retaining low rates of unemployment and inflation by greatly appreciated exchange rates (ranging from 15 per cent to 30 per cent). The high value of their currencies

lowered prices of imported goods, moderating the rise in consumer prices and wage rates and allowing for further rounds of appreciation and disinflation. This policy was arguably more important than incomes policy in attacking inflation, but it clearly cannot be generalized to all countries. For every group of countries whose exchange rate appreciates, there must be another group that is experiencing a relative depreciation. In this instance all four countries entered the 1970s with exchange rates that were undervalued relative to the U.S. dollar. More recently they have all experienced substantial depreciation of their exchange rates. Consequently, their ability to hold down inflation has come at the cost of increasingly high rates of unemployment.

- The economic performance of countries with long-standing tripartite practices has been exaggerated by the pundits. Looking at four indicators — economic growth, investment, inflation and unemployment — their records are not discernibly better, when examined as a whole, compared to the performances of most other countries.

The rate of growth of output for the European economy fell from an average rate of about 5 per cent in the late 1960s to 2-3 per cent in the mid- to late 1970s and to 1 per cent in the 1980s. Countries with tripartite practices (the first six in Table 9:1) do no better and sometimes worse than the OECD average.

Over the two decades of the 1960s and 1970s, excluding Norway with its exceptional oil investments, countries with tripartite practices have on average invested almost exactly the same proportion of total income

TABLE 9:1
Annual Average Growth Rates of Real Gross Domestic Product in OECD (%)

	1960-70	1970-73	1973-75	1975-79	1980-84
Austria	4.8	5.6	1.2	2.8	1.2
Germany	4.7	3.9	-0.7	4.0	0.8
Holland	5.2	4.5	1.2	3.1	0.2
Norway	4.3	4.6	4.7	4.2	1.0
Sweden	4.6	2.3	3.3	1.1	1.2
U.K.	2.8	4.1	-1.0	2.4	0.6
Japan	11.1	8.1	0.5	5.9	3.8
U.S.	3.9	4.7	-1.1	4.4	1.8
Canada	5.2	6.8	2.3	3.7	1.8
Total OECD	5.0	5.1	0.1	4.0	1.2

Source: OECD, *The Challenge of Unemployment*, Paris, 1982, p. 118; OECD, *Economic Outlook*, Paris, December, 1983, pp. 18-9, 152. Figures for 1983 and 1984 are based upon OECD estimates.

as have all European OECD members. All countries have experienced a discernible decline in capital formation since the end of the 1970s, and the tripartite nations have held up no better than the others.

The ultimate point of incomes policy is to hold down the rate of inflation while maintaining something close to full employment. Austria's rate of inflation averaged 6.4 per cent between 1973 and 1982 compared to 9.9 per cent for all advanced capitalist countries. Holland's performance (7.0 per cent) has also been exceptional. Germany's record has been better than average, although this cannot be credited to incomes policy. On the other hand, the inflation rates of Sweden (10.6 per cent), Norway (9.6 per cent) and the U.K. (14.2 per cent) have been no better or worse than countries without a history of incomes policy.

Except for the U.K. and the Netherlands, countries that have a practice of incomes policy have enjoyed a uniformly superior unemployment record. OECD statistics for the period 1973 to 1983 give the following average unemployment rates: Austria 2.2; Sweden 2.3; Norway 2.0; Germany 3.7; the Netherlands 6.5; all OECD countries 5.7. Yet these admirable results owe more to demographics than to job formation. As Table 9:2 shows, except for Norway and its oil boom, these countries have had remarkably little labour force growth in the 1970s. Consequently, a modest expansion in employment was sufficient to hold down their unemployment rates. Job formation in Canada has been far more rapid; but partly because of our much greater labour force growth, unemployment rates have been three to four times as high. While these countries' unemployment rates still remain low by North American standards, they have doubled since the end of the 1970s and are approaching the European average.

TABLE 9:2
Labour Force and Employment Growth Rates

	Labour Force % Growth Rate	Employment Average Annual % Growth Rate	
	1973-79	1975-79	1978-81
Austria	2.8	0.9	0.6
Netherlands	4.1	0.4	-0.4
Norway	15.9	2.3	1.6
Sweden	8.6	0.7	0.5
Germany	-1.1	0.7	0.2
U.S.	17.3	3.5	0.8
Canada	24.0	2.8	2.7
OECD Average	9.4	1.5	0.4

Source: OECD, Employment Outlook, 1983; OECD, *The Challenge of Unemployment*, 1982.

The Canadian Experience

Until the early 1970s neither the institutional requirements nor the economic conditions that gave rise to incomes policy abroad prevailed in Canada. In the context of the wage-price spirals of the 1970s, however, the Canadian Labour Congress (CLC) offered voluntary wage restraint in exchange for price and profit controls and the tripartite Council for Social and Economic Planning. Employers found the price too steep and the Liberal government chose monetarism instead. When the labour movement demonstrated that it did not have the strength to stop wage controls in the Anti-Inflation Board (AIB) period, the government took this as a signal that it had little to fear in unleashing monetarism to achieve the desired goal of wage moderation and industrial peace.

More recently, discussions of economic recovery commonly conclude that some form of incomes policy may be a necessary adjunct to other policies if the recovery process is not to be nipped in the bud by excessive wage claims. The particular concern is that unions will attempt to recoup real wage losses once employment begins to fall off. The Macdonald Commission calls for temporary controls; other interested parties urge the establishment of more permanent control structures.

Canadian enthusiasts of an incomes policy usually admit that because of the very different conditions prevailing here, the absence of centralized bargaining for example, it's not possible to import European models holus bolus. But far too often they then go on to construct amended versions that violate the basic tenets of these models. One recent effort, for instance, draws inspiration from the voluntary consensual arrangements of European corporatism, then proceeds to advocate the very thing, legislated wage controls, that these same European countries have studiously avoided as the very antithesis of building a "social partnership." Clarence Barber and John McCallum, the authors of the ironically titled tract, *Controlling Inflation: Learning From Experience in Canada, Europe and Japan*, concede that a voluntary consensus is not available in this country. It is their hope that through some immediate success of compulsory controls, coupled with a demonstration of even-handed administration and some inducements to both labour and capital, the necessary conditions for voluntary participation can develop.

Like its European counterpart, Canadian labour is opposed to legislative controls. The experience with the AIB and 6-and-5 program confirmed the previous contention that the burden of legislative controls falls almost entirely on labour. According to a study of the AIB, commissioned by the Conference Board of Canada:

> controls resulted in a significant shift in income distribution in Canada away

from persons and in favour of business compared to what would have occurred over the period (1975-1978) in the absence of the program. As a result, the composition of final spending in the economy shifted. Without controls, consumer spending would have been stronger and investment spending weaker than what actually occurred. Exports would have been lower, and imports would have been higher in the absence of controls.[23]

The level of average weekly wages was 7.7 per cent lower than would have been the case without controls, while controls lowered the price level by only 2.0 to 2.5 per cent. While net profit margins fell throughout the controls period, the authors conclude that this was due entirely to the economic recession and that in the absence of controls the level of corporate profits before taxes would have been 9.2 per cent lower than it actually was.

Ironically, while campaigning against Robert Stanfield's proposal to institute wage and price controls in the 1974 federal election, Prime Minister Trudeau faultlessly predicted this outcome: "You can't freeze executive salaries and dividends because there are too many loopholes to squeeze through." He noted that import prices couldn't be frozen. "So what's [Stanfield] going to freeze?" "Your wages! He's going to freeze your wages!"[24]

One of the reasons offered for controls is that they will help those on low incomes, those most victimized by inflation. Low-paid workers were permitted to receive an annual increase up to $1,000, but people earning low wages are in that situation because they don't have the power to improve their lot. Allowing them more than 10 per cent or more than 100 per cent is irrelevant unless they are also given the power to bargain for such an increase.

What's more, in ruling on applications for wage increases, "the AIB itself appeared to have discriminated in its treatment of labour groups depending on such factors as militancy, political and market power, and the effectiveness with which the labour organizations were able to argue their cases."[25] The AIB was more generous to groups which posed a real strike threat; low-wage workers found in the weakest unions and who posed no strike threat were more likely to have been treated "according to the book."

Canadian authorities prided themselves on the fact that, contrary to the experiences elsewhere, there was no post-controls wage bubble in Canada. But this was because Canada did not accompany controls with an expansionary fiscal and monetary policy. Wage restraint was introduced as a complement to a restrictive monetary and fiscal policy, and there was no pretence that incomes policy could be combined with a full-employment policy. There was no pent-up demand for labour when controls were lifted in 1978 because the unemployment rate was over 8 per cent.

Not long after the AIB was phased out, the federal government reintroduced a controls program, this time restricted to the public sector and without pretension about directly controlling prices. In the interim, inflation had slipped back up to 11 per cent, roughly the same rate that had prevailed when the first controls program was imposed seven years earlier. The other difference was that, while the AIB honoured signed agreements, the new legislation rolled back contracts negotiated before the program was announced. As well, in the first controls program collective bargaining was allowed to continue as usual with contracts normally turned back if they exceeded the guidelines. In the 6-and-5 program, collective bargaining agreements were merely extended so that management was excused from its duty to bargain and unions were denied the right to strike.

The alleged purpose of 6-and-5 was to set an example for private-sector wage settlements and to lower the federal bill for wages and salaries, allowing the savings to be reallocated "to the high priority needs for direct assistance of other Canadians." But, predictably, public-sector wage settlements did not spill into private wage settlements. While spill-overs are very important within the private sector, they emanate from similar industries within the private sector and not from the public sector.[26]

Inflation and wages fell sharply shortly after 6-and-5 was introduced. But the decline was produced, not by the 6-and-5 program, but by world recession and massive unemployment. As one author has remarked, "the federal government's wage controls can be seen as an attempt to take credit for reducing inflation without accepting the responsibility for creating high unemployment."[27]

Evidently Ottawa had judged that it was a politically opportune moment to engage in public-employee bashing since a Goldfarb public-opinion survey found that "there is a desire to see some measure of punishment of the civil service." Donald Johnston, then president of the Treasury Board, declared that public employees "represent a privileged community within this country," largely exempted from the restraints being imposed by private employers. It is fair to say that government officials knew this was not the case. Public wage and salary settlements were consistently below those in private industry between 1972 and 1981. And while regular federal employees are rarely laid off, this is not the case for the growing proportion of term appointments. After reviewing the evidence, one analyst concluded that besides sheer opportunism 6-and-5 was introduced as another chapter in the government's "grandiose plan" to permanently remove the right to strike from federal employees.[28]

In response to these compulsory wage-restraint programs, the Canadian Labour Congress put forward the conditions under which it would voluntarily agree to an incomes policy. Originally labeled "social corporatism," the CLC conditions included removing the business sector's "unilateral right to determine investment and pricing policies" and a system of economic planning in which labour would have "an equal share in the economic and social decision-making on a national basis with other partners — businesses and government." This formulation was adapted from what CLC officials observed to be the experience of West European countries where, as we have seen, tripartite councils were established, usually under the auspicies of social democratic governments and in circumstances where business had little option but to participate in such arrangements.

As previously noted, such circumstances have not prevailed in Canada and certainly do not prevail today. But let us assume for the sake of argument that tripartite councils of the kind the CLC proposes were established; in the main, the results would follow the European experience. But it is worthwhile identifying the structural realities from which these results flow.

Tripartism focuses on the process of decision-making rather than on its content. Corporatism presumes that the unit of production remains the private corporation whose owners retain direct control over the production process. In practice, this means that both the state and labour can at best influence pricing and investment decisions at one step removed. Retaining direct control, capital also retains its decisive economic power including its right to withhold investment to realize its interests. Tripartism may establish *de jure* equality among the three partners, but in the final analysis capital is the *de facto* senior partner. With the organization of production in private hands, the state is extremely restricted in its capacity to meet labour's main demands: full employment, income redistribution and investment priorities that serve social needs. Not being in a position to organize production itself, the state is forced to depend on corporate capital for economic development, and state policies are inevitably concerned with fostering the private accumulation of profit.

The "full and equal partnership" the CLC proposes can therefore be only an illusion. Whatever the original intent and the strength of its representation, labour can never be more than a junior partner in tripartite councils. This inequality is merely a reflection of the unequal power relationship between labour and capital that is a structural feature of an economy organized along capitalist lines.

This does not mean that labour can never influence decisions. Under conditions of full employment when labour's market power is at its strongest, and particularly when the state representation is sympathetic to its cause, labour can gain important concessions as the price for yielding to wage restraint. But when this begins to impinge on profit margins or threatens the countries' foreign balances, the room for manoeuvrability is greatly diminished. And during periods of slowdown and economic crisis it disappears altogether.

It is certainly possible to design models of income policy that produce an equitable treatment or that favour labour over capital. In conjunction with sustained full employment, such as has been experienced over extended periods in Europe, incomes policies have been known to produce substantial increases in wages, a rise of labour's share of national income and a squeeze of profits. However, the consequential decline in productivity and investment and the deterioration in foreign competition almost invariably force regimes to alter the terms of the policy. Most often this involves a freeze on wages, or some other drastic fiscal measures to halt the redistribution of income, and a shift in the priorities of state expenditures. Appeals to the national interest will likely be persuasive for a time, but sooner or later labour withdraws from the arrangement. Union leaders are unable to deliver industrial peace. Unofficial strikes and challenges to their leadership will force a change in union policy.

In sum, serious students of a quarter-century of incomes policy and social consensus have simply not found the unqualified success story reported by post-Keynesians in North America, who look longingly to the European experience. In almost every instance, incomes policy and tripartite structures have been notoriously fragile and subject to frequent breakdowns. Over the past half dozen years they either have become totally ineffectual and inoperative or, as in the majority of cases, have simply collapsed under the burden of the world economic crisis.

10 | Industrial Policy

Lurking in the background of the post-Keynesian argument for a new industrial policy is the long legacy of foreign ownership of the Canadian economy. The explanation commonly offered for this situation is that at the crucial turning point towards the end of the nineteenth century when other late-comers were launching an industrial strategy, Canada was dominated by a group of merchants, bankers and financiers who molded the political economy to suit their interests.

As merchant capitalists they accumulated wealth, not by producing goods, but by transporting and selling them. From their perspective, extracting raw materials for sale abroad was just as profitable as producing new industrial goods. The problem was not a shortage of entrepreneurship and risk-taking, as is commonly charged, but that entrepreneurship was located in trade and finance with their well-known penchant for liquid capital and quick returns. Locking up capital for long periods by investing money in new industries did not suit their interests.[1] To attract and absorb large numbers of people, more manufacturing was desirable, but it was more easily obtained by inducing foreign industrialists to set up shop in Canada. The National Policy tariff was designed to protect products rather than indigenous firms, thereby promoting industrialization "by invitation." This set the long-term trend: export of raw and semi-processed materials; import of foreign capital and foreign technology to assemble American industrial products for the Canadian market.

This "stunted form of industrialization" was obscured by the boom conditions that prevailed in all industrial nations throughout the 1950s and 1960s. Canadian prosperity, however, was not based on the development of new capabilities, new skills, new products, new technologies. Catering to the huge external demand for resources and a growing domestic demand for consumer goods, it found its traditional niche within this long-wave of postwar prosperity, creating an "environment of dangerous complacency."

Symptoms of Decline

Study after study began to reveal Canada's over-dependence on its finite resources, which were increasingly costly to extract and whose development generated relatively few jobs. These same studies revealed that the record of Canadian manufacturing in research and development and in productivity was inferior to that of its major competitors. This structural weakness in manufacturing showed up in various ways. First, in the early 1960s manufacturing accounted for more than a quarter of the new jobs created in the economy, but between 1966 and 1972 it generated barely more than 5 per cent of the new jobs. Second, in the 1950s Canadians enjoyed the second highest wages in the world; by 1980 the average Canadian wage had been surpassed by workers in Sweden, West Germany, the Netherlands and Belgium, with France and Japan quietly closing the gap. Third, in the mid-1950s Canada was second only to the U.S. in manufacturing exports per capita; by the mid-1970s Canada had been overtaken by Sweden, France, Japan, West Germany, Australia and Finland. Even "countries which most Canadians do not even think as industrialized — Spain, Yugoslavia, Portugal, Ireland and Mexico — were exporting a greater proportion of finished goods than Canada," according to the Science Council's report, *Uncertain Prospects*, published in 1977. Since then Canada's position has deteriorated further.

Where does Canada belong in the world economy? Are we an industrial, semi-industrial, or a non-industrial nation? Alfred Maizels, the economist who devised these categories, placed Canada among the industrialized countries because of the relatively high value of per capita manufacturing production and because, as he said, the Canadian and American economies are so closely related that "in many respects the two countries can effectively be regarded as a single economic system."[2] But from the perspective of his second criterion, proportion of exports consisting of finished products, Canada more properly belongs in the semi-industrialized countries along with Argentina, Australia, Brazil and India. And if dependency on foreign suppliers for finished products is also considered, Canada is in the same company as Burma. (See Table 10:1.)

Another commonly cited indicator of Canada's relative decline is the trade balance in end products. In 1971 the deficit of imports over exports stood at $3.6 billion. It grew to $10.3 billion in 1975 and doubled again to $20.9 billion in 1981. Over the decade the cumulative deficit was $100 billion dollars which had to be paid for with large surpluses in raw and semi-processed materials.

These trends suggest to the Science Council of Canada and others that Canada is moving backwards, "deindustrializing," confirming itself

TABLE 10:1
Finished Manufactures as a Proportion of Trade

	Exports 1955	Exports 1980	Imports 1980
Industrial Countries:			
Japan	64	71	11
Italy	47	61	28
West Germany	65	60	34
Sweden	33	53	45
U.S.	48	52	38
Great Britain	62	50	39
France	38	50	35
Canada	11	32	59
Semi-Industrial Countries:			
India	31	23	27
Brazil	0.4	22	29
Argentina	0.4	14	49
Australia	6.0	10	54
Turkey	0.4	7	39
Non-Industrial Countries:			
Egypt	3.0	4	35
Zaire	0.8	0.6	48
Burma	0.4	0.3	55

Source: A. Maizels, *Industrial Growth & World Trade;* UN, Yearbook of International Trade Statistics, as produced in G. Williams, *Not for Export,* p. 8.

as a nation of extractors, assemblers and retailers and falling desperately behind in high-technology industries.

The Global Challenge

Even more ominous, changing patterns in the structure of the world economy signal a further deterioration in Canada's competitive position. In response to the economic crisis, multinationals are moving and the cheapest location for the mass production of standardized products is becoming the Third World countries.

Almost all of the world's production of small appliances is now centred in and exported from Hong Kong, Korea, Malaysia and Singapore. At the same time, Taiwan, India, the Philippines and other poor countries have become the leading producers in clothing, footwear, toys and simple electronic assemblies. All of these products require substantial amounts of unskilled labour but little capital investment or technology. Workers in these countries earn no more than $25 per month. (Before the overthrow of the Somoza government, Nicaragua was advertising that its workers would assemble electronic components for 25 cents a day.) By the mid-1970s some of these countries were following Japan's earlier example and shifting their export mix towards more capital-intensive industries. Brazil, Mexico, Korea and Taiwan have become major producers of steel. Their share of world steel-making capacity rose from 9 per cent in 1974 to 15 per cent by 1980. Korea already has the largest shipyard in the world, and Brazil is becoming a net exporter of automobiles, commuter aircraft and hydro-turbine generators.

The changing international division of labour can be devastating for Canada because most of its industrial capacity is concentrated in the very same low-to-medium-technology assembly operations that are expanding in the newly industrializing countries. According to the Science Council, no amount of government subsidies and loan guarantees, tax breaks, wage cutting or tariff protection can save these industries from eventual extinction. Such defensive moves have been the dominant strategy in the U.S. which, according to Robert Reich, is also doomed to failure:

> America is trying to preserve its old industrial base but at the price of a gradually declining standard of living for its citizens. Barriers against imports are forcing Americans to pay higher prices.... Subsidized loans, loan guarantees and tax benefits are forcing Americans to pay higher taxes in order to finance these benefits. Rollbacks of environmental regulations are forcing Americans to breath dirtier air and drink dirtier water. Wage reductions are forcing Americans to accept less take-home pay.
>
> These declines in the U.S. standard of living would be more bearable if they resulted from positive steps toward a stronger industrial base and a higher standard of living in the future. But they will lead to nothing but further declines because they are conditioned on preserving American dominance in high-volumes standardized production, rather than on adopting American industry to flexible-system production.[3]

Other industrialized nations are confronting the competitive threat by shifting their industrial base towards specialized products and technologically advanced processes requiring skilled labour, the one remaining factor of production where they retain an advantage. To be successful in this field, what is required is a "flexible system" of production management that can respond quickly to new opportunities and is geared to "solving new problems rather than making routine the solution to old ones."[4]

Japan is cited as the most successful example of an economy that has shifted from capital-intensive, high-volume production to flexible-system production. It has scrapped its old plant and equipment and invested in new high-volume capacity in Korea, Taiwan, Singapore and elsewhere while retaining its higher paid workers for more skilled production at home.

Less successful, but moving in the same direction, West Germany shifted more of its production into specialty steels, pharmaceuticals, precision machinery, and technically advanced ships; France moved into satellite technology, electronic switching equipment, nuclear power generators and the design and fabrication of computers. In all instances, these conversions have involved massive state assistance both to phase out old industries and products and to support the emergence of new ones including, not only the development of new physical capital, but also the development of improved human capital.

The Cost of Dependency

State interventionists are convinced that Canada's relative decline is directly linked to its stunted economic structure and that this in turn derives from the overbearing presence of foreign ownership and dependency on foreign technology.

1. Canada's overwhelming reliance on resource exports arises from foreign capital's concern to secure a reliable and inexpensive supply of raw or semi-processed materials. Foreign capital's primary interest in secondary manufacturing has been to establish and protect a market position in Canada for its own technology and brand names. In many instances this maintains foreign capital's operations as a warehouse/ assembly type of facility. Canadian branch plants are restricted to the products, technology and markets assigned to them, and they are required to import most of their machinery, services, materials and components from suppliers prearranged by head office — nearly half of their requirements are imported from abroad — shutting out Canadian sources of supply. The technological multiplier effect that frequently arises from the relations between large firms and medium-sized ones is thereby lost. The purchasing patterns foisted on subsidiary firms is a major factor in Canada's huge import requirements: nearly three-quarters of all industry imports is accounted for by imports of foreign-controlled enterprises.[5]

2. Foreign-owned companies undertake less domestic research and development per dollar of sales than do domestically owned firms of a similar size. For instance, the ratio of research and development to sales for firms employing more than 500 workers is 2 per cent for foreign-owned firms compared to 10.3 per cent for Canadian-owned firms.[6] And the warmed-over technology foreign companies bring with them does not come without a price, as a look at "other service costs" in the balance of payments reveals.

TABLE 10:2
Canadian Processing of Primary Resources as a Per Cent of Other Selected Countries, 1976-80 (average)

	%
Australia	61
Austria	48
France	43
Germany	30
Italy	65
Japan	40
Sweden	33
U.K.	63

Source: Calculated from A. Rotstein, *Rebuilding from Within*, Table 3-5, p. 49.

3. As Table 10:2 shows, the degree to which Canada processes primary resources is notably lower than in all other industrial countries. Canada's low degree of processing together with its high tendency to import end products costs hundreds of thousands of jobs a year.

4. Canada's high manufacturing costs (on average 20 per cent higher than in the U.S.) is attributed to the excessive number of producers selling in the cramped Canadian market. Splitting up the small Canadian market among branch plants and their Canadian counterparts causes production runs that are less than efficient. This is further aggravated by a tendency towards excessive diversification — producing all the models supplied in the U.S. market. The fact that they have all managed to coexist is at least partly due to the Canadian tariff which has allowed them to raise their prices to cover higher costs.

5. The move towards multinational restructuring has benefited Canada very little. Since the mid 1960s, spurred on perhaps by the move towards freer trade, some multinationals have begun to rationalize their global operations to reduce these inefficiencies. Through world-product mandating, a subsidiary is assigned to develop and produce a few products or components for the world market. But a recent Science Council of Canada report indicates "very few [Canadian] subsidiaries have world mandates that account for more than a minor proportion of the subsidiary's total output."[7] More to the point, this is the same strategy through which multinationals are relocating some of their labour-intensive operations to Third World countries and closing down their Canadian plants.

The Canadian benefits of continental rationalization — whereby a limited number of products are selected for both American and Canadian markets — are also dubious. This scheme shifts no independent technological and marketing capacity to Canadian subsidiaries and at

TABLE 10:3
Changes in Manufacturing Productivity

	Output Per Hour[1]	
	1960-73	1973-81
U.S.	3.0	1.7
Canada	4.5	1.4
Japan	10.7	6.8
Belgium	7.0	6.2
France	6.0	4.6
West Germany	5.5	4.5
Italy	6.9	3.7
U.K.	4.3	2.2
Denmark	6.4	4.1
Sweden	6.7	2.2
Netherlands	7.6	5.1

[1] Results are expressed as per cent change.

Source: Lawrence Klein, "In Defense of Industrial Policy," in *Western Economic Review*, March 1984, p. 9.

its worst assigns them the least popular products while supplying the more popular and latest models from American-based plants. The experience of the Auto Pact stands out here. Assembling a smaller number of models for the North American market resulted in increased productivity and increased output. But it further reduced Canadian technological capability by transferring what little research, design engineering and testing there was back to American head offices. And by centralizing purchasing, it further crippled independent producers of parts and equipment. Similar results have occurred in the television industry with the television parts industry collapsing in concert with the disintegration of TV-set production. Over 3,000 jobs have been lost in that industry since 1973. The known effect of these schemes has been to preserve some jobs in the short-run while "guaranteeing long-run failure of the industry in Canada," according to the Science Council.[8]

6. Gross domestic product per worker grew by 30 per cent per decade in the period 1947-73; it was virtually zero in the decade 1973-83. A major part of the problem stems from the stagnation and depression faced by all industrial countries; under-utilized production capacity and under-utilized workers always drag down productivity. What is worrisome is that Canada's position has been deteriorating rapidly relative to other countries. (See Table 10:3.) Stagnant productivity combined with rapidly rising wages has produced a deadly combination, with labour cost per unit of output increasing by 9.6 per cent a year between 1973 and 1981. Most of Canada's trading rivals had better productivity records and/or more moderate wage increases.

TABLE 10:4
Productivity, Unit Labour Cost and Price: Electrical Machinery and Electronics Industry, 1975-80

	Productivity	Unit Labour Cost Local Currency	Unit Labour Cost U.S. Dollars	Producer Price
Canada	3.3	6.8	3.8	7.2
France	5.5	9.2	9.6	—
West Germany	5.0	3.0	9.5	2.0
Japan	14.0	−6.7	−1.5	0.4
Netherlands	7.8	1.5	6.5	1.6
Sweden	0.6	11.5	11.1	8.3
U.K.	1.8	19.9	21.0	13.4
U.S.	4.0	5.0	5.0	7.5

Source: Lawrence Klein, "In Defense of Industrial Policy," in *Western Economic Review*, March 1984.

Only a depreciating dollar kept us from falling further behind. This is portrayed in Table 10:4 which, for illustrative purposes, compares Canada's position with that of rival industrial countries in the electric machinery and electronics industry. In both productivity and per unit labour cost — which measures the combined effect of productivity and wages — Canadian industry ranked fifth among the eight countries cited. However, when Canada's depreciated dollar is taken into account, our unit labour costs are held down, ranking second only to Japan.

Nobel prize-winner Lawrence Klein, the source of this and other comparative data, says "the exchange rate is being used by Canada to cover up relative inefficiency."[9] It is obviously a short-term expedient at best if rising domestic production costs regularly wipe out the potential competitive gains of a depreciating currency. More fundamental changes are required to restore Canada's position in the world economy.

7. Relying mainly on unskilled and semi-skilled labour and fully developed and mature technologies, most products turned out in Canadian plants are the ones most easily transferred to low-wage countries, which often have more up-to-date facilities. Once Canadian markets for these products are saturated, foreign owners have little reason to put more investment in Canada. Retained earnings in their Canadian operations can easily finance whatever further expansion is deemed warranted. After a point, foreign subsidiaries siphon more capital out of Canada than the sum of new capital inflows from head office.

Up to the early 1960s new capital inflows accounted for most of the increase in foreign investment. During the 1960s they were still substantial but re-investment of subsidiary earnings was already financing slightly over half of the value of foreign direct investment. After 1970 net capital inflow was zero. The dollar value of Canadian purchases of foreign-owned companies exactly offset whatever new capital inflow that occurred. Over the past dozen or so years increased foreign investment has been entirely financed by Canadian savings in the form of retained earnings of foreign subsidiaries.

Looking at all international capital flows, during the 1950s Canada received roughly as much capital as it exported. Short-term and long-term capital inflows just about matched outflows of interest and dividend payments and service charges, such as license and management fees. After 1960, however, payments greatly exceeded receipts. For the period 1950 to 1982 as a whole, the short-term and long-term inflow of capital to Canada was nearly $35 billion. This was matched by an outflow of nearly $120 billion ($73 billion in interest and divided payments and $45 billion in "service charges"). The cost of our "structural deformities" is evidently growing. In the first three years of the 1980s Canada paid out $5 for every new dollar gained in foreign capital. This is a massive charge in return for a manufacturing sector that is nearly 20 per cent less efficient than its American counterpart. It absorbs nearly all of our trade surplus with the U.S., depriving Canada of an equivalent sum which could otherwise be invested in new plant or equipment or spent on new housing and consumer goods.

Beginning with the Watkins Report of 1969, these arguments have been refined and updated, and are now fairly widely accepted and certainly well known. The inevitable conclusion drawn is that, for all its short-term benefits, foreign investment can never be the agency for dynamic growth in Canada. While Canada is not alone in facing the threat of competition from low-wage countries, its combination of high costs and low levels of technological capability is deadly, and foreign multinationals have shown no inclination to develop Canada as a centre for the design and production of new products. The U.S. itself has been tardy in adjusting to the new international reality and is falling behind its European and Japanese competitors. "If the country which controls over 50 per cent of Canadian manufacturing is in trouble," the Science Council warns, "then it should come as no surprise that our manufacturing sector can look forward to continuing difficulties."[10]

A New Industrial Policy

The Science Council of Canada, which has been at the forefront of the state-interventionist school of thought, points to "technological sovereignty" as the key to breaking the vicious circle of export failure and import dependence: "technological," because the possession of new technology is seen as the overriding factor in ending Canada's dependency on imports for industrial goods and gaining access to foreign markets; "sovereignty," because foreign ownership is seen as the single most important obstacle to developing such technology.

A "buy-Canada" procurement policy is one obvious measure. Because departments and agencies of the state along with crown corporations are the largest purchasers of goods and services, by simply identifying Canadian suppliers for goods governments required anyway, a huge market for Canadian-made goods would be opened up thereby promoting the development and use of new technology.

The government, as a second measure, is urged to play an entrepreneurial role in identifying large projects that meet national needs while creating a market and facilities for the development of appropriate technology. Nuclear power and the communication-satellite program point the way to the benefits of the state taking the lead in identifying possibilities and co-ordinating programs. Establishing a "collaborative managerial framework" to carry out the energy and transportation mega projects scheduled for the next few decades would go a long way towards resolving the issues of regional specialization, labour and management antagonism, Canadian ownership, and the processing of resources. This is so because of the leverage generated by the sheer size and scope of these projects, their demands for novel technology and the necessary participation by government in financing and regulating them. For example, the government can influence private-sector purchasing policies by setting domestic purchasing performance standards for firms awarded contracts for such projects.

Following the example of the Syncrude tarsands project as a third measure, the state can become joint partners with private industry in very large and risky technologically intensive projects.

To increase the capacity for technological absorption at the enterprise level, as a fourth measure, government and industry should establish technology centres that would link small and medium-sized firms with new product ideas and know-how.

The Science Council of Canada, which has provided this blueprint of technological sovereignty, is very critical of the now-defunct Foreign Investment Review Agency (FIRA). While it was a noble idea, "the problems of Canadian industry were already firmly entrenched and too severe for FIRA to effect even the slightest amelioration."[11] As a fifth measure the council sees the need for a much more powerful agency which would supervise the activities of foreign-owned companies more stringently and in accordance with more specific guidelines than FIRA operated under. Thus, for example, the council would have the state declare certain strategic growth industries off-base to foreign investment or takeover. These protected industries would only be open to imported technology through licensing agreements and joint ventures.

While the state should attempt to modify the behaviour of foreign-owned companies, the council is pessimistic that such regulatory effort is the answer to what ails the Canadian economy. Nor does it advocate dismantling or buying out foreign firms. This would be a waste of resources because they are mostly involved in old-line industries whereas the future lies in building technological capacity in the growth industries of the next twenty to thirty years. "The long-term, the ultimate and the only solution to Canada's problems from its uniquely high degree of foreign ownership lies in the successful promotion of competitive Canadian-controlled firms and industries...."[12]

The Science Council and other industrial-policy advocates put great store in identifying and developing "core companies" as "chosen instruments" to generate technology. As criteria, the council suggests spheres of production appropriate to Canada's physical environment and geography, meeting the goals of national unity and national sovereignty and reducing the huge deficit in industrial machinery. Examples often cited include the billion dollar plus deficit market in hard-rock mining and pulp and paper; long-distance communication and transportation; cold ocean resource development; nuclear energy; electrical transmission; and raw materials processing.

Since establishing core companies usually involves integrating existing firms through mergers and joint-ventures, the possibility of using foreign subsidiaries is very limited. This strategy is thus linked to selecting existing Canadian-controlled firms that have the capacity to innovate and to be competitive in both domestic and foreign markets.

The neo-conservative alternative to an activist industrial policy is free trade. But, argue the post-Keynesians, the known results of the movement towards freer trade have been decidedly mixed. Between 1965 and 1978, the average rate of duty on imported goods was cut by 40 per cent. On the one hand, it dramatically increased the proportion of Canadian output exported rather than consumed at home. At the same time, it dramatically increased the degree of import penetration, with the rise of imported manufactured goods far exceeding the rise of exports. In medium- and high-technology industries, imports have all but replaced Canadian producers. For example, in 1964 Canada imported 14 per cent of its requirements in consumer electronics. By 1976, imports met almost 63 per cent of Canadian requirement. In computer and office equipment, imports moved from 56 per cent to about 90 per cent of domestic needs; general machinery from 65 per cent to 74 per cent; agricultural machinery from 76 per cent to 81 per cent. For the entire range of high-technology manufactures, the import ratio rose from 32 per cent in 1964 to 52 per cent in 1975.[13]

The problem with the free-trade argument, post-Keynesians say, is that it ignores Canadian realities. For instance, more than half of Canada's exports to the U.S. consist of sales by subsidiaries to their parent companies. Over 40 per cent of imports into Canada consist of purchases by subsidiaries from their parent companies. This is hardly a conventional exchange between trading parties dealing at arm's length. Multinational corporations are not the price-takers presumed by nineteenth-century free-trade theory. They are price-makers. At the very least, they set the prices of goods exchanged between themselves and their subsidiaries and they chose the products, technology, investment and spending patterns to maximize global profits rather than subsidiary profits.[14]

At the same time, post-Keynesians are not dyed-in-the-wool protectionists. They concede that higher tariffs will not solve Canada's problems. Most post-Keynesians would likely agree with the Science Council's call for a halt to further moves towards free trade until measures are taken to "restore firms to a degree of competitiveness [such] that they could benefit from bilateral or multi-lateral free trade, if introduced at a later date." In the absence of such measures, free trade, while favouring some industries, would cause more to survive "in a diminished form. The lower prices of their products — will be consolation only to those Canadians with jobs."[15]

Calls for "managed" trade are more consistent with the post-Keynesian perspective. A managed-trade regime includes domestic-content agreements of the kind the Canadian Automobile Workers advocates. Mexico requires auto manufacturers to produce in that country at least 70 per cent of the value of cars sold domestically. All told, twenty-eight countries have imposed similar content requirements on automakers.

The Japanese have negotiated co-production agreements to the same effect. In purchasing 100 F-18 fighter planes from the U.S., for instance, Japan negotiated the following deal: 14 of the planes to be made entirely in the U.S.; 8 delivered in kit form for assembly in Japan; 78 to be produced in Japan under license from McDonell-Douglas. While it would have been far cheaper to buy all the planes straight off the American production line, the Japanese calculated that the additional high-tech jobs and gains to its aircraft industry were well worth the extra price.

Counter-trade is another type of managed trade. The buyer of an imported product requires the supplier to market a like share of goods from the customer's country. When Sweden awarded a jet engine contract to U.S. General Electric, it required that GE market Swedish industrial goods of a like amount.[16]

Unlike protectionism, managed trade does not aim to reduce international trade. Rather it follows the principle that domestic purchasing power ought to produce domestic employment with the details left to bilateral agreements. Unlike free trade, commercial policy is adjusted to industrial policy rather than the reverse.

In sum, post-Keynesians look at the supply side of the economy but their conclusion runs counter to that of the free marketeers. Correction of Canada's inferior industrial position does not require superseding market forces; rather it is a matter of using positive state actions to create a new industrial environment which will promote a more favourable process of adjustment. With Canada's first-world wages we must also develop first-world technological capabilities or we will drift towards Third-World industrial status and quickly lose our high living standards. The solution is technological sovereignty, which will not happen without a major effort on the part of the state.

Post-Keynesians do not envision state enterprise supplanting private enterprise any more than state planning would replace the market. Rather, as in other advanced capitalist countries, the state would use its fiscal leverage to restructure and reshape the private economic sphere so that it can meet the current global challenge. Private ownership of industry is combined with "public" steering of investment through tripartite agencies of collaboration between representatives of labour, capital and the state. The goal is a state-supervised economic harmony between labour and capital to ensure that the economy serves the public purpose of industrial renewal and economic sovereignty.

Obstacles

Both the liberal and social democratic variants of industrial policy are almost exclusively concerned with means rather than ends: how to manoeuvre the existing structure of power to improve Canada's competitive position within the world economy, to increase our productivity and efficiency, etc. The assumption is that state intervention of whatever variety can achieve a more rapid and thoroughgoing restructuring than is otherwise possible by means of market forces. What are the obstacles in the path of this strategy?

It is presumed that the state has a unifying command structure with the capacity to identify the policies that serve the national interest and to develop and administer programs to implement them. But this involves more than an organizational and an intellectual capacity. It also involves an interpretive one that presumes an ideological coherence and consensus. But the great economic debate has surfaced inside the apparatus of the state and inside the executive levels of government. Lacking a unified command structure with a coherent ideology and political consensus, serious divisions inside the state produced a stalemate that stalled the development of post-Keynesian industrial policy during the final decade of the Trudeau era.

The development of an industrial strategy appears to have been the pet project of the Privy Council Office (PCO) developed by Prime Minister Trudeau as a counterweight to the parochial special interest concerns of line departments and the short-term perspective of the Department of Finance. The purpose of the PCO was to develop a general policy framework to help shape ministerial decisions, to identify future problems and policy alternatives and to systematize government priorities.

When Trudeau took over the reigns of government he brought with him the conviction that government-by-crisis and intuition could be replaced with government by rational planning. His hope was that by mobilizing "the many techniques of cybernetics" and systems analysis, government need no longer be "blind, inert pawns of fate.... With this knowledge we are wide awake,... capable of shaping the future.... With the refinement of techniques for forecasting and planning we are coming to realize that the image we hold of our future is itself an important element of that future."[17]

What Trudeau discovered, however, was that the central agency charged with mapping out and implementing government economic strategy, the Department of Finance, had an image of the future that was no different from its image of the present. Its intellectual roots lay in Keynesian economics: fine-tuning the economy through incremental adjustments to government expenditures and revenues and the money supply while allotting the allocation of resources to the market. Indeed, The Department of Finance has always been a champion of free trade and the free flow of capital. It presumed that structural problems would take care of themselves.

The finance department may be taken to represent capital's compromise with state interventionism. It emerged as the guardian of that compromise, and vigorously fought off the efforts of other departments and government officials to expand the horizons of state interventionism. Through its control over the budgetary process, it was positioned as the governing force in the state apparatus with dominance over other departments and with the means to impose its definition of the national interest.

The Department of Industry, later combined with the Department of Trade and Commerce, had been set up in 1963 to promote manufacturing. By the early 1970s it was offering a diverse range of promotional and incentive programs — alongside of the Department of Regional Economic Expansion, another new department designed to stimulate industrial development. Not surprisingly, "the flow of benefits through the line branches created a community of interest between program managers in government and their industry clients."[18] But while it meted out hundreds of millions of dollars in assistance, it was a program without coherence. It amounted to a proliferating collection of measures with no strategic framework.

The PCO was in large part established as a political directorate that could co-ordinate and develop a strategic framework for an industrial policy. No doubt it was spurred on by the souring economic picture of the early 1970s and the coming apart of the "special relationship" with the U.S. under the Nixon administration. In its approach, the PCO's interest in developing an industrial policy combined Trudeau's penchant for rational planning and the concerns of left-of-centre Liberals — like Walter Gordon, Tom Kent, Maurice Lamontagne and Herb Gray — for an active state role in reshaping Canadian industry, inspired by the examples of countries like Japan, France and Sweden.

While the PCO could outline the general contours of the policy, the policy itself was in the hands of the Department of Industry, Trade and Commerce. Its successive ministers were variously enthusiastic (Pépin) and luke-warm (Gillespie, Jamieson, Chrétien, Horner), but their deputies were uniformly resistant. They shared the same reservations about the wisdom and practicality of constructing an industrial policy as their colleagues in the Department of Finance. "They felt they were being asked to do the impossible and the undesirable."[19]

The debate inside the state was revealed at a meeting of the Cabinet Committee in Priorities and Planning to consider a 1972 memorandum submitted by Pépin regarding a general framework for state policy on industrial development. The meeting, described in Richard French's account of this whole process, featured a confrontation between Simon Reisman representing Finance and the planners in the PCO:

> Canada, said Reisman, already had an industrial strategy... the only one really open to a nation in Canada's circumstances. Because of the location of primary markets, the strategy was centrist in its emphasis and focussed almost completely on the United States. There was very little Canadian policy could or should do, said Reisman, to alter these basic realities of economic geography.... Thus, to promote a strategy implying that government "pick winners" (and thus, necessarily, pick losers as well) was to misunderstand profoundly the forces underlying industrial growth.[20]

As French remarks, this perspective led in directions — incrementalism, centralism, continentalism — that the PCO did not wish to go. This internal division resulted in a policy stalemate for several years.

The stalemate was partially broken when the Department of Finance lost its credibility in the fight against stagflation. A new opening was created with the setting up of the AIB; with the growing perception of the world economic crisis and Canada's incapacity to make the necessary industrial adjustments; and with a shift of many officials out of Finance and especially Industry, Trade and Commerce.

A new committee, which included the deputy ministers of all economic departments, was formed to institute consultations with industry (Enterprise 77); together they would formulate an industrial-development policy. Twenty-three sectoral task forces (Tier 1 committees) were established, each composed of representatives of management, labour, academia, and the federal and provincial governments. Twenty-three sectoral reports were produced with policy recommendations for each of the industries concerned. Altogether, these committees put forward over 800 recommendations calling for $4 billion worth of new expenditure and tax incentive programs. A Tier 2 committee with similar representation met to recommend broad policy initiatives that cut across industry lines. To co-ordinate the results of these consultations, a new cabinet committee, the Board of Economic Development Ministers, was created; it was supported by a high-powered staff of prominent civil servants (Ministry of State for Economic Development).

The planning machinery was finally in place but it had no plan and no mandate — except to cut expenditures and to review the collection of self-serving recommendations of the Tier 1 committees and the vague generalizations of Tier 2. Its sole accomplishment before the fall of the Trudeau government was a $750 million assistance program to modernize the forestry industry. After the Clark interlude and the momentary burst of activity aimed at Canadianizing the petroleum industry and increasing the federal share of oil revenues (National Energy Program), the quest for an industrial development policy again fell upon hard times. Industry, Trade and Commerce Minister Herb Gray called for new initiatives but that was dismissed out of hand. Instead, a new policy document appended to the November 1981 budget retreated to the old staples policy as the way forward:

> The leading opportunity lies in the development of Canada's rich bounty of natural resources...energy, food products such as grain and fish, forest products and minerals such as coal and potash. The 1980s will see substantial development of energy and energy-based industries such as petro chemicals, and further expansion of agriculture, forest-based industries and mining. These developments will involve massive investments in productive capability and in the transportation industry's capacity to ship bulk commodities.[21]

To help ensure Canadian content, the Task Force on Major Capital Projects to the year 2000 identified several major resource projects valued at over $100 million each. Jointly chaired by CLC vice-president Shirley Carr and Nova's Bob Blair, the task force identified supply obstacles such as transportation and manpower that might constrain Canada's ability to realize these opportunities; and mechanisms to ensure that Canadian industry and Canadian workers would be assured of full participation in these projects and the industrial opportunities linked to them.

The collapse in demand indefinitely postponed these major capital projects, but the federal government did proceed to reorganize the western transportation systems and to fund new manpower forecasting and training facilities including the Canadian Labour Market and Productivity Centre, jointly administered by representatives of organized labour and business. The only other tangible result of this ten-year quest for an industrial policy has been the restructuring of the Atlantic fisheries through government-supported mergers and consolidations.

Altogether, these achievements represent a pretty thin harvest. At one level, the blame may be laid on "insufficient ministerial concensus," the clash between the well-established "Keynesian intellectual system" housed in the Department of Finance and the "more eclectic, less mature intellectual bases" represented by the PCO. This is the explanation offered by Richard French and it has merit, for as Andrew Shonfield has written, "planning in a capitalist context" requires that all departments with significant long-term consequences be compelled "into a single intellectual framework determined at the highest level of administration."[22] While the PCO — the highest level of administration — wanted to introduce coherent industrial policy, it was unable to compel the co-operation of other ministers and their departments. The kinds of proposals put forward by the Science Council of Canada and others presuppose the subordination of the various parts of the economy (the state, enterprises, unions, etc.) to the pursuit of its objectives. Examination of the process of policy-making demonstrates that this cannot be taken for granted.

This view, however, is not entirely satisfactory. It cannot be the superiority of the Keynesian intellectual system that persistently allowed the Department of Finance to define the politics of the national interest — unless one is prepared to make the same claim for the monetarist intellectual system. When Keynesianism fell into disfavour, the department frantically grasped the mantle of monetarism, defending the Bank of Canada and shaping its budgets according to monetarist precepts.

What Keynesianism and monetarism have in common is the exercise of government policy at arm's length from business. Government intervenes at the most aggregative level while leaving the market as the dominant mechanism for allocating resources, including investment. Canadian business has always been receptive to non-discriminatory incentive programs and government provision of services which facilitates it in pursuing its self-defined objectives. The problem it has with industrial policy is that government decides what is the right course and uses its fiscal leverage to bend the private sector in this direction. Business is forced to yield its role as helmsman of the economy to the state.

The Department of Finance owes its dominance, not to its intellectual superiority nor even to its control over the budget, but to its position as the custodian of the economic power structure. Within the state apparatus, the department has taken on, and has been given, the task of official interpreter of the needs of capital. Industrial policy ultimately failed to get off the ground, not merely because of the divisions within the state, but also because it found little support within the economic power structure.

As part of this problem, French points to the absence of political will, a complaint also voiced by the NDP. But suppose that this problem is resolved with the election of a determined NDP majority government, the installation of a uniformally sympathetic bureaucracy and a planning system with a single intellectual framework. For the sake of argument we can further assume that the new government has successfully overcome industry opposition to the proposed legislation and that the new industrial policy is in fact enacted.[23] Having manoeuvred past all these obstacles, it cannot yet be presumed that the policy will be implemented, for it still requires the co-operation of large sections of capital and the thousands of managers who staff the giant corporations. It is presumed that they will co-operate and accede to encroachment on their prerogatives if the results desired by the state can be shown not to threaten their profitability and that they may even enhance opportunities to improve profits. But there is no evidence that capital would concede the economic leadership role to the state. Most owners do not see the control they exercise over investment as simply the means to achieve profitability. It is their ultimate preserve and in the final analysis represents the essence of their economic power. For them freedom has no other meaning.

Enforcing planning agreements through a variety of sanctions and incentives cannot work so long as enterprises oppose them. They can simply refuse to invest and move their capital elsewhere until the government comes to its senses. Most likely their actions will generate allies among the workers who lose their jobs, regional and local governments who lose their tax base, local businesses who lose their consumers and various companies who lose their supplies and their sub-contracts. This is precisely what occurred in France where the socialist government of François Mitterand was forced to retreat in the face of investment strikes. The same events occurred in Canada in response to the National Energy Policy.

The problem with these policies lies in the fact that they take no account of the existing distribution of power which ultimately rests with ownership. Even creating a few new crown corporations and nationalizing a few companies has not and cannot alter the arrangement of power, for the new corporate entities are easily absorbed into the status quo. To put the point more generally still, unless the dominant business class is woefully weak or temporarily dislocated due to war (France, Italy and Germany, for example), it is most unlikely that governments, no matter what their disposition, can impose upon capital a policy initiative which it firmly opposes. Insofar as an industrial policy is concerned, industrial leaders will find a way of confining their accountability to their shareholders.

Limitations and Constraints

There is obvious merit in some aspects of post-Keynesian analysis as well as in many of the specifics it proposes on industrial policy. But all varieties of post-Keynesians take as given the existing economic arrangements in restructuring industry. This means that in periods of economic crisis they inevitably end up accepting the same constraints as the free marketeers. Wage restraint is then necessary to reduce our labour costs; plant closure legislation is undesirable because it damages the investment climate; pensions cannot be increased, nor unemployment insurance extended, nor day care improved because this will drain the economy of resources that are needed for investment; manufacturing plants can't be located in the Maritimes because they will not be competitive since it is more efficient to force people to move from their communities than to bring jobs to them.

As the Canadian Conference of Catholic Bishops has said, restructuring the economy under the imperative of competitiveness reasserts "capital ... as the dominant organizing principle of economic life." So long as survival of the fittest remains the supreme law of economics, there is a tendency for people to be treated as having little or no significance beyond their economic contribution as factors of production. The bishops conclude: "as long as technology and capital are not harnessed by society to serve basic human needs, they are likely to become an enemy rather than an ally in the development of peoples."[24]

Thoughtful Canadians are beginning to doubt whether this economic model can secure meaningful jobs and provide all its citizens with the things they need. Can we develop an alternative economic vision, one which gives priority to serving the needs of all people and to the value of human labour, one in which capital no longer plays the dominant

208 The Great Economic Debate

role? In their "ethical reflections," the Canada Conference of Catholic Bishops ask:

> What would it mean to develop an alternative economic model that would place emphasis on socially useful forms of production; labour-intensive industries; the use of appropriate forms of technology; self-reliant models of economic development, community ownership and control of industries; new forms of worker management and ownership; and greater use of the renewable energy sources in industrial production?[25]

Not surprisingly, business and political leaders were aghast at the audacity of this line of thinking and dismissed the bishops as meddlers and utopians. But is the industrial strategy they propose so hopelessly naive?

11 | Industrial Democracy

As important as it is, overhauling the industrial structure is only one element of the post-Keynesian blueprint for economic recovery. In the post-Keynesian view our industrial relations system is as antiquated as our industrial structure is deformed — restructuring the workplace is as vital as restructuring industry. While the need for a new industrial relations system gets passing mention in most of their prescriptive accounts, it rarely receives the same detailed attention as incomes policy and industrial policy. It is therefore necessary to dig through the ample "quality of work life" literature to supplement post-Keynesian accounts.

Concern with the politics of the workplace goes back to the early 1970s when worker unrest gained Canada the distinction of being the second-most "strike prone" work force in the industrial world. Many analysts looked longingly to Germany, Japan, Austria, Sweden and Norway where they thought they saw a new era of social harmony and social partnership developing between labour and capital.

While an army of industrial relations experts went abroad to take a closer look at these systems in action, flurries of social research surveys reported that what lay behind the industrial turbulence, not only in Canada, but in North America as a whole was a generation of workers that were alienated and bored with their jobs. Declared the widely publicized report, *Work in America*, commissioned by the U.S. Department of Health, Education and Welfare:

> Dull, repetitive, seemingly meaningless tasks ... are causing discontent among workers at all occupational levels. Worker dissatisfaction, measured by absenteeism, turnover rates, wild cat strikes, sabotage, poor quality products and a reluctance by workers to commit themselves to work tasks is crippling productivity in the workplace.

Researchers concluded that what was causing this worker alienation was not so much that jobs have changed, but rather that the knowledge, skills and expectations of the workers have increased, and that in turn jobs have not been modified sufficiently to meet worker aspirations.[1]

When surveyed in 1974, 85 per cent of workers said they were satisfied with their jobs but only half said they would take the same job again; less than a third said they felt seriously committed and involved in what they were doing; and a third said they would sooner be on welfare than take the meanest and dullest type of job at the minimum wage. The survey also revealed that Canadians put interesting work and the means to do it at the top of their list of desirable job requirements — ahead of good pay and job security. Only among unskilled workers were these two economic factors placed first.

These results are consistent with Abraham Maslow's "hierarchy of needs." According to Maslow, as society develops people's needs mature. After the more elemental needs of safety, job security and adequate pay are satisfied, people seek opportunities for "self-actualization" — freedom to be creative, to develop their skills, to exercise some discretionary power, to experience a sense of belonging, mutual support and respect. While not all workers wish to climb Maslow's ladder, many do and their numbers are growing with the changing composition of the labour force.

But relatively few jobs provide opportunities to fulfill these needs. Most workplaces are still based upon extreme job fragmentation and an old army-like command. This is the "scientific management" style which assumes, in the words of Frederick Winslow Taylor, that "most men find work distasteful, are naturally lazy, solely motivated by fear or greed ... and always do as little work as possible for the largest possible wage."[2]

The Emergence of QWL

A new school of management, which calls itself the Quality of Work Life (QWL), emerged in the early 1970s. It views work not simply as a means of earning a living and as "an aggregation of codified actions," but also as "a factor fundamental to human development." In the language of one of the members of this school, "improving the quality of working life is tantamount to debureaucratizing the firm, stripping management of its exclusive rights and making managers of all employees."[3]

Eric Trist, a pioneer in the field, describes the difference in approach in the following terms:

> The old paradigm is based on the technological imperative; people are viewed simply as extensions of the machine, as expendable spare parts; work is simplified on the one man-one job principle; controls are externalized in supervision, functional staff and precise work rules and administrative

procedures; management is authoritarian; the pyramid is tall; the climate is one of internal competition and gamesmanship; risks are avoided; innovation is low.

The new paradigm is based on joint optimization; people are viewed as complementary to the machine and are to be developed for their own sake and as key organizational assets; jobs are grouped into operational subsystems with skills being broadened and controls internalized as far as possible in the primary work group; management style is participative; the pyramid becomes flatter, the climate is one of openness and cooperation; risk-taking is encouraged; and the level of innovation goes up.[4]

A major problem noted by some industrial-democracy advocates is the prevailing view that ownership carries with it absolute authority. The badge of authority is expressed in the management-rights clauses found in every collective agreement, and employers guard the language in this clause more ferociously than in any other. But for industrial democracy to work "management enjoys no sacred rights: in theory all facets of company life are opened to the workers, with access no longer contingent on affiliation with ownership but on skill and ability."[5] However, few employers are willing to share responsibility, let alone give away any authority.

Trade Union Resistance

Collective bargaining is another problem for QWL promoters. According to them, trade unions see themselves as the loyal opposition of the workplace. This is the basis of their concept of industrial democracy. If they became involved in management, there would be no one to oppose management. This adversarial relationship has been coded in our labour laws, writes Donald Nightingale.[6] Negotiations are a test of strength between two adversaries, and from this test comes a collective agreement, the outcome of which is "either domination or compromise, rarely an integration. With domination one side gets what it wants; with compromise neither side gets what it wants." In neither case is the conflict resolved. As soon as it can, the subordinate party will alter the balance of power in its own favour. In this "conflict trap" "common interests" are found to be superseded by "divergent interests." In the final show-down, when labour and management resort to their ultimate weapons of strikes and lock-outs, the outcome is determined, not by reason or fairness, but by staying power. This is a wasteful and irrational way of settling disputes, Nightingale concludes. In any case confrontation is an unlikely context to discuss the humanization of work.

Advocates of this new industrial-relations style contend that workplace democracy is not inherently inconsistent with trade unionism and that the relationship between labour and management need not be adversarial. They also point out that workers may be facing a harder time on their end of the adversarial stick. In an economic future of slower growth and the widespread use of robots and other labour-saving equipment, strikes will be more difficult to obtain. Growing taxpayer resistance will have the same effect on the public sector. Improved quality of life in the workplace could eventually be one of the few avenues open to unions to better the conditions of their members.[7]

Addressing both union and management concerns, Don Nightingale suggests that management and unions recognize the following realities: first, in unionized organizations no program of workplace democracy will produce results if directed against the union or threatens the union's relationship with its members; second, workplace reform should be jointly planned and implemented by the union and management; third, management should recognize that these reforms are not techniques to experiment with and then to discard when the results are not favourable; fourth, changes in work structures that do not also benefit the company will not be sustained because the employer has a dual commitment not only to increase worker satisfaction but also to improve profitability; fifth, workers must also bear responsibility for their decisions; should they decide in conjunction with management to delay the introduction of new labour-displacing equipment, they must bear the costs (lower wages and benefits) in lost profits.[8]

After surveying various experiments of worker participation around the world, another analyst noted still other elements for what he called "effective worker participation in decision making."[9] Among these he included management sharing of technical and economic information at the department, plant and enterprise levels and training programs to enable workers to interpret the relevant information.

A second element are "rights commonly associated with political democracy: Freedom of speech and assembly, petition of grievances, secret balloting, due process, ... immunity of rank-and-file representatives from dismissal or transfer while in office and a written constitution alterable only by a majority or two-thirds vote...." In cases of rule violation, for instance, due process would include the presumed innocence of the accused until the accuser could prove guilt, with the laws being applied equally — to managers as well as workers. It would also require judgment by peers, a joint tribunal consisting equally of workers and managers. As the author concludes, "employees will cling more closely to the participation system if they know that they themselves, not autonomous managers, have the last word on how its rules are applied, how basic rights are upheld, and how the opportunities for participation are guaranteed."[10]

Taken together the requirements for effective participation enunciated by its advocates are formidable: stripping management of its exclusive rights and making managers of all employees; ensuring that programs in no way threaten unions' relationship with their members; sharing technical and economic information; maintaining civil rights, including freedom of speech and assembly in the workplace, due process and judgment with peer representation.

With the possible exception of universities (and then only for faculty) no workplace anywhere comes even close to satisfying these conditions. But as the Ontario Ministry of Labour cautions: "QWL is no ideal. It is not something you either do or do not have; it is something you continually work toward." Among the things QWL is supposed to work towards are certain "workers rights" — including the right to a "good job" that has "optimal variety" and "ongoing opportunities to learn"; job security; and "real decision making powers ... based on joint control and shared responsibility."

The QWL movement encompasses a number of different reforms but essentially they break down into three distinct categories: worker representation on boards of governors, profit-sharing and the redesign of jobs.

Worker-Directors

Worker representation on boards of directors is concerned with who has a voice in deciding the broad strategies of company policy — investment, location, plant closures, allocation of profits, etc. This is the co-determination model. In Germany, one-third of the members of supervisory boards in enterprises with 500 or more employees must be nominated by the employees. In companies of more than 2,000 employees, worker representation is on a parity basis, although at least one employee representative must come from the ranks of management, and the chairman, who is nominated by the shareholders, casts the deciding vote. In Norway, workers have representatives on the boards of fully or partly government-owned enterprises. Worker representation is also recognized by statute in Sweden, Denmark, Holland, Austria and France, although in France worker representatives are not permitted to vote.

In Canada, except for crown corporations and worker-owned enterprises, worker-directors are effectively precluded by corporation law. Members of boards are obligated by law to protect the interest of shareholders. In Manitoba, the NDP government has recently permitted unions to nominate one or two representatives on the board of a few of its crown corporations.

There are at least five notable examples of employees purchasing failing firms, all from the 1970s. As an example, Timbec Forest Products of Temiscaming, Quebec, was established in 1973, a year after Canadian International Paper Ltd. closed the mill down. To keep it in operation, four mill managers entered a joint arrangement with the mill workers and the Canadian Paper Workers Union. They put up nearly 40 per cent of the capital and took four of the nine seats on the board of directors; the workers contributed just over 30 per cent of the capital in cash and lower wages and benefits and appointed two members to the board. The provincial government with 13 per cent of the capital also appointed two members and private investors nominated the other members. (Other townspeople are not represented on the board although they have 8 per cent ownership in the mill.) Ownership shares have modified since then with the workers owning 36 per cent, but board representation has not altered. Timbec has been a financial success under the new ownership arrangement and continues to function with worker representative on the board. Of the other four cases, one failed, two were successful. One of these has been sold by the employees and one other continues to operate under employee ownership.[11]

Profit-Sharing

Stock purchase, incentive and bonus plans based on profit have long been considered effective means of motivating executives but it is only recently becoming more widespread as a motivating device for production and clerical workers. In the U.S., for instance, a quarter of all manufacturing companies with more than fifty employees and a third of all retailers have profit-sharing plans. Altogether there are 350,000 registered profit-sharing plans, almost all of them available to rank-and-file workers. The practice is slightly less widespread in Canada (25,000 registered plans), but all but 5 per cent are limited to senior executives.

The NCR Corporation of Canada (formerly National Cash Register) is one example where all employees are eligible to participate in the plan. Employees of this company are permitted to purchase shares in the parent company worth up to 10 per cent of their annual salary and are given a discount of 15 per cent of market value.

In France companies employing more than 100 persons are legally obliged to distribute a portion of their profits to their workers according to a formula laid down by the law, the details of which are worked out through agreements concluded in each firm. As of 1982, 10,000 agreements covering a total of five million employees had been concluded.[12]

The idea behind profit-sharing or gain-sharing, as it is now being called, is that owning a share of the firm gives employees a sense that they and the company share common interests — thus "producing increased motivation, commitment and loyalty to the organization."[13] As owners of the enterprise, workers would be less likely to strike, to fight the boss at every turn and to resist changes on the shop floor. The other advantage of profit-sharing is that it is a non-inflationary form of compensation since it is tied to "the creation of wealth." Unlike wages, it is not built into the cost structure of the firm regardless of performance.

Alternative union-based profit-sharing schemes include the Quebec Solidarity Fund and the famous Swedish Meidner Plan. In 1983 the Quebec legislature passed a law enabling workers to deduct a sum from their regular pay cheques which would be entrusted to the Quebec Solidarity Fund operated by the Quebec Federation of Labour. Supplemented by money provided by the provincial government, the fund invests in Quebec enterprises that claim to have difficulty raising money in the capital market. To date, Quebec workers have been less than enthusiastic. Except for modest contributions pressed from union staff representatives, and smaller ones from union members, the bulk of the fund's 1985 capital was contributed by the Parti Québécois government.[14]

In its original form, the Meidner Plan would have transferred ownership/control to unions over a period of twenty to thirty years. Following Meidner, similar proposals were submitted unsuccessfully by labour federations of various countries. But in late 1983 Sweden did finally enact a much watered-down version. The five regional funds established are primarily compulsory savings schemes financed mainly from payroll deductions with board members appointed by government rather than elected by workers. Limits on the size of worker funds ensure that majority ownership remains in private hands. Despite the radical dilution of the original plan, the government still hopes that the fund will reduce distributional conflict, restrain union wage demands and secure greater worker acceptance of high levels of enterprise profits.[15]

Redesigning the Job

The third and by far most important QWL reform involves restructuring the organization of work. Because it occurs on the site where work is performed and has a direct impact on each and every worker involved, redesigning jobs is deemed to have the greatest potential effect on worker satisfaction, motivation and productivity. The central idea is to alter the boundaries of jobs so that workers are given more information, more variety, more decision-making power and more autonomy. This may be achieved through a variety of devices such as job enrichment, job enlargement, job rotation, or through the creation of autonomous work groups, which provide for varying degrees of group responsibility in the execution of tasks.

Job enlargement usually involves integrating auxiliary tasks with production tasks. For example, production workers can be made responsible for repair of machinery, preventative maintenance, quality control and custodial duties. Skill requirements, technology and cost, however, set limitations on the scope of job enlargement. Quality-control equipment may be too expensive to install at all work stations.

Job enrichment involves combining small operations to form a larger one, thereby extending the work cycle from a fraction of a second or a minute to a longer period. There are limits here too, however. Experience has shown that productivity is adversely affected if the work cycle for light assembly, for instance, is extended beyond twenty to twenty-five minutes.

Where technology does not permit the extension of the work cycle, job rotation may be an alternative way of relieving boredom. At the Laidlaw lumber mill in Thunder Bay, workers rotate jobs every two hours. A second possibility is for workers to move from one work station to the next, following the product as it moves through the production process.

While these devices provide workers with greater individual autonomy and variety, they do not by themselves involve them in the decision-making process. This is accomplished by setting up autonomous groups and is regarded as the highest form of workplace democracy. It can be introduced in a single department or on a plant-wide basis.

Perhaps the most famous example is the Volvo assembly plant at Kalmar, Sweden, where the traditional car-assembly line was replaced by an entirely new production system. The factory was broken down into small work teams of fifteen to twenty workers, with each team occupying its own area. Each team is held accountable for its own part of the assembly work and can decide for itself the division of work between team members and, to a certain extent, its own working methods. This concept of a "factory within a factory" in which five or six groups function independently of one another within the larger organization has been widely emulated. Besides spreading out the distribution of skills within the group, increased social contact is fostered, thereby creating a group identity and improved worker morale.

Industrial Democracy 217

The Laidlaw Lumber Company is one of several Canadian experiments in plant-wide self-regulating groups. Besides the Volvo features, work groups select their own team co-ordinaters; hire and train new recruits; counsel and discipline members who are prone to tardiness and absenteeism; and participate with management on the purchase of new machines, tools and machinery design. Pay scale is based on the principle of "paying people for what they know rather than what they do." This system was first practised at Norskhydro, the largest enterprise in Norway and was brought over to North America by General Foods at its Topeka dog-food plant. Under this scheme, the more tasks workers master, the more valuable they are. The aim is to build up an all-around capability in the work force which allows employees to be flexibly deployed according to the needs of a changing technological and economic environment. At Laidlaw Lumber there are three rates of pay: the starting rate, the team rate — given to workers who have mastered all tasks in the group — and the plant rate for workers who have mastered all tasks in the plant.[16]

The most celebrated Canadian QWL project is located at the Shell Chemical plant in Sarnia. In 1981 — eight years after the project was conceived and two years after it was introduced — a design team was formed along with a steering committee made up of senior executives, a consultant and a representative of the Oil, Chemical and Atomic Workers Union. Interviewed at the time by *Globe and Mail* labour reporter Wilfred List, the plant superintendent frankly admitted that the main goal was not to end up with happy workers. "We're doing it basically for the buck. To get production we need committed and dedicated people who will give a good day's work for a good day's pay."[17] The project consultant was more specific: in a continuous-process plant, maintaining the plant's expensive and touchy machinery at full capacity results in dramatic improvements in profits. The key is having a flexible and educated work force that can respond quickly in dealing with disturbances as they arise.[18]

Instead of the usual plant divisions, 108 production employees are divided into six shift teams with eighteen members each and a co-ordinator. In place of fixed job descriptions and set responsibilities, nearly all of the plant's functions are performed by the shift team with a pool of skills. Within the shift team, any member moves up the salary scale by passing examinations for a new skill level rather than being promoted to a specific position.

Behind the Sarnia plant's reforms is a "flexible labour contract." According to the seven-page collective agreement:

> Employees are responsible and trustworthy, capable of working together effectively and making proper decisions related to their spheres of respon-

sibilities and work arrangements — if given the necessary authorities, information and training.

Employees should be permitted to contribute and grow to their fullest capability and potential without constraints of artificial barriers, with compensation based on their demonstrated knowledge and skills rather than on tasks being performed at any specific time.

To achieve the most effective overall results, it is deemed necessary that a climate exists which will encourage initiative, experimentation, and generation of new ideas, supported by an open and meaningful two-way communication system.

Except for this statement of philosophy and the wage schedule, there is nothing much in the contract. All problems are pretty well left to the team co-ordinator to resolve, making a grievance procedure seemingly superfluous; and since everybody can train for all tasks, except for lay-offs, seniority provisions are also obsolete. Instead, detailed specification of norms, policies and practices are located in the "Good Works Practice Handbook" which can be changed from day to day.

There is a missionary quality to much of what is written about QWL, especially among its most zealous advocates. All too often, claims are exaggerated, a few success stories given all the publicity and the far more numerous failures rarely reported. Therefore it is necessary to strip away their pleasant-sounding verbiage and look at the QWL experience with greater objectivity.

Limits of the New Industrial Relations

During and immediately following the Second World War, the balance of power in the workplace shifted towards the workers. Union recognition and offers for participation followed demonstrations of strength, which found management in danger of losing control of the shop floor. Concessions were required to re-establish industrial peace and to regain control. Just this kind of thinking led one writer, while canvassing support from British employers during the war, to observe:

> It [joint consultation] provides higher management with an additional source of information, warning and advice.... It also provides the means for transmitting to employees information and explanations without which their attitude towards the work or their management is liable to be prejudiced. Thirdly, on the psychological side, *it canalizes the legitimate aspirations of labour* to have a voice in the industry to which it contributes so much.[19]

Immediately following the Second World War, German workers and their trade unions were also in a very strong position. A great many German industrialists had been disgraced by their open co-operation with the Nazis. The anti-Nazi unions had no such taint. In many districts workers on their own initiative set about rebuilding the economy, establishing works councils alongside their unions, and demanding nationalization. It was in this context that key steel enterprises rushed to offer "co-determination" rights to workers and their unions. In 1951 the principle was extended to the mines. But soon after, the Cold War eroded the influence of the unions, German capital reclaimed its traditional status and "subsequent co-determination laws (in 1952 and 1956) put the seal of subordination on the workers' powers within industry."[20]

Developments in Canada followed a similar pattern. The Great Depression, following the defeat of the Winnipeg General Strike of 1919 and more generally the defeat of industrial unionism, left Canadian trade unions feeble and divided. The Second World War changed the situation overnight. The massive wartime industrialization campaign combined with the mobilization effort created a labour shortage that finally tilted the balance of power. Workers flocked into unions and struck often to gain recognition for their unions and for some control of the workplace. To restore industrial peace, the federal government, by an order-in-council, instructed employers to recognize unions. These gains were secured and collective bargaining was affirmed as a permanent fixture in industrial relations after a series of bitter and prolonged strikes immediately following the war.

In practice, the collective agreement, with its no-strike clause and its multi-step grievance procedure policed by the union, has become a device for containing and channeling industrial conflict. With the union legally bound to the procedure, much of the conflict is removed from the workplace and relocated to management and union offices where it is disposed of in a quasi-legal fashion, largely out of reach of the workers most directly affected. There it can remain for months and even years before the results of particular grievances are determined.

Not all conflict is so easily routinized and so safely channeled. Most shops experience slow-downs, walk-outs, sit-downs and machine sabotage. These small scale eruptions act as safety valves for worker frustration. They also act as early warning signals for managers, alerting them to the location and nature of worker discontent and identifying shop floor militants who can be disciplined and reminded of their vulnerability to suspension and firing.

But such disruptions can be costly, especially when combined with unending grievances, high rates of absenteeism and turn-over, severe alcoholism and drug abuse and increased supervision to police disaffected workers. During long periods of prosperity, these costs can be absorbed without placing a serious squeeze on profits. They can, to a degree, be passed on to consumers in the form of higher prices. This was the situation until the late 1960s, when falling demand and intense competition seriously weakened the ability of firms to recover costs by raising prices. As well, after a long period of acquiescence, which featured a low incidence of strikes — averaging less than 250 a year and fewer than 1,500 lost "man-days" annually between 1948 and 1968 — the incidence and duration of official strikes rose dramatically in the decade 1965-76. The average number of strikes per year (723) nearly tripled and the average number of man-days lost (6,583) quadrupled.

Goaded by high inflation rates, strikes were particularly severe in the years 1973-76, equalling the record high levels of 1946. Moreover, a significant proportion of the walk-outs, as high as one-third in 1974, were illegal ones, occurring during the life of collective agreements. And they took on an increasingly militant tone. Despite fines, suspensions and the jailing of prominent leaders, trade unionists generally ignored back-to-work orders. As Robert Nielson, editorial writer of the Toronto *Star*, commented back then: "Defiance of back-to-work laws and injunctions is ... almost chronic in Canada today.... The law abiding traditions of Canadians, a tradition based on understanding of the moral weight and political rationale behind the laws, is being eroded."[21]

Between 1959 and 1965 the rise in manufacturing productivity had more than matched the rise in wages, resulting in falling labour costs per unit of output. Over the period 1959-70 labour costs rose by barely 1 per cent a year. But in the years 1971-77, with output per "man hour" crawling up at a rate of 2 per cent a year, unit labour costs were rising by more than 10 per cent a year. It cost the employer 76 per cent more to produce each unit in 1977 than in 1970.

Management responded in the traditional way with its short-term weapon of speed-up and increased discipline. The state responded by legislating striking workers back to work, jailing union leaders and by imposing wage controls. But these devices were expensive — speed-up requires more supervising personnel to discipline workers — and, except for wage controls, they were not very effective.

It was at this point that employers and the state sought to complement the "stick" with the "carrot," which included the introduction of QWL. Economic survival, concern for quality and improved efficiency all combined to cause some employers to look for a more harmonious relationship with workers, which would both reduce the costs of conflict and tap into the hitherto unharvested knowledge and experience of the work force. As one writer has said:

> That domain contains the intimate and irreducible knowledge that workers have of their tools, machines, and the products they work on. It includes the ability to report or not to report unforseen problems, and the ability to put out effort of all sorts that cannot be induced by coercion. This domain

represents the last "frontier of control" over work, the major boundary of conflict between workers and management.[22]

Joint Consultation

As a device to "canalize" the "legitimate aspirations of labour" for a voice in the industry, joint consultation costs employers very little, for it in no way dissembles any of their authority and might for a time increase worker co-operation or at least diffuse worker grievance. There are two other features common to all consultation schemes. First, workers are invited to participate at a low-level in the decision-making process where only the most local and immediate shop-floor issues are dealt with. Second, they are concerned at best with implementing measures that management has already decided to pursue. In fact, consultation procedures are often introduced to forestall trade-union formation or because of management's fears of the consequences of introducing changes without any consultation. The consultations themselves are generally used as a forum for company pronouncements and employee grievances. Some union activists regard consultative bodies with barely concealed contempt, dismissing them as "let's-all-cuddle" committees.

Job Rotation, Enlargement, Enrichment

Job rotation (changing workers from one job to another) and job enlargement (extending the range of jobs undertaken by a particular operator) offer some relief from boredom, but they have little impact on the hierarchy of authority in the firm. And because they involve some cost in rearranging the workplace and often generate only slight and short-lived improvement in job satisfaction and enhanced productivity, many in management balk at introducing them.

Job enrichment (giving workers a role in making decisions that were formerly the exclusive domain of supervisors and maintenance staff) offers considerably greater scope for participation and devolution of authority. Most experiments with job enrichment record a rise in quality and output, a decline in labour turn-over and absenteeism and a less antagonistic attitude to management.

While the power of top management remains largely unaffected, the delegation of greater responsibility to individual workers and work groups reduces the need for supervision, foremen and maintenance personnel. "The jobs of those remaining will be very substantially changed. Indeed they may feel that their last remaining vestige of status and responsibility has been stripped from them."[23] Supervisors who co-operate with this process can make it work well. Supervisors who fight the process can easily sabotage it. But because of their potential benefit, antagonism of front-line supervisors is unlikely to prevent the multiplication of schemes along these lines. They will likely be phased in as the old guard is retired or dismissed and their place taken by a new breed of supervisory personnel. Besides the tangible benefits they bring, these schemes can often be introduced unilaterally and involve no serious inroads into the policy decisions of top management. They are confined to small work groups and are largely concerned with the means of implementing managerial objectives.

Worker Participation

Participation schemes worked out in co-operation with unions involve a more serious sharing of decision-making power. Neil Reimer is one trade unionist who sees no problem with a blurring of the line between workers and management. "The way I look at it," he says, "if a fellow digs a ditch all his life, his focus won't be blurred. He will know that every morning he has to go out and dig a ditch. But what future is there in that? I can't see relegating 92 per cent of our work force to a non-participative life just so the lines will be clear and no-one gets confused. One answer to satisfying jobs is to allow the workers to take on more responsibility, not less. I don't believe in perpetuating present management styles and power."[24]

Many trade unionists are sceptical and some — like Jean Claude Parrot of the Canadian Union of Postal Workers — shun the new industrial relations altogether. Managers, Parrot says, are pleased to have union leaders working with them to solve problems especially when they decide to take decisions that are unpopular with workers; for then, whether they're conscious of it or not, it becomes the leaders' role to explain these decisions to their members.[25] Wayne Roberts, an officer with the Ontario Public Service Employees Union who formerly worked for the Ontario Quality of Working Life Centre, is also suspicious:

> Labour leaders can meet employers head to head, yuppie to yuppie, share concerns and consult with the best of them. But it's to the labour movement's tremendous jeopardy if they ever think they're in that luncheon room because labour and management are equals. They're there because either government or management fears that if they're not there they would be out creating a ruckus among the membership. As soon as union leaders forget that, they're entering those rooms powerless. One of the reasons why governments encourage task forces, luncheon meetings and forums is not to facilitate dialogue and the resolution of problems but to facilitate the separation of union leaders from their members.[26]

Hundreds of companies have tried QWL and some of them have been successful. But the vast majority in unionized workplaces fall apart in a year or two. A good example of a plan that failed is the experience of Canada Post. In 1976, to help resolve its horrendous labour-management problems, Canada Post introduced a scheme in which workers supervised themselves and planned their own work, with monthly consultation sessions held in every depot. Workers became involved in production problems and shop stewards became involved in personnel problems. Management, of course, always retained responsibility for decision-making. It worked well at first and Canada Post attempted to spread it throughout the system. All the unions got involved except CUPW. Through the process the other unions became sensitive to management concerns, began to identify more with management, and they settled negotiations quickly. CUPW, not nearly as conciliatory, ended up getting superior contracts on three successive occasions. Comparing results, participating unions concluded that QWL was harmful to their interests and decided to terminate their involvement in the program.[27]

A second example is a QWL-program launched with much fanfare in 1980 at a Ford automobile plant in Oakville, Ontario.[28] The experiment was initiated by management with the assistance of consultants from the QWL Centre of the Ontario Ministry of Labour. Top plant managers and senior local union leaders formed a steering committee to oversee the development of the project. Either side could veto the other and both had the right to veto suggestions coming from the plant floor. Management gave oral assent (but not written) to a union demand that no jobs were to be lost as a result of the experiment. Workers in the two work zones chosen as pilot projects elected project committees for indefinite periods to take suggestions from the shop floor, decide on their merits and priority and bring them to the steering committee, which had final say. One of the work zones selected had a history of good relationships between workers and supervisor. The other had been one of the most militant zones in the history of the plant where resistance to management had tended to be relatively successful and where supervision was particularly authoritarian.

In the final analysis, the company achieved most of its objectives in the first work zone and failed completely in the second. In the end, it decided that the process was far too costly and risky to implement throughout the plant. Committee meetings on company time, when multiplied for all work zones, would cause major increases in over-time pay. Zones with highly militant workers were not easily persuaded by management that some of their demands were too costly to implement. Their expectations having been raised, delays and vetoes only increased their frustration and antagonism and led to various outbursts of direct action. One senior manager said of the workers in the second zone, the company could spend a "billion dollars and never satisfy their needs."[29] Instead of proceeding with the joint program, the company decided to install Employee Involvement Programmes (Quality Circles), which are voluntary, by-pass the union structure and involve no process for choosing worker representatives.

Don Wells who researched the Ford situation outlines four functions that underly this QWL experiment.[30] All four, he says, "lead to the ultimate objective of encouraging worker commitment to the implementation of management goals."

The first function involves the controlled delegation of authority to workers which, Wells adds, does not involve "a shift in the balance of power between workers since decisions made by workers are always subject to management veto." He also notes that this delegated authority is restricted to a narrow range of decisions that are job-related: provision of tools, maintenance of machines, housekeeping practices, etc. The immediate objective was to get workers to think like proprietors, to think quality, paying attention to detail, looking after equipment.

The second function is management's improved access to worker knowledge by consulting about product design and ways of streamlining the work process.

The third function is the promotion of work-group identity, through common orientation sessions, separate eating areas, different colours of paint on the walls, etc. Group identity "allows management to tap the benefits of group pressure on individuals." "Rate-busting" loses its odour. As one worker is quoted as saying, "After QWL, nobody laughs at good workers." Or as a supervisor observed on the same point, "I feel for the first time zone peer pressure. For example, 'that guy doesn't fit. Why don't we get rid of him?'"

While cohesion within the work group is encouraged, linkages between work groups is not. "It is consistent with management's overall objectives that work groups be isolated and that ties between them wither and die. This will prevent ... the cohesion of work groups linking across the plant, a *plant-wide solidarity*. [This] is feared because it is far less easy to control."

The fourth function involves the promotion of product identity through job rotation (although this was vetoed for the second work zone) and consultation about product design, among other things.

From the evidence he collected, author Wells might have added a fifth and sixth function. The fifth function is to promote an identity of interests with management. At committee meetings, supervisors can explain the kinds of pressures they are under from management and, at a broader level, management is able to try to persuade workers that they are both involved in a common struggle for survival. As one worker is quoted as saying after attending one of these meetings, "I know what the company is going through. We need to keep profits up and we need to work together." Such sentiments may cause workers to make greater concessions than were made during contract negotiations.

The sixth function is to weaken the role of the union. As bodies soliciting workers' views and concerns, the project committees provide a forum for workers to articulate the kinds of grievances and needs that are not and cannot be covered in collective agreements, such as problems which arise from supervisory practices and work arrangements and which are often specific to an area or an individual. The QWL process provides a convenient device to resolve these very localized issues and in this way may operate to usurp union functions. Through QWL, management can thus deliver various improvements which remove some of the minor irritants that make life miserable on the job. And they can make various accommodations — like allowing workers to leave early if they exceed normal productivity levels — all of which make work more tolerable. If at the same time the company forces concessions in collective bargaining, "it reinforces the perception that the union is powerless while giving local management an image of concern for, and generosity to, workers."

The biggest problem QWL poses for unions is that in a climate of mass lay-offs there are strong pressures to pit workers in one plant against workers in another in a fight for scarce jobs. The immediate result of seeking job security through co-operation with management is to create massive disunity within the union, especially above local levels. The ultimate logic of these pressures is to foster company unionism or no union at all.

The Oakville Ford experiment is not likely to be trotted out as promotional material by QWL enthusiasts. But it does not represent an insignificant effort. What it reveals is not so much that QWL is an ideal but that in real life circumstances it is idealistic and even perverse.

It did not contribute to any meaningful improvement in the direction of good jobs. Aside from rotating a few boring jobs, the only improvements involved cosmetic changes in the work environment, such as new paint and piped-in music. Management refused most of the suggestions put forward by workers because they were too costly.

While job insecurity was the prime reason the union agreed to participate in the QWL experiment, management refused to provide legally binding guarantees that the QWL process would not eliminate jobs. The union is convinced that QWL did contribute to the loss of jobs in another part of the plant. Since the objective of QWL is to increase productivity, it is hardly surprising that in a period of declining sales this should be the outcome.

The only facet of company life open to the workers was that concerning the way jobs are performed. Decisions concerning investment, finance and product design were made in company headquarters, far removed from the QWL process. Having Douglas Fraser, former international president of the UAW, sitting on the board of directors of Chrysler could hardly be said to make any difference to decisions made at that level. But even at the lowest level where QWL does function, the workers could hardly be said to have enjoyed real decision-making power. Their demands were always subject to management veto.

Finally, to the extent that it is successful, QWL tends to undermine rather than enhance workers' power. By encouraging work-group identity, it develops peer pressures to ostracize both militants and less productive fellow workers. By promoting an identity of interest with management and sympathy for the plight of supervisors, it subverts the traditional form of workers' power — the ability to resist management initiatives through stoppages, slow-downs and sabotage. By providing an alternative vehicle to the union, by sponsoring work-group egotism as opposed to plant-wide solidarity and by setting the workers of one plant against the workers in other plants, it weakens the workers' only defensive organization.

Profit-Sharing and Worker-Directors

Two other programs, employee participation on boards of directors and profit-sharing, are also advocated as devices to recoup greater co-operation and commitment from the work force. On the one hand, profit-sharing schemes are little different from traditional bonus incentives. On the other, unless very much more ambitious schemes for employee ownership are envisioned — such as those corporate owners would never accept — the status of employee shareholders is little different from that of the small investor whose impact on company policy is marginal at best. When given the opportunity, it is not surprising that most employees end up selling their shares.

As for worker-directors, they have an opportunity to decide on the broad issues of company policy but they are restricted in at least two ways. First, in the absence of changes in company law, the prime function of the board remains that of protecting the interest of shareholders and creditors. Any worker participating at this level must formally take on a role indistinguishable from any other director. In practice, worker-directors may well seek to pursue policies that are in more accord with employee than shareholder interests. But as one critic has observed after studying the European experience, in the final analysis "they cannot help making the 'firm's interest' their own, taking on an essentially competitive world view *vis a vis* other firms and their workers."[31] Second, as a minority voice, worker representatives are placed in a position of having responsibility without power. Commenting on the decision to place workers on the board of nationalized steel companies, an editorial in the *Director*, the publication of the British Institute of Directors, pointed out: "The Government wants the unions to share in the responsibility for the working of a major industry. More important, they want unions to share the responsibility for some of the expected unpopular decisions."[32]

Conclusion

Historically, employers have been compelled to yield serious concessions to their work force during periods when the balance of power tilts against them, as occurs in periods of sustained full employment. The return of mass unemployment tilts the balance of power back in their favour. But if, as in the present circumstances, this is accompanied by intense international competition, they may still be forced to contemplate some organizational devices to increase productivity. Sharing control is one of these.

In workplaces with low levels of worker organization and power, management can quite likely gain worker co-operation with a minimum of concessions. When workers already exercise some degree of strength, however, management has to go to considerable lengths, approaching the QWL "ideal," to gain acceptance of their initiatives. Workers in these firms may demand more control over decision-making than management might wish to give. As Edwin Mills, director of the U.S. Productivity Commission's Quality of Work Programs, warned, the democratization of work programs could "open a Pandora's box from which there's no return. Pretty soon you'll have the workers managing the managers. It's a first step towards encroaching on management's prerogatives of controlling and directing the means of production."[33] At the first sign of this happening, of course, employers will have no alternative but to jettison the program.

But the workers may not go after more, at least not in the short run. Participation is a theme particularly attractive to white collar, professional and para-professional workers as well as to workers for whom the traditional strike weapon has been rendered ineffective by automation. It may also come on the agenda as a consequence of government-imposed arbitration and other forms of restricting labour's right to strike. Indeed, some West European governments have begun to legislate industrial democracy because it gives the appearance of an attractive low-cost quid pro quo to offset its increasing resort to restraining or outlawing disruptive aspects of collective bargaining.

The goals of workplace democracy cannot be faulted. Existing relationships within the workplace violate fundamental democratic principles, to say nothing of civil rights and liberties. But in the final analysis, labour will have to become much more powerful to even begin to fulfill the promise of the new industrial relations. Only then will unions be in a position of placing their own agenda on the conference table, whether it be technological change, shorter work hours or health and safety. Until that day arrives and indeed as part of the struggle for getting there, unionists can respond to employers' promises of a new trusting and equal partnership by demanding concessions that correspond to these claims: elimination of punch clocks, anti-speed-up guarantees and access to company books. They can attempt to translate the promises of QWL into the collective agreement. This would ensure that benefits gained would be legally binding and that they would be accessible to all, thereby reducing the chances of management playing favourites and setting worker against worker. A good example is the "justice and dignity" clause that the Steelworkers Union has incorporated into the collective agreement with the canning industry. It gives an accused worker the right to be considered innocent, staying on the job with pay, until proven guilty. This should be elementary, but in practice accused workers are presumed guilty and are punished until they can establish their innocence.

By taking the initiative in trying to improve the quality of working life and extending workers' control, unions directly challenge traditional "management rights." These are among the new directions unions will have to adopt to achieve the kind of power implicit in the new industrial relations.

PART V
Radical Political Economy

12 Income and Class

In the mid-1970s orthodox economists were stunned by the depth and duration of the economic crisis that threatened to strangle the Western world. The failure of their theories to explain, let alone solve, what was happening sparked a renewed interest in the radical tradition of political economy. Part V explores this tradition's analysis of how the capitalist economy works and ends up with its explanation for the emerging crisis.

It begins with capital, which is divided into competing blocks, each the domain of separate corporations. To remain in business, corporations must stay ahead of their competitors by lowering costs and/or stealing markets through the introduction of new and better products. All of this requires investment — in machines, technology, raw materials, labour management, product design, advertising and marketing. And investment requires profits. This leads to a simple but fundamental principle: capitalists relentlessly chase after profits.

This chase is called the process of capital accumulation. The reward for companies who complete the circuit is profit. It turns out that there are four main parts to the course, each with its own obstacles and opportunities: finding workers and supplies; combining them in a way to extract a surplus in production; finding buyers; turning sales revenue into profits.

Whether or not companies are able to finish the race (earn a profit) depends on such factors as the wages they must pay their work force and the prices they must pay for their supplies; the output they're able to extract from their work force; the interest they're charged on borrowed capital; the taxes imposed on them by government; the volume of their sales and the prices they're able to extract from consumers. Having successfully completed the course, they are obliged to enter the next race for another round of accumulation. Those who fail to complete the course can still enter the next race but this time with a handicap or under different colours.

The radical analysis flows from this brief description of the accumulation process. The long wave of prosperity following the Second World War was generated by highly favourable circumstances for capital accumulation: low wages and interest rates; cheap raw materials and energy; a steady rise in productivity due to technological innovations, improved management practices and industrial peace; the growth of mass consumer markets throughout the Western world; rapidly expanding international trade and capital flows; and a stable international environment led by an overwhelmingly dominant U.S. economy. In this buoyant economy growth was sufficiently great to easily absorb welfare-state expenditures without impinging much on profits.

The boom began to fade when profitable investment opportunities resulting from these favourable circumstances began to dry up. Sharp increases in wages and raw material and energy prices, when combined with increased industrial unrest at the point of production and smaller productivity gains, brought about a noticeable decline in profit rates. Government efforts to shore up profits by expanding the supply of money ended up causing inflation and ultimately stagflation. New mass markets were temporarily saturated and new technological breakthroughs temporarily stalled. With the erosion of U.S. superiority, international competition for a dwindling world market heated up. In this context of falling profits and increased competition underwriting the welfare state began to loom as a major burden.

According to the analysis, then, the crisis boils down to a crisis in the accumulation of capital. Capital's solution, in turn, amounts to a restructuring on both a national and a world scale. This involves a complex of reforms, including a redivision of capital to take advantage of cheap sources of Third World labour; rapid introduction of the "fourth technological revolution," namely, the energy-saving computer and its applications; and reducing union powers, government regulations and the welfare state.

The chapters that follow lay out the building blocks of this construction of events. We begin with an analysis of class and income.

Income Distribution and the Question of Class

In the history of economic ideas, there has always been a significant theoretical stream that focused on the distribution of power and income between the major classes as the key to understanding the dynamics of growth in capitalist societies. In the period of emerging industrialization, political economists like David Ricardo identified the parasitical landlord class as the enemy of economic growth. The struggle between the landlords and the manufacturers for the economic surplus was the critical battleground, with the future of capitalism hanging in the balance. For this generation of economists the working class was of no consequence in the outcome because it was too weak to secure more than a minimal subsistence existence. A subsequent generation, working in a period where economic and political dominance had passed to the industrialists, focused on the struggles between industrial capital and the growing proletariat as the determining factor. This was the emphasis given by Karl Marx and his cohort Friedrich Engels.

Towards the end of the nineteenth century, however, economics turned away from a focus on class divisions and emphasized the social harmony that was allegedly inherent in capitalist society. Class categories were shunned altogether and the individual became the fundamental unit. And instead of economic growth, which by then seemed unproblematical, the emphasis turned to allocational problems, expressing individual choices and preferences in market exchanges. Elaborate mathematical theories were devised to demonstrate that in a perfectly competitive economy everybody behaved in a manner that would maximize their satisfactions as consumers and their preferences between work and leisure. The free market operated to ensure, not only that the goods produced were the ones that matched people's preferences, but that they were produced in the least costly way. In these exchanges, the distribution of income was accepted as given but this presented no moral problem because still another theory was devised to show that in a market economy everybody received income commensurate with their productivity. Capital, labour and land were viewed as factors of production, each contributing something to productivity and receiving payment (profit, wages, rent) directly proportional to its particular contribution. The old notion of a surplus expropriated from the producing classes through ownership of the means of production disappears altogether.[1]

Writing in the depths of the Great Depression, Keynes turned back to the problem of economic growth but in doing so he did not challenge this neo-classical treatment except to target the rentier class as the enemy of progress. Subsequent Keynesians incorporated a social harmony analysis to produce the so-called neo-classical synthesis. In their effort to resurrect Keynes in response to the economic crisis and to monetarism, the post-Keynesians have returned to the older tradition that recognized the importance of class divisions. The reforms they propose, such as incomes policy and industrial democracy, take direct aim at moderating the results of class conflict, which they see as central to the emergence of the crisis and the present impasse. But they do so without questioning the fundamental institutions of capitalist society. Ironically, it was Pierre Elliott Trudeau, writing in 1956 about the early corporatism of Quebec society, who best summarized the inherent limitations of this approach: "Objective political economy and sociology have certainly not yet shown how a legal superstructure, which makes no essential changes in capitalist institutions, could reconcile the opposed interests of capital and labour, except in limited areas and for limited periods."[2]

What is the structural basis of these "opposed interests of labour and capital"? In the final analysis it still stems from the class divisions in capitalist society reflected in the conflict over the distribution of income, wealth and control of the workplace. As the young Trudeau remarked thirty years ago, these conflicts are too deeply embedded in the structure of capitalism to be overcome by "superstructural" reforms.

Dividing the Pie

After all the material expenses of production are dispensed with, the value of the products of industry are divided between the owners of capital and wage and salary earners. What is income for employees is cost for employers. Where it is in the interest of employers to minimize their wage costs, it is in the interest of employees to maximize their wage incomes. The outcome depends primarily on the power relationship between the two parties. This conflict persists regardless of the level of profits and wages that has been achieved. Businesses are compelled by competition to protect and increase their profits. Workers are compelled by a desire for a better lifestyle to demand higher wages.

Ideology plays a powerful role in shaping ideas about what constitutes reasonable pay. The expression "a fair day's wage for a fair day's work" assumes that workers have a moral obligation to their employer and takes for granted the existing distribution of income and the prevailing pattern of wage and salary differentials, which tend to parallel other inequalities in the workplace. The highest paid usually have the most pleasant working conditions, flexible working hours, secure employment and opportunities for advancement and creativity. The lower paid are often the most exposed to accidents and work-related diseases; they have the dullest jobs and the least job security and fringe benefits. Notions of fairness are as often as not used as euphemisms for preserving the status quo. As a British trade unionist remarked about this expression: "This paternalistic concept is the very opposite of all the union's objectives. There can never be anything fair about a master and servant relationship. All that any agreement ever achieves is a temporarily acceptable day's pay for a temporarily acceptable day's work. Both are always re-negotiable."[3]

Yet top salaries are rarely challenged. The salary of chief executive officers of top Canadian corporations stood at $500,000 plus in 1983. Seagram's Edgar Bronfman received over a million dollars in cash and security benefits; W.F. Light, chief executive officer of Northern Telecom, received a cash salary of $875,000; John Gallagher of near-bankrupt Dome Petroleum received a salary of $3.5 million; and the president of Dome, William Richards, received salary and security benefits amounting to $2 million.

But these compensations are only the beginning. A variety of schemes have been concocted to bolster their take-home pay, including interest-free loans, stock options, deferred pay which is given after retirement when taxes are lower. Lesser officers receive similar, if somewhat less splendid treatment: lavish offices with Persian carpets, sound-proof ceilings, bars and refrigerators, separate suites that serve as private dining rooms, and even private elevators round out the picture. The latest symbol to establish rank among chief executive officers is the private jet, replacing the private railway car and yacht. Apart from all this, the salaries of business executives and top-level civil servants are supplemented by travel, dinner, nights on the town and other expense account items.

Not all the fancy salaries and privileges are in the corporate sector. Senior deputy ministers in Ottawa make more than $100,000; in the provinces they take home $60,000-$75,000. Physicians and university presidents make $90,000-$100,000; lawyers and dentists, an average of $60,000-$70,000. Super-star broadcasters, entertainers and athletes have made it into the $100,000 (and over) league.

By comparison, the average wage earner makes $18,000. This ranges from $31,000 for hard-rock miners, $29,000 for school teachers, $27,000 for tool and die makers, $23,600 for automobile assembly workers, $21,000 for garbage collectors to $16,300 for senior office secretaries, $13,700 for sewing machine operators, $12,000-$13,500 for bank tellers, telephone operators, day-care workers, typists and shipping clerks, $10,000-$11,000 for female sales clerks, laundry pressers, crop farm workers, service station attendants, and kitchen helpers and $9,500 for charwomen.

It is hard to believe that the president of a corporation is thirty times more productive than a factory worker or forty times more productive than an office clerk. But except for economists, who ever said that income is a reward for productivity? If anything, these wage and salary figures understate the differences. The money received by people in the $40,000 and over category is virtually a guaranteed annual income because they are rarely laid off. The ordinary wage earner can expect to be laid off at any time — when inventories are excessive, when recessions occur or technology changes, or for disciplinary reasons. In fact, about one of every four workers lose their jobs at least once every year.

The division of income among various strata of Canadian society has remained largely constant between the 1950s and the mid-1980s, with

TABLE 12:1
Percentage Distribution of Families and Unattached Individuals by Income Fifths

Year	Bottom Fifth	Second Fifth	Middle Fifth	Second Highest Fifth	Highest Fifth
1951	4.4	11.2	18.3	23.3	42.8
1961	4.2	11.9	18.3	24.5	41.1
1971	3.6	10.6	17.6	24.9	43.3
1980	4.1	10.5	17.6	25.3	42.5
1982 (preliminary)	4.5	10.6	17.3	25.0	42.7

Source: Statistics Canada, Income Distribution by Size, Cat. 13-207; 1982 preliminary figures, Cat. 13-206.

the bottom fifth getting roughly 4.5 per cent of the income and the top fifth, at 43 per cent, getting nearly 10 times that proportion (see Table 12:1).

Despite all the allegations against the welfare state and the tax structure — as destroyers of the incentive system — taken as a whole, these intrusions by government have had remarkably little impact on income inequality. Income taxes are highly visible but other taxes also affect the distribution of income. The sales tax and medicare premiums, for example, are highly regressive, taking a larger fraction of the income of the poor than of the rich. And tax exemptions enjoyed primarily by the rich have removed much of the progressivity from the income tax. Thus the rich gain the ideological advantage of high nominal rates and the economic advantages of low effective rates.

The overall impact of the tax system leaves the distribution of income pretty much the same. Some redistribution occurs as a result of government-spending policies but much less than is commonly imagined because the cash benefits of social security programs are increasingly tied to the size of family income and because the rich tend to make more use of government-provided services like health and education. Taking into account all tax and spending programs in 1969, the last year for which detailed estimates are available, the state managed to redistribute only 3.6 per cent of the national income to the poorest fifth of the population. The freezing of welfare-state measures in the early 1970s, combined with radical changes in the tax structure benefiting the rich, has no doubt resulted in a sharp reversal in this already minimal redistribution exercise.[4]

Taxation statistics show that the average income earned by the richest 10 per cent of the population is forty to fifty times the average

TABLE 12:2
Estimated Wealth per Canadian Adult, 1980[1]

	Number of Adults	Total Net Worth of All Adults in Category ($ million)	Share of Total Assets Held by All Adults in Category (%)	Average Wealth per Adult ($)
Top 1%	165,000	146,361	18.8	887,040
Next 4%	661,000	187,623	24.1	283,847
Next 5%	826,000	110,549	14.2	133,837
(Total top 10%)	1,653,000	444,534	57.1	268,925
Next 10%	1,653,000	126,120	16.2	76,297
(Total top 20%)	3,306,000	570,654	73.3	172,611
Next 40%	6,612,000	200,857	25.8	30,377
Bottom 40%	6,612,000	6,228	0.8	1,002
Totals	16,530,000	778,519	100.0	47,097

[1] Figures on wealth per adult calculated by dividing wealth per household by number of adults in household.

Source: Lars Osberg, *Economic Inequality in Canada* (Toronto: Butterworths, 1981), p. 37

income earned by the poorest 10 per cent. But this disparity, wide as it is, pales in comparison to the inequalities of wealth holdings. (Wealth includes houses, automobiles, cottages, life insurance, pensions and bank deposits as well as ownership in corporate stocks which is even more concentrated than overall wealth.) Whereas the richest 10 per cent of earners receive nearly 30 per cent of the income compared to only 1 per cent by the bottom 10 per cent, they own over 50 per cent of the wealth while the bottom 10 per cent have negative wealth-holdings, which means they are in debt overall. Indeed, the bottom 40 per cent of adults own less than 1 per cent of the wealth (see Table 12:2). The average wealth-holdings in the top 1 per cent totalled nearly $900,000 in 1980 compared to an average of barely $1,000 in the bottom 40 per cent. Only a fraction of the population, a mere 8 per cent, owns any stocks at all and only 3.2 per cent are reported as owning $5,000 or more.

Even these statistics understate the degree of wealth concentration. A *Globe and Mail* reporter found that nine "super rich families and individuals" owned shares on the Toronto Stock Exchange with a market value of $9 billion out of a total index value of about $80 billion. The market value of the shares in which this group of nine held a controlling interest is $37 billion or about half of the value of the Toronto Stock

TABLE 12:3
Canadian Family Stock Holdings

Family	TSE Stockholdings Market Value ($ billion)	Value of Controlled Companies ($ billion)	Main Companies
Thomson	2.3	3.8	International Thomson / Thomson Newspapers / Hudson's Bay
Bronfman (CEMP)	2.0	5.0	Seagram / Cadillac Fairview
Desmarais	1.4	12.9	Power Corp. / Canadian Pacific / CP Enterprises
Bronfman (EDPER)	1.0	9.8[1]	Brascan / Noranda / Trizec / Labatt
Reichmann	1.0	0.6[2]	Hiram Walker / Abitibi
Weston	0.7	1.3	George Weston / Loblaws
Black	0.3	1.1	Argus / Dominion Stores / Norcen
Southern	0.2	1.9	ATCO / Canadian Utilities
Seaman	0.2	1.1	Bow Valley

[1] Although the Reichmanns own almost 50% of companies that hold trilon and related companies, control rests with EDPER Bronfmans.
[2] Excludes Hiram Walker.

Source: Dan Westell, "Big Chunk of Business in Hands of a Few," *Globe and Mail*, August 25, 1984.

Exchange's 300 composite index (see Table 12:3). As the reporter, Dan Westell, concluded: "Big business frequently seems faceless, owned by institutions and run by professional managers. But ultimately share certificates belong to people, and a surprisingly large chunk of Canadian business is dominated by very few."[5] Since his report was published, major acquisitions by members of the group of nine — the Reichman takeover of Gulf and Hiram-Walker, for example — will have further boosted their control over Canada's corporate wealth.

Much of this concentration of corporate wealth has occurred over

TABLE 12:4
Sources of Income among Top 2 per cent of Earners, 1981

	50-100		100-150		150-200		200-250		250 +	
	$ billion	%	$ billion	%	$ billion	%	$ billion	%	$ billion	%
Total Assessed Income	18.0	100	4.1	100	1.7	100	0.9	100	2.5	100
-wages and salaries	8.9	49	1.3	32	0.5	29	0.3	33	0.7	28
-professional income	2.0	11	0.7	17	0.2	12	0.1	11	0.1	4
-investment income	4.8	27	1.7	41	0.8	47	0.5	56	1.5	60
-other	2.3	13	0.4	10	0.2	12	0.0	0	0.2	8

Source: National Revenue, Taxation Statistics, 1983.

the past decade as a result of the takeover binge which saw the acquisition of well over $75 billion of corporate assets through a maze of holding companies and conglomerates. Over three-quarters of the wealth of the new "acquisitors," to use Peter Newman's apt phrase, added nothing whatever to the production capacity of the economy. Basically it derived from speculative "flipping" of paper titles, stock manipulation and corporate reorganization. The great new corporate barons, like Conrad Black, Edward, Edgar and Peter Bronfman, Paul Desmarais, Nelson Skalbania and Peter Pocklington, have yet to build a single new factory or open a single new mine.

These capitalists top the list of 5,800 individuals who, according to Revenue Canada's *Taxation Statistics*, earned more than $250,000 in 1981. Some 60 per cent of their income came from investment earnings and less than 30 per cent of their income came from salaries. Barely 2 per cent of all tax-filers have assessed incomes in excess of $50,000, over a third of which comes from investment earning (see Table 12:4).

A measure of the size of capital income may be gleaned from the fact that, if the investment earnings of the $50,000 plus club were directly transferred to the low-income population, it would be just sufficient to bring all poor households up to the low-income (minimum but adequate) cut-off line established by various social agencies. The Canadian Council on Social Development estimates that in 1981 this so-called poverty gap was $9.3 billion, exactly equal to the sum of investment earnings among the top 2 per cent. Transferring this privately held economic surplus would go a long way towards alleviating the purely financial aspects of low income. It is interesting to note that such a transfer would have had no such impact twenty or thirty years ago.

The most profound and massive inequalities do not stem from the occupational market of supply and demand, artificially designed or otherwise. Personal wealth in the tens and hundreds of millions of dollars cannot be amassed from salaried income, no matter how extravagant they may be. Rather, it derives from ownership of the means of production, as often as not, from absentee ownership. What gives this small capitalist class its power is not just the size of its possessions and incomes but also its control over the use of billions of dollars of physical assets, in short, its control over the productive capacity of the economy.

Explaining Income Differentials

The standard explanation offered by orthodoxy derives from "human capital theory," which originated with the American economist Gary Becker.[6] Basically, it treats individuals as petty capitalists, investing in themselves. They must invest time in obtaining higher skills, thus sacrificing present consumption, in order to earn higher future lifetime earnings. Wages are seen to represent returns to capital in the form of occupational skills. The assumption is that skilled labour is more productive than unskilled labour and since wages are allegedly determined by productivity, employers are willing to pay higher wages to skilled labour. Higher earnings are therefore a return for past individual investment decisions regarding academic and on-the-job training.

This is an economic theory in which economic institutions, like giant corporations, make no appearance. It cannot account for the fact that men are paid 30 to 40 per cent more than women with equal skills and training. It has no explanation for unequal resource endowments and unequal opportunities. Finally, while education and training certainly affect income differentials within a class location, human capital theory can tell us nothing about the systematic differences of income between classes.

Orthodox sociology provides an alternative explanation. It argues that income differentials are determined by the status or functional importance attached to different occupations on the one hand, and relative scarcity of qualified personnel on the other. All societies, in order to survive, must recruit their members to ensure that important positions are filled by the most qualified people. The most important and difficult-to-fill positions must carry with them the highest rewards. Alternatively, people with inherent talent must be sufficiently rewarded so they will acquire the skills and training necessary to fill society's most important tasks. Once there they have the bargaining power to sustain or raise their higher level income: "Social inequality is thus an unconciously evolved device by which societies insure that the most important positions are conscientiously filled by the more qualified persons."[7]

Besides rationalizing existing inequalities, this functionalist or income-by-merit argument has little to offer. First, in view of the obvious presence of ineptitude in some highly remunerated positions, it is obvious that the most important positions are *not* always occupied by the most qualified people.

Second, assuming that the most qualified people do occupy the most important positions, how do we measure relative importance? Is the $150,000 tax lawyer or accountant working on corporate tax deductions worth more to society than the $18,500 logger? Is the $125,000 marketing analyst developing an advertising campaign to sell more detergent worth more than the $24,500 truck driver? As one critic pointed out, "to suggest, for example, that managers are more highly rewarded than factory workers because they make a greater contribution to the productive system is to offer more of a value judgement than an explanation."[8]

Third, if we could establish some objective measure that would tell us which are the most important jobs, is it necessarily the case that unduly high rewards are required to induce them to take them? How unequal must rewards be? Must there be multi-millionaires and paupers? Could we function more effectively with spreads of ten to one? Five to one? Two to one? Put another way, to what extent must a society bribe its members into becoming high-ranking executives and administrators, movie and sports stars, physicians, scientists, corporation lawyers and university deans? It seems doubtful that people who are capable of doing creative work would be satisfied taking jobs that are repetitive, dull and physically exhausting.

The fundamental premise of Marxist theory is that within any given society (mode of production), income is determined in fundamentally different ways according to class location. Capitalists earn their income (profit) by maximizing the difference between the value of the products their employees produce and the value of the employees' power (wages). The capitalists' ownership of the means of production places them in a position to employ the labour power of others and to appropriate this surplus value. Petty bourgeois producers own their own means of production but employ only themselves. Thus all of their income is self-earned, generated by their own labour. Workers neither own their means of production nor control the labour of others. They depend entirely upon the sale of their labour power to others for their incomes.

Incomes within a given class location can vary according to a number of particular factors. For example, giant firms that employ large numbers of workers use advanced technology and enjoy a large degree of monopoly power in the markets they supply, earn greater profits than small firms that employ fewer workers, use average technology and compete in markets where they enjoy no monopoly power. Similarly, workers with better skills, training or talents or strong collective organizations earn higher incomes than workers with average skills and training and workers without collective organizations. Women and members of minority groups generally tend to receive lower incomes than white male members of the work force.

More precisely, class location determines a range of possible incomes. Within these class limits, income varies according to personal characteristics, market relationships (supply and demand) and organizational and technical factors. The implication of the Marxist analysis is that certain incomes are systematically more likely than others for each class location. The vast majority of working-class incomes range from $10,000 to $30,000 a year in 1985. Middle-management incomes range from $50,000 to $75,000, while the executive salary and investment income of large capitalists can vary from $200,000 to more than $5 million. These latter incomes are beyond the reach of people located in working-class positions. No amount of intelligence, education, scarcities or technical functions will garner a worker an income as high as that of a large capitalist, a senior manager or physician.

A second theme in Marxist distribution theory is that inequality among workers is an inherent feature of the capitalist labour market. While this is the same conclusion as the one derived from the human-capital theory, the reasoning is different. The Marxists argue that, since the intrinsic rewards of labouring are minimal or non-existent in most jobs, without an incentive system based on differential material rewards, workers are not likely to be motivated to toil diligently and to acquire and apply the skills necessary to increase their labour power. In order to remain economically viable, therefore, the capitalist mode of production requires significant inequalities in the distribution of labour income. If for no other reason it is needed so that "good workers" can be rewarded and "bad workers" punished. All of which is not to say that the extent of prevailing inequalities can be rationalized entirely along functional lines.

A necessary consequence of this analysis is that the welfare system, which by definition provides income without work, can never be allowed to provide an adequate living income. In a society that requires and depends on the wage incentive to force people to work, few would slave away at menial jobs if an adequate income were available without work. While in ordinary times, most social assistance recipients are either permanently disabled or ill (41 per cent) or families headed by an unmarried female (26 per cent), the remainder are to some degree or another employable.[9] During periods of severe recession, as many as half may be employable. Since adequate welfare income would clearly threaten work incentives, the welfare state cannot and has not significantly altered the structure of inequality in Canada or in any other capitalist country.

Inequality lingers on, Marxists argue, because capitalism both requires it and reproduces it. Any equalization introduced by progressive taxation, minimum wages, the welfare state and the like is easily overcome by market forces and the exclusive power that comes with business ownership. Business owners control their incomes because of the economic and political leverage of ownership itself. However well-intentioned, government intervention is bound to produce short-lived and modest results because it leaves unchanged the structure of ownership, the capitalist labour market and the profit system.

13 | Where Do Profits Come From?

When workers enter a factory or an office they must agree to a labour contract. To gain access to the premises and to the means of production owned by the employer, they must agree to relinquish all ownership rights to the goods and services they produce. They must also agree to carry on their work according to the employer's conditions, such as working hours and the organization and intensity of work. In return for selling their labour power under these terms the employees receive a wage or salary that covers their living expenses. This is the "natural" law of the workplace. Through hard struggles over the years, workers have been able to regain some control over their wages and work conditions. Capitalist income is based on workers producing more than the value of their labour power, more than it costs the employer to employ them. According to Marxist analysis, regardless of the specific form of capitalist income (profit, interest, rent or extraordinary executive salaries), the source of that income ultimately derives from this surplus value expropriated from workers.

Suppose a corporation buys labour, leather and machinery to produce shoes. Assuming that the corporation in question does not have a monopoly as a buyer of leather and that its supplier does not have a monopoly as a producer of leather, what it pays is the full market value of the leather — no more, no less. No profit is gained in the purchase of the leather. We make the same assumption about the purchase of machinery.

Let's also assume that the company pays $10 to cover the cost of leather and equipment used in a pair of shoes and that workers are paid $50 a day. In our example, they work for four hours a day and in that time each worker produces two pairs of shoes. The shoes sell for $35 a pair. Each worker, therefore, produces, on average, $70 worth of shoes per working day. The revenue exactly covers wages and other costs: assuming one hired worker, expenses per day include $50 in wages plus $20 in other costs (two pairs of shoes x $10 in other costs per pair) for a total of $70.

There are no profits here for the owner. If that was all there was to business, he would close up shop. But he is not without other options. The number of hours of work is a variable he controls. Because he owns the machinery and the materials and the workers own none, he can order them to work more hours. If they want to keep their jobs he can make them work, say, eight hours a day. Now they produce four pairs of shoes in a working day. The owner receives $140 on the daily output of each worker ($35 x 4). They still pay $50 per worker, and with an extra $20 to cover the additional cost of leather and depreciation, his total cost per worker per day is $90. That leaves a profit of $50 per worker. If he employs a hundred workers, the company earns a total profit of $5,000 per day.

This simple example illustrates one way of looking at the origin of profits. It derives from the extra time (surplus labour) workers spend on the job after they have produced enough goods to cover the value of their wages. Surplus value is the extra value workers produce beyond what is necessary to cover the value of their wages.

Studies show that G.M. workers must work 3 hours and 41 minutes each day to produce the value equivalent to their wages. The other 4 hours and 19 minutes they work for the owners. In 1979, G.M. (U.S.) produced a value-added of $31.6 billion. (Value-added is what's left over from sales revenue after payment to suppliers is deducted.) Of that total, $14.6 billion was paid to production workers. Of the remaining $17 billion, $2.9 billion went to profits, $4.2 billion to management salaries, $5.4 billion for investment and $4.5 billion to taxes. The surplus value produced in the 4 hours and 19 minutes was thus distributed among profits to the owners, management salaries and fees, investment in more capital equipment, and taxes.

What about machinery? Machinery does not add new value; its value is merely transferred into the value of the finished product. No doubt improvements in technology increase the productivity of the labour force — using new machinery, a worker can produce more per hour per day. The result is more surplus labour time and therefore more surplus value. Capitalists argue that since they put up the capital to invest in machinery they are entitled to the extra profits — in the surplus value — it contributes.

This argument raises serious questions. If the capital invested in machines comes from the surplus value produced by the company's employees, why shouldn't they have claim to the benefits the machinery provides? Why shouldn't the workers who produced the machinery also have a claim on the benefits? If the machinery increases productivity, shouldn't the workers who operate and maintain the machinery work fewer hours, since fewer hours are needed to cover the cost of the goods embodied in their wages?

The problem with the owners' argument is that while capital equipment is productive this says nothing about the productivity of the capitalist. It confuses capital as physical means of production and capital as legal claim based on property rights.

What about risks? Profit, investors argue, is their reward for the risks they take on when they start or expand a business. What they are risking, they say, is that there will be no profit, that the business will fail. What they ignore with this argument is that workers also bear the cost of failure. When a business is forced to close or when new technology makes a skill redundant, workers lose their jobs and their livelihood. If investors are entitled to a reward for risk-taking, don't workers have at least an equal claim? And if the money risked actually comes from the savings extracted from workers, why shouldn't the real savers get the full reward?

Finally, profits from risk-taking presume that losses are also being incurred. If nobody is failing, there can be little risk involved. The size of the reward for risk-taking depends on the odds of failure. Risk profits for successful investors are just counterbalanced by losses of unsuccessful investors. The total profit, as a return on risk, is, therefore, roughly zero.

In the final analysis, the Marxists argue, capitalists' claims to profit cannot rest on the productivity of capital or on risk. Profit is, rather, a price capitalists can command because they own the means of production and because the vast majority of people do not.

A number of factors can affect the amount of profit a firm can extract. For instance, a firm with monopoly power can buy its machinery and materials at prices less than their value and sell its finished product at prices that exceed their value. It can augment its profit at the expense of smaller, competitive firms. Monopolization does not increase the total amount of surplus value. Rather, through it the total surplus value generated in the sphere of production gets redistributed among different capitals.

Similarly, where workers have to pay monopoly prices for commodities that are part of their standard consumption, the monopoly price is paid by a deduction from real wages. Again, monopolization has not increased the total amount of value produced. But extra surplus value is appropriated from workers at the point at which they exchange their wages for consumer goods. This is the so-called "corporate rip-off" that stems from the ability of giant firms to charge prices far in excess of their costs. While it is not the source of "normal" profit, it is a major source of the super-profits regularly earned by firms that can use their favourable market position to extract high prices from consumers.

Firms that introduce advanced technology into their production processes are able to produce commodities with less direct labour time than firms who use average technology. For example, a worker in one shoe-manufacturing firm using advanced technology may be able to produce six pairs of shoes a day instead of four. The direct labour time involved per unit has been reduced by half. Since the firm has reduced its cost and is still able to sell at the prevailing price, it is able to realize extra transitional profits until other firms also introduce the same technology.

Finally, in periods of economic crisis when many firms go bankrupt, the surviving ones are able to purchase their assets at prices well below value. This again allows them to make additional profits.

What makes profits higher or lower? Six distinct factors come into the picture.

- Length of the working day. The longer it is the greater will be the labour time available to produce surplus value and, therefore, the greater will be the profits. If workers can shorten the working day, a greater portion of their time is spent covering their own wages and a smaller portion is left to produce profits.
- How hard workers work. The more workers can be pushed to speed up production or the more machines they can be forced to tend, the greater will be the profit.
- Level of workers' productivity. With more powerful machinery or a more efficient organization of work, workers need less time to produce a given amount of output with a given exertion of energy. Providing the new machines or methods cost less than the additional value of output made possible, profits will be greater. Greater productivity means that it takes workers less time to produce enough goods to cover the value of their wages.
- Pay level. The higher the wages, the lower the profit.
- Degree of monopoly power. In the age of monopoly capitalism, surplus value is appropriated from workers through at least two mechanisms — from the labour process itself and through the manipulation of monopoly prices. As well, giant corporations are also in a position to squeeze extra profits at the expense of firms in the competitive sector.
- Extent to which firms are able to socialize their costs. When the state assumes responsibility for financing the training of workers and maintaining their health it reduces the firms' employment costs, for employers would otherwise have to finance training from their own revenues and would otherwise have to pay higher wages so that workers could afford to pay for health care. Similarly, state capital investment in hydro-electricity, telephone, communication, and transportation facilities, etc., adds to private surplus value since these essential inputs would otherwise be sold to them at higher prices if they were produced by private enterprise. On the other

hand, some state expenditures support "non-productive" members of the population, and therefore absorb surplus value rather than add to it.

In the final analysis, it is the outcome of these different processes that determines the distribution of income. To a very large extent, it is decided by the balance of class forces: the economic conflict between capital and labour over the shares of profits and wages in national incomes and over the conditions and intensity of the work process; the competitive conflict between firms for profit; the political conflict over state policies, state expenditures and taxation.

Ever since capitalism began, workers have fought for higher wages, struggled to shorten the work week and resisted speed-up and stretch-out. Capitalists, in turn, caught in a constant competition among rival firms, have been forced to take whatever steps necessary to win the race for survival. Finally, on the political plane labour and capital have always, and particularly so in recent years, fought over the content of state expenditure and the distribution of the tax burden.

The factors affecting the profit level are examined in greater detail in this and the following chapter.

The Wage Level

Because workers are often paid by the hour and because pay appears to be related to productivity, the wages workers receive *appear* to depend on their hours of work and their productivity. But as in other instances, appearances are deceiving.

In a capitalist economy where labour power is a commodity like other commodities, its price, like the prices of other commodities, stays pretty close to the cost of producing it. Like other prices, if the labour-power price falls far below the "cost of production," sellers (workers) won't be able to put their labour on the market. If it rises much above its cost, the competition of other sellers entering the market will push it back down.

What is the "reproduction cost" of labour-power? Workers can't expend the energy to work unless they are fed. They can't show up to work unless they get there. They must also be housed and maintain their health. As well, they require for their spiritual subsistence some form of recreation. And if their work entails skills, these may have to be acquired through special training programs. All this costs money. If labour power is to be put onto the market, wages and salaries must be high enough to cover these costs.

If workers manage to push wages much above their costs, employers can fire them and hire workers prepared to work for less. Or they can decide that, at prevailing wages, the enterprise is not worth operating. They can close up shop or pack their bags and relocate in another region or country where workers are willing to take less.

In short, the advantage of being owners gives them the power to keep wages from rising much above the cost of worker maintenance. If wages fall much below that cost, on the other hand, workers can try to find employers who will pay them a higher wage. In any case, it is this cost of reproducing labour power, rather than the contribution workers make to production, that determines average wages.

This does not preclude some margin for manoeuvring and differentiation. In prosperous times, for example, when sales and profits are booming, employers are more likely to be willing to pay higher wages than risk a strike or work slow-down. Workers with skills that are scarce can usually bargain for wages that are considerably higher than the average. Workers in powerful unions or who are employed by particularly prosperous companies can sometimes win a wage bonus. On the other hand, women, youth and members of racial minorities generally receive wages well below the average and even below the cost of reproducing their labour power. Nevertheless, at any one time, there are fairly strict limits to the bargaining position of all but the most extraordinarily placed workers.

How can these generalizations be systematized?

Marxists look at the wage or salary of any category of workers as consisting of three component parts: the first representing the existing social standard for the average worker in society; the second representing a wage-privilege or wage-discrimination element; and the third representing the increased cost involved in reproducing labour's productive services because of better skills.

The Standard Wage

The existing social standard of living for the worker of average skills is a product of a variety of intersecting factors aside from climactic differences. They include the stage of technological and corporate development; the position of the national economy in the global world economy (for example, Canadian workers versus Guatemalan workers); the accumulated results of struggles between labour and capital both at the level of the enterprise and at the level of the state which, through minimum wage, industrial relations and other legislation, can affect the workings of the labour market.

With their large capital investments and long-term planning horizons, giant corporations require stable market demand but also a stable supply environment so that costs and in particular labour costs can be a known factor. This stable supply environment includes a reliable and disciplined labour force whose behaviour is socially controlled. From the beginning of the factory system, workers have been whipped into shape by the threat of being fired, by machine-paced production, by close and constant supervision and by crude systems of personally administered punishments and rewards. These control techniques become increasingly unsatisfactory with the expanding size of production units. Growing unionization meant that frequent threats and firings to maintain discipline resulted in long and costly strikes.

Adjusting to this reality, corporate employers totally restructured the organization of the workplace. Wherever possible they divided employments into those where productivity was related to tenure on the job and those where employment stability had no noticeable impact. Among the former they created career ladders and instituted rewards for tenure and seniority. In short, they offered a wage premium and a variety of fringe benefits — including pensions, longer vacations, decent cafeterias, better and safer working conditions — in order to build up a more reliable, stable and predictable work force. This system is usually codified in collective agreements and policed by trade unions. Long-term contracts guarantee a certain degree of labour peace for a specified period. While constraining the behaviour of management, unions also help regulate the supply of labour and the behaviour of the worker in a manner consistent with the goals of the enterprise.

Firms located in competitive industries with unstable markets cannot afford to pay a wage and fringe bonus. Their scale of operation is too small, their productvity too low, their survival always or frequently in question. In any event, with smaller investments in fixed capital and shorter time horizons, stable employee relations is less imperative. This is even more the case for firms located in seasonal industries. In other instances, large corporations that can afford to pay a higher wage deliberately attempt to isolate some of the jobs where tenure is less important for productivity — like keypunching, typing and messenger work — or they contract some of this work out to smaller companies.

Radical economists believe that the labour market is not homogeneous but segmented into two broad categories — the primary job market and the secondary job market.

Primary jobs pay better, offer greater job security and some opportunity to climb a job ladder of connected routine tasks. Employees' earnings rise significantly over a ten-to-fifteen year period. Because the path for advancement almost always depends on seniority within the firm, workers have a marked incentive to remain with one employer.

The biggest single group of the primary category includes the jobs of what may be called the traditional working class in mass-production industries; routinized jobs in auto and auto parts assembly and other transportation industries; steel making, rubber and tire manufacturing, electrical products, farm implement production, machinery manufacture, metal fabrication, some appliance manufacture, printing and publishing, consumer-products assembly, food and beverage industry, petroleum refineries, pulp and paper mills and the like. Other primary jobs are found in mining, transportation, utilities, retailing and wholesaling, and the myriad of occupations — clerical, maintenance and production — within the public sector.

Secondary jobs pay very low wages, offer virtually no job security or room for advancement and no protection from employer harassment. These essentially dead-end jobs include most farm labour, many production jobs in small-scale manufacturing, construction, many sales and service jobs in retail stores and restaurants, temporary and low-level jobs in offices and the jobs of attendants, guards, personal-care workers, janitors and messengers jobs. Within the manufacturing sector alone, about a third of all jobs are of this dead-end variety.[1] Within the economy as a whole, the proportion is likely a little higher.

Primary jobs tend to be unionized while secondary jobs seldom are. In fact, the dividing line between the two is probably as much a function of class conflict as of technology. Union organization can change secondary jobs into primary ones, and employers can shift jobs in the other direction. Californian farm workers were part of a classic secondary labour market until the United Farm Workers organized them and won higher pay, a seniority system, improved working conditions, a hiring-hall system and grievance procedures. Similarly, the unionization of Safeway, Dominion and other supermarket workers in Canada transformed some secondary jobs, as would the organization of the banks.

On the other hand, one of the features of the current economic crisis has been the mass lay-off of formerly secure salaried employees, the substitution of part-time for full-time labour and a greater tendency to contract out work formerly done in-house. The crisis is transforming many primary jobs into secondary ones.

The Privilege/Discrimination Factor

For those job slots that require a high degree of employee stabililty, employers use elaborate screening devices in their hiring. Certain groups, particularly women, young workers, immigrants and native people, are stereotyped as unreliable. They form a large undifferentiated pool of labour for the job slots at the lower end of the spectrum.

Women's salaries are, on average, about half those earned by men.

To some extent this has to do with the kinds of occupations women are concentrated in, but even within these occupations women on average earn only 62 per cent of men's wages. The dramatic expansion of clerical work and service jobs in the economy, particularly in health and education, has resulted in women flooding into the labour market. But more than 70 per cent of women employees work in routine and dead-end jobs, compared to less than 40 per cent of male workers. They type, file, answer phones, sort mail, key-punch, clean, cook, wait on tables, scrub floors, sort laundry, hairdress, sell, make coffee or clothes, bag groceries, count money, mind children and the old and the sick. Teaching and nursing, traditionally the two "best" jobs for women, account for a declining proportion of their work. More women than men work in the health and education fields, but since 1978 the overwhelming majority of additional female jobs in these professions have been part-time — and in teaching, women are losing ground to men. Women's location in management has increased substantially in recent years — from 18.7 per cent in 1975 to 25.2 per cent in 1980 — but three-quarters of these positions are in the service industry. As Pat and Hugh Armstrong write, "while some women have improved their position by moving into managerial jobs, these jobs are likely to be at the bottom of the pile, directing small beauty salons rather than large factories."[2]

But the discrimination/privilege component of the wage structure is not always negative. Temporary shortages of a specific category of workers can push the price of its labour power above the social standard. Permanent shortages produced by institutional restrictions can generate a so-called monopoly-rent through various devices, such as entrance and credentials requirements and control over training programs. This is particularly the case for the professions but also for certain skilled crafts. In the most extreme case monopoly-rent includes the half-million dollar contract that a Wayne Gretsky can command because his talents are unique.

A third form of positive discrimination favours those employees whose occupational position gives them a certain degree of control over their immediate labour process. Not only are they able to influence the pace of their work, but because of their involvement in planning, design, research, etc., their job requires that they do more than mechanically obey the rules set out by supervisors. Standard systems of managerial control may be effective in preventing misbehaviour and active disobedience, but they are not sufficient to stimulate the positive commitment and creativity that is required for satisfactory performance in these kinds of jobs.

Employers have traditionally attempted to wrest control from this layer of the work force by replacing employees through the introduction of technological devices. The increasing use of computers in design and planning functions in contemporary times erodes the autonomy of highly skilled technicians, planners and designers. But this procedure never completely eliminates this group of workers, and in any case it creates new positions, perhaps fewer in number, with high degrees of autonomy. As a result, employers have always relied on wage inducements to elicit creative and responsible behaviour from these employees. The extent to which their incomes exceed the social standard depends on the degree of autonomy their positions allow and their relative importance in planning and design activities.

Inducements are even more important a component in the salaries of managers and supervisors, for they not only influence their own productivity but also help regulate the labour efforts of others. The means by which this is accomplished is an elaborate hierarchial system with highly differentiated salaries attached to different positions. "Since income in a Capitalist society is the central criterion for status and success, large income differentials between hierarchial levels are essential for underwriting the legitimacy of authority."[3] For the same reason, managerial structures are also typically characterized by systematic gradations in the size and elegance of offices and other perquisites.

The Skill Factor

A skill costs something to produce and maintain, and unless the wage or salary of skilled workers more or less covers the costs, the skill will cease to be produced. In analytical terms, the skill factor is similar to the "human-capital" concept of orthodox economics, although radicals object to this expression, since they argue that the skills embodied in a worker cannot be sold or alienated from the worker in the same manner as physical machinery.

Defining the Social Standard

Today (1986) there are approximately 11.5 million job slots in Canada. Over a million more job slots were closed down between 1981 and 1983 — because the cost of keeping them open exceeded the profits they generated. Some were permanently eliminated, others temporarily.

Some of the job slots are seasonal and nearly 2 million of them comprise only part-time work. They are distributed unevenly around the country. The job slots vary by occupation and skill requirements. Some of them come with high wages and salaries, steady employment, good working conditions, job security and chances for advancement. Others offer low wages, unstable employment, poor working conditions, exhaustion and boredom, and little opportunity for advancement. What slot workers land depends on their skills, education and training, their age, sex and race, the wealth and position they have inherited, their connections in high places, and luck.

What level of income comprises the social standard? While there is no scientific answer to this question, we can accept as a rough approximation the "low-income" cut-off levels established by Statistics Canada and the Canadian Council on Social Development and the "standard of adequacy" defined by the Social Planning Council of Metro Toronto. In 1983 they ranged between $19,000 and $21,000 (before tax) for an urban family of four and $8,700-$10,000 (before taxes) for a single person working in an urban setting.

These income levels afford a minimally adequate standard of living. It is substantially above the minimal physical subsistence which, according to some studies, comes to $9,600 for a family of four and $4,000 for a single person.[4] The latter is roughly what people get on social assistance plus family allowance and child-tax credit payments.

What does an income of $20,000 afford? The family budget of Toronto's Social Planning Council includes a twelve-year-old colour TV set and stereo system, a fifteen-year-old camera, six movie admissions a year, a one-week vacation at a nearby rented cottage, urban transit, a few new items of clothing a year. With this income a family is not expected to purchase a home or a car, eat in restaurants, or accumulate savings beyond a contingency fund of a few hundred dollars.

Of the roughly 10.5 million paying job slots enumerated in the 1981 Census of Canada, a standard or "adequate" living family wage was attached to between 4 and 5 million of these. Even among the full-time job slots, fewer than 50 per cent provided the standard of adequate income required for that year (see Table 13:1). This is of course the population from which the so-called working poor are drawn. According to one study, there were more than a million Canadians living in working poor households in 1977, half of whom had one or more full-time wage earners. The working poor comprise nearly half of the total low-income population.[5]

Since there are less than 5 million job slots that provide a living family wage, it is only by combining the incomes of two or more wage earners that many families are able to secure an adequate income. Seven in ten non-poor households have two or more earners contributing to the family income, precisely the reverse situtation of the working poor. But even families with two wage earners cannot always secure an adequate income. While the combination of two minimum wage incomes would just enable a family to make a living wage, even a limited

TABLE 13:1
Distribution of Men and Women[1] by Income Group, 1981

Income Group	Women %	Men %
Under $1,000	5.8	2.9
$1,000 - 1,999	5.8	2.6
2,000 - 2,999	5.1	2.4
3,000 - 3,999	4.6	2.2
4,000 - 4,999	4.2	1.9
5,000 - 5,999	4.4	1.9
6,000 - 6,999	4.2	1.8
7,000 - 7,999	4.5	2.1
8,000 - 8,999	4.6	1.8
9,000 - 9,999	4.7	2.0
10,000 - 11,999	9.2	4.8
12,000 - 14,999	13.6	8.3
15,000 - 19,999	15.0	16.8
20,000 - 24,999	7.4	17.0
25,000 - 29,999	3.7	12.5
30,000 and over	3.1	19.1
Total	100.0	100.0
Average income ($)	$11,488	$20,382
Women/Men ratio	56.4	

[1] Whose major source of income is wages and salaries.

Source: Statistics Canada, *Income Distribution by Size in Canada 1981*.

bout of unemployment on the part of either breadwinner is enough to push the family income below the so-called poverty line.

Since women have the poorest access to the favoured job slots, the chance of their being members of the working poor is relatively high. One out of seven single adult women are among the working poor (nearly one out of every three is poor), compared to one out of ten for men. When women head single-parent families, their wage earnings are almost certain to place them in the low-income category.

In its study *Jobs and Poverty*, the National Council on Welfare concluded: "It is not their ages, education or geographic distribution that distinguishes low income workers. The single common factor which sets the working poor apart within our society is jobs!"[6] Over half of the heads of working-poor families are employed in service, sales, farming, fishing and clerical jobs — the occupations where the secondary labour market is concentrated.

A glance at Table 13:2 tells the tale. Assuming full-time employment, most of the jobs listed in the table generate better than a standard

TABLE 13:2
Occupations and Salaries

Occupation	Typical or Average Full-time Salaries, 1983	Comments
Corporate chief executive	$560,000+	Salary and benefits for Canada's top dozen corporations
NHL superstar	500,000+	
Corporate chief executive	300,000+	Salary and benefits for Canada's 50 largest corporations
Prime Minister of Canada	127,700	Includes salary as MP and PM plus allowances; $150,000 annual upkeep of 24 Sussex
Opposition leader	108,600	Includes salary plus allowances
Corporation executive, average	117,000	Salary only; excludes other cash remuneration and benefits
Chief Justice of Canada	112,000	
Senior Deputy Minister, Ottawa	105,000	
President, CBC	100,000	
NHL player	100,000	3 years in professional hockey
Senior corporate manager	95,000	Ranging from $80,000-$125,000 plus bonus averaging 20% of salary and other benefits
Ontario doctor, self-employed	98,000	Net income
Member of Parliament	70,000	Includes $16,800 non-taxable
Air Canada pilot	66,000	
Middle manager, corporate	64,000	Plus bonuses and benefits
Judge, Ontario	61,000	
Lawyer, private practice	60,000	Wide range
Union president	55,000	Ranging from $32,000 to $77,000
Stock salesman and trader	50,000	
CFL player, import	60,000	Average; average Canadian player, $40,000
Lawyer, salaried	43,000	10 years experience
Chemist, physicist, engineer, architect	40,000	Salary with 10 years experience

Where Do Profits Come From? 257

TABLE 13:2
Occupations and Salaries

Occupation	Typical or Average Full-time Salaries, 1983	Comments
Professor	39,600	Ranging from $27,000-$60,000
TV announcer	37,100	Ranging from $22,000-$150,000
Union staff representative	32,000	Ranging from $25,000-$40,000
Radio announcer	31,000	
Rock miner	30,800	Including overtime and bonuses
Principal dancer	30,000	National Ballet Co.
Police officer	27,800	
Elementary school teacher, female	27,500	$33,000, high school
Orchestra conductor	27,500	Average with wide range
Foreman, metal machine shop	27,500	
Tool and die maker	27,000	Without overtime and benefits
Machinist, union	26,200	Without overtime and benefits
Nurse	26,000	
Small store owner	26,000	Wide range
Insurance and real estate agency operator	24,800	Wide range
Urban transit bus driver, union	24,800	Non-union $13,700
Truck driver, heavy, union	24,400	
Social worker	24,300	Ranging from $18,000-$31,500
Computer programmer, senior	23,200	Junior, $19,000
Railroad conductor/brakeman	22,700	
Auto assembly worker, union	22,600	Plus benefits
Carpenter	22,000	
Retail salesman, top salary	21,600	
Mail carrier	21,100	
Professional librarian, female	20,200	Average male librarian, $25,200

TABLE 13:2
Occupations and Salaries

Occupation	Typical or Average Full-time Salaries, 1983	Comments
Ballet dancer	20,000	National Ballet Co., 5 years experience
Lab technician	19,400	
Cleric, United Church	19,000	Plus housing and car allowance
Computer operator, senior male	18,400	Junior male, $15,800 Junior female, $13,700
Timber cutter, union	18,500	
Symphony orchestra musician	18,000	
Average, all employees	18,000	
City garbage collector, union	17,900	
Supermarket cashier, female, full-time, union	17,500	Non-union, $9,900
Nurses aid	17,000	
Assembler (electrical industry, male, union)	16,400	Female, $15,800
Secretary/stenographer (senior)	16,300	Junior, $14,400
Director, day-care centre, female	15,000	
Sewing machine operator, female, union	13,700	
Shipping clerk, men's clothing	13,100	Top union wage, $19,600
Typist, senior	14,500	Junior, $13,200
Bank teller	12,800	
Telephone operator, union	13,600	
Day-care worker, female	12,000	
Janitor	11,700	
Service station attendant	11,300	Female, $8,900
Retail sales clerk, female	11,100	
Crop farm worker	11,000	
Presser, dry cleaning, female	11,000	
Office clerk, junior, female	10,500	
Sales clerk, female	10,000	
Char worker	9,000	Top wage, $13,500
Hotel-room cleaner	8,700	
Housekeeper	6,200	

Source: Department of National Revenue, Taxation Statistics; Statistics Canada Wage Rates, Salaries and Hours of Work; Paul Anisef and Elton Brichman, *What Jobs Pay*, Hurtig.

wage for a single person but only the most highly skilled, strongly unionized, semi-autonomous and professional job slots — the abode of the primary labour market — generate a standard family income. Most of the jobs clustered around $10,000-$13,000 belong to women, while most of the jobs clustered around $18,000-$26,000 belong to men.

Income, Jobs and Class

Dead-end (secondary), routine and craft (primary) work comprises about 85 per cent of the paid labour force. Aside from the thinning layer of craft employments (7.5 per cent), the jobs provide little or no opportunity for any control over the work they do. Their tasks are generally repetitive, routinized and machine-paced. The boss shadows them all day, prodding for greater productivity and constantly evaluating their performance. The skills required are limited, learned quickly (within hours, days or weeks) and are usually acquired on the job.

On average, routinized primary jobs pay about a half to two-thirds more than dead-end secondary jobs. Skilled and semi-autonomous jobs ("responsible employment") pay about a fifth to a quarter more than routinized jobs. A U.S. study has provided the following break-down of job characteristics in public and private sectors.[7]

There are more "responsible" (semi-autonomous) jobs in the public sector because of the large numbers of teachers and professional health workers. There are fewer dead-end jobs because the public sector is more unionized. If comparable Canadian figures were available, the results would be still more favourable to the public sector because it is more fully unionized than it is in the U.S.

What about the other 15 per cent of the labour force? Among the top ranks of paid employees, we can distinguish the million or so salaried professionals. They enjoy a great deal more on-the-job autonomy, job security and higher pay schedules than the vast majority of workers. Whereas nearly all doctors, dentists and lawyers had their own

TABLE 13:3
Job Characteristics, Private and Public Sectors

	Private Sector	*Public Sector*
Responsible employment	30.8%	41.3%
Routine employment	29.9%	34.9%
Dead-end employment	39.3%	24.7%

Source: David M. Gordon "Segmentation by the Numbers"; unpublished, New School For Social Research.

practices fifty years ago, by 1981 over half of the members of these elite professions had become employees of the state or corporations. They are increasingly losing control over their means of production, although they still enjoy almost complete autonomy with respect to their labour. Over 90 per cent of engineers, architects and accountants are salaried employees, and while they enjoy somewhat less autonomy than doctors, dentists and lawyers, their control over the work they do is still considerable. Teachers, welfare workers, nurses and librarians belong in the same "semi-autonomy" category, although in their case they are virtually all employed by the state. Finally, nearly 90 per cent of the artistic and literary professions — musicians, artists, photographers, writers and editors — are employees within the private sector and enjoy varying degrees of autonomy but much smaller incomes.

The rest of the top-paid employees (over 800,000) comprise the bosses' lieutenants. Depending on their rank, they are delegated differentiated degrees of authority, differentiated degrees of autonomy and a pay scale that is significantly higher than that received by subordinates. Excluding foremen at the lower rung of the managerial strata and the chief executive officers and vice-presidents af the very top, their salaries range from $65,000 to $125,000 plus bonuses and, in some instances, stock options, car expenses and other perquisites.

The intermediate layer, from middle management down to foreman, occupies what has been called a "contradictory class location." "Not only does it receive its petty share in the prerogatives and rewards of capital, but it also bears the mark of the proletarian condition."[8] Their function nevertheless remains one of extracting as much productivity as possible from their subordinates. So long as they remain in short supply they are easily exempted from the worst features of the "proletarian" situation. Once this circumstance changes, however, they are bound to be exposed to the forms of rationalization and control characteristic of the capitalist mode of production. When this begins to occur, despite their remaining privileges, they feel the same insecurities, frustrations and powerlessness that the working class has always lived with.

At the very top of the hierarchy, corporate executives merge with the capitalist class itself. They sit as chairmen, presidents, vice-presidents and treasurers alongside outside directors. Since board members are elected by shareholders, they are placed on boards of directors to represent the interests of the controlling ownership, to protect and enlarge its capital. Typical corporate executives are large shareholders, owning a quarter of a million to a million dollars of shares in the company they direct, and in many instances their investment earnings exceed their annual remunerations which, aside from the top few dozen, range between $100,000 and $300,000. Immediately beneath them in the corporate hierarchy are the senior managers and a small coterie of elite lawyers and chartered accountants whose remuneration ranges between half to two-thirds as much.

Worker Effort

The wage level is one determinant of profit. A second is the extent of worker effort. The problem has been defined in the following terms:

> When societies become divided into privileged classes possessing most of the power and property and ruled classes that did most of the work, the problem of the privileged class [was] how to make other people work effectively while turning over a good part of the fruits of their labour to the elite.[9]

One way of looking at this problem is that when owners purchase buildings, materials, tools and machinery, they can calculate their yield fairly precisely. These factors of production are fixed capital. But when they hire workers, they buy their labour time. The outcome is not so certain. In reality, they are really buying potential output. In this sense, labour comprises a variable capital. The size of workers' potential output is determined not only by objective factors — the length of the working day and the machinery and materials they have to work with — but also by a variety of subjective factors — how hard and efficiently they work; their training, intelligence, natural skills; and the owner's ability to get them to fully utilize these natural and acquired faculties. This is precisely the task of management. To what extent owners can extract their workers' full potential depends very much on workers' subjective state of mind, on their will to co-operate — or resist.

The labour contract is part of the answer. When workers enter their employer's establishment they yield full control over what tasks they may be required to do and in what manner and what penalties may be imposed when they fail to carry out their duties. This is the essential element of all labour contracts, and appears in every collective agreement as the management's rights clause which, for the employer, is the heart and soul of the agreement. The purpose of this clause is to establish union acknowledgement of the authority of the owner over the work force. It reasserts the traditional power relationship in the workplace, which the union must accept as its price for recognition. Here is a typical management's rights clause drawn from a 1983 collective agreement.

> The trade union acknowledges the employer's exclusive right to manage the enterprise and direct the work force including the following:

a) to maintain order, discipline and efficiency;
b) to hire, terminate, transfer (from, within and to the bargaining unit), classify, reclassify, direct, promote, test, appraise, demote, retire, lay-off, recall, discipline, suspend and discharge for just cause subject to the right of an employee to lodge a grievance in the manner and to the extent hereinafter provided;
c) to determine and administer all policies relating to the employer's operations and the discipline, general conduct and deportment of all personnel;
d) generally to manage the enterprise in which the employer is engaged and, without restricting the generality of the foregoing, determine the kind and nature of business, the right to plan, direct, inspect and control operations, determine the amount of overtime, assign work in accordance with the requirements determined by the employer, determine the standards of performance, the methods, procedures and equipment to be used, the scheduling, distribution and contracting out of work, the extension, limitation and curtailment or cessation of operations, and all other rights and responsibilities of management subject to the terms and conditions contained elsewhere in this agreement.

We can formalize this by saying that the employment relationship subordinates workers to a structure of control designed to maximize their effort and output in exchange for their wage. The point was made many years ago by the economist Alfred Marshall: "labour is often sold under special disadvantages, arising from the ... fact that labour power is 'perishable,' that the sellers of it are commonly poor and have no reserve fund and that they cannot easily withhold it from the market."[10] Employers have the franchise on jobs. A dissatisfied worker can switch jobs but this may not be easy in times of unemployment especially if that worker does not possess scarce technical skills or professional qualifications.

But the workers are not totally without power — if for no other reason than the employer is dependent on them to carry out the work. Regardless of their theoretical and legal authority, which is total and comprehensive, managers have to elicit from their subordinates some order of support, if not enthusiasm, for their goals. Within the system of rules and sanctions that operate in all workplaces, workers are able to impose their own informal rules on management as the price for their consent to the overall authority relationship.

Informal work practices have existed among work groups from the beginning of the factory system. There is, for example, the almost universal code of workplace conduct "whereby workers refuse to set back-breaking speeds of work which might be used to drive less healthy, adaptable or 'willing' workers to intolerable levels of strain. There are other 'rules' of a similar kind which prescribe that workers should protect each other from the attention of the foreman, should not squeal on fellow-workers who may breach company regulations, and so on. And there are informal but effective social sanctions which are applied to people who break unwritten codes."[11] Beyond these everyday forms of resistance, workers form unions to assert their collective interests. A union is therefore a "countervailing structure of control" that attempts to compel employers to take account of concerns and priorities at odds with their own.[12]

To counter worker resistance and more generally worker control over the job process, employers have adopted a number of different strategies over the years. Perhaps the first was employers moving the craftsmen out of the cottage and into the factory where they could dictate the hours, pace and quality of work. Another strategy involves introducing new technology like Henry Ford's 1914 assembly line.

Technological change reduces the element of human labour in production — in supplying the energy to operate tools and shape materials (powered machinery); in handling and transporting materials and partly finished products (assembly lines and transfer automation); in thinking about work (computers). By reducing the labour time expended per unit of output, workers could devote more of the working day producing surplus value. But the introduction of machinery and assembly-line technology also involved taking the skills out of work — in other words, separating workers from their skills and building these skills into machinery. By mechanizing skills, employers were able to regulate the intensity of work by controlling the speed of machinery together with the number of machines a worker could operate. To some extent, "technical control" through machine pacing reduced the need for personnel supervision and punitive devices. But it was obviously not sufficient because at the same time the mass assembly line was being introduced another system of control was beginning to spread — scientific management.

The father of scientific management, Fredrich Winslow Taylor, was absolutely clear about the problem that had to be addressed. The problem for employers, Taylor believed, was that the "workmen ... possess this mass of traditional knowledge, a large part of which is not in the possession of management.... The most experienced managers frankly place before their workmen the problem of doing the work in the best and most economical way." But leaving the initiative in the hands of workers meant that "the shop was really run by the workmen and not the bosses" and that they would deliberately set a pace of work far below the "optimum" that can be obtained from a day's work.[13] The solution, Taylor concluded, was to take the knowledge away from the worker by redesigning work.

First, managers had to gain control of all information about what was involved in each task performed by each worker, information which would then be translated into rules and regulations. Second, the work process could then be restructured, with managers using the information gathered to redivide the work, cut down on redundant motions, and discover speedier ways of getting things done. Third, owners could then remove to the fullest extent possible all matters of judgment from the shop floor. A separate planning department then designs the work down to the second, and the workers execute it. This separation of design from execution is essential. Fourth, once the planners design each task, every worker is given daily instructions describing in detail both the task to be accomplished and the means to accomplish it. Fifth, employers must find the right workers for the right jobs. From this principle arose the elaborate tests of aptitude, personality and skills which became part of the hiring practices of all large employers.

Scientific management centralized control, increased productivity and reduced cost. But like machinery, the new job structures reduced divisions among workers; the work force in most factories was now composed of unskilled and semi-skilled machine operators. This posed two new problems for owners: first, the assembly-line linked the entire work force of a plant, and in an integrated factory operation with a minute fragmentation of tasks, a relatively small group of disciplined workers could cripple the entire operation; second, with most workers doing roughly the same kind of job and getting similar pay, employees had a firmer basis for unifying against employers, forming industry-wide unions and striking. Frederick Winslow Taylor saw the likely outcome: "When employers herd their men together in classes, pay all of each class the same wages, and offer none of them inducements to work harder ... the only remedy for the men comes in combination; and frequently ... a strike."

Automated machinery, and in particular the computer, is the latest development in technical control systems. But as the same time it is being introduced, many employers have recognized that scientific management and job fragmentation have gone too far and are experimenting with the QWL techniques (discussed in chapter 11). The idea is that overall control of the work process, in danger of being lost through the rebelliousness of bored and alienated workers, can be retrieved by redesigning jobs and giving workers some limited shop (or office) floor autonomy.

The Role of Unions

Where do unions fit into this picture? The most commonly held view is that, as workers have mobilized themselves into trade unions with collective bargaining and the right to strike sanctioned by law, they have been able to gradually eliminate the serious imbalance of power between themselves and their employers. According to this picture, while industrial relations has by no means eliminated conflict, it has "created mechanisms enabling the contending parties, not too unevenly matched, to negotiate their mutual accommodations in a manner appropriate to a society which aspires to industrial as well as political democracy."[14]

This picture of a rough parity in the balance of power has itself the appearance of a balanced and fair-minded viewpoint. Unfortunately, it is grossly inaccurate. In the first place, the union's influence is greatly weakened where there is widespread unemployment and its members feel threatened by lay-off; where its members have diverse concerns because of differences in age, gender and skill; and where the labour movement as a whole is divided by warring factions of competing unions, by political discord and by separation into public-sector and private-sector unions. The potential and the cost of disunity is so great that it is little wonder that the rallying call for "unity" is so frequently heard from within the labour movement.

In the second place, "what unions demand in collective bargaining is necessarily constrained by what is considered realistic, and what is realistic is defined in terms of what the employer can be persuaded to concede in a negotiated settlement. This clearly does not extend to any radical alternative in the balance of power in industry."[15] Since wage claims normally (though not always) offer the most ample scope for compromise, they are more readily negotiable. There is a reasonable prospect for achieving a peaceful settlement. Similarly, unions can win some improvements in working conditions, reverse individual management decisions and impose certain limits on managerial prerogatives — the seniority principle is a case in point.

When compared with the plight of workers in most organized employments, these achievements are anything but negligible. But they cannot be said to represent more than a marginal rearrangement of life in the workplace when viewed in its total context. They do not challenge the right of the employer to exercise control and initiate change, nor the extreme division of labour and fragmentation of jobs, the hierarchial structure of organization, the massive inequalities of financial reward and status, the disposition of profits, the decisions around investment, location, technology, lay-offs, product design, marketing, advertising, and so forth.

These areas of control, which are of course the very heart of the private-enterprise system, are not negotiable. They are not at stake in collective bargaining. Should they ever be faced with demands that threaten the foundations of management power, privileges, values and objectives, owners can draw on their full reserves of strength. If necessary, they can call upon the coercive sanctions of the state which, in the final analyis, underwrites the contract whereby the worker must accept the sovereignty of the employer. Whereas unions can usually display enough economic power and have the sanction of the state to challenge management on a limited range of issues, they would need to mobilize far more power than they now have in order to garner concessions on what are widely regarded as the legitimate rights of management.

That they do not do so stems partly from an awareness of the employer's superior power, which makes the existing structure of authority seem inevitable, perhaps invincible. This awareness shapes workers' aspirations. Given the prevailing power relations, employees try to achieve what they feel they have some chance of achieving. But workers are also encouraged to see management's authority as not only necessary and inevitable but also legitimate and right. To embrace any but the most modest of objectives is to challenge everyday language and assumptions and to be seen as "subversive" or "irresponsible." Indeed, while the right of owners to shut down production is rarely if ever questioned, it is still cause to regard workers' strikes as irresponsible, unfair, wasteful, against community interests, contrary to the workers' own interests and unduly aggressive. "The morality which assesses strikes in these terms acts on employees so that they approach strike action with serious inhibitions."[16]

Out of necessity, therefore, unions play an ambivalent role in industrial conflict. This ambivalence was succinctly defined by C. Wright Mills nearly forty years ago when he described the union leader as a "manager of discontent.... He organizes discontent and then he sits on it."[17] Besides representing the interests of workers, union officials also seek to ensure the security of the union in its long-term relationship with the company and in competition with rival unions by curbing objectives that challenge the status quo. This is why in respect to what they do as distinct from what they say most left-wing union leaders perform not much differently than their more conservative counterparts. Their socialist beliefs are usually confined to distant goals and convention speeches and are not directed at challenging managerial control.

Modest aims are likely to be rewarded by a more accommodating live-and-let-live attitude of management. As Richard Hyman and Robert Fryer have written: "Where unions are willing to confine their objectives within ... comparatively innocuous limits, far-sighted managements have little reason to resist, and much reason to welcome union involvement.... For by articulating the many discontents generated by the workers' role within capitalist employment a union makes their behaviour more predictable and manageable. Resentment is not permitted to accumulate explosively, but is formulated in a manner which facilitates at least temporary solutions; and union involvement in any settlement increases the likelihood that its members will feel committed to the agreed terms."[18]

At the same time, this remains a highly precarious enterprise. A union that dampens workers' discontent too far runs the risk of destroying its own means for existence. And union leaders who repeatedly ignore workers' aspirations may find themselves out of a job. The underlying sources of industrial conflict sets limits on the extent to which union leaders can "manage discontent" by "sitting on it."

While the dominant values in society generally underwrite the legitimacy of those in positions of control, there are limits. Our culture also values freedom and democracy. Despite the nature of the labour contract, "workers do not assume that they surrender their autonomy absolutely during working hours." They are likely " to define their own obligations more narrowly than management would wish. If employers then seek to impose their own wider conceptions of authority, this will probably be perceived by workers as a naked exercise of power — and as such be resisted."[19] And many workers only partially accept the dominant social values; a minority does not accept them at all. Such an employee feels no compunction in "pressing every minor advantage, manipulating every rule, exploiting every loophole, harrying every managerial weakness or leniency in his continuous struggle against those whom he sees as exploiting his economic weakness for purposes about which he has not been consulted."[20]

In the final analysis, control over the work process with whatever techniques is never guaranteed. It shifts with the balance of class forces in the workplace. For this reason alone there is a powerful tendency for owners to replace workers with machines.

Monopolization

The extent of monopoly control over output is one of the factors determining the division of income between labour and capital and the division of profits between big and small capital. In 1983 not counting unincorporated businesses, independent professional practices and farm proprietorships, there were 391,000 enterprises in Canada operating nearly 400,000 (non-financial) corporations. The top twenty-five alone account for 33 per cent of all profits (23 per cent in 1975), 34 per cent of total corporate assets (22 per cent in 1975), 24 per cent of total sales (19 per cent in 1975), and about 13 per cent of all private-sector employees. The top 500 enterprises account for 70 per cent of total profits, 68 per cent of total assets, 55 per cent of total sales and about a quarter of all private-sector employees (see Table 13:4). These figures considerably understate the degree of ownership centralization because they take no account of intercorporate ownership. Eight holding companies have a controlling interest in at least a hundred of the leading 1,000 enterprises. Even so, the fact that 500 enterprises, representing one-tenth of 1 per cent (0.12) of the country's corporations, control nearly 70 per cent of the resources of Canada (and nearly a quarter of all jobs) — leaving the other 30 per cent to the remaining 390,712 enterprises — speaks volumes about the lopsided distribution of economic power among firms.

A hundred years ago, Marx predicted that the competitive process would itself propel this growing concentration of ownership and monopoly sharing of markets. Larger capitals tend to drive the smaller out of business. As technological progress raises the amount of capital required for optimal efficiency, small and medium-sized businesses are progressively excluded because of a lack of sufficient finance. The challenge of new competition is lessened as industrial entry is limited to those possessing large initial stocks of capital.

During the initial stages of industrialization, the size of enterprises was limited by both the availability of capital and the management capacities of the owners. Those limits were overcome by the establishment of the joint-stock corporation. Corporations enable owners to assemble capital far beyond their personal wealth holdings while vesting operational control in specialized managerial staff.

Increased concentration arises both from the initial growth of individual capitals and from the amalgamation of individual capitals through mergers. The entire process is facilitated by the growth of financial institutions possessing vast quantities of investable funds. While growing concentration is ongoing, it accelerates during economic crises when weaker firms are forced into bankruptcy or compelled to sell their assets to stronger ones. A glance at Table 13:4 illustrates the point. In the crisis years between 1975 and 1983 the hundred largest corporations increased their share of total enterprise sales from 34 per cent to 39 per cent; total assets from 39 per cent to 52 per cent; total profits from 41 per cent to 52 per cent.

The larger corporations that emerge are often able to get better discounts from their suppliers and make better deals with their customers — because of their monopoly power and because they can promise bigger orders on a large volume of goods. On the other hand, they are big enough consumers of certain products to become their own suppliers. General Motors makes most of its parts and components; most petroleum refineries produce their own oil; Safeway produces its own milk and bread, as do many other chain stores; newspapers often have their own pulp and paper plants; and some steel companies supply

TABLE 13:4
Percentage Control of Sales, Assets, Profits in Non-Financial Corporations 1975, 1983

	Number 1975	Number 1983	Sales 1975	Sales 1983	Assets 1975	Assets 1983	Profits 1975	Profits 1983
25 leading enterprises								
Foreign	12	9	11.5	9.5	7.5	5.7	12.7	14.9
Canadian	13	16	7.7	14.0	14.4	28.3	10.1	17.7
Total	25	25	19.3	23.5	21.9	34.0	22.8	32.6
100 leading enterprises								
Foreign	60	44	20.2	16.3	17.6	12.3	25.9	28.0
Canadian	40	56	14.1	22.9	21.6	39.9	15.0	24.4
Total	100	100	34.3	39.2	39.2	52.2	40.9	52.4
500 leading enterprises								
Foreign	280	240	30.0	24.3	28.7	18.9	39.2	37.4
Canadian	220	260	21.2	30.5	30.4	49.3	24.2	32.4
Total	500	500	51.2	54.8	59.1	68.2	63.4	69.8
All non-financial enterprises								
Foreign	3,887	3,399	37.8	29.6	37.9	24.3	48.4	43.6
Canadian	202,808	387,813	62.2	70.4	62.1	75.7	51.6	56.4
Total	206,695	391,212	100.0	100.0	100.0	100.0	100.0	100.0

Source: Corporations and Labour Unions Returns Act, reports for 1975 and 1983.

their own iron ore. By means of this "vertical integration," corporations can better control their costs and avoid sharing profits with suppliers. Threatening to go this route gives them additional leverage in bargaining with suppliers and customers.

The larger a corporation becomes the more flexibility it gains in being able to plan the allocation of its investment. Larger corporations can afford to move elsewhere if workers in one area get too powerful or if governments raise taxes or impose new regulations or if markets or suppliers are more readily available in other locations.

While concentration of production pays where there are large economies of scale, very large plants are more prone to industrial militancy and vulnerable to strikes. To a certain extent this dilemma can be solved by separating production of components. In the auto industry, for example, one plant produces engines, another produces transmissions and a third assembles them. Security and bargaining power are further increased by establishing more than one source for any crucial component.

With these advantages, the giant corporations form the centre of the modern business economy. Because of their large assets, cash flow and excellent credit ratings, they can raise the capital to buy out other businesses, to finance new labour-saving machinery, to develop new products and techniques, to establish nation-wide or world-wide marketing systems and branch plants and subsidiaries in other countries.

At the periphery of the modern economy is a myriad of small businesses, most of which have only local or regional importance. Many periphery firms serve as satellites to the dominant corporations, supplying them with inputs or channeling their products to the final purchaser. In the automobile industry, for example, a host of firms sell parts to auto manufacturers, while franchise dealers serve as forward satellites. They often act as subcontractors for dominant corporations.

Another set of periphery firms comprise the competitive fringe for centre enterprises, serving regional markets or producing single-line products. They typically surrender the power to make price decisions to the dominant corporation, but they may also be pioneers in developing new or improved products. A third periphery group fills in the cracks and crannies of the economy, usually in the repair, retailing, and service fields. Periphery firms are often labour-intensive, less productive enterprises and their management revolves around one or a few individuals who are also the owners. Their survival prospects are precarious; they are perpetually short of cash, feel both squeezed by government regulations, taxes, minimum-wage laws and unions and threatened by the prospect of elimination at the hands of larger rivals.

But there is also a third producing sector, the state. The modern state administers a variety of direct social services, but it also provides many inputs that are essential for industry, including transportation, communication, research, finance and marketing.

These are usually very large operations. While they aim to be self-financing and profit-making, many of them differ from other core firms because their profits are deliberately held below levels that privately owned firms would demand. Originally established under pressure from industrialists to ensure that these essential inputs would be cheaper, they in effect subsidize the private sector. Other state-owned companies often include failed private corporations nationalized by the state as a favour to their owners or because they were deemed either too large or strategically important to be allowed to dissolve. (Chapter 14 examines this process in greater detail.)

Outside the U.S. there has been a notable tendency towards state-owned enterprises. Within Fortune's 500 largest corporations outside the U.S., for instance, what has been called "state enterprise capitalism" accounted for 21 per cent of assets, 53 per cent of income and nearly 20 per cent of employees in 1976. Privatization in Britain and elsewhere have altered these numbers somewhat since 1980.

Within Canadian manufacturing industries, roughly 35 per cent of all goods are sold in markets controlled by a few giant corporations (see Table 13:5). Less than 20 per cent are sold in highly competitive markets and the remaining 45 per cent are sold in markets of a mixed character. Some sectors, like communications, utilities, petroleum and mining, are even more monopolized, while others, like retail and wholesale trade and construction, are less so.[21]

Small employers differ from large capitalist firms in at least three respects. First, the magnitude of their capital is such that it is usually very difficult for them to accumulate a substantial portion of their income in the form of profits. Second, small employers are themselves directly engaged in the process of production: the farmer-owner who hires farm workers is also a farmer; the shopkeeper who employs sales help is also involved in selling to customers. A substantial part of their income comes directly from their own and their family's labour and only a portion from the appropriation of surplus value from their employees. Third, as we have already seen, many are in a vulnerable position as franchise operations and as suppliers of the larger firms. A substantial proportion of their profits are redistributed to monopoly capital.

On the other hand, small employers located in very restricted and protected markets with high barriers to entry can usually protect their profits. Indeed, small employers who have their own collective systems of price determination, such as those engaged in the delivery of professional services, can themselves extract monopoly prices.

As for self-employed proprietors, the so-called petty bourgeoisie, their entire income is produced by their own labour and depends on

TABLE 13:5
Ranking of the 33 Major Industries by the Leading Enterprises, Measured by 1981 Sales

Rank Major Industries	% Sales accounted for by Top 4 Enterprises 1981	Top 8 Enterprises 1981
Tobacco products	92.3	99.8
Storage	81.8	86.5
Communications	71.0	81.0
Transport equipment	64.0	70.7
Petroleum and coal products	63.6	85.4
Primary metals	58.4	73.5
Rubber products	57.1	81.0
Public utilities	57.0	75.7
Metal mining	51.4	67.9
Transportation	49.1	53.7
Textile mills	41.0	48.4
Beverages	40.9	61.6
Mineral fuels	38.6	58.3
Paper and allied industries	38.5	52.0
Electrical products	36.4	46.4
Non-metallic mineral products	31.3	46.8
Chemicals and chemical products	25.8	38.1
Printing, publishing and allied industries	25.4	35.2
Machinery	23.0	30.8
Other mining	21.2	29.9
Leather products	18.7	30.5
Miscellaneous manufacturing	18.7	23.9
Food	18.2	27.0
Knitting mills	17.5	27.4
Wood industries	17.4	23.6
Retail trade	12.7	21.2
Metal fabricating	12.1	19.1
Furniture industries	10.3	15.9
Wholesale trade	10.1	14.3
Services	8.9	12.6
Agriculture, forestry and fishing	8.4	10.6
Clothing industries	7.8	11.2
Construction	3.6	6.1

Source: Corporations and Labour Unions Returns Act, Report for 1982, p. 47.

their skill and the market price they can obtain for the goods and services they supply. The most common outcome arising from market pressures is that the net incomes of the petty bourgeoisie seldom rise much above the cost of reproducing their labour power and are therefore not very much higher than the wages of workers of equivalent skill. Finally, except for a business that operates in a restricted market, neither small employers nor self-employed proprietors have any control over the prices of the goods and services they supply.

To understand the pricing process we need only look at the situation of a small firm that supplies a tiny proportion of the market for the goods or services it sells. This firm has virtually no control over its price. If it charges a price more than a shade above that of its competitors, it will likely lose all of its market to them. On the other hand, because it is so insignificant a producer the quantity it supplies has no perceptible effect on the total market — and it is presumed that it can sell all that it can produce at the existing price. Providing it can cover its costs at this price, it will stay in business. If the prevailing price is too low, it can attempt to introduce cheaper methods of production to reduce costs. If it is unable to raise productivity or, at any rate, not sufficiently, it will have to close down or produce something else. Raising productivity and reducing costs is also its path to increased profits. With increased profits it can afford to expand its operations — to sell more at the existing price level.

The large firm operating in a highly concentrated market faces a different situation. In the first place, it has some (but by no means total) control over its price. Within limits it can raise its price to achieve a higher rate of profit without having to fear that this will immediately attract new firms into the industry. Consumer loyalty for its brand, high capital costs, specialized technology, patents and labour and management skills throw up considerable barriers of entry into the industry. And it can presume that in normal times other firms in the industry will behave similarly, raising their prices as well to achieve maximum profits.

But unlike the small firm, it cannot be oblivious to the effect of the quantity of its production on the price. Specifically, each of a few large firms must take into account the effect of changes in its output on the market price. A firm that supplies 40 per cent of industry output, for example, cannot expect that it can increase its production and sales by 10 per cent, without having to lower its price.

The net result of open price competition and retaliation is that all companies are worse off. Since no company gains on its rival and since all suffer from the uncertainties that price wars produce, price-cutting is unofficially banned except under rare circumstances. It is replaced by some form of price leadership where price changes are initiated in a way that safeguards the best interest of all companies concerned. Even in periods of severe recessions, price cuts are seldom allowed. On the contrary, to offset reductions in sales and maintain cash flows, prices are usually raised. This contrasts with firms in competitive markets which fight to retain their sales by lowering their prices.

Competition among the giants, on the other hand, takes the form of product differentiation and massive advertising campaigns.

At the turn of the century, nearly half of all gainfully occupied people owned their own farms, businesses or professional practices. At present barely 10 per cent find themselves in this position. In the process of competition, the self-employed proprietors and small employers, who once supplied the overwhelming majority of goods, have rapidly diminished in importance. In other words, the overwhelming majority of the population has been "proletarianized." They do not own the means of production — land, materials and tools — that secure their livelihood.

In all of this, Marx's prediction of a hundred years ago turned out to be unerring. While many still dream of owning their own businesses, it is a dream very few will ever realize. And while the economic crisis has savaged all business, it is precisely among the independent proprietors and small employers that bankruptcy rates have been highest. The banks go to great lengths to reschedule the debts of their largest clients, but they do not hesitate to foreclose on the farmer and the small businessman.

This chapter has examined three factors determining the level and distribution of profits: the wage level, productivity and monopolization. Chapter 14 analyzes the state's role.

14 Business and the State

Following the work of James O'Connor[1] and other scholars, contemporary Marxists argue that the capitalist state must perform two basic functions: accumulation and legitimization. The first refers to economic functions, namely those of ensuring profitability, investment and economic growth. The second refers to socio-political functions, those of ensuring that the capitalist order appears just and fair according to the standards of the day and that social harmony is therefore maintained.

On this basis three categories of state expenditure can be distinguished:

- Social investment: projects and services that increase the productivity of labour or provide major inputs at prices below what they would have been had they been supplied by private enterprise — such as hydro, telecommunications, transportation and research.
- Social consumption: projects and services such as health care and education that lower the reproduction costs of labour. If these were not provided by the state, businesses would be obliged to pay higher wages to enable workers to purchase them.
- Social expenses: projects and services required to maintain social harmony, such as social-security payments, pensions, police, the army and judiciary.

The first two, which together may be called social capital expenditure, indirectly produce surplus value because they augment the rate of profit and accumulation in the economy. Social expenses are a necessary but unproductive expense draining money that could otherwise be used for capital accumulation.

There are obvious but important differences between this analysis of state expenditures and that of orthodox economics. Keynesians make no distinctions between kinds of state expenditures; they are only interested in its level and its consequent impact on total demand. Monetarists and supply-siders argue that with the possible exception of some social-investment expenditures, all other state expenditures should be minimized because they reduce the scope of profit-making activities (in any case, goods and services provided by the state are more efficiently produced by the private sector), and they interfere with the incentive system and the operation of the labour market.

The Marxist analysis has similar concerns but reaches a more uncertain conclusion about the impact of the welfare state on capital accumulation. On the one hand, labour employed by the state (other than in public enterprises) produces no surplus value. On the other hand, the services it provides can reduce the wages enterprises would otherwise be obliged to pay their employees, thus enhancing their profit.

Medical care that is wholly funded from income taxes and/or premium taxes levied on individuals illustrates the case. Total demand is unaffected since the taxes used to pay for health services are offset by reduced expenditures on private-health insurance. Families clearly gain since their taxes need not cover profit in the health industry that has been eliminated. Labour's gain is capital's loss even though labour bears the entire cost in the form of income and/or premiums taxes. But if as a consequence all employers can pay lower wages, they can re-appropriate part of the loss endured by the private-health industry. Surplus value is redistributed from the health industry to the rest of the capitalist sector.

In short, part of social services and payments provided by the state enters into the living standard of the labour force, contributing to the daily and generational reproduction cost of the working class no differently than the goods and services purchased with the wage packet. Such services and payments comprise the "social wage" which, together with the private wage and benefits packet, make up the value of labour power.

In the days before the welfare state, corporations offered their own welfare programs to their work force: pensions, medical and dental care, life insurance, libraries, social clubs and recreational facilities and the like. It was an investment to gain worker loyalty and industrial peace. But it was a heavy investment, amounting to as much as 8 per cent of profits and it failed to survive the Great Depression. The welfare state is corporate welfarism writ large, aiming to win loyalty to the social order while paying through general taxation for services formerly financed from corporate profits.[2]

But a substantial part of welfare-state services and payments is directed towards the non-working population and does not enter into the value of labour power. In fact, nearly every state expenditure is part social investment, part social consumption and part social expense. Roads, hydro, water, sewage, etc., are social investments but also enter into social consumption. Insofar as social services and payments contribute to the reproduction of the working population, they constitute social consumption. Insofar as they maintain other groups in the population or pay for the agencies of social control and coercion (social work, probation services, police, and certain aspects of the health and education systems), they are a social expense.

While it may be difficult to assign proper weights to the distribution of these expenditures, the consequence of these distinctions is important. The more state expenditures are allocated to the accumulation function — social investment and social consumptionm — the more they contribute to the long-term production of output. The more state expenditures must be allocated to maintaining social harmony — the more social welfare expenses grow — the less is available for future output.

In the conditions of advanced capitalist societies both functions have required a much greater involvement of the state in economic and social life. But because of the peculiar character of Canada's political economy, the state has played a major role in shaping affairs from the very outset.

The Age of Canadian Mercantilism

Until the Second World War the Canadian state had neither the revenue nor the administrative apparatus of modern governments. What it did have was vast natural reserves including land, minerals and timber belonging to the Crown, which it generously distributed to private capitalists. The best-known early example is the subsidy to the Canadian Pacific Railway Company which, in addition to 25 million acres of land, included a $25 million cash grant, nearly $40 million worth of government-constructed track, exemption from taxation, a monopoly over certain routes, the right to import construction materials duty free and other favourable terms. Besides choice agricultural land, the CPR came away possessing valuable real estate in virtually all urban centres as well as land rich in forest and mineral resources.

Far from being a unique case, the CPR was typical in the sense that underwriting railway construction was a well-maintained policy of Canadian governments from 1850 to 1911. No major Canadian railway was built without extensive government assistance. Canal construction followed much the same pattern before the age of the railway, while in the period following the Second World War government assistance for natural gas pipelines took the form of loan guarantees and cash subsidies.

As the dean of Canadian political science, C.B. Macpherson, has written:

> This embrace of private enterprise and government is not at all unusual in new countries. In Canada it is the direct result of the fact that the natural

resources, abundant but scattered, have always afforded the prospect of highly profitable exploitation and could most rapidly be made profitable by concentrating on the production of a few stables for export — fur and fish in the early days, wheat, forest products and minerals today. This required a heavy import of capital and heavy government expenditure in railways, power developments, irrigation, land settlement, and so on. To support such investment, governments have been driven to all sorts of further encouragement of various industries and regions, notably by way of protective tariffs.[3]

Traditional government measures to stimulate investment through private-capital accumulation also included tax concessions, cash bonuses, monopoly charters and mass immigration.

As described by Marx, this is part of the "primitive capital accumulation" process present in all capitalist economies in the earliest phase of their development. It is "primitive" in the sense that private wealth is built up, not by extracting surplus value from labour in the everyday process of production, but by means external to the production system itself. In an age of a petty mode of production, where labour productivity was still low and where the number of workers employed by a single capitalist was seldom numerous, substantial profit could not be made by investment in production. Moreover, with limited markets, it could only be made in trade by restricting the number of long-distance merchants, by exploiting local markets, by capitalizing on political advantage and by plundering native populations in underdeveloped countries. Until the new mechanical age, the vast potential of extracting surplus value from investing in the employment of wage-labour was not apparent.

In Europe the period of "primitive capital accumulation" covered nearly 300 years and involved various forms of theft, seizure, coercion, imposed monopolies and bribery. The most important sources of these early fortunes included the seizure of ancient treasure from India and the Americas; piracy on the seas; the slave trade; usury; the expulsion of peasants from the land; local trade monopolies; colonization; long-distance trade monopolies granted by state charter and secured by the military apparatus of the state.

Profit was understood to be the result of an advantage gained from buying cheap and selling dear. On a national level this meant importing as little and as cheaply as possible and exporting as much and as expensively as possible. The central aim of state policy was therefore monopoly control of both domestic and export markets and a structure of production in colonial territories geared to the production of the metropolitan centres. The name given to state policy in the age of primitive accumulation is mercantilism. This system of state-regulated exploitation through trade played a highly important role in the adolescent state of industrial capitalism everywhere.[4]

Before they had attained a clear economic and political superiority, the merchant and incipient manufacturing class was forced to seek alliances with non-capitalist classes and, in fact, to play off the antagonisms of different groups to its own advantages. When it finally emerged triumphant, it worked to establish a form of government that would ensure the kinds of laws, tax structures, tariffs and services required to maintain and expand a capitalist-type economy. This government had to be made responsible to the electorate, but the franchise did not need to be universal and it was vital that it was not until the broad masses more or less accepted the rules of the capitalist game.

The heyday of Canadian mercantilism was the 150-year period between the arrival of the Hudson Bay Company and the completion of the CPR. The Hudson Bay Company, later joined by other fur-trading companies, was given a charter to plunder the native population. The exhaustion of the fur supply marked the end of the first stage of primitive capital accumulation in this country. The second stage revolved around the vision of a newly created mercantile class to develop the St. Lawrence water system as a transportation route linking North America to Britain, with Montreal as the trading capital. State-financing of canals and other infrastructure and complex tariff arrangements were essential ingredients of this development project. Indeed, early state-craft was occupied with little else.[5] There was an alernative vision of a laissez-faire state and a self-sufficient economy comprised of small-scale farm and industry proprietors. When the 1837 rebellion ended in ignoble defeat the vision disappeared from political consciousness. The victory of a state-sponsored capitalist development, with the state actively facilitating the private accumulation of wealth, has endured to this day.

While developing a material base to serve the economic needs of the motherland, British colonial governments used the vast lands and resource assets of the Crown to create a dominant economic class that would reproduce a Tory-style hierarchical and undemocratic political and social system. Since state patronage was fundamental in establishing Canada's first generation of business enterprises, government involvement in economic development bore the stamp of legitimacy from the earliest days. In the social structure of nineteenth-century Canada, accumulation and legitimization — the two functions of the state — merged. "Accumulation was legitimization," as Reg Whitaker has written.[6]

Indeed, from the time of the Family Compact of the 1820s, to the end of the century at least, economic and political elites were almost always one and the same. The same personnel occupied both the offices of the state and the boardrooms of capitalist enterprises. Special privileges, pay-offs and other forms of corruption were standard instruments in the early accumulation of wealth. Public office and private profits were two sides to the same coin.[7]

To secure its privileged position, the dominant mercantile class maintained control over the executive branch of government while confining the elected assembly to a strictly advisory capacity. Having granted responsible government around the middle of the century, it fought against popular representation until well into the nineteenth century. Universal male franchise was finally conceded only during the First World War in the struggle for military conscription.[8]

Like many other such dreams, the "empire of the St. Lawrence" was never realized, but it was not too long before the ruling elite set about implementing another national dream, which came to be known as the National Policy. This was the third exercise in primitive capital accumulation, a national development scheme aimed at creating an east-west economy linked by a national railway with central Canadian industrialization protected by tariffs (an average of 30 per cent on dutiable imports by the end of the century) and a state-supervised settlement of the prairies earning foreign exchange through trans-Atlantic wheat exports while providing a captive market for eastern manufacturers and merchants.

The first requirement was to purchase Rupert's Land for a sum of $1.5 million. This territory — essentially the Canadian prairies and the north — had been granted to the Hudson Bay Company 200 years earlier. The second requirement was to expel the native population from fertile lands so that it could be parcelled out to land developers and railway companies for settlement. The third requirement was to subsidize the building of a national railway; the fourth to bring in overseas peasants to farm the land and to find a cheap source of immigrant labour to construct the railroads and cities and to stock the labour pool demanded by the anticipated industrialization. The final requirement was protectionist and incentive programs to stimulate new industry and encourage the expansion of existing ones.

From Protectionism to Continentalism

The east-west economy envisioned by the National Policy was short-lived. Its anchor — protective tariffs — had never been popular outside of the industrial heartland of central Canada. Farmers and businessmen in the Atlantic and prairie regions viewed them as a transfer tax which shifted wealth from themselves to the manufacturing and financial centres of Ontario and Quebec. To accommodate regional demands and as a means of co-opting the large contingent of Progressive members western members had sent to Parliament, the Liberal government of Mackenzie King undertook a series of selective tariff reductions in the mid-1920s. After the failed effort of the Bennett Conservatives to "blast" Canada's way into the markets of the world with a substantial tariff hike, King resumed the Liberal project of dismantling the old National Policy.

The dismemberment of the east-west economy and its displacement by a continental economy was closely associated with the growing Americanization of the Canadian economy. The National Policy's protective tariffs were clearly meant to attract foreign capital to help build Canadian industry. But John A. Macdonald did not have the branch-plant model in mind when he designed the policy. Indeed, most of the foreign capitalists who took the bait in the early years of the National Policy did move in with their capital; absentee ownership of the branch-plant variety came later. It was at this point that continentalism began to assert itself. From 1919 to 1928 an average of fifty American-owned firms were established per year, rising to ninety per year in the early 1930s.

The pulp and paper and mining industries developed mostly by American subsidiaries to serve the American market and the component-importing branch-plant manufacturing firms to serve the Canadian market sealed the doom of the old Tory vision of a national economy which would unite the country. Ontario and Quebec developed a highly ambivalent attitude towards preserving an east-west economy, Ontario as the prime location of American branch-plants and Quebec along with Ontario as the prime exporter to the U.S. As they cultivated their own continental trading patterns based on new staples, other provinces did so as well. The collapse of the wheat economy in the 1930s lessened the prairie commitment to the national economy. Finally, the development of hydro-electric power in a provincial context also promoted a sense of provincialism. With the extensive economic and political co-operation between Ottawa and Washington during the war years, the idea of a north-south continental economy became commonly accepted as natural and inevitable.

The first postwar expression of the new continentalist policy was the Hyde Park Agreement of October 1950. It declared that the two governments agree "to cooperate ... to the end that the economic efforts of the two countries be consummated for the common defence, and that the production and resources of the two countries be used for the best combined results...." Linking up Alberta's fertile oil fields to the oil-short American West was an immediate pay-off. Besides forging a continental energy deal, Hyde Park began the process of standardizing weapons and equipment with the U.S., which led to the NORAD Agreement in 1957 and to the Distant Early Warning (DEW) Line whereby political sovereignty over part of Arctic was transferred to the U.S. In 1959 came the Defence Production Sharing Agreement which opened up U.S. defence subcontracting to Canadian industry. U.S. defence contracts processed in Canada were soon to account for more than a quarter of inedible end products exports to the U.S. The Canada-U.S. Auto Pact was signed in 1965. Along with the Defence Production Sharing Agreement, it fundamentally altered Ontario's historical role as the supplier of industrialized products to the rest of Canada. Before the Auto Pact, Ontario's factories produced most of the motor vehicles that were used in Canada. After the pact, 70 per cent of Ontario's output was exported to the U.S., while the western Canadian market was largely supplied from the U.S. The St. Lawrence Seaway, originally built to carry Quebec iron ore to America steel mills, and the mammoth James Bay Project, which converted Quebec into a permanent supplier of power to New York State, were other state-sponsored projects hitching regional economics onto the American growth wagon.

In the wake of the National Policy's demise, economic historians have looked in vain for signs of a coherent economic-development strategy followed by the Canadian state. Vernon Fowke held that, the purpose of the National Policy having been fulfilled by 1920, federal governments gradually evolved a new national policy consisting of provisions for social welfare, regional equalization, agricultural price stabilization and monetary management.[9] This interpretation has long since been dismissed because these are stabilization, not development, policies. In a recent article, Lithwick and Devlin insist that since 1945 there has been no explicit economic development policy.[10] This blindness is surely indicative of the fact that continentalism is now so pervasive that it is looked upon as natural rather than as the end result of deliberate policy decisions accelerated by postwar governments.

The Accumulation Function: Corporate Welfarism

Whatever the explanation for these events (an area of heated debate among economic historians), American capital came to be the main beneficiary of state efforts to promote industrialization. Late nineteenth-century municipalities engaged in fierce competition to attract manufacturing concerns, offering cash bonuses, tax holidays, utility concessions, cheap or free land to induce firms to locate within their municipal boundaries.[11] Provincial and federal governments also offered cash bonuses to stimulate the production of a variety of products. Iron and steel producers alone received federal subsidiaries of more than $17 million by the time this program ended in 1912.[12]

This policy was renewed in the period following the Second World War. While continentalism brought rapid economic growth for a time, even its architects recognized some defects. For one thing, it did not spread growth evenly across the country, but accentuated already existing disparities. A study by geographer Michael Ray showed that nearly two-thirds of U.S.-controlled manufacturing employment was concentrated in an area within 300 miles of Toronto, compared to two-fifths for Canadian-owned firms.[13] Bonusing firms to locate in have-not regions was designed at least in part to counter this imbalance. Between 1968 and 1980 well over $500 million of federal subsidies was pumped into private companies to support regional expansion.[14] And repeating the bonusing competition of the nineteenth century, most provincial governments set up state development corporations to subsidize manufacturers and resource companies.[15]

Government promotion of research in the private sector began in 1917 with the establishment of the National Research Council. But large-scale subsidization of research and development is a more recent phenomenon. In fact, it was not until the 1960s and 1970s that most government programs got under way. Altogether more than $1.4 billion of federal funds has been granted to private industry since the establishment of these programs.

Another source of indirect transfer to support capital accumulation are the free services provided by federal and provincial governments to the private sector. Departments of Agriculture became the first significant industrial service ministry, providing drainage programs, experimental farms, weed and pest control schemes, grading and quality control standards and numerous other services. When the wheat pools collapsed in the 1930s, the federal government created the Wheat Board, which became a state monopoly in the 1940s. Since then the state has established marketing boards to regulate the production and prices of most major agricultural commodities. Similar provisions were extended to mining and forestry industries, including assay offices for miners, forest fire protection, geological surveys and research; and to manufacturing and commerce sectors, including market surveys, the provision of technical schools and the upgrading of skills.

The task force on program review headed by Deputy Prime Minister Erik Nielsen uncovered 172 separate federal programs, employing 34,000 civil servants, engaged in providing subsidies, assistance and grants to the private sector. The task force estimated that in 1985 these handouts totalled $11.2 billion, nearly as much as corporations paid into federal taxes, and equivalent to more than a fifth of all private investment expenditures (excluding housing). When combined with massive tax relief measures, state provisioning of the private sector assuredly deserves the designation "corporate welfarism."

State-Enterprise Capitalism

Unlike in the U.S., Canadian governments have never rejected public ownership as an instrument of state policy. Indeed, public ownership is more prevalent in Canada than in many, if not most, west European countries. Herschel Hardin went so far as to claim that Canada "is a public enterprise country, always has been and probably always will. Americans have, or at least had, a genius for private enterprise and Canadians have a genius for public enterprise."[16] Hardin is probably right that Canada's resorting to public enterprise is almost unique within the advanced capitalist world. But his explanation for this phenomenon — "Canada's public enterprise culture," "Canada's public enterprise ethic" — owes more to romantic notions of the public purpose than to a class politics that pragmatically viewed public enterprise as a convenient tool to sustain or accelerate private accumulation. There were exceptional circumstances and some notable examples where the public purpose was the primary objective, but usually it played a decidedly auxiliary role.

Most Canadian public enterprise originated from private failures and were motivated as much to bail out shareholders and banks as they were to serve any public purpose — or they were inserted into the breach where profit possibilities were negligible or non-existent — or they resulted from pressure by private industry to nationalize price-gouging utility monopolies.

Going back to 1840, the government rescued the Welland Canal Company which had become a cesspool of corruption and a plunderer of public funds. Its legendary promoter, William Hamilton Merritt, began the project to increase the value of a parcel of his land. Sixty years later the federal government amalgamated the bankrupt Grand Trunk and Canadian Northern railway companies and formed the CNR. If the government had not paid the Canadian Northern $10.8 million for worthless shares, its creditor, the Canadian Bank of Commerce, might have been in trouble. The same situation caused the federal government to nationalize the Canadair and de Havilland aircraft companies a half century later and to bail out Chrysler, Dome and Massey-Ferguson with massive loan guarantees in the late 1970s and early 1980s. Similarly, Nova Scotia bought up the failing Sydney Steel Company, Manitoba the failing Flyer Industries bus company and British Columbia the Pacific Great Eastern. The list of government rescue operations is endless.

The movement for public power began in 1902 when the government of Ontario nationalized private operations and created a state monopoly. As the historian H.V. Nelles has written this was hardly an experiment in socialism:

> From the outset, the crusade for public power was a businessmen's movement; they initiated it, formed its devoted hard-core membership and, most importantly, they provided it with brilliant leadership. By the phrase "the people's power," the businessmen meant cheap electricity for the manufacturers.... The socially and politically influential manufacturers turned readily to public ownership primarily because the private electric companies ... refused to guarantee them an immediate, inexpensive supply of a commodity on which they believed their future prosperity depended. In this, as in countless other cases ... when the market economy failed to satisfy the immediate necessities of the business community, it appealed without the slightest hesitation to the state for public provision of the service.[17]

Shortly after, and for much the same reason, the Manitoba and Saskatchewan governments took over the telephones of the Bell Company and Winnipeg City Hydro was formed. Somewhat later most of the other provinces followed the same route. Even W.A.C. Bennett, who regularly campaigned for re-election with attacks on the "heavy hand of state socialism," took B.C. Electric over in 1961. Perhaps the only exception to this particular path towards "hydro socialism" was Quebec, where René Lévesque created Hydro-Quebec as an instrument of economic nationalism.

The creation of Trans-Canada Airlines (Air Canada) followed from the unwillingness of private enterprise to become involved in the airlines on terms set by Transport Minister C.D. Howe. But just as soon as traffic volume permitted, the public monopoly was broken and CP Air was given permission to compete on domestic flights.

During the Second World War, the state decided that public enterprise was the most expedient instrument to build a war-based industrial infrastructure in a hurry. Twenty-eight crown corporations were established over a five-year period. Only a few of these survived after the war; their assets were sold off to private industry at a fraction of their true value.

In the postwar period, new ventures in public ownership usually involved the state taking over the failures of the private sector. But there were some exceptions. For example, Saskatchewan's NDP government nationalized a major segment of the province's potash industry, which would allow it to enforce price-fixing arrangements and maintain price and income stability for both producers and the government. Several provincial governments established a public monopoly in automobile insurance, and the federal government formed Petro-Canada as a "window" on an oil industry dominated by foreign owners. Saskatchewan set up Sask Oil and Manitoba established Manoil with the same purpose in mind.

Of all the public enterprises created over 150 years, cultural agencies like the National Film Board and the CBC are perhaps the best examples of the ones that unambiguously serve the public purpose, although the CBC was also originally established because no private operator was willing to risk its capital in establishing network broadcasting for a thin Canadian market which stretched over thousands of miles.

Summing up his study of Ontario Hydro, Nelles wrote that government ownership posed no threat to the business community. "In this Hydro was not an exception, for it was run by businessmen, for businessmen, in what was always referred to as a 'businesslike' manner."[18] The conclusion Nelles drew from the Ontario experience can stand as a general statement for what has been called "state-enterprise capitalism" in Canada:

> the positive state survived the nineteenth century primarily because businessmen found it useful. The province received substantial revenue from the development process and enjoyed the appearance of control over it, while industrialists used the government — as had the nineteenth-century commercial classes before — to provide key services at public expense, promote and protect vested interests, and confer the status of law upon private decisions.... It seemed to me on looking at the evidence that the structures established to regulate business in the public interest ... contributed to the reduction of the state — despite an expansion of its activities — to a client of the business community.[19]

Linkages at the Top

The Liberal Party continued the Tory tradition of building private enterprise at public expense. And as proprietors of a much expanded state, postwar Liberal governments maintained an intimate relationship with the business community. As the purchasers of vast supplies of goods and services from the private sector, the Liberal Party was able to finance itself "by levying a percentage on government contracts, or by straight patronage rake-offs where tenders were not involved."[20]

While the more complex corporate and continental economy it presided over could not possibly duplicate the fusion of economic and political elites in the nineteenth century, the connection was still profound. It extended from Mackenzie King advising John Rockefeller, to C.D. Howe, to corporate lawyer St. Laurent, to the Pearson-Trudeau cabinets of corporate elite members (Winters, Richardson, Drury,

Sharp) to John Turner who went from cabinet to the boardrooms of more than a dozen major corporations, and to Brian Mulroney who went almost directly from the corporate boardroom to the prime minister's office.

Since the days of the Second World War when C.D. Howe brought a large number of businessmen to manage government departments and to head public enterprises, the links between the state bureaucracy and the corporate bureaucracy has also been intimate. In recent years the old career civil-service model has been replaced by a cross-pollination, with senior civil servants being encouraged to spend periods of time in the corporate sector. Sociologist Wallace Clement has found in his investigations that nearly 40 per cent of the current members of the economic elite or their close kin spent at least some part of their careers somewhere in the state system.[21] The new Tory regime of Brian Mulroney will maintain these links and undoubtedly intensify them.

The switching of roles among members of the corporate, political and bureaucratic elites and financial dependency on big business by the two main political parties ensure that government will always lend a sympathetic ear to business needs. But the privileged status of the business community does not rest on these intimate connections. To a very large degree they merely reinforce another more profound conditioning factor.

Indeed, most politicians act to enhance the prosperity and stability of business without seeing this as favouring a particular class or group. Ralph Miliband remarks:

> If the national interest is in fact inextricably bound up with the fortunes of capitalist enterprise, apparent partiality towards it is not really partiality at all. On the contrary, in serving the interests of business and in helping capitalist enterprise to thrive, governments are really fulfilling their exalted role as guardians of the good of all. From this standpoint, the much-derided phrase "What is good for General Motors is good for America" is only defective in that it tends to identify the interests of one particular enterprise with the national interest. But if General Motors is taken to stand for the world of capitalist enterprise as a whole, the slogan is one to which governments in capitalist countries do subscribe, often explicitly.[22]

This stance does not require that government officials prefer the capitalist system. It is sufficient that they accept private enterprise and profit-making as the foundation stone of the economy. The consequence of this acceptance, however reluctant and conditional it may be, is that in the final analysis, when national goals like full employment conflict with the requirements of capital accumulation, the national goals are bound to be abandoned. This is why even governments pledged to far-reaching reforms, and elected to office precisely to introduce these reforms, more often than not fail to carry out more than a small part of their program. Their failure cannot be blamed simply on the shortcomings of leaders or the machinations of civil servants — which is not to say that these factors do not play an important role in many instances. The more fundamental cause is that the private-enterprise economy imposes certain structural constraints on public policy which cannot be ignored or evaded whatever the colour worn by the government of the day.

Legitimation Function: Towards the Welfare State

It may appear paradoxical that while the state acts as an essential instrument for capital accumulation, and all that this implies for the well-being of the corporate sector, it has also acted as the primary organizer of reform. The explanation lies in the fact that in a private enterprise/liberal democratic society, while workers require no special inducement to work, they must consent to their status or at the very least give it a passive acceptance. If this condition is absent, social unrest, unruly behaviour, even violence and revolution, are possible. The police and the army can be used to compel acquiescence. The use of the army to defeat the Winnipeg General Strike in 1919 is only the most dramatic incident in Canada's extensive history of using force to bring labour to heel. But in a liberal democracy acquiescence cannot be won on a sustained basis with the use of force. Nor can high levels of productive performance. In particular, the state is forced to intervene if only to stem capital's self-destructive character. With "its unrestrainable passion, its werewolf hunger for surplus labour,"[23] capital might destroy its own basis, the labour power of the workers, if the state did not intervene.

The alternative is for the state to institute a program of reforms to ameliorate the social conditions of labour and avert social and political unrest. As Gladstone put it in the nineteenth century in England, "Please to recollect that we have got to govern millions of hard heads; that it must be done by force, fraud or goodwill; that the latter has been tried and is answering." Kaiser Wilhelm I, grandfather of state health insurance, discovered the same lesson in nineteenth-century Germany: "The care of social ills must be sought not exclusively in the repression of social democratic excesses, but simultaneously in the positive advancements of the welfare of the working classes."[24] Thus virtually all democratic states take a major role in providing such essential services as education, health and housing; in the provision of income support, such as unemployment insurance, welfare, family allowances, family and child social services; and in establishing minimum standards in hours of work, wages, holidays and work and safety conditions.

Until the shift in class forces impelled the state to chart a different course, however, social expenses of this kind were minimal. It was taken for granted that the working classes were obliged to work and that this obligation should, if necessary, be enforced by law. The solution to poverty caused by the first experience of mass industrial unemployment in the 1880s was mass exodus to the U.S. Where assistance was provided, it was available only at the municipal level and was restricted to the sick, elderly and women with dependent children. Pressure from the women's movement finally secured provincial assistance, beginning in Manitoba in 1916, but it was usually available only to widows who were "fit" mothers and was otherwise restricted by asset limits, citizenship and the age of dependent children. The federal Old-Age Pension Act was introduced in 1927, but it too was highly restricted, available on a means-test basis and only to British subjects aged seventy or more who had resided in Canada for at least twenty years. These programs and workers' compensation, established in virtually all provinces between 1910 and 1920, were all there was to assist people without a regular pay cheque. And workers' compensation was not, strictly speaking, a state-welfare measure since it was paid for by contributions from employers.

Government policy reflected the prevailing economic orthodoxy that unemployment was the responsibility of the unemployed: if workers would only accept lower wages and take work where it was available, they could always find jobs. The most popular solution was back-to-the-land where farm employers were always on the look out for cheap labour. As for unemployment relief, the common view, accepted by both manufacturers and farmers, was that the surest way to create unemployment was to bonus it.

Next to the back-to-the-land policy, the most popular solution was poorhouse relief. It took a variety of forms. Back in 1919, an Ontario royal commission, established to investigate the crisis of unemployment, had recommended the setting up of "industrial farms" modeled along the lines of penitentiaries. Vagrants and unskilled workers would be required to work "in exchange for security against ... destitution." This solution was to surface time and time again over the next twenty-five years. For example, during the Great Depression R.B. Bennett's labour minister, Gideon Robertson, recommended that the best solution for the transient problem was to put the men into relief camps where they could work under "supervision equivalent to semi-military control." Those who refused to go would forfeit their right to state assistance. Bennett agreed and the assignment of setting up relief camps went to Andrew McNaughton, chief of the Army General Staff. At its height, 20,000 single men toiled in relief camps for 20¢ a day. Besides combatting the "dole mentality" and preserving the work ethic, the relief camps were meant to serve an overriding political objective. "By taking men out ... of the cities," McNaughton noted, "we are removing the active elements on which the 'red' agitatiors could play." Without relief camps, he argued, it was "only a question of time until we have to resort to arms to restore and maintain order."[25]

In fact, resort to arms was already commonplace. In 1931 in Saskatchewan, the RCMP were called in to break up a coal-miners strike. Led by the Communist-sponsored Workers Unity League (WUL) three workers were killed; several others were jailed. Two years later the WUL organized a general strike in Stratford, Ontario, that was finally broken up when four machine-gun carriers and 120 soldiers answered the mayor's appeal for military aid. Municipal police were called in regularly to break up hunger marches, rallies and sit-ins at city halls throughout the country. To combat "incorrigible" and "dangerous agitators," the government drafted an order-in-council that empowered the minister of defence to establish "camps of discipline" for those who refused to enter relief camps or to perform the work assigned to them.

One of the first acts of the King administration when it returned to office in 1935 was to abolish the relief camps. But King had nothing in mind to take their place. King regarded Roosevelt's New Deal as a move towards "dictatorship" and "state socialism." Resorting to public works sufficient to absorb the 330,000 employables on relief was rejected as inconceivable outside of a "philosophy of socialism."[26] "More than a change of economic structure, what is needed," he proclaimed, "is a change of heart."

It was the belief of both the King and Bennett administrations that the strain which the cost of relief placed on municipal finances and on local tax-payers would act as a powerful check against generosity in setting minimum standards of living for the jobless. With organizations of the unemployed springing up all over the country, leading angry parades to city hall and electing aldermen and mayors, municipal governments were vulnerable to pressures to raise relief rates. Desperate to regain control of the labour market by leveling down the living standards some of the unemployed had won through hard-fought political action at the municipal level, businessmen looked to Ottawa as the last bastion of financial and political stability. The banks had long been among the most ardent supporters of a contributory unemployment insurance scheme. They feared that the debts carried by the provinces and municipalities threatened the entire credit system. An alternative to the existing relief system was required "for our general self-preservation," the president of the Bank of Montreal had written to Prime Minister Bennett.

Using constitutional jurisdiction as his excuse, Mackenzie King still resisted the unemployment insurance route and his second act in office was to slash federal assistance and to set maximum relief rates well below local wage rates for unskilled labour. As he wrote in his diary, this would force local authorities to accept "the truth of the saying that 'everyman must learn to earn his bread by the sweat of his brow'."

It was not depression but war that finally convinced King to enact unemployment insurance. The return to full employment would enable employees to contribute to the plan without hardship, and an unemployment insurance scheme, financed partly by the pay cheques of workers, seemed like an effective way of broadening the government's tax base. As late as 1940, less than 5 per cent of working Canadians earned a taxable income. Labour, which was doing so much for winning of the war, would expect the government to make provisions for its needs once the war was over, King noted in his diary. The alternative was losing control to the socialists, already rising rapidly in the opinion polls.

Why has the Canadian state been such a laggard in the provision of social services and income security while breaking trail in the field of government support for economic development? Certainly not because nobody had thought of it. Liberal reformers, the workers' movement and the women's movement had advocated welfare-state measures since before the turn of the century. And Mackenzie King who ruled the country as prime minister for more than a quarter of a century before 1946 was one of the first writers in the Western world to theorize about the advantages of the welfare-service state and of forging a social partnership between labour, management capital and the state.

Within his 1918 *Industry and Humanity* and his declared "Law of Peace, Work and Health" can be found descriptions of sweeping new innovations — old-age pensions, unemployment insurance, a national health scheme, minimum wage and safety laws — in fact the whole paraphernalia of the welfare state — along with detailed descriptions of profit-sharing, worker-directors, joint councils, and most other quality-of-work-life devices. Yet it was nearly thirty years before elements of the welfare state was in place and sixty years before the state pursued QWL and liberal corporatism. The reason for this delay, as Leo Panitch has written, is that

> ideas, if they are socially disembodied in the sense of not correlating with the nature and balance of class forces in a society, can themselves have little impact. The fact that in the pre-Second World War period the petite

bourgeoisie was the largest subordinate class in Canada and that there was less need on the family farm for the kind of benefits associated with the welfare state, was a major factor in explaining Canada's retardation in this respect. Another key factor was that labour did not pose a *centralized* threat with which the state was forced to deal. The major conflicts of the interwar years were regionally isolated. It was only during the Second World War, with the tremendous growth of popular radicalism and union consciousness, that the Canadian state turned in a deliberate way towards welfarism.[27]

Faced with this pressure and the distinct possibility that, as King noted in his diary, unless "our people ... realize that labour has to be dealt with in a considerate way,... we will begin to have defections from our ranks in the House to the CCF," the Liberals finally began building the foundations of the welfare state. They did so in the most minimal of ways, as the disappearance of the national health plan until its re-emergence in the 1960s testifies. The provinces were another source of pressure for, within the division of responsibilities handed out in the constitution, it was the provinces who were in the front lines in having to respond to the demands of labour for social service. Without an adequate revenue base, it is not surprising that they should call upon the federal government to take over responsibility for funding these programs. To a degree, the welfare state involved the nationalization and rationalization of welfare schemes and social services that were sprouting in chaotic fashion throughout the dominion.

In sum, these social policies have invariably been put into place as a concession to working-class pressure and in order to maintain the system in the face of a threat or potential threat to its stability. At the same time they provide employers with a better-trained and educated, more healthy and quiescent labour force. Despite these advantages to employers, social-reform measures have generally been strongly and even bitterly attacked by some, if not all, elements of the dominant economic class; for even if it is true that such reforms must in the long run be accepted to preserve social order, the price to finance them is often unpalatable. There is always the question of how much reform is necessary to ensure social stability and there is the possibility that in some circumstances, reforms — far from stilling discontent — will encourage demands for more. Above all the state must be stopped from conceding so much that profit margins and the labour market are threatened.

These are matters that businessmen, with their eyes fixed on immediate interests and requirements, cannot be expected to handle properly. As the primary organizer of reform, the state therefore needs some elbow room to manoeuvre. The reforms introduced have for the most part been easily accommodated and have proved problematic only in times of economic stagnation and crisis.

Securing Labour Peace

Attitudes towards trade unions partly mirrored the approach towards income security. Prior to 1872, the formation of trade unions and the use of the strike weapon had been treated as statutory offences under the restraint of trade laws. The 1872 Canadian Trade Unions Act removed this restriction but it did nothing to require employers to recognize and bargain with unions. On the contrary, throughout the first decades of the century the extensive use of naked force by the state in defence of employer's resistance to unionization became a hallmark of Canadian labour history. From Cape Breton to Vancouver, the state resorted to military intervention and mass arrests dozens of times, culminating in the use of military troops to break the Winnipeg General Strike in 1919. At least one union organizer, Ginger Goodwin, was shot dead by a member of the special federal police corps.[28]

The 1903 Royal Commission on Industrial Disputes in British Columbia recommended that "radical socialistic" unions should be outlawed because they were not "legitimate" trade unions and because their officials were "not trade unionists but foreign socialist agitators of the most bigoted and ignorant type." It condemned picketting and urged that certain "reprehensible" actions of labour should be banned, such as sympathy strikes, boycotts of employers, intimidation of non-union workers, and the circulation of lists of strike-breakers or "scabs." Various of the labour actions targeted by the royal commission have since been outlawed. In 1917 the federal government abolished strikes and lock-outs for the duration of the war and outlawed fourteen radical organizations.

With the passage of the Industrial Disputes and Investigations Act (IDIA) of 1902, under the auspices of Mackenzie King, the state introduced a system of compulsory conciliation, a "cooling-off" period to allow for "reasonable" bargaining between parties. Between 1907 and 1911, 101 disputes were handled under the IDIA and in nearly all cases strikes were averted. Claiming itself an "impartial umpire," the state used this strike-delaying legislation to enforce industrial peace. In the words of one student in the period, it amounted to "an ad hoc suspension of hostilities" in the context of "a generalized defence of private property rights of the Canadian state."[29] While unions were deprived of their main bargaining weapon, there were no effective restraints placed on employers to prevent familiar practices of imposing yellow-dog contracts, black listing, discharging union members and employing non-union members or strike breakers.

Instead of encouraging the formation of unions, the state promoted joint councils and welfare works as devices to bring harmony in the relations of labour and capital. It was not until the 1940s that it would replace coercion and containment with legislation that recognized the principles of freedom of association for workers.

We can conclude from this that, until wartime conditions altered the balance of class forces, the state's policy in the area of both income security and industrial relations was entirely aimed at enhancing the private accumulation of capital. Its concerns for legitimacy was confined to the ideological precepts of business. The working class was still too weak to force the state to expend significant revenues on social harmony. The coercion of market forces, backed by police force if necessary, was deemed sufficient to maintain "law and order and good government."

The Postwar Settlement

The manifestation of worker power during the war and the promise of a better life after the war pressured the state to assist workers in establishing a recognized bargaining relationship with employers and to provide the rudiments of an income-security program. A wartime federal order-in-council (PC1003) giving unions legal recognition, sanctioning collective bargaining and guaranteeing the right to strike was hastily duplicated in all provinces. But the very same legislation also subjected unions to detailed government regulations and supervision. The price imposed for state assistance included continuation of the compulsory conciliation and work-stoppage delay features of the earlier legislation, along with a broad set of new legal restrictions. These provisions delineated eligibility for union membership, procedures and conditions under which unions could be granted certification as bargaining agents, outlawing of strikes for the duration of contracts and liability for unions and their members if illegal strikes occurred.

Hedged with so many regulations and restrictions, many of them working to the disadvantage of labour, the term "free collective bargaining" is a particularly inappropriate title for the new industrial-relations system. It suggests a relationship between two evenly matched adversaries playing out a game under rules that do not prejudice the outcome. Obscured from view is the structural inequality between labour and capital, the restrictive character of the rules particularly regarding labour and the fact that in the final analysis the state stands ready to use its coercive powers to protect the prerogatives of capital.

The terms of this postwar truce were graphically described by Justice Rand in his famous 1946 ruling on union security:

> In industry, capital must in the long run be looked upon as occupying the dominant position.... Any modification of relations between the parties here concerned must be made within the framework of a society whose economic

life has private enterprise as its dynamic.... It is the accommodation of that principle ... with evolving notions of social justice in the area of industrial mass production that becomes the problem for decision...."[30]

The truce established by corporate and union leaders through the mediation of the state lasted for twenty years. The unions were clear about the advantages to labour. They paid less attention to corporate gains. The truce was obviously designed to secure, under new conditions, what Justice Rand aptly called "the framework of a society whose economic life has private enterprise as its dynamic." More particularly, the restrictions built into the legislation to cool labour militancy allowed management to win back much of the leverage it had begun to lose.

Employers took their cue. Management-rights clauses soon appeared in nearly all contracts. Many corporations insisted that wage gains be tied to increases in workers' productivity. Effectively this meant that unions promised not to increase workers' wages at the expense of surplus value. It was a perfect arrangement. Tying wage increases to productivity induced employees to work hard and competitively; management-rights clauses left decision-making about production as management's exclusive prerogative.

The period was haunted by Cold War anti-Communism, by the American Taft-Hartley Act and later by the Landrum-Griffin Bill that together undid much that had been accomplished by the famous Wagner Act of 1936, American labour's so-called charter of rights. Encouraged by the state, certain union activists seized the issue of anti-Communism as their claim to union leadership in Canada. Battles for control were particularly savage in the new industrial unions. When they failed in their efforts to defeat the Communists and those closely associated with them, the targeted unions were summarily expelled from the "official" houses of labour. The spectacle of raids, counter-raids and expulsions scarcely recommended unionism to union members, much less to others. With more money and energy devoted to battles for control and less to winning better settlements and working conditions, labour was rendered a greatly weakened force. Little wonder it had no resolve to fight the restrictive legislation introduced in this period.

The first flurry of postwar restrictions came in the immediate wake of Taft-Hartley. The restrictions aimed to stop the spread of trade unionism, to confine trade unions to the sphere of large-scale industry, which they had more or less already successfully organized. The chosen instrument was a certification procedure that allowed a determined employer to so obstruct and delay certification that the union would likely give up or be destroyed. As well, regulations dealing with "unfair labour practices" were so cumbersome as to make traditional "union-busting" methods available to any employer that wanted to employ them. The legislation and its application went a long way towards denying collective bargaining to hitherto unorganized workers. It was particularly effective in keeping trade unions out of small-scale and small-town employments.[31]

More far-reaching were the legislative restrictions introduced from 1958 to 1962 to weaken existing unions. Alberta prohibited strikes in "essential services." Manitoba and British Columbia required government-supervised strike votes. Many provinces confined picketing to striking employees during a "legal" strike, thus outlawing "secondary boycotts" and sympathy strikes. Three provinces placed limits on the ability of unions to provide funds for political parties.

Except in Saskatchewan, no public servants enjoyed bargaining rights until 1965. By the mid-1970s public-sector employers in all jurisdictions had been granted some form of bargaining rights. Federal employees were conceded collective bargaining rights in 1967. This was no mere gift granted by benevolent governments. It was sparked by the extension of bargaining rights to Quebec's public-sector workers in 1965. This was one of the fruits of the Quiet Revolution in Quebec — a new deal for public employees purchased by the Lesage government to broaden its coalition. When federal employees in Quebec demanded equal treatment and the movement for public-sector bargaining spread to other parts of the country, the die was cast. The real question was how "free" collective bargaining would be. The answer was not long in coming.

Both federal and provincial governments imposed restrictions beyond those placed on private-sector workers. In the federal area such vital issues as pensions, job classifications, staffing, technological change and the use of part-time employees were wholly or partly excluded from the scope of bargaining. Serious consideration was also given to denying federal workers the right to strike. But the outbreak of a number of "illegal" strikes in the Post Office persuaded the government that making strikes illegal was no guarantee that they would stop. Most provincial governments similarly set a number of crucial issues outside the scope of bargaining, and in the case of Ontario, Alberta, Nova Scotia and P.E.I., civil servants, hospital employees and others were denied the right to strike.

Regarding the capital-labour relationship, the state has been forced to compromise its accumulation function to a degree by legislating a space in the economic and social order for trade unions and by regulating collective bargaining as a means by which workers could affect the terms and conditions of their labour. With the onset of the economic crisis, however, and particularly since 1975, the state felt compelled to retract many of these concessions or at least to temporarily suspend them through ad hoc interventions terminating collective bargaining or overruling its results. Given the favourable economic environment of the first postwar decades, the outcome of free collective bargaining and various legislative provisions could be fairly readily accommodated without impairing profit margins. When that environment soured, the state decided it could no longer afford to compromise its accumulation function. Moreover, it was encouraged to believe that trade unions were at least partially responsible for the economic crisis.

Legitimacy versus Accumulation

This process of retraction began in October 1975 when wage increases were restricted according to a complex formula implemented by the Anti-Inflation Board (AIB). Whatever the extent of the AIB's success in holding down inflation, all commentators agree that it did suppress wage gains and protect profit margins. While the AIB exercise did not suspend collective bargaining or the right to strike, it severely restricted the results of collective bargaining and rendered the strike weapon all but futile.

A second round of wage controls, targeted specifically at public-sector workers did suspend collective bargaining and the right to strike. Beginning with Alberta in January 1982, B.C. in February and the federal government in June, within a year all but one of the provinces had adopted some form of wage restraint for public-sector workers. In some instances, Quebec in particular, these workers were forced to accept significant wage cuts. For most of the last decade, then, public-sector workers have been governed by legislation that has severely undermined the already circumscribed collective bargaining rights granted public-sector workers over the previous decade. With the exception of the 1975-78 period, governments seemed content to allow rising unemployment and the threat of mass lay-offs to take care of wage bargaining in the private sector.

The use of statutory wage control has been accompanied by legislative acts to remove the right to strike from an increasingly broad group of public-sector workers, including greater resort to suspension of strikes and increasingly onerous penalties — such as prison sentences for union leaders and members defying the law. Between 1975 and 1984 anti-union emergency legislation was used in forty-one occasions, far more than it was used over the previous twenty-five years.

In addition to ordering striking workers back to work, the legislation included Nova Scotia's infamous Michelin Bill. It quashed union certification by requiring the simultaneous organization of all plants in "integrated" structures, tailor-made to keep Michelin union-free and almost certainly brought in at the request of company officials. It also

TABLE 14:1
Back-to-Work Legislation, 1950-84

Years	Federal Jurisdiction	Provincial Jurisdiction	Total
1950-59	2	1	3
1960-69	4	9	13
1970-74	4	9	13
1975-79	6	16	22
1980-84	1	18	19

Source: Royal Commission on the Economic Union and Development Prospect for Canada, Volume 2, p. 680.

includes Alberta's legislation that allows unionized construction companies to circumvent collective bargaining by setting up non-union subsidiaries, and the whole host of anti-union legislation brought in by B.C.'s Socred government.

It would be wrong to characterize all legislation introduced since the mid-1970s as anti-union. Quebec passed legislation limiting the use of strike-breakers; B.C., Ontario, Quebec and Manitoba established provisions for improving first agreements on recalcitrant employers; Ontario and Manitoba prohibited the use of professional strike-breakers; most jurisdictions passed legislation allowing workers the right to refuse unsafe work.

Most of this legislation came before the seriousness of the economic crisis dawned on policy-makers. As the 1970s wore on, the pronounced shift towards undisguised coercive measures became undeniably apparent — so much so that its negative impact on the carefully crafted post-1945 industrial-relations system was noted by then federal labour minister, André Ouellet:

> The frequency and predictability of government interventions in both strikes and wage settlements may have created a contradiction. On the one hand, the political process has sanctioned a wage determination system that is based on free collective bargaining which guarantees the right to strike. On the other hand, ad hoc measures have been taken that may have paralyzed the system and removed various rights essential to its functioning.[32]

The state had clearly reached a crisis of legitimacy in its relationship with the labour movement. To repair the damage, the federal Department of Labour was given "almost carte blanche to initiate programs which would appease organized labour."[33] It responded with a fourteen-point program which included the establishment of the Institute for

Occupational Health and Safety, a task force to study paid educational leaves, grants to unions to conduct labour education, a QWL program and various improvements in employment standards in the Canada Labour Code. Most of these programs were enacted along with tripartite agencies: the sectoral task force and Second Tier Committees, Major Projects Task Force and advisory committees in the automotive, aerospace, forestry and petrochemical industries.

Before its demise the Liberal government was groping towards an attempt to "merge the capital accumulation and legitimation functions of labour policy" or more precisely "to use legitimacy measures to promote the accumulation functions." As noted by Stephen McBride, this attempt was demonstrated in the decision to include the Department of Labour in the economic, rather than in the social-affairs expenditure envelope on the grounds that "a harmonious work environment is essential to the economic well being of Canada."[34] This approach meshes well with the philosophy of the Mulroney government and will no doubt be pursued in the years ahead.

Whether or not it will work is another matter. While participation in tripartite councils appeals to certain elements within the leadership of the labour movement and goes a long way to meet their desire for legitimacy, it is widely distrusted elsewhere. The opposition that arose within the executive council of the Canadian Labour Congress to former President McDermott's agreement to participate in a government-sponsored committee to advise on cut-backs in the federal civil service is a case in point. More generally, whatever the predispositions of particular labour leaders, pressures from within the ranks will make it difficult for them to continue to participate in collaborative exercises with governments that resort to coercive interventions and that rely on heavy unemployment and social-service cut-backs to discipline the work force.

A glance at the data reveals why the Canadian welfare system state has also been vulnerable to attack in recent years. The first wave of welfare-state measures was easily absorbed. Expenditures on health, education and income security took up 8.2 per cent of total expenditures in the economy of 1950. Expanded to include Old-Age Security (1952) and the Disabled Persons Act (1954), it had drifted up to 13.1 per cent by 1965. The second wave, which included Medicare, Canada Pensions, the Canada Assistance Plan and the Guaranteed Income Supplement, was not so easily absorbed. The welfare state bill rose to 18.7 per cent in 1970 and, with the addition of a generously overhauled Unemployment Insurance Program (1971), to 23 per cent in 1976, where it remained until 1981 when it took another jump.

While the welfare state was never warmly embraced by the Canadian business community, so long as it could be financed painlessly out of the growth dividend and on the margins of higher incomes, it was passively accepted. Business criticisms remained muted until the mid-1970s. From the 1960s on, tax-relief measures awarded to the corporations and to the rich enabled them to reduce their share of the tax burden, shifting the increased cost of the welfare state onto working-class and middle-income earners.

Once stagnation set in, however, it was inevitable that the narrower tax base could not generate sufficient revenues to cover the cost of the program, which were further bloated by the impact of mass unemployment. Since in the eyes of the business community it is the size of the deficit (together with high wages) that ails the economy, the deficit had to be brought down. This could only be achieved either by raising tax rates, including the business community's and/or eliminating tax breaks or by cutting down government spending. Not surprisingly, those programs that make no contribution to profits — like public assistance for the arts, universities, human rights, ecology and especially income security — became their primary targets of business.

We have come some distance in examining the factors that affect the profitability of private investment: wages, monopolization, worker effort, the state. In the following chapter this analysis is put to use in helping chart the history of the current economic crisis.

15 | The Economic Roller Coaster

The Canadian economy has roller-coasted over at least twenty-five business cycles in the past century. Continuous economic growth is good for jobs, but it turns out to be bad for profits. And capitalism is based on production for profit, not for employment. Corporations, as their executives are the first to admit, count their earnings in money, not in the jobs they create. Even the thirty years of postwar boom were marked by occasional recessions. The official unemployment rate rarely fell below 3 per cent in the period, but over the last decade, the decade of the Great Stagnation, it seldom fell much below 10 per cent, and even the most optimistic forecasters cannot foresee a time over the decade ahead where it will return to postwar norms.

It now appears that the entire capitalist world is caught in the downslope of what is known as the Kondratieff wave. Nicolai Kondratieff was a Soviet economist whose thoughts on the long-wave cycle were published in the 1920s. He was exiled to Siberia in 1930 and his long-wave theory disappeared with him. Only recently, in the wake of the current crisis, has it been rediscovered.

While by no means universally accepted, economists who see something in it have plotted four long waves over the past century and a half. Engulfing the entire capitalist world, each cycle has a duration of roughly fifty years: from 1815 to the mid-1840s, from the mid-1840s through the mid-1890s, from then to the Second World War, and from the war through at least the late 1980s.

Within each wave, long periods of expansion and prosperity are followed by substantial periods of depression and stagnation. During the expansion phase, recessions tend to be short and mild; during the long down cycle, they are both frequent and severe with recoveries only partial. Each period of expansion is characterized by its own special features: a particular propelling industry, technology and labour process; specific forms of enterprise and competition; a certain international division of production with one country emerging as the leading nation; a well-defined role for the state; specific class organizations, class alliances, political forms and ideologies. Each period of crisis is also unique with its own mechanism of adjustment and institutional restructuring.

Why are a million and a half Canadians currently out of work? In a nutshell, unemployment results when the owners of business cannot foresee sufficient profits and therefore cut back their operations and shelve plans to build new factories and buildings or to open up new mines and stores.

When Marx described this process he did so in much the same way as a businessman would. He pictured it as an accumulation circuit with three distinct phases. In the first phase, businessmen use money to hire labour and buy the materials and equipment needed to start up production. Money capital is turned into variable capital (labour power) and constant capital (means of production). The second part of the circuit is located entirely in the place of production rather than in the maketplace. Labour power, materials and equipment are combined and turned into finished products. It's here where surplus value is generated. In the third phase, capital — now embodied in finished goods — must complete its metamorphosis back into money. This occurs in the marketplace where goods are bought and sold. Its here where surplus value is realized.

After the completion of each circuit, there must exist those who are willing and able to resell their labour power and others willing and able to buy it — the core of the capitalist relationship which must be retained and reproduced. On the one hand, workers remain *able* to sell their labour power because they are paid a wage high enough to ensure continued fitness to produce. They remain *willing* to resell their labour power because their wage is not sufficiently high enough to enable them to purchase their own means of production or to obtain a living income by other means. On the other hand, businessmen are *able* to hire workers out of the resources they command from past output, and they are *willing* to employ them because they make a profit by selling the commodities that workers produce.

We can trace the problems that may arise from the point of view of business. First, employers have to discover a source of labour, materials and equipment. If workers are unwilling to work at wages employers are prepared to pay or if the needed material inputs are unavailable or too expensive, the circuit is cut off before it even starts. Of course, employers search the market for cheap sources of labour, machinery and materials. Some businesses may even discover occasional bargains and thereby gain an advantage over their rivals. But chances are that they will not be able to retain their advantage for long. Employers who find cheap sources of fuel, for example, or cheap supplies of labour or technologically superior equipment will profit from the discovery, but unless they can keep other firms from using the same new source, their advantage will be wiped out quickly. Moreover, as others take similar advantage of the new discoveries, the price of fuel and the price of labour is bound to rise. This process will be accelerated if the suppliers organize themselves into cartels and unions. Windfall gains may persist for a long time but not forever.

Once money capital is successfully converted into labour power and stocks of materials and equipment, management must obtain the maximum effort and diligence of its work force in order to maximize the volume of its saleable output. Any interference with labour discipline, such as absenteeism, sabotage, slow-downs, vandalism or indifference, will reduce the quality and/or quantity of the finished product, thereby lessening its capitalized value. Employers can manipulate the length of the working day and increase the intensity of work, but these measures are not without risk. In unionized shops, particularly when alternative jobs are available, such strategies can provoke resistance, causing a reduction in work effort. To entice greater worker co-operation, management will often have to resort to the more sophisticated techniques of industrial relations and control that we have previewed.

Having successfully completed the fabrication process, the firms must sell what they produce, likely through merchants who act as intermediaries between producers and consumers. The firms may have produced too much given the state of the market and may have to sell the product at a price below its cost of production. Changes in buyers' needs and tastes is another daily risk; marketing analysis can help but it is never foolproof. A new product or product design or a new marketing technique may attract a new buying public, but new customers are easily stolen by rival firms that put superior products or cheaper ones on the market.

To complete the circuit of capital, the firms must turn sales revenue back into new investment, and in this they face still other obstacles. Besides paying out dividends to shareholders and salaries to officers, sales, staff, accountants and lawyers, as well as fees to advertising agents, they still have to pay out interest on loans from the bank and taxes to the government. If governments impose higher profit taxes, less remains for reinvestment. If corporations are successful in convincing governments to shift the tax burden on to the general public, lower disposable incomes may cut into sales markets.

Whatever is finally left after all these deductions is called retained earnings. Just as soon as they are counted they have to be ploughed back and the entire process repeated in the hope that they will again re-emerge as an ever-expanding quantity.

Breakdown

The odds of this happening are not at all high, but a breakdown in the overall economy can occur in several ways.

- Too much production. When an economy expands it can at first produce more output with the existing productive capacity, since so much of it is lying idle from the previous recession. But at some point it will have to produce new machines and buildings to supply the demand for additional goods. When enough of them are built to support expanded production of consumer goods, the demand for machinery and buildings dries up. With few orders coming in, the capital goods industries cut back in their volume of production. Laid-off workers lose their ability to buy consumer goods. With shrinking consumer demand, consumer-goods industries find their inventories piling up. They cut back production too, laying off more workers. Soon the economy is in general recession.

  Alternatively, overproduction may appear first in the consumer-goods sector as the volume of production expands faster than consumer demand. If this is the source of the problem, the recession is likely to be brief, just long enough to enable firms to reduce their excess inventories.

  The problem of matching demand and supply may be a general one: the total amount of purchasing power generated in phase one may be insufficient to absorb the total value of goods produced in phase two. Perhaps products can only be sold at prices less than their worth, dampening expectations of further profits and thereby causing firms to hoard their profits rather than investing in more production.

  On the other hand, the problem may be in the overproduction of only some commodities. If these are important enough in the overall economy, pockets of depression can spread into other sectors. The general point is that, because of the interconnectedness of the system on the one hand and the disconnected way investment decisions are made on the other, whatever happens to reduce demand or profits anywhere quickly reverberates throughout the system.

- High wages. In the early phase of an economic expansion there is always a substantial amount of unused capacity and unemployed labour — a legacy of the previous recession. There are few bottlenecks to expanding output and large numbers of unemployed workers prepared to hire their labour out at prevailing wages. All of this permits rapidly rising profits, which swell the income of the rich and allow for a reinvestment in more equipment, raw materials and the hiring of more workers.

But as the economy grows, bottlenecks begin to appear. In particular there is a growing shortage of labour. Unless new supplies of labour are uncovered, the reserve pool of labour dries up. Workers gain bargaining power: their ability to demand higher wages and better working conditions increases; their productivity falls off, not only because machinery is overused and tends to break down more frequently, but also because of the increasing time lost in strikes and grievances as workers become more demanding and less manageable. As long as firms can raise their prices to affect rising labour costs they can protect their profit margins. At some point, however, workers' growing power begins to cut into profit. As profits decline, employers cut back on production and dismiss a part of their work force. A recession begins.

- Too much machinery. One way firms can attempt to offset higher labour costs is to introduce labour-saving machinery. This could work to protect profits providing the savings gained from reduced labour costs exceed, over an appropriate period, the cost of the new machinery. With lower than average per-unit cost, an innovating firm will find itself earning above average profits. Sooner or later, however, most if not all firms will have been forced to adopt the new machinery. By then, the industry price will have been adjusted downward to cover the new lower average unit cost plus the normal mark-up. Any advantage the pioneering firm had gained will be wiped out.

If labour-saving machinery is introduced extensively throughout the economy overall profits may shrink rather than expand. Profit derives from surplus labour time. Machinery enhances productivity and therefore increases the amount of surplus labour time per worker. But the rapid reduction of the number of workers can negate this gain and cause a decline in the total amount of surplus labour time. As a consequence, profits shrink rather than expand. But the impact of the machinery on profits is more complicated still. Under continued pressure of labour-saving machines, cut-throat competition among workers likely reduces the wage rate. A more productive work force which also receives lower wages could increase profits despite the narrowing foundation of surplus labour time. This is an empirical question, the final result depending on the quantities and proportions that emerge in practice.

- Too little consumption. If employers respond to a profit squeeze by lowering wages or by investing abroad to take advantage of a cheap labour supply, they run the risk of workers and their families, who are the consuming public, not having enough money to purchase all the commodities produced on the market. The source of profits may be the point of production, but profits are finally realized in the marketplace.

Owners could spend all of their profits on consumption goods for themselves and so eliminate any surplus of consumer goods. But this denies their function as capitalists, which is to reinvest their profit in more and more capital. If consumption spending fails to keep up with production, it's still possible for the gap between supply and demand to be filled by increased spending on capital goods. As indicated above, however, this can only be a temporary solution. A final possibility is that domestic shortfalls in demand can be offset by net export surpluses. This outlet is obviously not available to all, since the export surplus of some countries comes at the expense of trade deficits of others.

In short, given the combined pressures of competition and worker militancy, employers search desperately for ways to control workers' wages. They'll hire unorganized workers, blackmail unions, move their plants, among many other options. But as they succeed they could find that the demand for their product is shrinking. What appears to be a rational solution for one capitalist turns out to create chaos in the market place if the same solution is tried by all capitalists. Businesses can reduce their prices in the hope that this will generate greater sales. But this might result in lower rather than higher profits. Declining profits cause firms to cut back in production. We are in a recession.

The contradiction posed to the system is obvious enough. Profit is served by keeping wages low, but low wages limit the size of markets. High wages create larger markets for products, but at some point they put the squeeze on profits. To the extent that employers are successful in keeping wages down, their selling problems are worsened by the lack of consumer purchasing power; to the extent that workers are successful in driving up wages, capitalists have smaller profits to reinvest. Periodically there develops an imbalance between the capacity to produce and the capacity to consume.

- Not enough liquidity. Periods of prosperity usually spawn a boom psychology. Not only are existing businesses eager to expand their operations, but new businesses multiply to stake their claim to the profits bonanza. Many firms go into debt to finance their expansions, and new businesses are financed on credit. Meanwhile, consumer purchases are blown up by inflation of retail, installment and mortgage credit.

Shortages of labour and materials finally give rise to bottlenecks in production and to inflation. With inflation eating up cash faster than expected and with sluggish collection of accounts receivable, corporations turn more and more to the banks. The banks in turn sell off their investment in government bonds to get hold of more money to lend to businesses, consumers and speculators. Banks are then forced to raise their lending rates to attract new savings in the light of rising prices, because of their expectation that repayment will be in depreciated currency and because of the higher risks involved when borrowers face critical cash-shortage problems. The financial structure becomes more and more fragile. It is supported by hope and faith that the boom is not coming to an end.

Consumers depend on continuous employment to provide them with the income to meet interest charges and eventually to pay off their debts. Manufacturers count on uninterrupted growth in sales and profits. Commodity, real-estate and stock-market speculators operate on the assumption that prices will keep on rising. And the banks depend on continuous prosperity to enable them to repay depositors and savers the money they've been lending.

All have become speculators involved in a precarious enterprise. Any slow-down in the economy causes the credit structure to tremble. The accumulation of excess inventories, the over-investment in new plant and equipment, the overproduction of consumer goods relative to demand, squeezed profits, the inability of banks to extend further credit — any of these factors or some combination can bring the economic upswing to an end. As incomes, sales and employment drop off, lenders press their claims and the scramble among debtors to collect funds begins. The fact that debt has been piled upon debt produces a domino effect throughout the economy. When the short-term liability sections of their balance sheet reach dangerous proportions, businesses must curtail their operations, and many will be forced into bankruptcy.

The possibility that the economy will grow smoothly — adjusting easily to these problems and finding readily accessible escape routes — is very, very remote.

Marx on Crisis

Marx offered two perspectives on crisis under capitalism.[1] The first extends over the course of the business cycle; the second is the long-run tendency towards a falling rate of profit.

Why is the business cycle a necessary feature of capitalist development? Firms are compelled to accumulate, that is grow, in order to safeguard their position against rival firms. In the course of this expansion they search out all sources of labour power from which to wring more surplus value. Engaging extra workers poses no problem so long as the wages do not encroach on surplus value. Through increased productivity, real wages can easily rise while the rate of surplus value is maintained or even increased. But as all available sources of labour power become exhausted, the law of supply and demand will push up wages to the point that they do finally encroach on surplus value. When this point arrives, capitalists will have little incentive to reinvest in expanding their output. On the contrary, they will contract. This is the crisis phase of the business cycle with workers being laid off thereby bringing down the level of real wages. This swelling of this "reserve army of labour," Marx wrote, is the pivot upon which "the law of demand and supply of labour works."[2]

Besides holding wages in check, unemployment enables management to exercise greater discipline on the factory floor. The crisis also permits major structural changes in the economy. Weaker firms are destroyed as is much of the debt built up in the boom. Some of their assets are purchased at below their value by the financially stronger surviving firms. Capital is thereby further centralized and concentrated. The sorry state of business lessens the demand for bank credit. The banks gradually regain their liquidity and interest rates fall. Other costs are also lowered as markets that were too tight become slack once more. In short, the crisis creates the condition for a revival of accumulation and the cycle turns upwards again.

But like the classical economists before him, Marx was mainly interested in exploring "the laws of motion" of capitalist society, the forces governing its long-run movement. In the final analysis, long-run movement rests with the consequences of capital's compulsion to expand. Capitalism, Marx argued, is controlled by competitive relationships, the conflict not only between labour and capital but also between capitalists themselves. Competition manifests itself in the continuous threat that each enterprise poses to every other. The only certain defence is an expansive strategy. Self-preservation, then, forces each individual "capital" to seek to expand. "Accumulate, accumulate! That is the Moses and the Prophets."[3]

This property, Marx thought, imparts to the capitalist system as a whole a particularly precarious growth path. As all enterprises seek to augment their capital, they compete for access to labour power, causing wages to rise and surplus value to shrink. They then attempt to cut costs and maintain profits in the only way open to them, by substituting machinery for labour — or, as Marx put it, substituting dead labour for living labour.

Self-protection compels this response but its cumulative effect is also self-destructive, for the introduction of machinery will achieve the expected results for a time but, when it is substituted for labour across the system, the results can be adverse. Machinery can never be the source of surplus value. While machinery increases the amount of surplus value extracted from workers, "the rate of exploitation," by replacing the work force it also narrows the base from which surplus value can be drawn.

Marx called the proportion of machines and raw materials to workers employed in production the technical composition of capital or, measured in value terms, the value or organic composition of capital. Capitalism's precise path, therefore, depends on the outcome of the race between an increasing organic composition of capital and an increasing rate of exploitation. If the former rises faster than the latter, the rate of profit will fall and beyond a certain point further capital accumulation would be impossible.

For Marx, the "law of the tendency of the rate of profit to fall" was "in every respect the most important law of modern political economy and the most essential for understanding the most difficult relations."[4] But it is only a tendency, for "the same influences which produce a tendency in the general rate of profit to fall," he wrote, "also call forth counter-effects which hamper, retard and partly paralyse this fall."[5] The outcome that emerges from these conflicting forces cannot be mechanically predicted. Marx in fact listed five major counteracting forces which have the effect of either raising the rate of exploitation or lowering the organic composition of capital.

The rate of exploitation can be raised by compelling workers to toil more intensely, running an assembly-line faster or increasing the number of machines a worker operates; by depressing wages below the value of labour power, to sweat labour where conditions permit; by reorganizing work methods with such techniques as "scientific management," like time and motion studies or elaborate job ladders; by eliminating work practices that reduce managerial flexibility; and most important, by continuously introducing new technology that raises productivity.

The organic composition of capital can be lowered if the new machinery being introduced is more capital-saving than it is labour-saving. Although more machines are in use, their value (the labour time needed to produce them) is less. Similarly, the elements of constant capital can be cheapened by the discovery of more efficient ways of extracting raw materials or by discovering cheaper sources of raw materials. Further, improved techniques of organizing, planning and communicating economize in the use of constant capital by increasing its rate of turnover. Finally, during business cycles, machinery, inventories and raw materials of bankrupt companies can be purchased below their true value. In sum, while the physical quantity of machines and raw materials used up in production has grown prodigiously, the proportion of total value they represent has obviously increased nowhere near as much and in some periods not at all.

Another counteracting force is the constant pressure to extend the geographical scope of capital accumulation both inside national boundaries and without. The rate of exploitation of the population living in these territories is generally higher and the organic composition of capital generally less than in the advanced industrial countries and regions. Surplus value can also be transferred by means of "unequal exchange" of goods through the monopolization of trade channels and the ability of multinational corporations to transfer price profits to their subsidiaries in low-tax havens.

These counteracting influences are nothing else than the ongoing restructuring of production in the face of competitive pressures on profits. They make it impossible to foretell either the timing or the extent that the rate of profit will actually fall. All that Marx wanted to express is that as mechanization displaces the ultimate source of profits, profit rates will always be subject to erosion. The counteracting influences can modify the outcome and reverse it for a time. But the tendency, however invisible, is always operative. It only becomes visible when the ongoing restructuring process is not sufficient to overcome it.

In fact, the crisis is itself a vehicle for accelerating the counter-tendencies. Competition for smaller markets intensifies, and weaker enterprises crumble. Massive unemployment and the ever-present threat of lay-off forces workers to accept lower real wages, a speed-up of production and a relaxation of shop-floor restrictions on management control.

Supervising the Crisis: Limits and Possibilities

Marx did not consider in any detail the state's role in managing the economy. In his time it was relatively minor. This is a hotly debated subject among contemporary Marxists. The most useful contribution has been that of the German school, which argues that the role of the state is governed by the "logic of capital" itself, by the particular requirements and consequences of capital accumulation as they have themselves evolved and changed.[6]

In the example of research and development, where knowledge and technology cannot be privatized, it tends to be underproduced by capital; where the risks are great or where the organization and financial resources required surpass even the capacity of large enterprises, it again will be underproduced. At a time in the history of capitalism where advancing technological development is critically important in the race for survival, the state and its agencies take over the function of producing science and technology and subsidizing its development.

Similar factors have caused the state to socialize the reproduction of labour power by providing education, training and health care; to build various types of capital-intensive infrastructures; to take over unprofitable but important spheres of production. All of these expenditures have the effect of countering the falling rate of profit as do certain redistribution devices built into the tax system and tariffs structure.

On the international plane, states of leading capitalist nations use their diplomatic offices, and if necessary their military apparatus, to safeguard existing spheres of investment, sources of raw materials and unequal exchange relations. This function has become particularly important in recent years as multinational corporations split up their production empires, hiving off labour-intensive operations to Third World countries, where low wages and minimal regulations provide extraordinary rates of profit which can offset declining rates of profit in advanced countries.

Overlaying these interventions in the production sphere are the state's economic management functions in the market sphere: regulating effective demand through the automatic stabilizers, credit and budget management, and the maintenance of an apparatus for economic analysis and forecasting. Government can increase demand temporarily through its spending and deficit finance. But unless the barriers to accumulation are overcome, the outcome is likely to be more of an increase in prices than in output. In any case, since these techniques have never been very effective, they have often been supplemented by more direct measures like incomes policy.

Incomes policy emerged in late capitalism as a direct consequence of the cumulative impact of capital accumulation on the labour force. The progressive concentration of capital has the effect of concentrating workers and stimulating their organization into strong unions. This, in turn, reduces the competition between workers, improving both their collective bargaining position and their political weight. The state is brought in as a third party in wage negotiations to persuade workers not to take their full potential gains.

The consequence of capital accumulation has imposed still further obligations on the state, which take the form of what previously has been called social-harmony expenditures. Thus the welfare state also emerged from the increasing political and economic strength of the working class as well as from the dissolution of traditional forms of income maintenance, such as the family farm, the extended family and private charity. As well, ecological damage in the wake of capital accumulation forces the state to undertake expenditures that reproduce the natural environment and repair urban blight.

Industrial concentration in most favoured regions and the promotion of large and innovative capitals in favoured growth sectors lead to demand for state subsidization of industry in more backward areas and for assistance programs that benefit small business. Owners of failing firms, the corporate victims of capital accumulation, demand subsidies or outright nationalization. The explosive growth of privatized consumption, essential as outlets for the mass production of goods, imposes major fiscal obligations on the state in building a complimentary collective infrastructure: roads, city planning, new schools, protective services, etc.

From the point of view of capital accumulation, all such social-harmony expenditures are unproductive. They contribute not even indirectly to surplus value, but maintain social harmony at the expense of capital accumulation, a social contract whose terms become increasingly unaffordable as the rate of profit declines and accumulation slackens.

At some point, the state is forced to reconsider these public obligations, perhaps shifting its emphasis away from pacification towards a more repressive strategy, for when accumulation slackens, it must supervise the crisis so as to shift more revenues towards capital. Under these circumstances, this can only be financed by reduction of the real incomes of the broad mass of people. This is likely to be accomplished by imposing a regime of wage controls, strike bans, tax exploitation, privatization, retrenchment of income security and other social-harmony expenditures. In short, as the crisis unfolds in its severity, the state may be compelled to discard its veneer of social reform and openly take the side of capital.

These policy moves are inevitably accompanied by manoeuvres in the ideological sphere. Concepts like universality, social security, equal opportunity and full employment are replaced in the lexicon of politicians, the media and texts with the more traditional and conservative values of selectivity, self-reliance, family, "right to life," women's place in the home, thrift and fiscal responsibility.

But the shift is anything but smooth, risk-free and certain. Slashing or dumping social security and equal opportunity measures, which represent the hard-fought gains of popular movements past and present, is bound to provoke a hostile public reaction. The possibility of electoral defeat could temper the enthusiasm of politicians in the manner and extent they are prepared to implement a wholesale policy of retrenchment.

And while in the crunch government may be able to move decisively against organized labour since this represents the common class interest of business, other steps inevitably draw government onto terrain where business interests conflict. Reducing or eliminating fiscal support for have-not regions, for weak or dying industries and for various services; terminating uneconomic public enterprises; weakening support for the arts and science communities and for universities — all of these kinds of retrenchment measures are bound to provoke a hostile response among some business and community interests.

Indeed, restructuring the state apparatus is also bound to create conflicts within the state bureaucracy which was built up to service these many competing interest groups. Nor is it likely that any one strategy for crisis management will be acceptable to the different wings of the political parties, each of which has its own ideological biases — thus the continuing controversy over universality versus selectivity, and over monetarist, supply-side and state-interventionist measures. The goal may be the same — a substantial shift towards capital — but there is plenty of room for debate over how best to regulate the crisis to achieve this objective.

As a consequence of these three factors — working-class and popular resistance against wholesale retrenchment and the limitations on state actions imposed by democratic political structures; competing interests within the business community and the state bureaucracy; and conflicting views on how best to restructure the economy — no unified and consistent strategy is likely to emerge. The policy outcome is more likely to be a series of compromises and a "muddling through." Whether the resulting mix of partial measures and partial programs will add sufficient weight to the counteracting tendencies is always problematic.

During such periods, it is almost inevitable that the party in office will face constant cabinet disputes and charges of economic mismanagement and that most countries will experience frequent changes in political representation. Each change in government involves attempts to introduce a new consistent policy system, which the new government then fails to implement. Such failure represents, not the peculiarity of a particular party or its leadership, but the problems inherent in a class-divided society, further fragmented by intra-class and regional divisions. As the Italian Marxist Antonio Gramsci wrote in his *Prison Notebook*, a "crisis consists precisely in the fact that the old is dying and the new cannot be born; in this interregnum a great variety of morbid symptoms appears."[7]

These strains are emerging most vividly in Thatcher's Britain, but the B.C. and federal governments in Canada have not been immune. Only in Washington has the state been allowed to reorganize social and economic life with seeming impunity.

How does the Marxian analysis make sense of present circumstances? The following chapter applies this conceptual framework to trace the development, emergence and political management of the crisis.

PART VI
The Economic Crisis

16 From Depression to Prosperity and Back

The Great Depression was a traumatic experience for nearly everyone. At its height more than 30 per cent of the regular labour force was unemployed. The recovery was painfully slow and woefully incomplete. By 1939 economic activity had still not reached 1929 proportions and unemployment was still pervasive. Then came the war. Almost overnight there was work for nearly everyone and soon there were severe labour shortages. New heavy industry sprang up, largely built with public money. And there was a new political environment. Government strategies believed that the war could not be won unless millions of ordinary people were convinced that their country had something better to offer than the enemy — not only during the war but after as well. Expectations, like investment and jobs, soared.

It was in this politically charged atmosphere that the Liberal government pledged its commitment to full employment, established the welfare state and gave unions the legal recognition they had sought. Then came the postwar scramble for jobs, cars and houses. It seemed as if good times would go on forever.

Why did the depression return? When will we once again enjoy prosperity? If the analysis offered here is correct, then it should be possible, in describing the factors that made the long boom possible, to describe also the barriers that developed to block further accumulation and to restructure the economy.

The Long Boom

In the final analysis, the long waves of prosperity and stagnation are rooted in the way capital is accumulated. The gross value of output minus the cost of material and equipment must provide, not only wages and services for workers, but also salaries and bonuses to management, all the cost associated with selling, interest to banks and taxes to government. Capitalists claim the remainder as profit which they have a strong incentive to reinvest but only if they can expect to realize a satisfactory rate of return.

What, then, were the specific conditions that gave rise to the long postwar expansion?

A Stable International Order

Capitalism seems to work best when there's a nation that establishes a global system around its orbit. With its currency universally used as the currency for international exchange and its industrial supremacy clearly established, international economic unity and order is more likely to be achieved. When its economic supremacy is challenged, this unity is likely to collapse leading to trade wars and international political tensions.

While most the capitalist world was devastated during the Second World War, the U.S. (and Canada) emerged from the war having doubled its industrial capacity. American supremacy included economic takeover of the former colonies of Europe and Britain and their ultra-cheap sources of raw materials; the expansion of the transnational corporations into all corners of the globe and military outposts in forty countries linked to their "ultimate headquarters in the war room of the White House."[1]

In 1940 an editorial in *Business* magazine declared that it is doubtful "whether the American capitalist system could continue to function [unless we can organize] the economic resources of the world so as to make possible a return to the system of free enterprise in every country." While the U.S. was unable to win back every country to the free-enterprise system, with the help of close to $200 billion in military and economic aid, along with selective interventions of the marines and the CIA, few countries were lost to the other side.

In a classified memorandum written in 1948, George Kennan, who was the policy planning director of the U.S. State Department, clearly enunciated the American position and intent: "We have about 50 percent of the world's wealth, but only 6.3 percent of its population.... Our real task in the coming period is to devise a pattern of relationships which will permit us to maintain this position of disparity."[2]

From the beginning, American business interests saw massive export surplus and investment in other countries as alternatives to increases in government expenditures, which they opposed. At an international conference at Bretton Woods (New Hampshire), the leading industrial countries agreed to a new international money system with the value of other currencies effectively pegged to the U.S. dollar (formally speaking, to gold). Dollars had to make up the greater part of other countries' reserves because the production of gold, at the fixed price of $35 an ounce, was insufficient to provide for both its industrial and monetary uses. More important, other countries found dollars not only as good as gold, but better, since they could earn interest on their dollar holdings.

This arrangement left the U.S. in a highly privileged position, since the only way other countries could accumulate needed reserves was if the U.S. provided them, by spending more abroad than it received. This is just what the U.S. did. Thus, in the early postwar years when the rest of the world had a desperate need for industrial goods and little industrial capacity to produce them, the U.S. was able to extend loans, credit and aid to provide the dollars that were needed. As well, it was able to massively increase its industrial presence abroad. Between 1946 and 1963 the value of American-owned plant and equipment abroad jumped from $7.2 billion to $40.6 billion. Profits from foreign investment rose from $2.1 billion in 1950 to $7.3 billion in 1965, amounting to 22 per cent of domestic profits, compared to 10 per cent in 1950.

Dollar hegemony enabled the U.S. to finance the aid as well as to roam the world seeking out the most profitable investment opportunities and to finance overseas military expeditions to keep the world free for U.S. capital and goods. So long as the rest of the world accepted increased dollar reserves, the U.S. was not required to pay these foreign bills by selling goods abroad. It seemed to be buying business and influence abroad with mere pieces of paper. Of course there was more involved than this, for behind dollar hegemony was American industrial supremacy, a competitive edge in terms of knowhow, manufacturing techniques, products and marketing — all of which made investment abroad profitable.

Europe was valued as a profitable source of markets and investment outlets. But Washington was also concerned with the widespread social and political turmoil prevalent there in the chaotic years following the end of the war. Extreme hardship provoked major working-class unrest.[3] Factory councils in Germany organized ballots on nationalization without compensation, with voting in the mines typically 90 per cent in favour. In Italy, where coal mining, railway, telephone, electrical supplies and part of the banking industry were already nationalized, capital was stymied by a political paralysis, with the Communists and Socialists together securing an assembly vote (in the spring of 1946) marginally greater than the Christian Democrats. In France the Communist Party emerged from the November 1946 National Assembly election as the largest party. The Left, including both Communist and Socialists, had nearly 50 per cent of the vote. As part of a coalition government, the Communists did attempt to restrain working-class demands, but to retain working-class support its ministers were obliged to oppose government wage-control policies and were summarily dismissed by the prime minister. In Japan too the working class was out of control, demanding higher wages in the face of roaring inflation and starvation pay. Workers struck for more than six million person-days in 1946 and a quarter of a million workers engaged in "production control," challenging management rights.

West Europe and Japan were not about to topple into the Russian orbit, but there was a clearly perceived danger that deteriorating economic conditions were breeding desire for socialization, planning and workers' control. A U.S. official put the point clearly at a business meeting in February 1947: "If the American program for world trade were to fail, its failure would hasten the spread of nationalization among the other countries of the world.... We cannot insulate ourselves against the movements that sweep around the globe. If every other major nation were to go Socialist, it would be extremely difficult, if not impossible, to preserve real private enterprise in the United States." As we shall soon see, with the help of American aid and selective intervention, worker militancy and political radicalism were very quickly quelled.

Within the new international order, Prime Minister Louis St. Laurent and his economic lieutenant, C.D. Howe, secured a special place for Canada as an exporter of natural resources to feed materials-hungry industrial mills of the U.S. and as an importer of high technology goods and parts to supply the assembly-line operations of mainly American-owned branch-plant manufacturing firms.

The special importance of exports had been recognized in the 1945 White Paper. Successful application of a full employment policy, it said, would be largely dependent on Canada's ability to recapture prewar export markets and to find new ones. By 1956 nearly 60 per cent of the Canadian exports went to the U.S., compared to only 40 per cent before the war. Rising exports to the U.S. were accompanied by heavy foreign investment by American transnational corporations, particularly in the resource industries so heavily engaged in export trade — like metals, petroleum and forest products. These exports were more than matched by imports from the U.S., the vast majority of which consisted of machinery and other capital equipment required in the resources industries and in manufacturing assembly plants. The inflow of American capital offset the trade deficit. These arrangements secured Canada's international payments position until the mid-1970s.

This role conceded to Canada in the international division of labour with its extreme emphasis on resource extraction and reliance on the export of a few staple products attracted critical concern in some circles of government — so much so that C.D. Howe flirted with the idea of requiring manufacturing subsidiaries to export a greater proportion of their output. But, as the president of the Dominion's Progressive Conservative Association said in response, "he might as well go bay at the moon.... It is contrary to the policy that brought people here who set up industries in Canada."[4]

Howe's plan fizzled and died. The matter was raised a decade or so later by Finance Minister Walter Gordon. But Gordon's solutions for stimulating exports in the face of export blocking were among those that forced him out of the cabinet. In the boom conditions of the 1950s and 1960s, no government saw any point in pursuing the matter. Canada's appointed role as supplier of raw materials for U.S. consumption and importer of American capital and machinery seemed to suit the country's requirements. The growing domestic market for consumer goods and services fully occupied the labour force (or nearly so) and Canada's international payment position was in reasonable order.

Profitability

Within this *pax Americana* a number of factors combined to make accumulation highly profitable and more rapid than it had been before.

- Cheap labour. In the immediate aftermath of the war and in most countries for sometime afterward, wages were relatively low. In Europe the slump of the 1930s, followed by the ravages of the war, created a large pool of unemployed. Europe, Japan and North America also took in millions of refugees who were available for wage work. By 1948 eight million refugees from areas incorporated into Poland, Czechoslovakia and the Soviet zone of Germany had flooded into Germany's western zones. Six million refugees from Japan's Asian empire had also returned home.

In all countries rural agriculture provided a large pool of disguised unemployment. Many farms had more family workers than could be fully employed, so migration into the cities could occur without loss of food output. Mechanization in the countryside also reduced labour requirements. In all, between 1950 and 1970, the number of self-employed farmers fell by 50 per cent in the advanced capitalist countries while the number of unpaid family workers fell by 70 per cent.[5] When these sources dried up, West Germany absorbed two million foreign workers between 1958 and 1971. A similar number was absorbed by France, Switzerland and the Benelux countries over the same period. Finally, all countries experienced an exceptional influx of women into wage labour.

Even so, output was rising so rapidly that demand for labour was threatening to outpace the supply. To counter the pressure on wages, business accelerated its scrapping of old plants and equipment, not merely substituting capital for labour, but increasingly mechanized forms of capital. Workers expelled in the process contributed significantly to the pool of available labour.

Clearly, without this vast supply of labour, postwar capitalism could not have achieved its formidable expansion of output without a significant decline in the rate of profit.[6]

- Weak worker organization. After a considerable demonstration of worker strength in the years immediately following the end of the Second World War, employers led a counter-offensive that quickly re-established the balance of class forces in their favour. In turning the tide, they received no little help from the state, the Cold War and inter-union feuding.

In France, a strike of mine safety crews in the autumn of 1948 was broken up when the government dispatched troops to remove strikers from the pit-heads; miners did not strike again for another fifteen years. Contributing to the defeat was the division of the trade-union movement, which occurred when a third of the membership of the Communist-led Confédération Générale La Travail split to form the Force Ouvrière, presenting employers with a golden opportunity to use divide-and-rule tactics.

In Italy, a similar split within union ranks hampered the labour movement's fight against employers who were in the midst of launching an assault on the power of the unions at shop-floor levels. As in the case of France, money contributed by right-wing U.S. unions helped finance the split-off and employers invariably favoured the weaker non-Communist unions.

In Germany, trade-union demands for socialization of key industries were undermined by U.S. insistence that Marshall Plan aid was conditional on their being dropped. Unemployment rates reaching 11 per cent in 1949 and divisions produced by ousting Communists from union executives weakened efforts to improve wages in the face of very high profits.

In Japan, following American advice, the state deliberately moved towards retrenchment. The Japanese League of Employers declared its intent "to dismiss all those who ... interfere with the normal management of enterprise" and to favour unions who support "labour-management collaboration." In 1950 the occupation instigated a "red purge": 12,000 Communists were sacked; the Communist-dominated union federation was destroyed and a rival one established in its place. By 1951 industrial productivity had surpassed prewar levels while real wages were well below.[7]

In the U.K., employers never launched a frontal attack on the labour movement comparable to what was occurring in France, Italy and Japan, but as a result of a wage freeze, real wages fell continuously from 1946 to 1951. In 1948 the government announced a purge of Communists in the civil service, and in 1949 the powerful transport workers disbarred Communists from holding office. As elsewhere, this anti-Communisst witch-hunt weakened the trade unions, although the failure of employers to launch a thorough assault against the labour movement at this time probably hurt them in the long run, for breaking the back of union power was a precondition for the investment boom of the 1950s in continental Europe and Japan.[8]

In the U.S. the Taft-Hartley Act of June 1947 radically curtailed trade-union rights: it outlawed the closed shop strikes by federal employees, secondary strikes and boycotts; it required a sixty-day cooling-off period before a contract was ended and allowed the president to seek an injunction to postpone for eighty days any strike deemed to affect "national health and safety"; it allowed employers to sue unions for breach of contract or for illegal strikes or boycotts; it forbade union contributions to candidates in federal elections; and it required union officers to swear that they were not members of the Communist Party or supporters of other "subversive" organizations. At the time the Communist Party controlled unions making up roughly a third of the CIO membership. Within a few years Communist leaders were purged from office or their unions were purged from the "house of labour." The witch-hunt helped diffuse the postwar strike wave, ease the implementation of Taft-Hartley and consolidate the position of union leaders prepared to reach an accommodation with business.

In Canada, governments were somewhat less thorough in their efforts to restrict unions, but amendments to provincial labour codes had similar effects. And, as elsewhere, rival trade-union leaders used the Cold War to cleanse the labour movement of Communist influence which, if anything, was even more deeply entrenched than it was in the U.S. With labour's energy sapped by inter-union wrangling and its strength further weakened by a heavy overload of unemployment through most of the 1950s and early 1960s, employers were able to proceed with their business with little hindrance from labour.

Together with the ample supply of labour, the industrial and political weakness of the working class meant that workers were forced to accept employment on terms favourable to capital. These were the terms upon which the postwar settlement between labour and capital was based. Yet modest as wage increases were, after a decade and a half (four decades in Europe) dominated by war and depression, the postwar settlement offered a new security and steady improvements in living standards which seemed bountiful at the time.

Not only were wages restrained, but even more important, firms had enormous freedom to adopt new techniques of production and to alter work practices to increase their profits. A second consequence was that, while real wages gradually rose, the proportion of total product taken by personal consumption expenditure fell (from 63 per cent of Gross Domestic Product in the advanced capitalist countries to 59 per cent between 1952 and 1973), leaving a higher proportion available for private investment.

- Cheap raw materials. From the early 1950s through the 1960s, industrial countries benefited greatly from improving terms of trade with primary Third World producers. In 1951, the terms of trade for primary products (the ratio of the average price of primary products to the average price of manufactured products) stood at 119 and fell steadily to 81 in 1968, where it remained until 1971.[9] Worsening terms of trade for undeveloped countries represents a direct transfer of value to the industrial metropolitan centres. An abundant supply of cheap raw materials — especially oil — boosted profitability, directly through its impact on the cost of production and the organic composition of capital and indirectly by helping to raise real wages at no cost to industrial capital. Its impact on the Canadian economy, however, was decidedly mixed, since so much of Canada's economic activity is resource-oriented.
- Capital, technological innovation and management practices. Spurred on by low interest rates and high retained earnings, the stock of fixed capital in advanced capitalist countries rose nearly two-and-a-half-fold between 1950 and 1973. The means of production per worker more than doubled over the period. It was as though each worker was confronted by two machines where one stood before. But the machines changed as well. New capital embodied important innovations — high-productivity machines replaced low-productivity machines. The principle of an automatic continuous process of production and the construction of automatic calculators derived from cybernetic principles — developed primarily during the war and applied in the arms economy — created a potential backlog of technical knowledge that revolutionized the electrical, aircraft, vehicle and chemical industries. These innovations, accompanied by improvements in management practices, resulted in large gains in productivity and new mass markets.

The combined effect of all of these factors produced highly favourable conditions for capital accumulation. It explains how profit rates were maintained at a steady level for most of the period until the mid-1970s when they began to drop.

The rate of profit is the product of two ratios: the ratio of profits to the value of output and the ratio of output to capital (P/K = P/O . O/K). The first depends on the outcome of the race between labour costs and productivity. Since the real cost of employing labour did not outpace productivity, there was virtually no change in the profit share between the early 1950s and the mid-1960s.[10] Similarly, the quantity of the means of productions in use and the level of output grew very closely in parallel so the ratio of output to capital remained fairly constant.[11]

Rapid accumulation could sustain the boom for such a long period only if there were adequate outlets for sales. The mass consumer market fueled by rising real wages allowed consumer-goods industries to grow more or less in line with those producing the means of production.

The steadily rising growth in investment spending was another important sales outlet for the realization of surplus value. As people began to live in the suburbs, for example, massive opportunities for profitable investment were centred in the automobile, petroleum, construction and durable consumer-goods industries. Investment rose sufficiently to absorb the rising proportion of income being saved, a tendency that restrained consumption growth and that would otherwise have resulted in a slacking in the growth of output.

Exports is another outlet but only if it is not offset by imports. For the advanced capitalist countries as a whole, the export surplus with the rest of the world was quite small. For some countries like Japan and Germany, however, it played an important role. For Canada, export surpluses and deficits more or less offset each other from 1950 to 1965.

Government spending is the final outlet. Its impact depends largely on how it is financed. To the early 1970s the overwhelming mass of state expenditure was financed by taxation, taking the advanced capitalist countries as a whole. Contrary to those who ascribe great importance to Keynesian policies, the boom was in no sense based on government deficits. It should be added that to the extent taxes are met by reduced saving, rather than by cut-backs in spending, the overall impact is still expansionary — in which case increased government spending does contribute as a sales outlet for the realization of surplus value.

It was the coincidence of these material forces, rather than a commitment to a particular monetary-fiscal regime by the state, that laid the basis for expanding long-term investment opportunities and international trade and the consequent long wave of prosperity. And it has been the exhaustion of these forces, rather than errors of policy, that brought an end to it.

This is not to suggest that the state was of little consequence. On the contrary, immigration policy played an important role in holding down wages. Industrial-relations policy regularized conflict and so established a long period of industrial peace. Social-investment expenditure in capital infrastructure and research and development financed the overhead costs of the whole process of capital accumulation, without which capital would make no profits at all. Social-consumption expenditure in education, retraining and health lowered labour costs.

Throughout the period, Keynesianism was rarely put to test. Detailed studies of government policy suggest that, where deliberate Keynesian demand management was used, it was as destabilizing as it was stabilizing.[12] But because of the underlying buoyancy of the economy such errors could be offset by the automatic stabilizers that operate irrespective of the particular configuration of government policies. Here the only condition for success is quantitative. Providing the size of state revenue and expenditure is sufficiently large, the automatic stabilizers can effectively moderate slight swings in the economy without deliberate government intervention. This quantitative condition was achieved as a consequence of the enduring influence of the Second World War and the rise of the welfare-warfare state.

The net effect of the favourable material conditions was to raise and sustain high levels of investment and international trade for nearly a quarter of a century. The use of fiscalism as an instrument of employment policy had been conditional on sustained levels of high employment being maintained by high investment and buoyant international trade, and subject to the variety of forces considered above.

To put the matter differently, a full-employment policy was not responsible for prosperity; prosperity made it easy for the state to commit itself to a policy of full employment. A more balanced interpretation of state policy over the period is that it supervised the postwar reorganization of the economy by adopting tax structures, immigration policy, credit expansion, labour legislation, unionization laws and international monetary institutions to support and sustain the capital accumulation made possible by underlying material forces.

Until the mid-1960s there was no generalized cycle in the western economies. The U.S. and Canada went through recessions in 1948-49, 1953-54 and 1957-58, but in Europe and Japan it appeared that the business cycle has been permanently conquered. The most these countries experienced was an occasional slackening in the rate of growth of output, never an actual fall in output. The first synchronized cycle occurred with the recession of 1966-67 followed soon after by another drop in 1969-70, the roaring inflation of the early 1970s, the great recessions of 1974-75 and 1980-82 (and another one predicted to be just around the corner). From the mid- to late 1960s, then, the world economy began its long downward slide with short booms giving way to a prolonged stagnation with frequent recessions and partial recoveries.

When favourable material conditions were exhausted, the limitations of Keynesian fine-tuning became apparent. In the absence of these conditions, anything approaching full employment could only be achieved by sustaining budgetary deficits even more massive than they are at present and imposing the kind of "comprehensive socialization of investment" hinted at by Keynes in the final chapter of his *General Theory*. The socio-political and institutional ramifications and consequences of this sort of policy combination, to say nothing of the constraints imposed by the international money market, are such that, with the possible exception of the Mitterrand government, no government has even seriously considered it as a realistic option. And within the first year of its term, the Mitterrand government found it impossible or inconvenient to buck the tide of restraint.

The Tide Towards Depression

For as long as it lasted, however, these were capitalism's golden years. The economies of the advanced capitalist world grew by an average of nearly 5 per cent a year between 1950 and 1973. With this scale of growth rate, output doubles every sixteen years. Over the period each generation enjoyed a standard of living twice as high as its parents and four times as high as its grandparents. For the first time automobile workers, for example, could own their own cars and carpenters their own homes. Some of them could also send their children to university, and higher education was a ticket into expanding white-collar, technical and educational sectors of employment. Canadian disposable income doubled on average over the period even when discounted for inflation. The fact that the richest 30 per cent of income earners captured almost half of this new income while the poorest 50 per cent received only 20 per cent went mostly unnoticed. Distributional questions lose their bite when all, or nearly all, are making reasonable gains.

But such a rapid rate of accumulation could not be sustained forever. For one thing, a growing imbalance between accumulation and the supply of labour and raw materials led to increasingly severe labour shortages and to shortages of strategic materials, particularly energy resources. The normal capitalist response to these circumstances is to scrap old plant and equipment and replace it with labour-saving and material-saving technology. This is precisely what happened, but the capitalist system has no mechanism guaranteeing a smooth transition. In the late 1960s and early 1970s the initial effect of over-accumulation was a period of feverish growth that resulted in rapidly rising wages and prices and wildly speculative ventures. These temporarily masked but could not suppress the deterioration in profitability. As the new reality finally dawned, the confidence of capitalists was undermined, investment collapsed and the world economy was in crisis. One casualty of the process, which also contributed to it, was the breakdown of stability in the capitalist world system as U.S. producers found themselves facing the challenge of European and Japanese rivals in increasingly competitive world markets. In the pages that follow each of these developments are briefly examined.

Profitability

Rising worker militancy: By the mid-1960s, the cumulative impact of high rates of capital accumulation and economic growth produced full employment situations in all of the advanced capitalist countries. The main result for business was increasing pressure for higher wages and loss of control over the shop floor. To regain control and restrain wages, several countries experimented with incomes control and tripartism but, as we have already seen, these experiments failed. A wave of strikes swept across Europe between 1968 and 1970 and strikers won huge wage increases, about twice those of preceding years. In the graphic words of one account:

> The May 1968 events in France triggered a three-week general strike. Next year Germany and the Netherlands were drenched by waves of wildcat strikes, and Italy sweated through a Hot Autumn of industrial unrest. In the United Kingdom the Wilson government's income policy broke down in 1969-70 in a "Winter of Discontent."[13]

In Canada and the U.S. the strike-wave broke out a few years earlier, simmered for a while and erupted even more ferociously in the early 1970s, when Canada had taken over as the second most strike prone country in the world. As in other countries, North American workers won very large wage increases. Employers everywhere resisted but in the end they were forced to concede because they could not find substitute labour and because, with burgeoning sales, they could not afford long interruptions of production.

One of the consequences of increasing worker resistance was the expansion in the number of supervisors required to police and maintain the work force. The amount of supervisory and management time devoted to each hour of direct labour by production workers rose significantly. As well, new layers of middle management were added to collect, analyze and interpret the flow of information on sales, sales cost, advertising, production cost, loans customer service, and so forth. An army of clerical workers was employed as support staff to the bureaucracy. These rising costs of controlling workers and collecting and monitoring information were not paying for themselves by generating enough of an increase in workers' output and sales.

The combination of more rapidly rising wages and declining productivity was bound to cause a major increase in labour cost. In the period 1966 to 1976 when the tide was turning decisively towards depression, the value of labour compensation (wages and fringe benefits) per person in the Canadian goods industries nearly tripled while the value of output per person employed rose by less than 50 per cent. Unit labour costs in the goods-producing sector, which had not risen at all between 1950 and the mid-1960s, exactly doubled between 1965 and 1976 — and rose by almost a third again between 1976 and 1980.[14]

If aspirations rise faster than productivity, attempts to realize them through higher money wages will squeeze profits; and capitalists will seek to protect their profits by raising prices. Should they succeed, this will further frustrate labour's demand for a higher real wage and workers will seek further increases in money wages.

In sum, by the late 1960s the labour reserves so vitally important to the long wave of prosperity were largely exhausted. The balance of strength between labour and capital shifted momentarily to labour. The political and religious divisions which had earlier so weakened the labour movement were finally overcome. Workers' aspirations for a better life and a better job expanded. A rising tide of worker militancy swept away a generation of union leaders that had grown somewhat complacent during the years of the labour truce. Trade unionization became widespread in the rapidly growing public sector. Union membership in Canada jumped from 30 per cent in the mid-1960s to over 35 per cent of the non-agricultural labour force in the mid-1970s and to nearly 40 per cent by end of the decade. Between 1966 and 1976 three times as much working time was lost each year due to strikes compared to the period 1950-65. Individual acts of resistance and job avoidance were on the rise too. When worker productivity stagnates or declines, any increase in real wages eats into profits. But powerful corporations are not about to share their surplus value with their workers. With workers unable to prevent corporations from raising their prices and corporations unable to prevent workers from obtaining money-wage increases in excess of the rate of productivity growth, the result is a wage-price spiral.

Technological Stagnation: Productivity increases derived from technological innovations could have offset or partly offset rising labour costs. But a number of factors combined to slacken its influence. First, European and Japanese producers had been able to make spectacular gains by following the technological leader and adopting the best technology, which in most cases has been that of the U.S. By the late 1960s they still lagged behind in many industries but as the technological gap was clearly narrowing, the adoption rate of new technology was bound to slow down.

Of course, this catching up cannot explain the slow-down in the U.S. It can be argued that American corporations, so long unchallenged by foreign rivals, had become somewhat complacent. No doubt much of the new technology developed during the war had already been incorporated into the capital stock. But with huge investments sunk in this capital stock, firms were understandably reluctant to invest new funds in developing new technologies. Unlike the situation in Europe and Japan, American wages were rising only modestly, implying a weaker pressure to scrap old plant and equipment and replace it with new.

Furthermore, American researchers had become used to energy-intensive and labour-using technologies. When energy prices had shifted and wages pushed up, they were slow to launch out in new directions. Scientists and researchers become accustomed to one technology; developing another involves a long process of intellectual adjustment and scientific re-tooling. Reflecting the depletion in the pool of inventive possibilities, the patent rate had been falling since 1969. The "fourth industrial revolution," computerization, was in the embryonic stage in the late 1950s. A decade later it was still on the horizon, not quite sufficiently profitable for widespread adoption.

Rising Material Costs: With the scale and extent of industrialization so much greater than ever before, it was only a matter of time before the accelerated demand for raw materials would begin to exhaust cheap sources of supply. The uneven distribution of resources around the world was bound to eventually create a politics of scarcity in which the bargaining power of the primary producing nations would improve.

The commodities boom began in 1972, triggered by the sudden increase in world demand caused by the synchronization of an expansionary fiscal and monetary policy in all the industrialized countries. Producers were slow to adjust mainly because of years-long under-investment due to deteriorating terms of trade between primary and manufactured products and fear of investing in politically volatile Third World countries.

Major grain exporters began to cut back production because of mounting stocks. The big four wheat producers — the U.S., Canada, Australia and Argentina — all offered large subsidies to farmers as incentives for acreage reductions. Their combined wheat production fell from 80 million tons in 1968 to 60 million in 1970. A crop failure in 1972; the mysterious disappearance of anchovies from the Peruvian coast (an important protein for animal feed); and a massive sale of U.S. grain to the U.S.S.R., equivalent to a third of annual U.S. grain exports, all combined to reduce grain stocks to dangerously low levels and to bump up the price of food. A year later came "the oil crisis" when war broke out in the Middle East and OPEC announced a 10 per cent cut in oil exports and selective embargoes. Oil prices quadrupled during the winter of 1973-74. Predictably, all of this activity attracted speculative funds that contributed significantly to the commodities boom. By 1974 primary products were on average 45 per cent more expensive relative to manufactured products than they were two years earlier.[15]

While the terms of trade stabilized somewhat a few years later, they still had not been entirely reversed by the end of the decade. The commodity-price explosion transferred wealth to the primary producers (1.5 per cent of world purchasing power was transferred to OPEC at a stroke) and eliminated a major source of easy wage increase. Without cheap food and materials, wage increases absorbed an increasing proportion of productivity gains at the expense of profits. But its impact was unevenly felt within the industrialized world. Commodity exporters, including Canada and the U.S., benefited from the boom. Major importers, especially Japan, suffered from it. A number of European countries were faced with massive increases in trade deficits. More generally, the additional exports required to earn the extra foreign exchange to pay for increased import bills drained domestic incomes. Since this deduction would have to come from either wages or profits it worked to intensify distributional struggles and reduce the rate of accumulation. Balance-of-payment problems also forced governments to deliberately repress domestic growth and to cut back on social expenditures.

Insurgent oil prices in particular also caused a restructuring of profit within some of the industrialized countries. Chase Manhattan estimated that the world-wide rate of profit for leading oil companies rose from 7.9 per cent in 1972 to 19.2 in 1974 and 24.0 per cent in 1979.[16] American oil majors were suddenly awash with one-third of total corporate profits, "crowding out" other manufacturing sectors. Canadian oil barons took nearly a quarter of all corporate profit, nearly double the proportion in 1970.

Market Saturation: By the mid-1970s the consumer durable goods markets, which had been the prime engines of growth in all the western economies, had everywhere reached near saturation. Whereas the 1960s North American and European car markets grew at 12-13 per cent per annum, they fell off to replacement rates of 2-3 per cent yearly. In a country like France, the percentage of workers owning cars grew from 21 per cent in 1959 to 60 per cent in 1974; television sets from 9 per cent to 81 per cent; washing machines from 21 per cent to 73 per cent. Equivalent middle-class consumption rates were all above 90 per cent.[17] It was inevitable that, until a new generation of consumer goods took their place, these industries would face a situation of excess capacity which was bound to have a multiplier effect that touched all industries.

For instance, it clearly dried up the demand for related plant and machinery.

Contradictions in the Welfare State

When the economy is growing rapidly it can afford to be generous towards its outcasts. Social-harmony expenditures go hand in hand with stimulating business enterprise by placing an extra amount of purchasing power in the hands of those who spend — without too much of an adverse burden on the "contributors." To maintain its own legitimacy the state had little option but to respond positively to rising demands for new welfare programs emerging from an increasingly politicized labour movement and newly politicized movements of poor people.

Redistributional transfer payments in Canada, for example, doubled in the five years between 1966 and 1971 and tripled over the next five years. This acceleration reflects in large part the new layers of welfare programs introduced in this period. The magnitude of these programs can be measured by the fact that transfer payments had only doubled in the ten years between 1947 and 1956 and that it took another ten years for them to double again.

No doubt the state's rising share of output was due not simply to the expansion of the state services, but also to the fact that productivity has risen so slowly in the service industry, of which the state sector is a major part. And while productivity in the state sector has lagged — partly because it has not been subject to a technological revolution comparable to industry and agriculture, and partly because most public-sector services are shielded from the laws of competition — wages there reached approximate parity with wages in industry because of a new-found militancy among public-sector workers. Thus the state came under pressure to freeze salaries in the public sector — both as an economy measure and as a means of support to industrialists trying to reduce their wage bills.

Whatever positive role was played by growing state expenditures in aiding the realization of profits was now overwhelmed by its negative effect — a worsening in the conditions for the production of profits. Not only did it reduce, in the net, the resources available for private investment ("crowding out"), it also acted to bolster the strength of labour and, by extending credit to salvage poorly operating firms, the interventionist state also curbed the disciplinary impact of market forces on inefficient firms.

In the Marxian terms of the previous chapter, the "counteracting" forces were now failing to offset the falling tendency of the rate of profit. Sluggish technological advance, the explosion of raw material prices and the extension of state credit to salvage inefficient firms all worked to raise the value of constant capital. Meanwhile, rising worker militancy pushed down the rate of exploitation by raising wage gains relative to productivity. Working in the same direction, increasing food and raw material prices also forced up the value of labour power. Finally, more and more of the economy was devoted to sales, distribution and advertising that add nothing to value and to welfare expenditures, which are also unproductive of value an surplus value. Therefore capital accumulation was bound to suffer.

Breakdown of the International Order

American leadership had provided a certain order and stability to the international economy. A unique set of circumstances allowed the U.S. to perform this happy function. First was the fact of its overwhelming economic superiority. Through its contribution to world trade and investment, its dynamism helped support the reconstruction of the war-devastated economies of Europe and Japan. Second was the fact that its relatively high self-sufficiency allowed the U.S. economy to easily accommodate the rising shares of world manufacturing trade of Europe and Japan. For as late as 1970, only about 8 per cent of U.S. GNP circulated in the world market.

But the U.S. was not capable of maintaining forever its overwhelming economic superiority and the corresponding unchallenged superiority of the dollar. By the end of the 1960s, Europe and Japan were competing on an equal footing and challenging American supremacy in world markets. In 1948 West German exports were only 6 per cent of U.S. exports; by 1969 they stood at 78 per cent. Japan's exports rose from 2 per cent of those of the U.S. to 43 per cent, Italy's from 9 per cent to 31 per cent in the same period. In 1950 West Europe and Japan had a combined gross national product that was only 39 per cent of the U.S.'s. By 1969 their combined total was 70 per cent of that of the U.S.[18]

The fundamental problem for the U.S. economy was that rival economies were accumulating capital at a far faster rate and were doing so on the basis of wage costs which until 1970 were still far lower. Capital stock in U.S. manufacturing rose by 57 per cent between 1955 and 1970 compared to 116 per cent in major European countries and 500 per cent in Japan. And whereas in the U.S. average productivity rose by less than one-half, it doubled in Europe and it rose three and a half times in Japan.[19] The U.S. economy was actually devoting slightly more of its gross national product to research and development than

Europe and Japan but 40 per cent of it went for military and space purposes. Industries that benefited most from this government-funded research and development, aerospace and electronics, maintained their world lead. Other industries, such as steel and automobiles, lagged behind.

The signs were already out in the late 1950s that Europe and Japan, helped by the aid programs and the transfer of American capital and technology, were on their way to full recovery and in a position to begin their challenge. It was the Vietnam war that accelerated the process.[20] At the time the war was Americanized in 1965-66, the North American economy was close to fully utilizing all the available plant and labour force. Bottlenecks were already appearing; wages and other costs started to squeeze profits.

An already fully employed economy was overheated by vast expenditures on military and military-related outlays. It was further aggravated because the Johnson administration decided it could not afford the political costs of taxing the American public to pay for the war. Instead, the war was financed by borrowing and cranking the money-making machines. The result was an economy about to burst, and the consequent inflation whittled away at America's competitive position in world trade. In 1971 it experienced its first trade deficit since the turn of the century. On top of the disappearing export surplus were the huge outlays of foreign and military expenditures abroad. Policing the American empire had become a financial burden of the first order. In the process the U.S. economy was becoming increasingly dependent on the outcome of international trade and capital flow.

We can retrace the events linking a weakening American economy to a growing international instability. Taking advantage of the reserve currency status of the American dollar, the U.S. could ignore its rapidly growing deficits. European countries had already grown resentful of the (much smaller) deficits that had emerged before the escalation of the war. In effect, the U.S. had been printing dollars and using them to buy European industry. Now it was using the same method to share the burden of the Vietnam war with other industrial countries. But once these countries had built up their U.S. dollar reserves to adequate levels, there was nothing to be gained from further increasing them. Only an imperial nation can impose such conditions on its creditors, not by outright coercion, but by persuading them that they have no alternative to accepting the imperial currency. The entire financial structure of world capitalism might otherwise crumble.

Tipped off by the U.S.'s growing trade deficits, holders of American dollars finally speculated that a devaluation was imminent. Faced with the resulting massive flight of capital (between April and June 1971 speculation against the dollar ran at an annual rate of $14 billion, increasing to $35 billion between July and September), the U.S. was required to sell off billions of dollars of gold to maintain its old exchange rate. At the beginning of 1971 U.S. gold reserves had been sufficient to cover 32 per cent of foreign dollar holdings. Twelve months later they could only cover 18 per cent.

President Nixon finally announced the suspension of the convertability of dollars into gold and a series of measures including surcharges and quotas on imports into the U.S. A few months later, in December 1971, there was the "Smithsonian realignment" of the major currencies. Further exchange rate adjustments in the 1973 finally ended the Bretton Woods system, with all currencies now allowed to float. The result of this chain of events was that European and Japanese currencies were revalued relative to the American (and Canadian) dollar, making North American goods cheaper in the world market and relieving for a time the American deficit problem.

The aggressive measures of the Nixon administration ushered in a period of uncertainty and dissension. Meant to recoup American leadership, their immediate effect was to unleash a trade and currency devaluation war, fuel a general inflation, cause a swift breakdown of the old order and a jockeying around for new leadership roles.

The quadrupling of oil prices between 1973 and 1974 was another wild card thrown into the increasingly confusing and unstable game of international finance. It created huge pools of foot-loose dollars, which were added to the already vast sums of Euro-dollars. Much of it was recycled to money-starved Third World countries, especially those that were net importers of oil. Third World debt grew from $97.3 billion in 1973 to $425.2 billion in 1980. So long as inflation was rising and the prices of primary commodities continued to increase, nobody was bothered by the risks involved. Inflation effectively reduces the size of debt overtime; increasing prices of primary commodities enhances the value of Third World exports. But, as the crisis set in, the problem of Third World debt would threaten the world financial structures.

At present the position of the U.S. relative to Europe and Japan bears a resemblance to that of Great Britain to Germany and the U.S. at the end of the nineteenth century. That rivalry resulted in the Great Depression sandwiched between two world wars over thirty years of almost continuous social, political and physical devastation. It would be wrong to insist that such a cataclysmic series of events is bound to happen soon again. But with the arms race heating up, signs of a second cold war between the U.S. and the U.S.S.R., and new trade wars among the highly industrialized capitalist economies, it is unlikely that the international economic order established after the Second World War will survive intact.

Caught up in the changing reality, we can already observe a divided, international ruling class unable to stop the further drift of countries out of the capitalist orbit. There were flickers of rebellion in Third World countries back in the 1950s. Iran elected a nationalist prime minister who announced his intention to nationalize the oil industry — the CIA arranged for his overthrow. A few years later, in 1956, Guatemala elected a president, Jacobo Arbenz, who announced his intention to nationalize the United Fruit Company — the CIA responded similarly. Rebels threatened the stability of the Middle East in 1958 — the U.S. marines landed in Lebanon. Cuba got away despite the Bay of Pigs invasion by opposition forces sponsored by President John F. Kennedy. In 1964 the U.S. helped sponsor a military coup in Brazil to thwart the populist tendencies of the elected government of Joav Goulart. The U.S. marines invaded the Dominican Republic in 1965 to suppress a nationalist and leftist rebellion in that country. Most important, the U.S. escalated its involvement in Vietnam in a frantic effort to protect its client regime against mounting insurrection.

In Chile, Allende's Popular Unity government was elected in 1970 but was effectively deposed with U.S. assistance in 1973. Guerilla movements launched serious offences in Argentina, Uruguay, Bolivia and elsewhere, but they were successfully contained. After the Arab defeat in the 1967 war against Israel, a radicalization of the PLO led to an intensification of sabotage and guerilla operations, but the PLO was momentarily crushed by King Hussein of Jordan.

The late 1960s and early 1970s also witnessed the rise of a variety of nationalist regimes that made some moves in an anti-imperialist direction: Peru (1968); Iraq (1968); Libya (1969); Syria (1970); Ghana (1972); Jamaica (1972). Most of these regimes were pro-capitalist but their nationalistic impulses led them to move against foreign-owned multinationals. There was a total of thirty-four takeovers between 1965 and 1974, compared to only three between 1951 and 1965. And it was in 1973 that OPEC rose to prominence using its oil weapon to try to break the Middle East stalemate.

While the American imperium successfully defended its territories, the cracks were beginning to show. The dam that had blocked the anti-imperialist movement really burst in the mid-1970s. Saigon finally fell in 1975. The Portugese empire collapsed as guerilla movements liberated Guineau-Bissau, Mozambique and Angola. Nicaragua, Ethiopia and Afghanistan were other losses. In *The Making of the Second World War*, author Fred Halliday lists fourteen losses in all in the period 1974 to 1980. This shrinking of the capitalist world system, together with stagnating markets and trade between industrial countries, has the effect of intensifying the growing rivalry between capitalist nations as well as recharging the Cold War between the superpowers in the context of liberation struggles.

The U.S. had to consider the possibility that the balance of world forces could be tipping the other way. Challenged from within the capitalist orbit by Europe, Japan, the OPEC nations and Third World nationalist regimes, from without by the spread of revolution it could not check and by Soviet attainment of a rough parity in the nuclear field, new American strategies seemed inevitable.

In this wider context, Canada's payments equilibrium began to come undone in the 1960s. Whereas U.S. direct investment had contributed positively to the alleviation of Canada's balance of payments problem in the 1950s, it began to constitute a net drain in the succeeding decade. More dollars were being remitted as profits and service payments to company head office than was being brought into the country by the transnational corporations. In effect, these companies were by then financing expansions of their Canadian subsidiaries with profits earned in Canada while still having substantial amounts left for remittances to head office.

The implications of this change was twofold. First, in the future, deficits in the trade and services account would have to be met by borrowing money abroad and this meant setting the Canadian interest rate significantly higher than the American level. Henceforth Canadian governments would be less free to stimulate the economy by applying the traditional monetary measure of lowering the interest rate.

Second, profit remittances abroad and interest payments on foreign loans soared. They nearly doubled from the 1950s to the 1960s and quadrupled from the 1960s to the 1970s. These outflows, together with parallel increases in royalties, consulting fees, patent rights and other service payments to parent companies, and the net loss on travel expenditure, constitute an enormous drain on the Canadian economy. While merchandise exports also showed sizable increases, it was a rare year when trade surpluses were sufficient to pay for these obligations. The difference increasingly required long-term borrowing, adding to the amount of interest charges which must be paid every year to foreign lenders.

There are three ways out of the debt trap. One is to restructure Canadian industry to increase the export of finished goods. A second is to lower dependence on imported manufactured goods. The third is to increase exports of raw materials while holding down domestic income through fiscal and monetary restraint, thus repressing the demand for imported goods. Canadian governments have in the main followed the third course. In 1971 Canada was importing $3.6 billion more in manufactured products than it was exporting. By 1976 this figure rose to $10.1 billion. In 1981 it had reached $20.6 billion. These imported goods represent 350,000 permanent jobs that are missing in Canada. In a sense, the chickens had come home to roost. The structural dependence negotiated after the war laid the basis for some of Canada's most enduring problems, which were to place severe obstacles to economic recovery.

Inflation: Postponing the Crash

The exhaustion of expansion forces reached critical proportions over the decade following the mid-1960s and resulted in declining rates of profit and a reduction in the share of post-tax profits throughout the advanced capitalist world. Given the combined claim of the state and primary producers, and the ability of the working class to resist attempts to have their consumption reduced by similar amounts, what remained for profits was greatly diminished.

The manifestations of crisis were postponed for a time by the dramatic increase in the supply of money, evident throughout most of the capitalist world by the late 1960s and early 1970s. As we have seen, this process actually began during the Vietnam war when Lyndon Johnson, rather than confront the negative response of a rise in taxes, financed the war by deficits fueled by large increases in the supply of money. The devaluation of the American dollar, designed to reverse some of the negative trends that characterized the U.S. economy in the 1950s and 1960s, also fed world inflationary pressures.

But it was the 1972-73 mini-boom that finally burst the dam. Between the first halves of 1972 and 1973 world capitalist industrial output grew by 10 per cent. It was stoked by unprecedented increases in money supplies (12 per cent in 1971 and slightly more in 1972), a halving of interest rates and enormous increases in international liquidity generated by the exodus from the dollar. Concurrent elections in the U.S., Canada, Germany, Italy and Japan prompted "give-money" budgets and expansionary policies.

TABLE 16:1
Business Net Profit Rate

	Advanced Capitalist Countries	Europe	Japan	U.S.A.	Canada
1951-69	16.4	14.4	22.4	18.3	10.4
1970-73	13.9	12.0	24.8	14.2	9.1
1974-81	11.0	8.6	14.7	12.6	7.5

Source: Calculated from data in P. Armstrong et al, *Capitalism Since World War II*, Fontana, 1984, p. 465.

Price acceleration clearly began in the goods market with wages only beginning to catch up and threaten a wage-price spiral in 1973. The very speed of the upswing caused bottlenecks and rising costs, pushing up prices which fed through the system. The commodities boom came on top of these forces. Indeed, it is doubtful if OPEC could have successfully imposed its price increases in the absence of the high levels of demand accompanying the mini-boom.

Higher prices can protect the rate of profit from forces that push it down. Thus, if businesses could always adjust their prices to any level they wish, a crisis could be avoided. This possibility did not escape Marx's attention, but he observed that capitalists could not protect themselves in this manner as long as the value of national currencies were linked to gold, which has an intrinsic value of its own. When the "discipline of gold" is relaxed, however, this constraint is removed.

To avoid a decline in profits, firms typically avail themselves of bank credit to pay their bills while passing the burden of higher costs, wages and taxes on to consumers (and thus back to wage earners). Consumers similarly avail themselves of consumer credit to afford the higher payments. The result is a massive expansion of private indebtedness, far greater even than the rise of public indebtedness. Indeed, government borrowing was not responsible for this expansion of credit.

Up to this point the advanced capitalist countries were in rough budgetary balance. But governments allowed the banking system to respond to demands for credit and interest rates were held down to below the rate of inflation (declining "real" interest rates). Even though investments earned less overall, by financing an increasing proportion through borrowing at negative real interest rates, corporations helped maintain the profitability of shareholders' funds.

Sales, employment and profit margins were more nearly maintained, but only at a higher level of average prices. The consequent inflation momentarily disguised the fact that expansionary forces were exhausted. Credit extension kept solvent high-cost, inefficient firms that would otherwise go bankrupt or be forced to undergo major restructuring. High costs and unrealistic capital values were built into pricing structures. Similarly, credit extensions maintained high levels of employment keeping pressure on wages in all sectors of the economy.

On the surface, this explanation of inflation resembles the monetarist explanation. Thus the rise in prices appears to be based on an expansion of the money supply. To the monetarists this appearance is mistakenly taken to be the basic cause. But the underlying cause is not the extension of state expenditures and the expansion of the money supply. Instead it is the falling rate of profit, which necessitates an increase in the money supply and state credit to enable production to be sold at higher prices. It represents an attempt by the state to regulate or moderate the crisis.

For essentially four reasons the inflationary strategy did not work. The first, as Jacob Morris has written, is that it worked well enough while it was an insider's strategy.[21] Once it became general knowledge and more people started to do something about protecting themselves or taking advantage of the strategy, inflation turned into an agency for chaos and disorder.

After a few beatings, union wage demands began to take account, not only of past losses in purchasing power, but of future losses as well. Inflation's moderating effects in distributional struggles progressively weakens as the illusion of money fades with growing experience of inflation. Others are also caught up in the inflationary psychology — building up inventories in anticipation of price increases, speculating in land and commodities, expanding plants and equipment, office buildings, and luxury highrises, and buying out other firms — mostly on borrowed money.

As the Belgian economist Ernest Mandel correctly asserts, "an inflationary atmosphere promotes a cumulative expansion of credit because the devaluation of money, counted on by every capitalist, makes it lucrative to buy on credit today and repay with devalued money tomorrow." This is the explanation, he adds, "of the seeming paradox that in times of growing inflation, when the banks are lending an increasing amount of money, it is sometimes possible for there to be a 'shortage of money' which drives up interest."[22] Banks and other moneylenders raise their interest charges in anticipation that loans will be paid off in depreciated currencies. And they refuse to lend for more than short periods of time. The result is a piling up of short-term debt at very high interest rates. The banking system becomes extremely vulnerable to any event that might impair its liquidity: the failure of a large customer; the collapse of the real estate market or the commodities market.

The process feeds on itself. Business firms that have made the right financial moves are swimming in profits, while many others are facing insolvency. To abort bankruptcies of major firms, heavy pressure is placed on government to relieve crises of liquidity by still more inflation. When inflation and inflationary expectations reach such proportions that they weaken the whole internal discipline of capitalist production, pressure to constrain it becomes irresistible.

Jacob Morris summarized this point neatly:

> When inflation has finally reduced the capitalist system to a condition of more or less permanent internal chaos, it can no longer serve as an efficient substitute for the industrial reserve army. The system no longer responds

well to inflationary drugs (which now seem to affect it as a poison), and it begins to heave convulsively as it attempts to restore the basic inner relationships and balances which it needs for continued survival.[23]

The second and third reason that the inflationary strategy ultimately failed are bound up with international finance and international competition. With stagnant domestic markets, the struggle for international sales intensifies in the form of new trade wars. Each nation-state must contain its own inflation for fear that it will undermine its competitive position and experience a loss of both home and overseas markets. When the vast American balance-of-payments deficit, which flooded the world with unwanted dollars, threatened the financial stability of Western capitalism, financial authorities finally pressed collectively for a containment of credit expansion.

The fourth reason that the inflationary strategy had to be scrapped is that it became a political liability. While most groups ultimately adjust their incomes and protect their purchasing power, not all are in a position to do so. Even those who succeed find the psychological cost of an inflation-induced anxiety difficult to bear. At some state the electorate demands that government do something to bring inflation under control.

To summarize the argument to this point: large and growing deficits combined with credit expansions succeeded in maintaining high levels of demand and employment but did not address the new obstacles to capital accumulation. These policies helped to disguise the fact that the expansionary forces responsible for the long wave of prosperity had exhausted themselves. Left to itself a crisis would have accelerated the restructuring process needed to pave the way for economic renewal. Government-sponsored inflation blocked this process. But all it succeeded in doing was postponing the day of reckoning and aggravating the crisis by converting stagnation to stagflation. When this situation finally "reduced the capitalist system to a condition of more or less permanent internal chaos," to quote Morris, restructuring could not be put off any longer.

The Crash

The crash began in the summer of 1974. In the first half of 1975, output in advanced capitalist countries fell 3.5 per cent from what it had been a year earlier. Recovery was rapid at first, almost regaining 1973 levels by the spring of 1976, but it lost its momentum thereafter. By 1979 output was 17 per cent above the 1973 level, when the second round of oil price increases took its toll. OECD output grew by less than 1 per cent a year over the period 1979-82. Between 1973 and 1982 it rose by only 1.9 per cent a year compared to 5.5 per cent in 1960 to 1973. Symptomatic of the economic slow-down has been the re-emergence of mass unemployment — from 8 million at the end of the mini-boom to 15 million in 1975 to 32 million in 1983. This is equivalent to an OECD unemployment rate rising from an average of 3.5 per cent in 1973 to 5.5 per cent in 1975 to 8.4 per cent in 1983.

What were the elements of the slow-down?

Rising unemployment and declining real wages caused a reduction in the growth of consumer spending (from 3.5 per cent a year from 1960 to 1973 to 1.4 per cent a year between 1973 and 1982). Worsening terms of trade caused a slight reduction in the value of export surpluses between the advanced capitalist countries and the rest of the world. On the other hand, growing government deficits helped reduce the extent of the general decline. These were invariably caused by the slow-down in government revenues induced by the economic slow-down rather than by increased goverment spending. Overall, government spending was deliberately repressed.

Most important has been the collapse of business investment. Profits had been falling for some years but until the crash business confidence remained fairly buoyant. To be sure it had been bruised by the wage explosions and industrial unrest of the late 1960s. But it was increased international financial insecurity symbolized by the break-up of the Bretton Woods system and the oil crisis that seems to have triggered the run on major stock exchanges, signifying the collapse of business confidence. The crash in share prices between September 1973 and September 1974 was greater than that of 1929. Revelations of the Watergate affair, which dominated the world's media in spring 1974, did not help. "The country with the largest single vote on the IMF, the largest recipient of OPEC funds and the key issue of international money was being run by a president whose attentions were more and more focused on saving his own skin."[24]

Profits collapsed after the mini-boom. In 1975 the rate of profit was only 60 per cent of the 1968 level; it rose slightly in the recovery as capacity utilization inched up and pressure from wages and import prices eased and fell back again in 1979. By the early 1980s business profit rates were still no higher than what they had been in 1975 and manufacturing profit rates were considerably below the 1975 level.

By comparing the 1981 level with the average level obtained in the 1951-69 period, the full extent of the drop can be readily observed (Table 16:2). In each bloc, business profit was 50 to 60 per cent of the 1951-69 average, and the manufacturing profit rate only 30 to 50 per cent. The drop in Canada was notably less. The fall in profitability

TABLE 16:2
Profit Rates, 1981 Compared to 1951-69

	Advanced Capitalist Countries	Canada	U.S.A.	Europe	Japan
Business					
1951-69	16.5	10.5	18.3	14.4	22.3
1981	10.2	8.2	11.8	7.6	14.2
1981/51-69	0.62	0.78	0.64	0.53	0.64
Manufacturing					
1951-69	23.1	19.5	27.5	17.3	31.5
1981	8.9	13.9	10.3	5.2	13.3
1981/51-69	0.39	0.71	0.37	0.30	0.42

Source: Calculated from Armstrong et al, ibid.

summarized the fact that conditions for capital accumulation had seriously deteriorated and had thus far failed to improve.

Retained earnings is the major source of investment funds, but it is not the only source. In the face of falling profits, corporations can finance investment by issuing shares or borrowing. Share issues were discouraged by the depressed state of the stock market. The alternative was borrowing from banks or issuing bonds. Most businesses made use of these sources especially since, until 1981, real interest rates were low and often negative. But nominal rates were high even in these years and loans could become very costly if inflation subsequently fell. Therefore, many businesses resorted to short-term borrowing. In any event, corporations did not feel sufficiently confident about future returns to borrow on a scale that would offset declining retained earnings. Consequently, the accumulation rate failed to recover.

The Canadian crash shadowed the world crash. But there are a few special points worth noting. Whereas other governments deliberately deflated their economies in 1974 to repress inflation, the Liberal regime attempted to buck the tide. Believing that inflation was world-wide in origin, it decided to let other governments fight inflation while Canada went on prospering. Canadian profit rates had risen spectacularly since 1970 (by 42 per cent in manufacturing and 25 per cent overall) and the government hoped that by by-passing the world down-turn it could help sustain capital accumulation. But by late 1974 and early 1975 unions, having lost ground over the previous years, were suddenly winning big settlements. It was to help prevent corporations from forfeiting their gains that wage controls were imposed at this time.

TABLE 16:3
Canada: Average Annual Spending in Constant 1971 Dollars

% Change

	Total	Consumption	Gov't	Business Investment	Housing Investment	Government Investment	Net Exports
1950-73	5.3	4.4	6.1	6.8	6.7	6.8	−0.4
1974-84	2.5	2.8	1.6	2.3	−0.1	1.2	0.8
1974-84/ 1950-73	0.47	0.64	0.26	0.34	−0.01	0.18	2.0

Source: Calculated from Department of Finance, Economic Review, April 1985, p. 69.

By now it was clear to the government that it could not isolate Canada from the world crash. Henceforth, Ottawa joined other governments in deflating the economy to stem the inflationary tide. To encourage investment, it expanded its offering of tax-incentive schemes which, however, were notably unsuccessful. Thanks to the boom in commodity prices — lumber, metal and mineral prices more than tripled between 1972 and 1980 — overall investment held up fairly well until 1982. With their disastrous drop, investment collapsed totally, producing a much sharper down-turn in Canada than in the U.S. And, contrary to previous economic recoveries when investment always surpassed its pre-recession peaks, to date capital formation lingers well below the high reached in 1981.

The overall circumstance in the depression period 1974-84 is presented in Table 16:3, on the previous page, which shows that all sectors except net exports have contributed to the decline.

While economic performance has varied from country to country in recent years, in late 1986 the capitalist world remains stuck in the quagmire of stagnation. In the next chapter we examine the strategies adopted to break out of the crisis. A few preliminary observations are in order. First, none of the advanced capitalist countries has escaped the crisis. Second, all have recognized the need for major restructuring. Third, all have accepted the conclusion that a prolonged policy of economic restraint is a necessary part of unblocking the obstacles to economic renewal. The specific policy instruments have differed from country to country. Thatcher's Britain has persisted with both monetary and fiscal restraint, while in Reagan's America restraint has been tempered by tax reductions and the impact of the arms build-up. Some countries have placed greater emphasis on fiscal restraint than monetary restraint. Others have tried wage restraint as a complement to monetary and fiscal restraint. The Canadian state is one that has used a combination of monetary, fiscal and wage restraint. Whatever the policy or policy combinations, the priority of the state has clearly shifted to the single one of acting as an instrument for the restoration of profit.

17 | The Road to Recovery?

We may now ask what the ingredients are of a successful capitalist restructuring. As already noted, preconditions for a long-term sharp increase in the average rate of profit include a major erosion in real wages and worker militancy; dramatic reductions in the share of state expenditures allocated to non-productive purposes; the elimination of inefficient firms of all sizes; radical reductions in the cost of equipment and materials; massive applications of new technological innovations; and the restoration of order in international economic relations.

While the economic crisis is symptomatic of the collapse in accumulation, paradoxically it is also a necessary element in the path to recovery. By removing the main obstacles to further accumulation it allows for an acceleration of the restructuring process. Restructuring occurs at five levels — at the level of the plant, the enterprise, the national economy, the international economy and the state.

Plant Level

Management uses the crisis to change the organization and reward system of production. It introduces new technology, new methods and intensification of work, and new incentive schemes; it takes back control over the work process, the concessions and benefits won by workers in better times; and it relaxes safety standards. Supportive of this effort is the state's role in rewriting labour laws and managing the crisis to sustain unemployment, which weakens workers' morale and their ability to resist wage cuts and the reorganization of work.

An example culled from recent British experience is Rupert Murdoch's moves to destroy the print union in four of Britain's leading newspapers. The Australian millionaire demanded a collective agreement that would abolish the closed shop, prohibit strikes and industrial action for any reason whatsoever, roll-back wages, and give management total power to classify and reclassify workers and "dismiss, suspend, discipline and lay off workers as it seems fit." Obviously, Murdoch never expected the print unions to accept the agreement. When they struck, all 6,000 printers were sacked the same week and production immediately shifted to a new plant far removed from Fleet Street, with a thick barb-wire fence and tight security measures. Production was maintained by non-union workers. New industrial relations law introduced by the Thatcher government strengthened Murdoch's hand by outlawing all forms of secondary action in a strike. By splitting up production in six satellite companies, union picketing was declared illegal; the union's financial assets were seized and its leaders faced imprisonment. Burdened with a past image of having effectively used their position as highly skilled workers to win wage rates far above the industrial average and having denied access to women and non-whites, the union failed to garner much support outside the printing trade.

In North America, the restructuring of industrial relations has come primarily in two forms: quality-of-work-life schemes/quality circles and concession bargaining. They usually go together. A typical example is LTV Steel Company's Cleveland works. The company signed a pact with the United Steel Workers as the bargaining agent for yet-to-be hired workers in a new plant. The contract provides hourly wages and benefits that are $5 to $10 less than industry rates and a gain-sharing plan with a formula measuring productivity, quality and work attendance. It contains no grievance procedure; allows management full flexibility in scheduling hours and work; replaces job classifications with four skill levels and job rotation; and gives workers a voice in hiring and firing.[1]

Concession bargaining has been by far the most widespread system of bludgeoning labour costs. While companies have always used recessions to try to rid themselves of practices that reduce their flexibility, they have never before been so successful in their efforts.

In a feature article "A Work Revolution in U.S. Industry," *Business Week* lists several important work rule and benefit concessions granted by American unions in the recession years: cutting size of crews; enlarging jobs by adding duties, eliminating unneeded jobs (steel, autos, railroads, meatpacking, airlines); giving up relief and wash-up periods, working more hours for the same pay, allowing management more flexibility in scheduling daily and weekly hours (steel, autos, meatpacking, rubber, trucking, airlines, textile); restricting the use of seniority in filling job vacancies, bumping rights during lay-offs and picking shifts (steel, autos, meatpacking, rubber); reducing piece-work and bonus incentives (steel, rubber); offering straight-time wages for weekend work performed within the regular forty-hour work week (rubber, textile, trucking).[2]

These efforts continued into the recovery stage. Nearly 40 per cent of American workers covered by settlements negotiated in 1983 specified a wage freeze in the first contract year; nearly 20 per cent had no increases over the life of the agreement. In 1984, 12 per cent were covered by agreements specifying no wage increases throughout the life of the contract and 5 per cent took decreases (averaging 10 per cent) as first-year wage adjustments. Nearly 10 per cent of all settlements also included two-tier wage structures under which new employees are paid lower wages than existing employees doing the same jobs. Many contracts also provided lump-sum one-time pay bonuses and profit-sharing plans in place of base-rate wage increases.[3]

Union locals turned out to be powerless to halt or even slow down the process. As described by three researchers who surveyed the scene:

> In most situations, management accompanied its demands with threats that were linked directly to negotiation outcomes. The threats were generally clear and specific, including stated intentions to close particular plants, liquidate specific business assets, shift operations to other facilities, implement massive lay-offs (with specific members indicated) or, in a few cases, file for bankruptcy .... In order to obtain work rule changes, it was common for management to use whipsaw tactics by comparing rules and productivity information between plants and threatening to shift or outsource work if recalcitrant locals did not agree to changes.[4]

According to these authors, national union-staff representatives, testifying to the credibility of management threats, promoted the concessions and "used political muscle (eg. threats to withhold resources needed by local leaders, implied threats to careers of local officers) to induce unwilling local leaders to support concessions." Yet, "even when concessions were granted and the union argued that they were temporary and necessary to obtain job security, many employers returned in a matter of months seeking additional concessions, continued to close plants, or to outsource work."[5]

Recent decisions by the Supreme Court and the National Labour Relations Board (NLRB) strengthened management's hand in this concessions environment. The NLRB has ruled that companies can demand concessions from their unions in the middle of contracts and, if unions refused, close their plants and move operations elsewhere. Prior to this ruling such moves would have been deemed unfair labour practices. The Supreme Court has ruled that contracts can be abrogated if companies claim that they are financially burdensome. For all practical purposes, companies now have the right to unilaterally break contracts which effectively means decertifying the union.

The looked-for break-up of existing American industrial relations structures has been succinctly outlined by the Canadian-born publisher of *US News and World Report*, Mortimer Zuckerman:

> We will have to do nothing less than transform the industrial culture in America. We must involve management and labour in a much more collaborative effort to be competitive. For example, we should explore moving away from a system characterized by stable compensation and unstable employment and toward a system of stable long-term employment and variable compensation. This involves all employes [sic] sharing in the ups and downs in terms of their pay rather than the top sharing the upside through bonuses and stock options while the bottom absorbs the downside through layoffs. Variable compensations would signify a de facto end to industry-wide unions. Unions would have to accept responsibility for the performance of individual companies in order to help their members increase their compensation.[6]

This scenario would see the end of unionism and collective bargaining as we have known them in favour of company or enterprise unionism similar to that in Japan with wages fluctuating with the state of the market and enterprise profits. It was exactly this approach that was on the agenda of the big three auto companies in their negotiations in the early 1980s. Indeed, it was precisely the acceptance of this agenda by the American UAW that led the Canadian region to break away from the international to form the Canadian Automobile Workers (CAW).

Canadian unions in general have been somewhat more successful in holding the line against concessions. This has been partly due to stronger union resistance but also to less stringent labour legislation and to a lesser degree of industrial deregulation. But with a few years lag many of the same features are spilling over to Canadian agreements. For example, in 1984 there were a total of 136 settlements involving nearly 300,000 employees, almost double the 1983 total, where wages were either frozen or cut in the first year of the contract term. They represent over a quarter of all employees covered in major 1984 collective bargaining settlements. Lump-sum cash payments, profit-sharing plans, paid vacation and holiday reduction, and two-tier wage systems, etc., are also becoming fairly common. In mining, the United Steel Workers has signed contracts with Inco, Cominco and Hudson Bay Mining and Smelting that provide for no general wage increases with wage improvements tied to volume and metal prices. Its contract with Kaiser Aluminum reduces wages by an average of $1.84 an hour with 85 per cent of the concessions to be returned to employees in the form of Kaiser stock. Several businesses have scuttled industry-wide labour contracts in favour of more versatile and tailored agreements. Included among these are CN, CP, building contractors and meat packers where, for the first time in forty years, separate agreements rather than a single master contract were signed in 1984.[7]

These concessions notwithstanding, industrial relations observers note worriedly that restructuring of capital-labour relations has not been nearly as thoroughgoing in Canada as in the U.S.

> Unlike in the United States, there have been very few initiatives in Canada towards flexible compensation systems or any real reassessment of the growing cost of employee benefits. Nor has there been any systematic attempt to improve long-term productivity growth through accelerated modernizing of plant and equipment and by changes in work methods and in managerial efficiency. More importantly, there is little evidence of any major change in traditional collective bargaining relationships.[8]

The concern is that, not having broken the back of trade union resistance, employers will be forced to deliver the catch-up increases unions will demand as the recovery gathers strength.

Enterprise Level

Firms shed unprofitable or less profitable branches and products on the one hand, while on the other diversifying in more profitable directions by taking over or merging with other firms. They decentralize or, as the case may be, centralize production in the most efficient locations. This process may be supported by the state in a passive manner, by giving a free play to market forces during the recession à la Thatcher and Reagan; or in an active way by assisting state-mandated companies in technologically advanced or otherwise strategic industries, by encouraging mergers, industrial reorganization, consolidation and branch relocations with financial assistance, state equity or even nationalization. The objective of nationalization under these circumstances is, not to feather the nests of lame ducks, but to increase productivity. Once enterprises have been put back on a profitable basis with state funding they could be returned to private enterprise. As for existing state-owned enterprises, their unprofitable parts are eliminated and their profitable parts privatized. This has been a major priority of Thatcherism and one that the Mulroney government is emulating.

To date the Thatcher government has sold off $35 billion of public assets including British Gas, Jaguar, British Telecom, British Petroleum, among others, and 600,000 housing units. These sales transferred half a million workers to the private sector. Canadian privatization has been puny by comparison. But having sold off de Havilland, Canadair and Northern Transportation, several others will be dumped soon including Teleglobe and Eldorado Nuclear. All of these companies were put on the auction block by the former Liberal government. The Tory plan is more impressive. It calls for a massive sale of shares in Petro-Canada, Air Canada, CNR and public properties worth billions.

Where state-owned enterprises are not sold off they are subject to the same rationalization process as private-sector enterprises, as French steel workers discovered to their dismay when the Mitterand government decided to shed tens of thousands of jobs in the process of modernizing France's debt-ridden steel industry. Ottawa's measures to restructure the railway industry, including the establishment of VIA Rail, the elimination of the Crow rate for farmers, the cancellation of unprofitable routes — all moves towards the deregulation of the industry — have eliminated tens of thousands of jobs. Transforming the Post Office from a public-service-based institution to a profit-based one is another goal near the top of the Tory agenda.

The phenomenon of plant closures is an important element of restructuring at the private-enterprise level. During the depths of the 1980s recession, most plant closings were related to insolvency. More recently, a growing number have been shuttered as part of decisions to rationalize production. In 1981, before the recession hit, 130 Ontario companies with fifty or more employees shut down or reduced their operations, terminating 20,000 jobs. Over the next three years, 470 companies closed for good or eliminated part of their operations, putting 77,000 people out of work. Nearly 90 per cent of the plant closures involve subsidiaries of U.S.-based corporations and in many cases Canadian production is transferred south by the U.S. parent company.[9]

The Black & Decker case is fairly typical.[10] In April 1985 it closed Canada's largest housewares and small-appliance plant, permanently laying off 600 workers. Originally owned by Canadian General Electric, the Barrie, Ontario, plant was sold to Black & Decker a year earlier as part of G.E.'s planned rationalization. Helped by a million dollar interest-free loan from the Ontario Development Corporation and a world product mandate, it was by all accounts a modern and profitable plant. Black & Decker closed it to escape the union (at a meeting with MPPs, company officials admitted they had closed every unionized plant they had acquired in North America) and as part of its corporate reorganization to move all of its production out of Canada. Black & Decker has already reduced its Canadian product lines from twenty-seven to seven, having shifted the other products to its operations in the U.S. and offshore.[11] Union efforts — which included an illegal walk-out, lobbying of MPPs, forming a community coalition and pressing a court order to force Black & Decker to comply with its undertaking to FIRA which had approved the original plant sale — all proved fruitless. As Jim Turk, research director of the United Electrical Workers concluded: "Their campaign generated massive press coverage and widespread sympathy. They had invalidated all the company's justifications for the closure. But in the end, there proved no legal impediment to the company doing what it wanted."[12]

Capital's tendency to migrate from areas with strong traditions of union militancy is fairly universal. It played a part in the shift away from urban centres to smaller towns in the U.K. in the 1960s. The movement of U.S. manufacturing to southern sunbelt states has been similarly motivated. Subcontracting work to small non-unionized companies is another part of the same picture. In Japan, for instance, the average large manufacturing firm has 160 subcontractors. It's the primary means used to avoid over-commitment to life-time employment which is confined to less than a third of the Japanese work force. When sales slacken, the unemployment problem is passed down to smaller firms. Another advantage to contracting out is that workers' pay is less than 60 per cent what it is in large factories.[13]

National Level

Restructuring involves the deindustrialization of some sectors and regions and the development and redevelopment of others. It also includes deregulation of industry, one of the major priorities of the Reagan administration.

Regulations established in the 1930s to provide a measure of stability and order in the transport, banking and telecommunications industries have been stripped away to introduce greater competition and thereby force companies to cut costs and prices. Since labour costs are usually the largest controllable expense, workers bear much of the pain of adjustment. Similarly, governmental agencies like the National Labour Relations Board and the Occupational Safety and Health Administration, set up to provide a measure of protection for workers, have been gutted. As *Business Week* magazine reports, "the proliferation of new competitors is doing to deregulated industries in the U.S. what foreign competition has done to the manufacturing sector. Since deregulation, shipping costs have been slashed, the airline industry has increased its output by 19 per cent with fewer than 1 per cent more employees."[14] Borne on the backs of workers, it amounts to a significant shift of resources to capital.

Deregulation along these lines is a policy thrust that the Mulroney government will not be able to resist. But the first priority of the Tory regime, which would involve a massive restructuring of the entire economy should it succeed is, of course, the free-trade agreement with the U.S.

International Level

Largely through the instrument of the multinational corporation a new international division of labour is gradually taking shape. In the current crisis, the multinationals have begun to reorganize their global operations in two specific ways. First, some are abandoning the old branch-plant system which produces a wide range of goods exclusively for national markets and replacing it with a world-mandate system in which branch-plants produce a narrow range of products or components for the world market. For example, the Ford/Lynx was designed by Germans, Americans, Englishmen, Swiss and Spaniards; its components are produced in a chain of twelve different countries from Japan to Yugoslavia. Using the entire globe as their field of alternatives, automakers determine where each part can be produced most profitably.

Second, some multinationals are separating off their most labour-intensive divisions and in many instances all their manufacturing operations — either contracting out to off-shore producers or re-establishing them in Third World areas where labour is cheap and employment less regulated. Thus a dual labour market is evolving on a world scale. Taken together, these departures amount to a restructuring of the international division of labour.

State Level

Whatever the state's strategy for managing the crisis, restructuring involves a revision of the tax system in favour of corporations and the rich, a shedding of the most expendable social services and cut-backs or freezes in others, a reordering of commitments to various programs, and a rationalization of the internal organization of work in government departments and state agencies.

As in the case of deregulation, the Reagan administration has led the way in restructuring government tax and spending systems. Between 1982 and 1988 top marginal tax rates in the U.S. will have been reduced from 70 per cent to 28 per cent as a result of the Economic Recovery Act of 1981 and the Tax Reform Act of 1986. The first gave highest income households a tax saving exceeding $21,000; the second lopped off another $7,000. While the 1986 bill removes 6 million low-income families from the tax rolls, per household saving comes to only a hundred dollars or so on top of the $60 saving from the 1981 bill. The $30,000-$70,000 income earner who carries the great bulk of the tax load in America gets little or no reduction.[15]

The basic thrust of the 1986 tax reform is a radical movement away from the liberal ability-to-pay taxation principle first established in 1913 towards a regressive flat-rate tax system. For now, a two-bracket tax system, 15 per cent and 28 per cent, replaces the progressive income tax; the corporate tax rate, already among the lowest in the world, is reduced from 46 per cent to 34 per cent. But the tax bill also repeals or reduces many tax breaks. Largely as a result of increased exemptions, exclusions, credits and deferrals written into the 1981 Economic Recovery Act, corporate income taxes contributed only 9 per cent of federal revenues in 1984, helping to widen the U.S. deficit. The new tax plan is supposed to shift some of the tax burden from individuals to corporations and put the corporate share of income taxes back to 1970s levels.

By drastically reducing tax rates and "leveling the playing field" among industries and individuals, the Reagan tax reforms provide one more test for supply-side economics. As of 1984, Reaganomics had already succeeded in nudging income distribution in favour of the rich. In 1984 the wealthiest fifth of families had an average disposable income 6.4 times larger than families in the poorest fifth, compared to 5.1 times in 1980.[16]

State expenditure has been similarly reoriented. While military spending — which basically means government investment in a dozen or so high-tech corporations — has soared, cuts in spending have been directly aimed at the poor. Altogether income-assistance programs targeted to the poor fell by nearly 4 per cent in real terms between 1980 and 1983. For instance, families with incomes below $10,000 had their incomes reduced by 7.5 per cent ($375). At the upper end of the scale, $80,000 or more, social-spending cuts amounted to only $131 or 0.1 per cent of income.[17]

The Thatcher government has introduced a similar change in tax regimes: the top rate of income tax was cut from 85 per cent to 60 per cent giving the richest households a 25 per cent increase in take-home pay, while the overall tax burden to the average worker rose from 44 per cent to 48 per cent between 1979 and 1983.[18] As a consequence of these and other measures, the wealthiest 50 per cent now own 80-84 per cent of all wealth compared with a share of 79-83 per cent in 1979. This represents "a decisive reversal since Mrs. Thatcher came to power in 1979 of the long-term trend towards a more equal distribution of wealth."[19]

While other governments have been much more constrained in cutting social programs, they have moved in the same direction: freezing social-security benefits (Holland); cutting hospital beds (Belgium); imposing hospital-user fees (France); deindexing or partial deindexing of welfare payments (France, Denmark); delaying scheduled pension increases

(West Germany); cutting back health services (Holland, Britain); cutting back unemployment benefits, grants to local authorities and education (Britain).[20]

We have already examined the extensive tax restructuring in Canada introduced by the Liberals and extended by the Tories. Except for substantial cuts in post-secondary education, federal Liberal governments in Canada were content to allow inflation to pare down the real value of welfare and social-service expenditures. From 9.5 per cent real growth in the previous decade, the advance in social spending was cut to well under 3 per cent a year after 1975, considerably less than the expansion rate of the economy. As a consequence, social spending has fallen to just 22 per cent of GNP, its lowest in a decade and well below the spending levels of most European countries. Canada, in fact, has dropped to fifteenth on a list of the nineteen major industrialized countries in terms of its expenditures on social programs. More severe cuts can be expected from the Mulroney administration. Deep cuts have already slashed the budgets of the CBC and arts agencies, the Science Council and the National Research Council, including the elimination of its environment protection secretariat. The twenty-one volume (Nielsen) report of the Task Force on Program Review and the Macdonald Royal Commission are notable examples of attempts to develop new agendas for restructuring the state.

Since the crash of 1974 the crisis has indeed accelerated the restructuring process and helped remove or reduce some of the obstacles to further accumulation. Wage freezes and cuts and the reorganization of work inside plants raise the rate of surplus value.

The reorganization of capital at the enterprise, national and international levels concentrates production in those regions, countries and enterprises where labour is most productive of surplus value. The crisis eliminates the weakest firms, destroying their capital or transferring it at vastly reduced prices to financially stronger rivals.

Mass unemployment weakens workers' ability to resist cuts in real wages (variable capital) and intensification of the work process. The reduction of social expenditures and the redistribution of the tax burden away from corporations and the wealthy increase the proportion of total income available for accumulation.

The "slaughter" of capital values, the elimination of debt, the repression of wages, the rise in productivity, etc., all have the effect of dampening inflation. More importantly they have the potential of reversing the decline in the rate of profit. With profit being concentrated in a diminished number of firms that are both financially and industrially strong, it is more likely that profitable investment opportunities and available cost-cutting but expensive technologies will be taken advantage of.

The ground-work for radical changes in technology has been laid by the recent developments in micro-processing. New propelling industries that might constitute the basis of a renovated accumulation can be anticipated: atomic and solar energy, space, genetics, synthetic food production, sea bed exploitation, etc.

Is Restraint Working?

Due in part to the cyclical upturn (1983-85) but also to the restructuring process, labour costs have declined significantly in most countries (see Table 17:1). Because of the appreciation of the American dollar against the currencies of all other countries except Japan, unit labour costs fell in all the advanced countries when measured in U.S. dollars. The decline represents the combined effect of increased productivity — reflecting vigorous recovery in output with weak employment growth — and declining real wages — reflecting wage growth less than inflation.

Whether these improvements will spark a sustained growth in investment spending is not at all certain, however. The advanced coun-

TABLE 17:1
Unit Labour Costs in Manufacturing

Average Annual Percentage Change

	1960-73	1973-81	1982	1983	1984
National Currency Basis					
United States	1.9	7.7	6.6	−0.8	0.1
Canada	1.8	9.8	13.5	0.3	−2.3
Japan	3.5	2.3	−1.8	−1.7	−5.3
France	2.6	10.3	11.1	7.6	3.7
Germany	3.7	4.7	4.0	−0.5	−1.0
Italy	5.1	15.6	18.1	14.0	3.9
Sweden	3.5	10.5	4.2	0.6	5.3
United Kingdom	4.1	17.1	4.0	0.5	3.8
US Dollar Basis					
United States	1.9	7.7	6.6	−0.8	0.1
Canada	1.9	6.3	10.2	0.5	−7.0
Japan	4.9	3.1	−13.0	3.1	−5.7
France	2.4	4.5	−8.1	−7.1	−9.5
Germany	6.1	4.4	−3.4	−5.4	−11.2
Italy	5.4	4.8	−0.7	1.6	−10.1
Sweden	4.3	2.8	−16.0	−17.6	−2.3
United Kingdom	2.6	9.2	−10.2	−12.9	−8.4

Source: US Department of Labor, Bureau of Labor Statistics.

tries are still burdened with much surplus capacity — over 20 per cent in the U.S., 22 per cent in Canadian manufacturing and much more in mining. A seemingly vigorous U.S. investment growth, for example, is clearly deceiving. It shows that by the second half of 1985 capital investment had advanced beyond the pre-recession 1979 level by 30 per cent when measured in constant dollars. Yet, when examined in detail, all the investment growth is concentrated in two narrow components, office equipment and business purchases of automobiles. Investment in most other durable goods industries such as manufacturing and other machinery is still well below 1979 levels. This is likely too narrow a base for sustained recovery.[21]

On a world scale, the question at this point is whether the old structures and relationships have been sufficiently uprooted to spur a full recovery; whether the labour movement has been inflicted with a defeat severe enough to prevent it from fighting back effectively when and if economic conditions substantially improve; whether competition, conflict and uneven strength among advanced countries can be resolved before breaking down into a vicious trade war and severe protectionism; whether technologically induced unemployment will be sufficiently great to drag down consumption, break the welfare state, spark political unrest among the young; whether the piling up of corporate debt and/or Third World debt can be managed and brought under control before causing a major financial crisis.

International Imbalances

While a certain degree of restructuring on a global scale has taken place, corporate investment in less developed countries only amounted to $11 billion in 1980 compared to $800 billion in the advanced capitalist countries.[22] As such it provides still limited possibilities for accumulation. Moreover, new trade patterns have aggravated the problem of uneven development within and among advanced capitalist countries. The fact that the less developed countries (LDCs) are large net importers of manufactured goods from the advanced countries provides cold comfort for hard-pressed first-world producers of clothing, footwear, electronic goods and TV sets. And while LDCs are selling consumer goods mainly to the U.S. and Europe, they are buying most of their capital goods from Japan. The resulting friction reflects the fact that competition between the advanced countries is being fought on their terrain.[23]

There are three great international imbalances — in trade, in savings and investment, and in international finance. They reflect the uncoordinated financial, trading and fiscal actions of the leading capitalist countries. The American recovery, far more vigorous than any other, has been entirely fueled by the massive increase in military expenditures and the tax cut. They have produced America's huge budgetary deficit, $176 billion in 1984 and over $200 billion in 1985; and they are largely responsible for America's unprecedented trade deficit — $123 billion in 1984, up from $60 billion in 1983, and $36 billion in 1982 — making the U.S. the leading debtor nation. No other nation can afford to go into hock on such a spectacular scale.

One of the ironies of the present situation is that Japan, the country most heavily under attack for its trade surpluses ($65 billion in 1985), is doing the most to provide the capital inflows that are keeping the U.S. international payments system in rough balance. Japan is the big holder of U.S. dollars which it has used to purchase dollar-denominated bonds and securities. West Germany ($40 billion trade surplus) has also been pouring its surplus dollars into the American economy. If they were all part of the same country, tax cuts and public spending would stimulate consumption and jobs in all regions. But the U.S., Japan, Europe and the Third World do not have a single government or a common currency. This is why "the threat of international crisis-protectionism, third world debt and currency misalignments will continue to rumble beneath the surface of the world economic recovery, as long as the present imbalances of trade, financial flows and fiscal policies persist."[24] As long as the American economy expands, interest rates stay up and the dollar is in demand, capital inflows into the U.S. may be kept up, but any puff of wind can cause a collapse.

The situation began to develop when, fueled by the size of its arms-led deficit and by tax cuts to business, the temporarily impressive American recovery led to heavy demands for credit for new business investment. This came on top of the requirements of government and consumers and what was demanded for mergers and acquisitions (up from 1,500 in 1980 to 3,000 in 1985 and $125 billion in 1984 and 1985) and speculation of all kinds.

The increased supply of money that would have been needed to accommodate such demands without raising the rate of interest was beyond what the money authorities had been willing to allow. As a consequence, prime interest rates were pushed up to 13 per cent in 1983. With inflation running at less than 4 per cent, the prime rate in real terms was 9 per cent, at least double the historical average. High interest rates sucked in billions in foreign capital raising the foreign-exchange value of the dollar, up 15 per cent between 1983 and 1984 and 65 per cent between 1980 and 1984 against the other ten leading OECD currencies.

The super-dollar has had two contradictory effects. On the one hand, it opens the door to more imports from abroad, helping the recovery of other countries while penalizing American exports, with American industry facing an enormous price disadvantage. On the other hand, the super-dollar further worsens the terms of trade of countries trading with the U.S. Except for the small part of their exports which are sold in the U.S. at American dollar prices — Canadian forest products for example — other countries have to sell more in exchange for the same quantity of their imports from the U.S. For Canada, Japan and the countries of western Europe the advantage of a trade surplus outweigh the disadvantages of worsening terms of trade. For debtor countries, the high foreign exchange rate means a further increase in the burden of their debt. They have to export still more and/or import still less. For them, a trade deficit helps their economic development. All the benefits of a trade surplus are absorbed in helping them pay the interest and principle on their foreign debt.

The consequence of America's ballooning trade deficit creates further contradictions. First, it involves a massive transfer of resources from other countries, in particular the Third World nations — a Robin Hood in reverse. Roughly a third of the increased consumption of goods enjoyed by Americans since 1982 has been supplied by other countries. And the U.S. now absorbs 8 per cent of all the money saved in the non-Communist world. On its current course this will rise to 15 per cent within four years unless the U.S. adopts drastic policy changes. Second, it maintains pressure on U.S. interest rates. Ostensibly raised to curb inflation they are now also necessary to attract the required capital from abroad to pay for the trade deficit. The effect is not only harmful to domestic recovery and to the global debt problem; it also has perverse effects on the recoveries of other countries. It removes capital which otherwise might have been invested at home and it forces other monetary authorities to maintain interest rates at levels much higher than they would like.

Economists at New York's Morgan Guaranty Trust have worked out several alternative scenarios, none of them reassuring. One is a stage-by-stage devaluation of the American dollar which would wipe out the trade deficit as it dropped. To accomplish this by the end of the decade would require a 12 per cent devaluation each year, 50 per cent overall by 1987. Devaluation on this scale, however, could bring back inflation with a vengeance and cause a major recession in Europe's export-dependent economies.

A second alternative is a government-imposed austerity program, drastically cutting the budget deficit over four years or placing a surcharge on imports. However, the austerity program would have to be so severe that unemployment would rise to 15 per cent while import surcharges would have to be so high that they would be bound to set off a trade war.[25] If other governments, especially Japan and Germany, would expand their economies while the Reagan administration practised austerity, some of the load would be taken off the American economy. If this was accompanied by allowing Third World countries to follow more stimulative policies supported by flows of commercial and official funds, the huge transfers of funds now taking place from poor to rich countries would be at least partially relieved. These are the objectives of the initiatives launched by U.S. Treasury Secretary James Baker. So far, they have had a cool reception.

Notwithstanding the likely outcome, the Reagan administration appears to have chosen the first strategy. Between February 1985 and August 1986, the U.S. dollar has been allowed to devalue by 35 per cent. Meanwhile, as a leading Wall Street analyst has put it, the world economy is like an aircraft flying at minimum speed. Aerodynamic theory shows that it can stay aloft but that the slightest shock could send it crashing down.[26]

The Hollow Corporation

Behind the rapid deterioration of America's international position lies what has been called "the hollowing of American industry." In the words of Akio Moritu, chairman of the Sony Corporation:

> American corporations have either shifted output to low-wage countries or come to buy parts and assembled products from countries like Japan that can make quality products at low prices. The result is a hollowing of American industry. [27]

An insightful special report of *Business Week* magazine described the evolution of a new kind of company, manufacturers who do little or no manufacturing. Precisely to shore up their bottom lines, U.S. manufacturers are in fact pursuing with a vengeance the strategy discussed earlier, buying parts or whole products from other producers both at home and abroad. So-called outsourcing replaces the traditional policy in which firms make virtually all critical parts. Vertical disaggregation replaces vertical integration. The result is the post-industrial corporation, industrial companies without industrial production. Companies long identified with making goods of all sorts now often only produce the package and the labels.

For example, General Electric spent $1.4 billion in 1985 importing products sold in the U.S. under the GE label. Virtually all of its consumer electronics are made in Asia. RCA, with the biggest share of the American VCR market, gets its machines stamped with the RCA logo in a Hitachi factory. Indeed, no video recorders are currently being made in the U.S. Forty per cent of automobiles marketed in the U.S. are foreign-made including nearly 20 per cent sold under Detroit labels, and even the cars Detroit assembles carry a huge proportion of imported parts.

"The hollowest option of all," says *Business Week*, "is to axe manufacturing altogether and instead serve as the marketing arm for a foreign-owned factory. Yet more and more industrial giants ... are choosing this course for its almost instant rewards."[28] There are more profits in marketing, finance and distribution than in manufacturing — but what is proving to be a perfectly rational profit turn-around policy for individual businesses will have a devastating long-term impact on the American economy and aggravate the imbalance in the international economy still further. For it has always been the industrial sector that has been both the leader in U.S. productivity growth, and innovation and the backbone of the country's high living standards. Manufacturing now accounts for only 21 per cent of the U.S. gross national product, a 30 per cent drop since the peak year of 1953.

Business Week quotes one economist as saying: "For corporate managers the central question is not necessarily what products their companies make but whether their companies make profits. If Ford Motors, for example, can make money by making loans, it will become a bank and let the Japanese make more and more of its cars." No doubt this is a commonly held view and the service sector has indeed expanded spectacularly (from 60 per cent of GNP in 1960 to 68 per cent in 1985). But another economist quoted is more nearly correct: "If you lose your industrial base, you can't be a prosperous service economy. The US is too big to be a niche economy.... In a global input-output model, it may not matter where the goods come from, but a huge core of this economy depends on what's made on these shores."[29]

A vast array of services, from trucking to banking to computer-programming to utilities and health services, are directly linked to the goods-producing industries. GM's largest single supplier is not a steel maker or tire manufacturer but Blue Cross.[30] Despite the incredible growth in service employment — it provided 80 per cent of all jobs created since the 1981-82 recession — the pace cannot be kept up if manufacturing withers.

Other factors strengthen doubts that the service economy can replace the industrial economy as the linchpin of American recovery. First, the U.S. share of global trade in business services, such as brokerage, consulting and engineering, has fallen from 15 per cent in 1973 to 8 per cent in 1983, putting it behind France, Germany and Britain. Second, dogged by the same competitive pressures that face manufacturers, managers are scanning the globe for cheaper labour to undertake service functions.

Third, the average hourly pay in service employments is 11 per cent lower than in manufacturing employments, putting pressure on consumer markets. Cashiering, the occupation predicted to supply the largest number of jobs through 1995, pays 60 per cent of the average American wage. Future wage gains in general will be restrained by the fact that the fast growth industries are more competitive than traditional manufacturing industries and can't afford premium wages. In this environment unions that once drove up wages are easily frozen out. In the U.S., the secondary labour market of part-time, low-productivity, sex-segregated, poorly paid jobs is fast over-taking the primary labour market and may already predominate. Automation will no doubt accelerate the process. American prosperity since the Second World War has been built upon rising mass-based consumer markets developed from a high wage/high productivity work force. But the "affluent worker" is fast becoming a depleted species in the era of the post-industrial corporation.

By lowering its wage base, outsourcing, and by literally turning industry inside out — hollowing — American corporations may be temporarily reversing their profit decline, but only at the cost of shrinking the American industrial mass consumer base. What's rational for individual corporate entities struggling for survival in the global economy turns out to be irrational for the national economic entity.

Technological Unemployment?

The fully automated factory appears to be an obvious route for North American companies in the struggle for survival. Linking all functions of the factory and corporate headquarters, manufacturers could conceive new products on a computer-aided design (CAD) system; pass the data electronically to a computer-aided engineering (CAE) system for verification; extract from the data the information needed to make the product and send it to a computer-aided manufacturing (CAM) system which would send electronic instructions for making the product to computer-controlled machine-tools, robotic assembly stations and other automated equipment on the shop floor; co-ordinate with computerized management systems to keep track of parts and equipment and to schedule production; continuously update corporate data banks used by marketing, finance, purchasing and other functions of headquarters. Besides giving corporations the ultimate in product flexibility, the fully automated factory would bring down labour costs to virtually zero. Other offshore savings, such as cheaper materials and lower overhead, would be overwhelmed by the benefit of quick turn-arounds and low inventories. "The computerized factory could produce things in Indiana for less than they cost to import from India."[31]

The fully automated factory does not come cheap. A mini-version costs $5 million (U.S.). So far only about 250 U.S. companies have come even close to full computer integration. In Canada only GM's planned Auto-Plex qualifies. However, several thousand American companies have already installed CAD/CAM systems — in Canada 500 of 43,000 manufacturers — and robots are more pervasive again. At the end of 1984, U.S. installations totalled 13,000 compared to Japan's 64,600; France 3,380; Britain 2,620; Sweden 2,400; Canada 940. Chrysler's Windsor, Ontario, plant increased production output by twenty units an hour with the help of robots and no additional workers. Boosting production to this extent with the old technology would have required another 600-700 workers. With its $400,000 investment in CAD/CAM, Chrysler estimates that it will trim $2,500 from the production cost of each vehicle.[32] But computer automation extends far beyond the factory. Its greatest application will be in the office where the productivity of workers has increased only 4 per cent over the past two decades compared to 85 per cent for factory workers.

Every long wave of prosperity in the past has involved the introduction of radical new technologies which have altered the entire shape of the economic and social environment, slashed production costs, and opened up an array of new profitable investment opportunities: the railroad, steam engines and steamships of the mid-nineteenth century; steel, electricity, turbines and internal combustion engines of the late nineteenth and early twentieth centuries; electronics, synthetic fibres and plastics in the post-1945 boom. The new technology of the late twentieth century is undoubtedly the computer-chip. Its impact on productivity is both spectacular and pervasive. Quite apart from its direct contribution to productivity, it also permits a closer monitoring of worker effort by recording key strikes, production, sales completions, etc. Better able to monitor materials, parts and inventories of all sorts and because it also uses less energy resources, computer technology may be capital-saving as well as labour-saving. Whether its capital-saving feature outweighs its labour-saving feature remains to be seen. Even if this proves not to be the case, the dramatic improvements in productivity it promises (increased rates of surplus value) could easily offset any increase it brings in the organic composition of capital.

But profits generated in production must be realized in exchange. Who will buy the mountains of goods produced by the new technology? The ultimate Achilles heel could well be the massive reduction of productive employment implied by the new wave of automation. Japanese studies estimate that robotization will eliminate one-third of the existing jobs in that country's industrial sector. The massive number of workers expelled from industry could theoretically be absorbed in an expanding service sector. But that sector is also the subject of radical restructuring through the application of micro-processing in office work, finance, administration, telecommunication and the retail-wholesale trade.

The overall employment effects of the micro-processor revolution cannot be forecast with any precision. They depend on too many unknown variables: the speed of its application or diffusion; the growth of the domestic and world economy; new jobs created by technology. In the U.S. current estimates range from an annual job displacement of 60,000 to a total of two million. A feature article in *Business Week* in August 1981 estimated that 45 million jobs in North America would be either lost, de-skilled or otherwise transformed through automation in industry over the next ten to fifteen years. The Rand corporation predicts that by the year 2000 only 2 per cent of the North American labour force will be employed in manufacturing, down from 25 per cent in the 1970s. In a paper called "The Rocky Road to 1990," the federal Ministry of State for Science and Technology forecast that between 1 and 2 million jobs will disappear in Canada by the early 1990s including up to one-quarter of the jobs in finance and insurance.

In the 1970s a German study estimated that 40 per cent of white-collar workers could lose their jobs through automation. The Nora Minc report commissioned by the French government estimated that 30 per cent of bank and insurance workers could be displaced. An international study published by a British consulting group predicted a 15 to 20 per cent reduction in hotel employment. Such predictions struck a chord of fear because the service sector typically accounted for 80 per cent of the new jobs in the 1970s. In Canada it accounted for up to 90 per cent of the new jobs and 97 per cent between 1973 and 1983.

The most accurate way of determining the impact of technology is to compare the total number of hours provided. Focusing on jobs can underestimate the impact because of shorter work weeks, increased part-time work and increased paid vacations. An American study found that despite a growth in manufacturing output of close to 40 per cent between the 1969 and 1979 cyclical peaks, total manufacturing hours worked grew by only 1.5 per cent. Hours worked by production workers fell slightly. Similar results were found in Europe. Between 1972 and 1978, the index of manufacturing production in France and Germany rose from 99 to 113 and from 101 to 113, respectively. Hours worked fell by 11 per cent in France and 10 per cent in Germany. In Japan the total number of manufacturing person-hours declined by 17 per cent between 1970 and 1979.[33]

A Canadian study focusing on jobs rather than hours estimated that a total of 626,000 jobs in the business sector were lost due to technological change between 1971 and 1979. This amounted to 10.5 per cent of 1971 employment. Through economic growth, overall employment nevertheless rose but not nearly enough to avoid a steady increase in unemployment. In absolute terms the biggest losses by industry were in transportation and storage (100,000), agriculture (86,000), electrical-products manufacturing (58,000), retail trade (53,000), transportation-equipment manufacturing (43,000), textile manufacturing (39,000), communications (35,000), wholesale trade (34,000) and clothing manufacturing (33,000).[34]

As Table 17:2 reveals, the process of shifting from labour-intensive to capital-intensive technologies accelerated during the 1970s. For example, $1 million of capital investment employed 208 manufacturing workers in the late 1970s compared to 425 a decade earlier; it employed 57 forestry workers in the recent period compared to 130 in the late 1960s. The result is that only a portion of the work force laid off in a recession is recalled and workers who leave through normal attrition are frequently not replaced.

As a consequence, bigger pools of unemployment collect at the height of each successive period of economic recovery. The unemployment-rate floors have risen since the mid-1960s but particularly so in the recent recovery, at least partly because of the incidence of technological change (see Table 17:3).

Looking into the future, the overall impact of technological change on jobs is bound to be much greater than it was in the 1970s which absorbed only the first wave of the micro-electronic revolution. There are at least four related reasons why the impact of automation will increase. The first is that survival in an environment of growing international competition among industrialized countries and from low-wage developing countries makes the adoption of new technologies imperative. The second is that companies will have had the time to phase out their investment in old equipment and to plan the necessary changes in work deployment that accompanies the use of micro-electronic technology. The third is the vigorous competition within the micro-electronic industry itself, which has resulted in both dramatic reductions in size and price and improvement in quality of the new technology, as well as in the discovery of more and more applications. In the last two decades micro-electronic components have fallen in size and price by approximately 100,000-fold while processing signals travel faster and more reliably and using far less power than their predecessors. The fourth reason is that automation has only now seriously penetrated the office and service industry, the largest and fastest growing employment sectors.

TABLE 17:2
Average Annual Employment per Million Dollars of Real Capital

	1961-65	1966-70	1971-75	1976-80
Forestry	175	130	96	57
Mining	24	18	14	8
Manufacturing	106	92	76	48
Construction	431	425	377	208
Utilities	7	6	5	—
Transportation	61	59	57	12
Finance	109	83	67	40
Trade	240	243	245	166
Services/Public administration	63	60	55	42
All industries	92	83	66	37[1]

[1] Non-agricultural employment.

Source: Statistics Canada.

TABLE 17:3
Unemployment Rate "Floors"

1966	3.4%
1969	4.4%
1974	5.3%
1979	7.5%
1984	11.3%

While numerically controlled machines decimate production jobs among machinists, metal workers, garment workers, etc., and robots decimate assembly-line jobs (by 1990 the robot's cost could drop to the equivalent of one dollar an hour), the new technology also threatens other factory employments. Maintenance and repair work is reduced and what remains is effectively deskilled because fixing is increasingly being reduced to substituting one micro-electronic component for another. Factory foremen could become redundant, not only because the number of people working in the factory is dropping, but because computer monitoring of machines largely eliminates the need for supervision.

Middle managers are also rendered redundant as top managers discover that much of the information collected, analyzed and interpreted for them can be obtained faster, less expensively and more thoroughly by computer. In automated offices the all-round manager is being replaced by computer specialists who can design, manage and apply data communication systems. While the job impact on management employments has yet to surface and, in fact, is still on the rise, clerical employment growth has already slowed almost to a halt. In public administration, for example, it grew by less than 1 per cent between 1975 and 1980.

The impact in the service sector will be more severe again. In the banking industry, which accounted for as many as 152,000 jobs as of 1980, the first phase of data processing in the early 1960s actually expanded employment as new services became available and bookkeepers, ledger keepers and file clerks became key-punch operators, computer operators and tape librarians. The second phase also added new services, but it consolidated the tasks of several people — the teller, the supervisor and the data-entry clerk — into tasks for one person and it further automated the delivery of a variety of bank services. By the time automated tellers started to be installed in the late 1970s, bank employment had already begun to fall. By 1990, at least half and perhaps all North America's large banks are expected to install automatic transaction machines. An automated teller can handle 2,000 transactions a day, works 165 hours a week and costs about $22,000 a year to run, compared to human tellers who can handle up to 200 transactions a day, work 30 hours a week, get a salary ranging from $8,000 to $20,000 (U.S.) a year, plus fringe benefits, coffee breaks, vacation and sick time.[35]

The retail trade, another mainstay of job growth in the 1960s and 1970s (a million jobs in the mid-1980s), has just begun to level off. According to one estimate, the electronic cash register, optical scanner and other devices have resulted in the following savings at peak shopping times: 21 per cent easier register balancing; 21 per cent increased productivity through automatic weighing and pricing; 14 per cent improvement through reduced errors in price reading.[36] Since cash register data yield instant information on stock taking, inventory monitoring, cash-flow analysis, productivity, and overall record keeping, the jobs of stock clerks and supervisors are threatened and even the status of store managers is undermined. Likely the job impact will be uneven, for as the new electronic devices spread throughout the supermarket chains the major employment effects will first be felt through job losses in other stores rather than by direct loss in the store being automated.

Similar trends will have their impact in libraries, hotels, hospitals, insurance companies, telephone companies and throughout the service economy. The overall impact of these trends depends on a number of variables: the growth of the economy, productivity increases and the speed of adoption of the new technology.

Heather Menzies has provided some calculations for clerical labour within the service sector.[37] Assuming a 3 per cent growth of output in the 1980s and 2.5 per cent in the 1990s, she allowed for variations in clerical productivity growth, 33 per cent (low) and 50 per cent (high), and two diffusion times, twenty years (slow) and fifteen years (fast). For the year 1990 the results ranged from a work-force requirement above 1980 levels of 1 per cent and 15 per cent; for the year 2000 it ranged from 15 per cent to 29 per cent. These results were then compared to the size of the female clerical labour force to the year 2000. For purposes of estimating potential unemployment, she assumed that the proportion of women seeking clerical employment will remain at the 1970s level and used three different participation-rate projections offered by different economic forecasters.

The results show that with the slow diffusion, low productivity assumptions, unemployment among clerical workers in 1990 would range from 11.5 per cent with no increase in participation rates, up to 25.3 per cent, if the high participation rate projection is realized. The middle projection gives a 16.7 per cent unemployment rate. For the year 2000 the respective results are 7.8 per cent, 15.6 per cent and 32.2 per cent. With the fast diffusion and high productivity assumptions the results are, of course, much more severe — 22.5 per cent, 27.0 per cent and 37.6 per cent in 1990 and 18.3 per cent, 25.2 per cent and 39.9 per cent in the year 2000.

All of these scenarios suggest that unless economic growth exceeds the projected rate and/or women are steered towards other work, there will be an alarmingly high rate of unemployment among female clerical workers in the years ahead. This would likely include an increasing trend towards part-time employment, a trend already evident in the early 1980s.

The question, of course, is what will be the source of alternative employment opportunities. By all accounts direct production jobs will continue to stagnate and possibly decline. Most of the products and processes to which micro-electronics are applied are labour-saving. In addition, as an International Labour Organization (ILO) report argues: "If the all-pervasive nature of the technology is taken into account..., the compensation theory which maintains that job displacement in one sector will be affected by employment opportunities in another begins to look distinctly unsound."[38] New products and whole new industries may be projected from space, underwater mining and nuclear energy, etc., but these are as of yet a matter of speculation. As for the expanding market for pocket calculators, home computers, video recorders, among other things, it seems improbable that they will not make much of a dent on the unemployment problem.

> It is hard to envisage new products, whether consumer or capital goods, which are of sufficient volume and value to absorb the labour displacement

put forward [10-15 per cent or more of the work force] at least in the same time scale. Studies of the labour-displacement effect of electronic watches versus mechanical watches ... or of the portable calculator versus the reduced demand for the electromechanical disk machines, suggest that the negative labour effect is much higher than the relatively trivial positive labour requirements for, say, electronic TV games.[39]

All Canadian analysts agree that high-tech industry will not create many new jobs in Canada. Using conventional definitions, it presently provides only 1.1 per cent of all jobs, most of them in Ontario and only 2.4 per cent using the broadest possible definition.

While "high-tech" industry is relatively important in Ontario already ... it is not important as an employer, nor it is likely to become much more important in this respect than it now is under any plausible set of circumstances. Even successful "high-tech" industries initiated in Ontario are likely, in the end, to establish their major production facilities elsewhere, either for cost reasons or to gain access to large markets: witness Northern Telecom and Mitel. There simply will not be enough "high-tech" industrial jobs to go around, and it is folly to pretend that there ever will be.[40]

The education industry has also ceased being a growth industry and in fact will be a rapidly falling one with the declining school-age population. Hospitals, day care and care for the elderly on the other hand are labour-intensive service industries whose employment will expand as will the restaurant and fast-foods industry, specialty shops, entertainment and a great variety of personal services, janitorial and sales clerk employments. Unfortunately most of these are low-paying with a lot of part-time seasonal jobs. At the other end of the scale, there will be a great need for specialized personnel, particularly computer analysts and electronic engineers.

The net outcome of all these trends remains in some doubt. The reduced growth in the labour force projected over the next decades will ease the burden, as would massive expenditures in training and retraining. But without a return to long-term prosperity it seems very doubtful that the overall unemployment rate in Canada will have declined much below the present 10.0-12.0 per cent by the 1990s. Depending on the diffusion rate of the new technology, it could be even higher. It is most unlikely that the unemployment situation will be any better among other industrial economies.[41]

To ease consciences many have convinced themselves that a majority in this standing army of the unemployed do not need work (married women, older men), do not want work (the young and the "welfare bums") or are unfit to work (the handicapped, the unskilled and untrained). The same people comfort themselves with anecdotes about the difficulty of finding casual help — "they can't be that hard up then" — and about the new fashion of graduate students on the dole.

These are convenient myths — for those currently in work and in business. Reality lies elsewhere. Without a return to an earlier world of 5 per cent growth and/or a radical reduction of work-time, the most likely scenario is that for the remainder of this century a significant minority of Canadians, perhaps as many as a third, will find themselves drifting in and out of the paid labour force in part-time, casual, seasonal and low-paying jobs. Many of them will be women and most of them will be young workers. Already in 1985, 27 per cent of working women and 29 per cent of young workers (under twenty-five) held only part-time jobs even though a third of them would have preferred to be working full time. And nearly a quarter of the officially unemployed were without work for three to six months and another quarter for over six months.

With the number of new slots offering full-time jobs in regular (primary) employments so scarce, it is safe to assume that a majority of young people coming into the labour market will not have access to these job slots for the first ten years of their working lives. They will comprise a new "lumpen-proletariat" with middle-class aspirations that cannot be realized, many of them over-qualified for the temporary and part-time jobs they find. Even more dismal scenarios are commonly being drawn for Europe.[42]

Third World Debt Crisis

This does not yet exhaust the obstacles in the path of full recovery. Continuation of the wild deflationary policies adopted since 1979 could plunge the capitalist world into a financial collapse, the final result of which is difficult to predict.

In the Third World in 1982, twenty-two countries were forced to negotiate debt rescheduling because they could not meet their contractual payments. Default was avoided because of prompt and energetic rescue measures taken by the U.S. government, central bankers, the International Monetary Fund (IMF) and the World Bank. But these were mere stop-gap measures to rescue the banks and not the countries themselves. By supplying quick money and helping to arrange stretch-out schedules for repayment, international financial agencies shifted part of the risk to the public. By applying strong-arm pressure to force debtor countries to reduce imports and restrict mass consumption, they hoped to generate a climate to encourage the banks to resume their lending operations. But a year later at least thirty-eight nations were in arrears on their debt payments. *Time* magazine's January 1983 cover story, "The Debt Bomb," declared, "Never in history have so many nations owed so much money with so little promise of repayment."

Private bankers acknowledge that they no longer expect governments to repay their debts. "Paying it back isn't the issue," says a senior vice-president of Citibank. "The issue is the borrower's remaining credit worthy and able to service and carry the debt ...." [43] Servicing the debt would of course supply the lending banks with an indefinite flow of net income, for it can be mathematically shown that even under the most favourable of assumptions, the debt can never be paid off. The real question is in fact whether or not they can be serviced.

Third World debt jumped from $100 billion in 1973 to $400 billion in 1979 to $600 billion in 1982 and to $800 billion in 1984. After the oil price increases in 1973-74 the OPEC countries had so much spare cash that most of it was deposited in western banks. Awash with OPEC dollars plus unwanted American dollars arising from the growing U.S. balance of payment deficit, the banks showered countries like Brazil, Mexico and Argentina with offers of large loans at very low rates of interest. Because of rising raw material prices and expanded manufacturing, the risk seemed minimal. The loans would be paid off by the export earnings of the debtor countries, more specifically with the extra dollars earned from the surplus of exports over imports. In practice, the banks were making so much in interest charges and commissions that they were quite content to keep the debt rolling over, increasing the amount being owed.

Whereas 56 per cent of the debt undertaken in 1972-73 was needed to meet the service charges on accumulated debt, this figure climbed gradually to 59 per cent in 1978. But after the second big rise in oil prices in 1979, the position of debtor countries rapidly deteriorated. They had to find a lot more money for oil imports. Adding to their troubles, in 1980 the terms of trade began moving decisively against raw-material-producing countries. While they had to pay more for imported manufactured goods, commodity prices had collapsed, dropping 22 per cent from 1980 to mid-1982. International commodity prices fell to their lowest level since the Great Depression. As well the severe recession reduced the demand for their exports.

With rising expenditures and falling incomes, the only solution was to borrow more. But as a consequence of monetarist policies, money borrowed when interest was 6 per cent a year began to cost much more — 16.5 per cent in 1981. In addition, a larger proportion of the debt was short-term, with a consequent increase in annual amortization payments. Borrowing money to compensate for falling export revenues, some countries found that they could not even afford to pay the interest, indicated in Table 17:4.

TABLE 17:4
1983 Debt Ratios*

	Medium and long-term	Medium, long-term, short-term
Argentina	58.1	199.5
Philipines	31.6	173.5
Uruguay	25.3	159.6
Israel	32.7	156.8
Mexico	56.7	146.5
Portugal	29.2	141.2
Chile	55.9	140.4
Ivory Coast	44.5	138.4
Columbia	38.8	118.9
Ecuador	39.9	118.6
Brazil	51.7	113.5
Peru	35.2	109.7
Venezuela	18.8	106.4

* Debt payment as percent of export earnings.
Source: *Wall Street Journal*, June 22, 1984.

A decade ago, analysts worried when a country had to spend more than a fifth of its annual exports making payments on its medium- and long-term debt. At present more than forty countries have debt-service ratios higher than 20 per cent. If short-term debt obligations are included in the debt-service payments as more cautious analysts prefer, fifteen countries would have to devote more than 100 per cent of their current export revenues to service their annual debt.

Two developments accentuated their difficulty in obtaining capital. The first is that the growing insecurity of Third World countries caused multinational capital to shift their funds towards safe havens, especially the U.S. whose record-high interest rates made investment there very attractive. By 1983 underdeveloped countries as a whole were paying back $21 billion more to their creditors than they received in new loans.[44] As well, however, they also experienced a massive capital flight as wealthy individuals and businesses among them sought safer and more profitable locations for their money. The recent revelation of the Marcos billions is one example. Wealthy Mexicans are estimated to have removed $40 to $45 billion to Europe and the U.S. Altogether, rich Latin Americans and Latin American corporations are estimated to have deposited at least $100 billion abroad in 1981 and 1982.[45]

Loans extended to these countries far exceed the capital stock of most of the world's major banks, including all of Canada's six large banks. For example, loans by the Chase Manhattan Bank to three major Latin American countries reached 149 per cent of bank equity by 1983. The figure was 153 per cent for the Bank of Montreal.[46] When they refused to lend any more money, countries were forced to go to the IMF and the World Bank for large loans. But their loans are conditional on the willingness of debtor countries to take draconian measures to solve their problems. Taking as given falling export prices, falling demand and rising interest rates, which are the cause of most of the global debt crisis, these measures place all the burdens and sacrifices of adjustment on the debtor countries themselves.

While monetarist measures have been tempered when applied in western economies, in Third World countries they are applied full force. Standard prescriptions include wage cuts; elimination of subsidies on basic consumer items; reductions in imports; devaluation of currencies; elimination of import quotas, exchange controls, and controls on foreign investment; reduction of public spending, particularly in health, education and welfare spending.

These policies, taken to an extreme, can reduce the debt burden and so provide temporary relief for western banks. They are obviously not designed to help Third World countries restructure their societies to become more self-reliant. Instead of allowing them to reduce imports by imposing direct controls, for example, the IMF insists that they be reduced by devaluation and austerity measures. While lowering wages will result in a reduced overall import bill, it does so at terrible cost to the majority of people. Moreover, if it results in improved domestic profits, it likely results in increased luxury imports. Devaluation raises the cost of imports which make it more difficult to overcome bottlenecks that constrain productive capacity. Restrictions on public investment further frustrate attempts to develop domestic substitutes for investment. The dismantling of exchange controls allows capital flight to continue when debtor countries desperately require this capital to build up their economies. Trade liberalization weakens the ability of local industry to withstand the competition of multinationals. "Export at any cost" policy means that farmers produce cash crops for rich countries while the local population goes hungry.

The IMF is essentially an instrument to police the global investments of the advanced capitalist countries. The banks turned to it when they found that they could not impose conditions required to secure their investments. "There certainly is a need for [the IMF] to be in there as ... a disciplinarian and that's the thing all of us like about the IMF," says the vice-president for international operations of the Royal Bank. "The more strings they have on their bow, the better," adds the chairman of the Bank of Montreal.[47]

Governments that have accepted IMF conditions have been almost invariably faced with stiff opposition. In response to general strikes protesting IMF policies, which would have resulted in a 400 per cent increase in consumer prices, Bolivia was forced to reimpose subsidies on basic consumer items and to accept a 130 per cent wage increase to compensate for losses caused by an earlier austerity program. A general strike in Peru obligated the government to delay big increases in the price of electricity and food and to begin a job-creation scheme. In his inaugural address, President Alan Garcia announced that Peru would dedicate no more than 10 per cent of its export revenues to debt service and would refuse to negotiate with the IMF. Other measures included a one-time wage increase of 18 per cent followed by price controls; import restrictions and foreign exchange controls; an increase in local food production to replace costly imports. In June 1984 more than 80,000 Argentinians marched in support of the government's firm line in negotiations with the IMF and international banks. A banner in front of the parliament building read "National Unity Against International Usury." Strikes and slow-downs in Brazil forced the government there to rescind legislation making it illegal for employers and unions to negotiate wage hikes that would match the rate of inflation. In the Dominion Republic more than fifty people died when rioting broke out against IMF-inspired price hikes, which had doubled and tripled the price of essential items. The General Workers Confederation, the group that led the campaigns against IMF policies, demanded an alternative economic program, including a definitive break with the IMF and its policies; a ten- to twenty-year moratorium on debt payments; government control over foreign currency and foreign trade to end the flight of capital out of the country; a reorientation of the domestic economy, including land reform to develop local industry and agriculture for the domestic market; price controls on basic consumer items; and diversification of the sugar industry to produce other products than sugar for export.[48]

Similar programs emphasizing the need for self-reliant development are circulating throughout Latin America. As the editors of *Monthly Review* have observed, "the dilemma facing the international enforcers of 'sound finance' is how far the Third World countries can be squeezed without provoking social revolutions ... and possible debt repudiation."[49] Should Mexico and Brazil default on loans or declare a unilateral moratorium, the nine largest U.S. banks and at least two Canadian banks could be forced out of business since over 100 per cent of their capital would then be needed to keep the banks in operation. This is, of course, a worse-case scenario. In any case, the Federal Reserve and the Bank of Canada would likely act promptly, and rescue operations through international financial organizations are reportedly in the works to keep bankrupt banks in Canada and elsewhere afloat.

To date most Third World governments, while denouncing international creditors, have in the end complied with their wishes. Talk of forming a debtors cartel has come to nothing since "political and economic dependency on the United States is much stronger than ties among the Latin American countries."[50] But Third World countries have the power of debt, for — paraphrasing John Maynard Keynes — "if I owe the bank $1,000 I have a problem; if we owe several billion the banks have a problem."

The international investment community is beginning to recognize that the positions at the bargaining table have reversed. In the words of Albert Friedberg, director of a Toronto brokerage firm, "the creditors are weak and don't know it yet, and the debtors are strong and haven't mustered enough courage to force their terms."[51] Before they do, several analysts have suggested that the banks take the initiative in accepting their responsibility by writing off Third World debts as they would any bad debt. To head off a global financial collapse they advise that they be phased out gradually with the cost being born by banks and taxpayers. Several other reform proposals are also in circulation, including converting loans to long-term, lower interest bonds held by central banks; exchanging loans for equity ownership in the raw materials, state corporations and public properties of debtor countries; IMF and World Bank guarantees for private financiers; rescheduling debts over a realistic time period.

Even without total debt repudiation, such moves can provide much-needed breathing space for debtor nations and for some time at least they can stave off the collapse of the international financial system. But the ultimate problem would not have been resolved and the financial system remains as vulnerable as ever. The decline in oil prices helps oil importers, but only sharp reductions in interest rates and increases in commodity prices and world trade can reverse the downward tide in Third World countries. The long-run solution must involve independent industrialization oriented towards domestic needs. As a leading Peruvian economist has said:

> For the majority of the continent's poor, the problem isn't the debt; it is their countries' overall political and social structure ... the debt debate is, in the final analysis, a debate among elitest groups who have always tried to dominate the continent's history.[52]

In the meantime, the IMF's solution of importing less and exporting more is riddled with contradictions: certain imports are essential to have the supplies to produce exports; and how can everyone at the same time reduce imports and increase exports, especially in the face of growing protectionism in the West? The Third World's debt crunch itself has had the effect of reducing world trade by forcing debtor countries to put their dwindling foreign exchange towards debt payments rather than import purchases. According to the North-South Institute, Canada alone lost 135,000 jobs and $451 million in exports between 1981 and 1983 because developing countries were unable to maintain their buying power. Austerity policies imposed by the IMF can only create a further drag on recovery from the world crisis.

Domestic Debt

While no bank has yet come a cropper on Third World loans, record numbers of banks are foundering because of bad domestic loans. There were 79 bank failures in the U.S. in 1984, a total of 189 since 1980. Banks were better able to weather the storm in the 1970s (only fifty-six failed) because companies were rescued by double-digit inflation, a depreciating dollar and interest rates lower than inflation. In the different environment of the 1980s many corporate borrowers cannot push through the price increases needed to repay their loans. The stronger American dollar is shutting off export markets and pulling in cheap imports that cut into domestic sales. High real interest rates make it hard for companies to service their debt.

As *Business Week* notes in its special issue entitled "What's Really Behind the Banking Turmoil," "the most troubled industries — electric utilities, real estate, agriculture, mining and shipping — all have one thing in common: over-capacity, born of the 1970s illusion that inflation is forever and nurtured by lavish credits from bankers caught up in the same mania." But the problem is pervasive, "shared by thousands of U.S. industrial companies" whose balance sheets "are the weakest ever at this stage of a recovery.... A growing share of corporate income is dedicated to interest payments" rather than investment in new plants and equipment.[53]

The merger and acquisition phase was one of the factors behind the build-up of corporate debt. Encouraged by the negative real interest rates and inflation of the 1970s, corporations went on a buying spree to diversify and expand their holdings. Much of the financing was done through loans, which goes a long way in explaining the rise in overall corporate debt to record levels. As often as not, the resulting mammoth conglomerates performed poorly. The worst performers were those that acquired firms outside their traditional field, or plants built in the 1970s that they could not use profitably in a less inflationary environment.

Bank deregulation has been another part of the problem. Removal of ceilings on interest rates that banks offer depositors was designed to allow banks to compete with mutual funds and other investments which had deprived banks of their wealthiest customers in the high-inflation 1970s. But as banks raised their interest rates to attract depositors they have also been forced to raise their interest rates on loans to pay for the higher cost of attracting money. Finding it more difficult to find customers at these higher loan rates, banks have tended to overlook risks. Regulation had made banks into a risk-free public utility. Deregulation puts them in the same boat as the corner grocery store. The dilemma has been noted by the much-quoted Wall Street economist Henry Kaufmann: "When you encourage the entrepreneurial drive of the banks, the only way that drive can be disciplined is by allowing banks that have behaved improperly to fail. That's a key issue. Are we willing as a society to have major institutions that hold savings and temporary funds fail so that the proper discipline can be exerted on them?"[54]

The problems created by deregulation go beyond the banks. Everywhere it has been introduced it has left behind a string of bankruptcies as the competition of new entrants forces down prices, price wars lower profit margins and jeopardize companies' ability to modernize their plant and equipment. Since deregulation, for example, more than 300 trucking firms, many of them sizeable, have gone bankrupt. Braniff and a number of smaller airlines have failed and several more are struggling for survival.

Throughout the 1970s bankers and industrialists were crying out for low inflation and deregulation. Reaganism gave them both. While a certain amount of dislocation was both expected and accepted as a necessary cost of priming and enlivening American industry, the extent of business turmoil they created was unimagined. As we have already seen, corporations have taken radical steps to shore-up their bottom lines including the installation of computers to reduce their inventory and labour costs and outsourcing to the point of "hollowing" their entire operations or liquidating entirely. To reduce their debt, many corporations have begun to divest themselves of certain assets, divisions and product lines acquired a few years earlier. All told, U.S. companies sold off 900 divisions and subsidiaries in 1984, a jump of 40 per cent in four years. As a result assets are being reconcentrated into the hands of companies that dominate industry output. Reagan's relaxed anti-trust policies, part of his deregulation, encourages companies to grow through acquisition in their own basic industry rather than through diversification. Overall corporate debt has declined from 50 per cent of total capitalization (equity) in the 1970s to 39 per cent in 1985. A good part of the reduction has been accomplished by write-offs and by acquisitions by domestic companies flush with cash from generous depletion allowances or from asset sales of their own and by foreign buyers enriched by huge trade surpluses and spurred by fears of protectionism.[55]

While these different moves have no doubt reduced the crisis of liquidity, whether it has been entirely resolved remains to be seen. To avoid further chaos and bank failings, pressure is already mounting to reverse course and reflate the economy, a policy reversal that would be strongly resisted in Reagan's America.

Corporate indebtedness is far worse in Canada. Total debt to equity stood at 70 per cent in 1980 rising to 95 per cent in 1982 and falling back some to 83 per cent in 1984.[56] Between 1974 and 1981 corporations were forced to allocate 20 to 30 per cent of their income to interest payments, an historical high. In 1982 this rose to over 50 per cent and has only fallen back slightly since then. As a consequence and because of the existence of massively under-utilized productive capacity, a relatively small proportion of their resources is available for investing in new capital goods. The decline of investment growth, -12.4 per cent and -9.1 per cent in 1982 and 1983, and the fact that investment growth since has been weaker than in any recovery period in recent history are no mere coincidence.

In part, the high indebtedness can be attributed to the phenomenal takeover activity of the late 1970s since much of it was financed by borrowing. There were more mergers in Canada between 1970 and 1980 than in all of the preceding seven decades, reaching all-time highs in 1982 and 1983, which saw over 1,200 acquisitions. The eight largest Canadian conglomerates managed to more than double their assets (from $25 billion to $52 billion) in the troubled years of 1975-80 and about 40 per cent of this spectacular growth was due to takeovers. All this represents a merger movement that is proportionately far greater than the similar one occurring in the U.S. over the same period. While some Canadian companies have begun to write-off bad debts, further major acquisitions in 1985 and 1986 have not been divesture-driven as in the U.S. but represent further efforts by conglomerates to expand through diversification.

Two important tax incentives have encouraged Canadian firms to put their money into takeovers: since 1972 corporations have been allowed to tax-deduct the interest on funds borrowed to finance acquisitions; secondly, companies are allowed to pay the shareholders of an acquired firm in the form of company shares instead of cash. This makes them more willing to sell their stock at a low price since they do not have to pay capital gains tax when they give up their shares.

Another source of rising corporate debt has been the astronomical loans to the petroleum industry, which alone increased from $333 million in 1970 to $5.7 billion in 1980, encouraged in no small part by the

Canadianization incentives of the federal government. The decline in energy demand, falling off of energy prices and high interest rates left the oil companies with huge debts in relation to the bank value of their assets.

The weakest balance sheets are found in the small independent firms, among whom almost one in five had more debt than assets. A rising incidence of corporate bankruptcy was inevitable. Between 1980 and 1983 there have been 37,000 corporate bankruptcies, an average of over 9,000 a year which compares with less than 3,000 in the 1974-75 recession.[57] The number of official farm bankruptcies rose from 125 in 1979 to 551 in 1984, but for every official bankruptcy farm organizations estimate another ten sell out "voluntarily." They estimate that 6,000 family farms are lost per year.

Analysts suggest that total problem loans should be less than 1 per cent of bank assets. In 1985 they represented 2 per cent of assets of the major six banks, a decline of 15 per cent from 1984 mainly due to a rise in write-offs of bad loans, many of them in the energy field. An independent assessment of the loan portfolio of the failed Canadian Commercial Bank concluded that in mid-1985 nearly half of the bank's loans were of little or no commercial value.[58] While the Canadian Commercial Bank and the Northland were the only banks to go under, Canada's liquidity problem remains, for should another severe recession occur soon, "many corporations certainly do not appear to have the balance sheet resiliency to easily withstand it."[59]

Conclusion

These results are neither surprising nor unexpected. They are textbook illustrations of neo-conservative restructuring at work: they merely demonstrate the folly of assuming that, once unions have been shackled and enterpreneurs liberated, markets will automatically and quickly generate expansion. Diminishing the state's economic role and conquering inflation are supposed to create the climate for recovery. Yet the means to that end — crashing the economy through monetary, fiscal and wage restraint, dampens economic activity, killing off some efficient firms along with the inefficient ones and reducing consumer spending even among those who manage to hold onto their jobs. For as long as the crisis lasts, bringing deficits under control proves to be much more difficult than imagined. Raising tax rates to compensate for falling tax revenues only deepens recessions, and slashing welfare benefits and social services in the face of rising unemployment and poverty is too risky for most regimes. Meanwhile, global and domestic debt hang over the Western economies, hampering both investment and trade and the uneven character of recovery creates seemingly insoluble contraditions within the world economy.

These questions and possible consequences are worth considering.

- Can the regularly employed two-thirds of the labour force provide a consumer-base large enough to fully absorb the economy's growing productive capacity? Unquestionably, this problem is exacerbated by capital's ability to use the standing army of the unemployed to hammer down wage gains. Weak consumer demand drags the recovery and prolongs the crisis.
- Will the regularly employed two-thirds, already pressed with bills they cannot pay, come to resent having to transfer an increasing portion of their income to the unemployed and under-employed and to support a rapidly aging population? It is among those who see their power diminished, their profits and incomes squeezed, their mobility curtailed and their security endangered that Reaganism and Thatcherism find their social base. They are also part of the base that gave Mulroney his smashing electoral majority. Thatcher and Reagan's appeal to the Victorian virtues of hard work, law and order, self-reliance and the family has clearly won substantial backing within the beleaguered working class, the petty bourgeoisie and small employers. The New Right movement in America is an amalgam of fundamentalism, Catholic orthodoxy, the white backlash to integration, affirmative action, hostility to women's liberation, abortion and gay rights and the ultra-nationalism evident in the jubilant response to the invasion of Grenada and in the Los Angeles Olympics, which became a Reaganite spectacle with its endless chant of "USA! USA!" In Canada the New Right includes some of the same constituencies along with the Anglophone aversion to bilingualism.
- As volatile young workers turn into a marginalized and hard-core social minority, will they remain content to wait their turn for the dwindling number of good jobs? Excluded from the established social institutions that provide avenues for orderly protest and opposition, will they turn towards more confrontational and disruptive individual and collective actions?

The upshot of this analysis is that, the longer the crisis is prolonged, the further the state will retreat from the liberalism of the post-1945 era and the more likely will be the drift towards a more repressive society. The political consequences of a domestic upsurge in joblessness and international-economy disarray cannot be wished away. "Beggar-thy-neighbour" American trade policies and the economic policing role of the IMF could generate new revolutionary pressures in Third World countries and new threats of default on bank loans. From Reagan's perspective, one remedy is military adventurism. Imperialist pomp and blood-letting in the South Atlantic worked for a time for Margaret Thatcher. In the name of "national security" Americans would be asked to accept austerity and to obey authority. Detente, presumably the product of American weakness in the 1970s, has been scrapped in favour of a "resurgent American" policy. Robert Tucker, the analyst who coined the term "resurgent America" claims that "reasons of pride and historic tradition" justify U.S. meddling south of the border. In planning for the fiscal 1985 Pentagon budget, Deputy Secretary of Defence Paul Thayer "has ordered the armed forces to plan for expanded operations in Central America and has placed new emphasis on projecting American military power to the Persian Gulf," according to the *New York Times*.[60] The skirmishes off the Libyan coast and the massing of American troops in Honduras confirm this prognosis.

After the decade-long war against Vietnam had been lost, American leaders became extremely wary of getting into a similar situation. It was likely the "Vietnam Syndrome" that kept the years 1973-82 relatively free of overt U.S. interventionism. U.S. intervention in Nicaragua would be a long and bloody affair — precisely what created the "Vietnam Syndrome" in the first place. But the U.S. crusade against changes in the global status quo would at some point almost certainly result in confrontations with the U.S.S.R. — always perceived as the source and instigator of the revolutions that threaten to overturn the status quo. In a moment of madness, this could easily erupt into a world war.

Afterword: Another Way Forward

If and when Reaganism, Thatcherism and their various imitators fail, then what? One predictable response will be an urgent call for a return to old-fashioned Keynesian expansionism. This is, at best, a simplistic and short-term solution which would eventually come up against some of the very same barriers that made Keynesian crumble in the 1970s. Any future strategy will have to develop a policy on interest rates, exchange rates and levels of demand. But their impact on markets is bound by what happens in production. The ultimate limitation of Keynesianism is that it has nothing to say about the sphere of production where wealth and value are created.

Others are calling for a sharp turn towards more direct state-interventionism. Post-Keynesianism, with its emphasis on industrial policy and industrial democracy, in addition to incomes policy, does enter the sphere of production. But it does so on terms which do not challenge the dominant position of capital. It presumes an ultimate harmony of interests between labour and capital, which is belied by real world experiences and confirmed by the fact that corporatism has broken down throughout Europe over the course of the crisis.

What about socialism? It is evident that today's socialists are as bereft of ideas as the liberals, which is why their governments are falling like ten-pins or merely emulating New Right solutions. A good example is the experience of the Mitterrand government, which followed a mixture of Keynesian, post-Keynesian, social democratic and socialist prescriptions. These involved boosting consumption by raising the minimum wage and social-security payments, increasing public investment and expanding public employment, nationalizing the banks and some other strategic industries. But in the context of the crisis these measures produced inflation, balance of payments problems and capital flight. To reassure capitalists at home and to preserve confidence in the currency, the regime was forced to retreat. Retrenchment severed the government from its popular base, resulting in a major electoral defeat.

In the 1930s socialist movements were at least confident of their solutions — state planning and regulation, nationalization and the welfare state. No such statist formula is available today.

The role of the modern state is one of the great perplexities of our times. Its strongest opposition comes from the Right rather than the Left even though, Friedmanites to the contrary notwithstanding, the capitalist state has always functioned to allow capitalist relations of production to flourish. On the one hand, the welfare system to a degree insulates the population from the harshest consequences of unemployment. To this extent the Right's hostility to the welfare state has a rational basis. Starvation would no doubt allow employers to reduce wages, break strikes and attack the position of workers far more than is the case today. On the other hand, such a result would generate a degree of dissatisfaction and a mobilization of the oppressed that might threaten the social order. The cost of maintaining a relatively passive citizenry seems small compared to the risks that would be entailed if the free market were given full sway.

State provisioning of services on a universal basis has broken the connection between ability to pay and the availability of amenities like education and health care. It's an accomplishment that few would like to see surrendered. The record certainly shows that any Canadian government that strays too far from the interventionist ethos does not last too long. On the other hand, the state in its massiveness is seen as unaccountable, its services inadequate or subject to inexplicable delay, its officials too often arrogant, patronizing, secretive, snoopy and dictatorial. Most members of the working class do not view the welfare state as *their* state — largely because statism as such has never been synonymous with democracy.

Nationalization has always occupied a top place on the agenda of the Left. Public ownership is already a well-accepted institution in Canada's statist tradition. For socialists nationalization is supposed to achieve three objectives: to dispossess the big capitalists; to divert profits to the public purse and/or to provide services with a public good rather than a profit criteria; to make management accountable to employees. Nationalization under capitalist auspices has achieved virtually none of these goals. Capitalists are indeed dispossessed but only after they have been fully compensated, with the result that the distribution of wealth is not significantly affected. Moreover, public utilities set prices which effectively provide a subsidy to industrial consumers. Nationalization is not seen as particularly advantageous by employees and, like regulatory, hospital, child services and college and university boards, crown corporations are accountable neither to users nor to employees. They are hierarchical, secretive and nearly as closed to public involvement as almost any in the private sector. Moreover, their boards are dominated by the big bourgeoisie and professional classes, hardly a cross-section of the Canadian population.

The whole apparatus of state activity is generally perceived as an ever-increasing burden on the incomes of ordinary workers. Meanwhile, except for a tiny minority, the "actually-existing socialism" of the Soviet-bloc states has lost its attraction. Instead of withering away, the state has become a gigantic and cumbersome bureaucratic force, swallowing up nearly all other institutions and imposing itself on the people — sometimes with tanks — in the name of "The People." Hence, it is not surprising that programs offered by socialists that simply call for more social services, more government intervention, more nationalization have failed to win an enthusiastic response.

What are the alternatives? A few general ideas are introduced here. A more thoroughgoing account will be available in the successor to *The Great Economic Debate*.

Alternatives include:

- The predominance of social ownership of the means of production. To provide spaces where workers can more easily take charge, "small is beautiful" is the guiding trend in social ownership. Central state ownership is confined to activities where bigness and national/provincial co-ordination are required for economic efficiency. Worker co-operatives and community enterprises will otherwise be the norm with private ownership subject to strict limits.
- Worker control of the shop/office floor level with management responsible to the work force outside the limited area of private enterprise; tripartite responsibility for product, investment and most other policy decisions in community enterprises and big state-owned enterprises; and workplace environment boards to participate in and monitor all decisions affecting the safety of the workplace, including stress factors and physical and chemical hazards.
- Conscious limits on permissible inequalities. While a degree of material inequality is unavoidable, private fortunes are neither required nor morally justified. Except for the indigent and otherwise unemployables, virtually all income will be earned. Maximum allowable differentials will be established along with equal pay for work of equal value with the details determined at enterprise levels.
- Guaranteed employment for everybody wishing to work, universal day care to help broaden the employable base. With a statutory right to work in place, elected local labour boards will be obliged to find or create jobs for all who register, in the same way that local school boards are obliged to place each child registering for education. The boards would not necessarily themselves employ people. Their funds could be bid for by private employers, co-operatives, community arts

and recreation centres, health clinics, day-care and senior citizen centres, local government services, trade unions and other voluntary associations. Successful bidders would receive employment subsidies and matching capital grants to initiate new projects. Only the residually unemployed would have to be employed directly by the boards. Subsidies would have to be regulated to ensure that employers pay the going union rates and that private employers do not abuse the privilege by drawing all or most of their workers from the board pool.

- Reducing the domination of work. While it is essential that nobody should be denied work, happiness is surely not having a job. Given the tremendous potential of labour-saving technology, there is no reason why work should continue to dominate our lives. The objective is to produce socially useful goods and services to satisfy unmet but real material needs. This no longer requires that we devote so much of our time to paid labour. Indeed, we can likely to without a lot of the things currently produced. Many present jobs are redundant; they supply a multiplicity of brands of the same product. More serious is the considerable amount of work that contributes to environmental destruction. A universal four-day week is an immediately feasible objective. Further reduced work time as we approach "retirement" would lessen retirement shock. Many European countries have annual vacations of four to six weeks for all workers and sixteen to twenty-one statutory holidays. Paid educational leave (up to four years over a lifetime) to include vocational retraining, art, music, recreation and literacy as well as degree courses would be a beneficial and popular means of reducing unemployment.
- Plant-closure legislation to maintain the stability of community life. This would include a warning time sufficiently long so that the enterprise decision could be scrutinized and possibly reversed by means of community audit reviews committees that consider social costs and social impact in addition to owners' financial interests. It would include a provision requiring firms to pay into a community lay-off fund; severance pay; and the right of the state to take over plants and wherever feasible find alternative uses for them.
- Conservation and renewal. Another threat to community life stems from the proliferation of chemical and nuclear waste and from other deadly materials used in production processes and shipped around the country. We should have no-pollution-without-representation legislation establishing the right of communities through referenda, town meetings or city councils to bar the production, disposal or transshipment of hazardous or environmentally destructive material. Further, community right-to-know legislation is required to compel businesses operating in a community or transshipping goods

through it to make available full information on the chemical properties of potentially hazardous substances they use or transport.
- Prices to be determined by market forces reflecting both cost and consumer demand — except for a list of "free" and subsidized goods and services, to be worked out through the democratic political process. To guarantee the widest possible consumer choice, firms are obliged to compete for customers. Excepting sectors exempt from market criterion, commercial viability will be the norm, with social cost-accounting to be applied wherever appropriate.
- Central planning of aggregates including savings and investment, credit, wages, taxes, pensions, foreign trade, regional disparities, and so on. The centre (federal and provincial) will also have prime responsibility for investment and pricing policies of large state-owned enterprise and monitoring, through bank and credit institutions, enterprise viability and closure proceedings. It will make funding available to local labour boards for capital grants, employment subsidies, training and the like. Provincial governments will continue to assume overall responsibility for health and child care, education, etc., with responsibility over resource development reverting to the federal level. Formal mechanisms for federal-provincial co-operation will be required, and a new mechanism will have to be put in place involving trade unions and the state for determining allowable overall wage increases.
- Conscious efforts towards greater national and local self-sufficiency. At the national level this means reducing our dependence on a narrow range of resource exports, processing our resources before they are exported and, where economically possible, replacing imports with domestic production. At the local level it means matching labour and materials with locally determined needs and priorities.
- Creating new avenues for the exercise of popular sovereignty including base-level popular assemblies, more frequent use of referenda, elected local planning councils, labour boards, health care and child services boards, etc. The purpose is not to pre-empt the powers of democratically elected parliaments and municipal councils but to enlist the direct participation of people in decision-making at levels where they can most appropriately be involved.

What is the name of this alternative society? Some writers have called it "market socialism," others "feasible socialism," others yet "democratic socialism," and still others prefer "economic democracy." If it had better ring to it, my own preference would be for "participatory socialism." Clearly, it has elements of all of these.

Even if these new institutional arrangements were magically in place, it would be foolish to believe that fundamental disagreements would disappear. We should know by now that it is only in fairy tales that people live happily ever after. So long as there is scarcity there will be conflict. And we can eliminate scarcity no more readily than we can eliminate personal jealousies, power-tripping, drunkenness and all other human foibles and inadequacies. Nor can we command people to attend meetings and take hold of their social lives. All we can do is to encourage them to do so while providing them with both the means and the opportunity.

Where will the money come from to finance the programs outlined here? The first point to note is that some of them do not involve additional resource commitments. They either are self-financing or arise from redistributional gains, democratic reorganization, or re-allocations due to different priorities. Included among these are higher minimum wages, limits on pay differentials, equal pay for work of equal value, worker- and community-owned enterprises, reduced work time, and nationalization. While there would be some obligation to provide partial compensation for former owners in the socialization process, it could be done on a sliding scale with definite maximum — $1 million ($5 million?) — which any individual or family residing in Canada could in toto receive. Foreign-owned assets could be traded off for Canadian investments abroad, the difference to be paid over a period of time. Some of the programs, like more day-care facilities, child pay for single parents, and a vast expansion of community facilities, do involve net additional expenditures. But the resources they require are readily at hand. At present they are simply being wasted.

The proponents of pro-business economic strategies assume that a profit-based private-enterprise economy is more efficient than any other alternative. In fact, it is enormously wasteful. What other conclusion can be reached when, over the past several years, a million to million and a half workers have been rendered unproductive by forced idleness; when over a third of our productive capacity is sitting unused; when billions of dollars of our savings are being squandered to finance corporate takeovers and mergers, and investment abroad — all of which add nothing to our capacity to produce — when 2 per cent of our GNP regularly goes to advertising which contributes nothing to our knowledge about the quality of goods we buy; when so much creative energy is lost fighting the boss and so much labour is devoted to policing an unco-operative work force?

In its submission to the Macdonald Royal Commission, the Manitoba Political Economy Group estimated that if we could fully retrieve these wasted resources the capacity of our economy to produce would be expanded by 40 per cent. Under the best circumstances, all the waste could not be retrieved overnight. Moreover, this is only a ball-park estimate. But even if it is too large by half, it reveals the enormous sacrifice of potential output we make in order to maintain the prevailing economic system.

The important point is that we do not face a zero-sum situation where one goal must be totally sacrificed for another. Because of the enormous waste embedded in the capitalist economy we can, by instituting major reforms, have greater efficiency and greater equality, greater output and reduced work-time, more social services as well as more private goods, more consumption and more investment. There are limits of course. We cannot achieve *any* quantity we wish. Choices still have to be made. Priorities must be decided. But by reorganizing the economy and democratizing it, the room for choice is enormously expanded; more priorities can be met; and decisions can be made which reflect the public interest rather than the interest of a few.

In the abbreviated form they appear in above, these alternative arrangements may have the appearance of being a frustrated professor's "wish list." They are much more than that. Nearly all of them derive from solutions posed in the course of recent popular struggles and many of them have already been put into practice. I can only give a few examples here.

Spain's Mandragon is by all accounts an effectively run co-operative conglomerate with management directly elected by the work force. Until it was abolished by the Thatcher administration, the Greater London Council (GLC) offered an interesting example of municipal democracy. Controlled by the Labour Left, it gave financial support to applicant enterprises providing they involved union and city officials as equal participants in designing enterprise plans that included employment levels, training, investment and new technology. The GLC also gave emphasis to "socially useful products" which built on existing but underemployed skills and met social needs as established by community-based social audits. This latter idea arose out of the efforts of Lucas aerospace design engineers, who developed their own models of socially useful products which their employer could manufacture as an alternative to mass lay-offs in the event of a recession. Both the Canadian Postal Workers and the Ontario Public Service Workers Union have adopted similar strategies to preserve public-sector jobs.

Similarly, the principle of pay equity has already been accepted although its application is partial at best. "Solidarity wage" policy which raises the pay of low-wage workers more rapidly than those of high-wage workers is a longstanding practice in Sweden. A Work Environment Board with a large budget and a mandate far wider than health and safety committees was briefly put in place at the Crown-owned Potash Corporation of Saskatchewan. Sweden's Workplace Environment Act gives union health and safety representatives the legal right to be involved in plant design and planning processes from the first stages. The principle of self-reliance has emerged as one of the major recommendations of the Canadian Council of Catholic Bishops; the Science Council has also argued for greater self-reliance; and the National Energy Program, with arguable means, was designed at least partially to increase self-sufficiency in oil. The Canadian Automobile Workers (CAW) content proposal requiring corporations wishing to sell in Canada to commit themselves to a certain share of jobs and investment here would be a move in this direction. The ten-point program for economic recovery proposed by the Canadian Union of Public Employees also embodies a desire for a more self-reliant Canadian economy, and it is a central theme of the community development strategy of many native organizations. In response to a spate of plant closures, the CAW demanded job protection legislation including the establishment of tribunals to assess social costs, financial penalty clauses, and the right of the state to seize abandoned plants and find an alternative use for them.

Perhaps this is sufficient to demonstrate that these ideas are not merely the product of my or somebody else's imagination. They are emerging from social struggles in Canada and elsewhere in the ongoing fight against the neo-conservative program of austerity, free trade and deregulation. It is precisely the function of intellectuals of the Left to elaborate upon and formulate these fragments into a coherent alternative policy agenda.

If it still sounds utopian, the answer is: of course, but it's far less so than the never-never-land of the neo-conservatives. At the very least we are looking to the future rather than to the past. If I can paraphrase Simone de Beauvoir: "Socialist Canada? There are moments when I ask myself whether it is not a utopia. But each idea not yet realized curiously resembles a utopia; one would never do anything if we thought that nothing is possible except that which already exists."

Notes

1: Ways of Seeing

[1] This section was inspired by an article that appeared in *This Magazine*. The author, Thomas Walkom, was at the time an economics reporter for the *Globe and Mail*. Shortly after the article appeared, Mr. Walkom was transferred to the newspaper's Tokyo office. One suspects the coincidence of events was not accidental.

[2] Quoted in Robert Kuttner, *The Economic Illusion*, Houghton Mifflin, 1984, p.13.

[3] See Michael Mann, "The Social Cohesion of Liberal Democracy," *American Sociological Review* 35 (1970).

[4] John Porter, *Vertical Mosaic*, University of Toronto Press, 1965, p.3.

[5] Erik O. Wright, *Class, Crisis and the State*, New Left Books, 1978.

[6] William Johnston, Michael Ornstein, "Social Class and Political Ideology in Canada," Institute for Behavioural Research, York University, 1982.

[7] Charles E. Lindblom, *Politics and Markets*, Basic Books, 1977, p.46.

[8] According to Bachrach and Barantz, the ability to control the public agenda reveals the location of power as much as the ability to get people to do things they otherwise would not do. Some groups are so lacking in power that their concerns never get on the agenda. Peter Bachrach and Morton S. Barantz, *Power and Poverty: Theory and Practice*, Oxford University Press, 1970.

[9] See Samuel Bowles and Herbert Gintis, *Schooling in Capitalist America*, Basic Books, 1975; Ivan Berg, *Education and Jobs: The Great Brain Robbery*, Beacon Press, 1971.

[10] See Melvin Kohn, *Class and Conformity: A Study of Values*, Dorsey, 1969.

[11] The *Toronto Star* supported the NDP in 1979 and returned to the Liberal fold in 1980.

[12] Quoted in Adam Przeworski, "Material Bases of Conduct, Economics and Politics in a Hegamonic System," *Political Power and Social Theory*, vol. I, p.21.

[13] A. Przeworski, op cit., p.27.
[14] Ibid., p.34.

2: Economic Theory and Ideology

[1] Karl Popper, *The Open Society*, vol. 1, Routledge & Kegan Paul, 1962, p.213.
[2] Joseph Schumpeter, *History of Economic Analysis*, Oxford University Press, 1968, p.42.
[3] Harry Johnson, *Theory of Income Distribution*, Gray-Mills Publishing, 1973, pp.220-1.
[4] Joan Robinson, *An Essay on Marxism Analysis*, Macmillan, 1969, p.18.
[5] William Beveridge, *Full Employment in a Free Society*, George Allan Unwin, 1944, p.18.
[6] Robert Kuttner, op cit., p.91.
[7] See C.W. Gonick, "Foreign Ownership and Political Decay," in Ian Lumsden (ed.), *Close the 49th Parallel*, University of Toronto Press, 1970.
[8] Frederich List quoted in John Eatwell, *Whatever Happened to Britain*, BBC, 1982, p.73.
[9] Ibid.
[10] John Maynard Keynes, "National Self-Sufficiency," *Yale Review*, Summer 1933.
[11] In the heady days of the early postwar period, Keynes dropped his vision of national self-sufficiency. In the ensuing years, it was rarely mentioned, even in footnotes.
[12] Robert Heilbroner, "Economics as a 'Value-Free' Science," *Social Research*, Spring 1973.
[13] J.M. Keynes, *The General Theory of Employment, Interest and Money*, Macmillan, 1957, p.383.
[14] Adam Smith, *An Inquiry into the Nature and Causes of the Wealth of Nations*, Modern Library, 1937, p.674.
[15] Ibid., p.435.
[16] Anthony Downs, *An Economic Theory of Democracy*, Harper & Row, 1957.
[17] Ben Fine, *Economic Theory and Ideology*, Edward Arnold, 1980, p.13.
[18] Charles Lindblom, op cit., p.173. The argument that follows draws from Lindblom's account.
[19] In some of the Marxist literature, the state is accorded "relative autonomy" to mediate between competitive factions of capital. See,

for example, N. Poulantzas, *Political Power and Social Classes*, New Left Books, 1975.
[20] See Ralph Miliband, *Capitalist Democracy in Britain*, Oxford University Press, 1982, for a balanced version of this interpretation.
[21] Quotes are from volumes I and II of the Macdonald Commission on the Economic Union.

3: Orthodoxy and Its Reformers

[1] Thomas Kuhn, *The Structure of Scientific Revolution*, University of Chicago Press, 1962, p.74.
[2] Ibid., p.77.
[3] Adam Smith, *Wealth of Nations*, Modern Library, p.128.
[4] Ibid., p.250.
[5] Ibid., p.329.
[6] Ibid., p.734.
[7] Ibid., p.249.
[8] Ibid., p.66.
[9] Ibid., pp.66-7.
[10] Ibid., p.79, 674.
[11] *Theory of Moral Sentiments*, Part IV, chapter 1, quoted in R. Heilbroner, "Homage to Adam Smith," *Challenge*, March-April 1976.
[12] Nassau Senior, *Three Lectures on the Rate of Wages*, preface.
[13] Nassau Senior, *Journal Kept in France and Italy from 1848 to 1852*, Henry King, 1871, pp.150-2.
[14] Ibid., pp.4-5.
[15] N. Senior, *Conversations with M. Thiers, M. Guizot and Other Distinquished Persons during the Second Empire*, Hurst & Blackett, 1878, vol. I, p.169.
[16] J.B. Say, *A Treatise on Political Economy*, p.135
[17] Lionel Robbins, *Great Depression*, 1934, p.73.
[18] In D. Brown, ed., *The Economics of the Recovery Program*, 1934, p.16.
[19] John Stuart Mill, *Principles of Political Economy*, Longman, Green, 1963, p.21.
[20] Ibid., p.945.
[21] Ibid., p.208.
[22] Ibid., p.234.
[23] J.S. Mill, *Dissertations and Discussions: Political, Philosophical and Historical*, 1973-4, Henry Hold, vol. 3, 59.
[24] J.S. Mill, *Principles of Political Economy*, p.774.
[25] Ibid., p.207.
[26] J.S. Mill, *Socialism and Utilitarianism*, p.127.

[27] J.S. Mill, *Principles of Political Economy*, p.951.
[28] Ibid., pp.804-5.
[29] J.S. Mill, *Socialism and Utilitarianism*, p.127.
[30] J.S. Mill, *Autobiography*, Henry Holt, 1875, p.232.
[31] Barry Commoner, *The Closing Circle*, Bantam, 1971, p.167.
[32] Quoted in Bruce Doern, "The Political Economy of the Hammond Beaudry Reports," *Canadian Public Administration*, March.
[33] Labour Canada, *Employment Injuries and Occupational Illnesses*, 1984.
[34] Bob Sass, "The Labour Process and Health: An Alternative Conception to Occupational Health and Safety," unpublished.
[35] Quoted in ibid.
[36] K. William Kapp, *The Social Cost of Private Enterprise*, Harvard University Press, 1950, p.231.
[37] Ibid., p.233.
[38] Ibid., p.251.
[39] R.W. Souter, "The Nature and Significance of Economic Science in Recent Discussions," *Quarterly Journal of Economics*, May 1933.
[40] David Ricardo, *The Principles of Political Economy and Taxation*, Dent, 1962, p.1.
[41] K. Marx, *Capital*, vol. I, Foreign Languages Publishing House, p.645.
[42] K. Marx, *Economic and Philosophical Manuscripts*, in E. Framm, *Marx's Concept of Man*, Fredrick Ungar, 1961, pp.141-2.

4:Keynes' Vision

[1] J.M. Keynes, *The Means to Prosperity*, Harcourt, Brace, 1933, p.3.
[2] J.M. Keynes, *The General Theory*, Macmillan, 1957, p.381.
[3] J.M. Keynes, "Democracy Efficiency," *New Statesman and Nation*, January 28, 1937.
[4] J.M. Keynes, *Essays in Persuasion*, Norton, 1963, pp.132-4.
[5] J.M. Keynes, *The General Theory*, viii.
[6] Keynes clearly accepted the orthodox view that in the short run, with a given amount of productive capacity and with existing technology, a rise in employment would require a fall in the purchasing power of wages (real wages). But he doubted that cuts in money wages could actually depress the real wage rate. First, where collective bargaining is highly fragmented and where unions fiercely protect wage differentials, any union would resist a wage cut even in the face of heavy unemployment. Secondly, even if trade union leaders

could be induced to negotiate lower money wages, this might not be sufficient, for what is important for employment is the level of real wages. Unions may have some influence over money wages but they have very little influence over prices. While it is true that a wage cut in one firm would likely depress the real wages of workers employed in that firm and might encourage its owners to hire on more workers, what happens with a general wage cut affecting all workers? The answer, Keynes said, is that competition would force firms to reduce their prices in proportion to the drop in costs. Real wages and profits would therefore be unaffected and employers would have no incentive to hire more workers. The solution he offered is that workers (suffering from "money illusion") would accept lower real wages if it came in the form of a price increase rather than a wage cut. Creeping inflation induced by government expansionary policy was therefore built into his solution of increasing short-term employment.

[7] Quoted in Robert Kuttner, *The Economic Illusion*, p.83.
[8] J.M. Keynes, *The General Theory*, p.320.
[9] J.M. Keynes, ibid., p.378.
[10] J.M. Keynes, *Essays in Persuasion*, p.318.
[11] J.M. Keynes, *The General Theory*, p.129.
[12] J.M. Keynes, ibid., p.322.
[13] J.M. Keynes, ibid., p.220.
[14] J.M. Keynes, ibid., p.375.
[15] J.M. Keynes, *Essays in Persuasion*, p.268.
[16] J.M. Keynes, *How to Pay for the War*.
[17] Quotes are cited in J.A. Trevithich, "Keynes, Inflation and Money Illusion," *Economic Journal*, March 1975.
[18] This correspondence and others referred to are cited in Lord Kahn, "On Re-Reading Keynes," *Proceedings of the British Academy*, vol. 60, 1974, pp.385, 387.
[19] J.M. Keynes, *The General Theory*, p.381.
[20] J.M. Keynes, ibid., pp.382-3.
[21] J.M. Keynes, *Essays in Persuasion*, p.324.
[22] J.M. Keynes, *The General Theory*, pp.378-9.
[23] J.M. Keynes, *Essays in Persuasion*, pp.369-70.
[24] J.M. Keynes, *The General Theory*, p.376.
[25] J.M. Keynes, ibid., pp.383-4.
[26] Michael Kalecki, "Political Aspects of Full Employment," *Political Quarterly* IV, 1947.
[27] Quoted in Beveridge, *Full Employment in a Free Society*, George Allen & Unwin, 1945, p.195.

5: Was There a Keynesian Revolution?

[1] The account of this debate is taken from Sidney J. Alexander, "Opposition to Deficit Spending in Income, Employment and Public Policy," *Essays in Honour of Alvin Hansen*, 1947. Such considerations were debated well into the decade by highly reputable members of the economics profession. In an article entitled "Full Employment At Any Cost" (*Quarterly Journal of Economics*, August 1950), Jacob Viner took issue with a report reproduced for the United Nations by a panel of five economists — J. M. Clark, A. Smithies, N. Kaldor, P. Uri and E. R. Walker. "There are many costs I would not be prepared to pay for 'full employment' even if the alternative were failure to attain it by a significant margin — although I would have the unemployed generously taken care of," Viner wrote. He would be satisfied with measures to preclude "mass employment" such as "to strengthen rather than to undermine the foundations of what remains of a free market, free trade, free enterprise world."

[2] Wm. Beveridge, *Full Employment in a Free Society*, 1945, pp.273-4.

[3] Wm. Beveridge, ibid., p.158.

[4] *Saturday Night*, September 1, 1945.

[5] See James Struthers, *No Fault of Their Own, Unemployment and the Canadian Welfare State, 1914-1941*, University of Toronto Press, 1983.

[6] James Struthers, ibid., p.206.

[7] James Struthers, ibid., p.191.

[8] R.M. Campbell, "From Keynesianism to Monetarism," *Queen's Quarterly*, Winter 1981.

[9] Scott Gordon, "A Twenty Year Perspective: Some Reflections on the Keynesian Revolution in Canada," in S.F. Kaliski (ed.), *Canadian Economic Policy Since the War*.

[10] Irwin Gillespie, "Post War Canadian Fiscal Policy Revisited, 1945-1975, *Canadian Tax Journal*, May-June 1974.

[11] Irwin Gillespie, ibid., p.275.

[12] M. Kalecki, op cit.

[13] J.M. Keynes, "The General Theory of Employment" in S. Harris (ed.), *The New Economics*, Alfred A. Knopf, 1947, p.185.

[14] Anthony Crosland, *The Future of Socialism*, Schocken, p.79.

[15] Quoted in A. Gunter Frank, *Reflections on the World Economic Crisis*, Hutchinson, 1981, p.68.

[16] Milton and Rose Friedman, *Free to Choose*, Avon, 1979, p.331.

6:Monetarism and Supply-Side Economics

[1] M. and R. Friedman, *Free to Choose*, Avon, 1979, p.5.
[2] Ibid., p.135.
[3] Ibid., p.109.
[4] Ibid., p.215.
[5] Thomas Courchene, "Towards a Protected Society: The Politicization of Economic Life," Department of Economics, Research Report, University of Western Ontario.
[6] Michael Crozier, et al., *The Crisis of Democracy: Report on the Governmentality of Democracies to the Trilateral Commission*, 1975, p.164. See also Samuel Britton, *The Economic Consequence of Democracy*, Temple Smith, 1977.
[7] Friedman, op cit., p.24.
[8] F.A. von Hayek, *New Studies in Philosophy, Economics and the History of Ideas*, p.13.
[9] Friedman, op cit., p.227.
[10] Friedman, ibid., p.223.
[11] Richard G. Stapleton, "Why Recessions Help Britain," *Economic Affairs*, 1981.
[12] Bank of Canada *Review*, April 1982.
[13] Michael J. Prince, "Whatever Happened to Compassion? Liberal Social Policy 1980-1984," in Allen Maslove (ed.), *How Ottawa Spends, 1984: The New Agenda*, Methuen.
[14] Eugene Swimmer, "Six and Five," in A. Maslove, ibid.
[15] George Gilder, *Wealth and Poverty*, Basic Books, 1981, p.259.
[16] Ibid., p.188.
[17] Ibid., p.203.
[18] Ibid, p.202.
[19] Ibid., p.218.
[20] Ibid., p.29.
[21] Department of Finance, "The Corporate Income Tax System, A Direction for Change," May 1985, ibid., p.5.
[22] Linda McQuaig, *Globe and Mail*, March 30, 1984.
[23] Ibid.
[24] Ibid.
[25] Department of Finance, op cit., p.6.
[26] Calculations in National Welfare Council, "Giving and Taking: The May 1985 Budget and the Poor," July 1985.

7:The New Right: Theory and Practice

[1] Ramesh Mishra, *The Welfare State in Crisis*, Wheatsheaf Books, 1984, p.62.
[2] Michael Moffit, "Chicago Economics in Chile," *Challenge*, September-October 1977; O. Letellier, *Chile: Economic Freedom and Political Repression*; Robert Carty, *Chile: Miracle or Mirage?* Latin American Working Group.
[3] F.A. von Hayek, "1988's Unemployment and the Unions," Institute of Economic Affairs, p.23.
[4] "Monetarism and UK Monetary Policy," *Cambridge Journal of Economics*, December 1980.
[5] I. Bukker and R. Miller, "State Expansion and Economic Decline: The Policy Debate," unpublished manuscript, p.15.
[6] Cited in E. Black, "The Assault on Unemployment Insurance," *Canadian Dimension*, July-August 1986.
[7] Martin Feldstein, "Supply-Side Economics: Old Truths and New Claims," *American Economic Review*, May 1986, p.29.
[8] Jerry Hausman, "Income and Payroll Tax Policy and Labour Supply" in L.H. Mayco (ed.), *The Supply-Side Effects of Economic Policy*.
[9] Richard Bird, *Tax Incentives for Investment*, Canadian Tax Foundation, 1980, p.2.
[10] Department of Finance, *The Corporate Income Tax System, A Direction for Change*, p.22.
[11] Robert Kuttner, *The Economic Illusion*, p.51.
[12] Ibid., p.72.
[13] See W. Magnusson, et al. (ed.) *The New Reality, The Politics of Restraint in British Columbia*, New Star Books, 1984, for a full treatment of this subject.
[14] John Malcolmson in ibid., pp.75-87.
[15] W. Magnusson, et al. (eds.) op cit., p.275.

8:The New State Interventionists

[1] Robert Reich, *The Next American Frontier*, New York Times Books, 1983, p.239.
[2] Abraham Rotstein, *Rebuilding From Within*, James Lorimer, 1984, p.1
[3] John Bossma and D.P. Dungan, "The Government Deficit: Too High or Too Low," *Canadian Tax Journal*, Jan.-Feb. 1983.
[4] Science Council of Canada, *Forging the Links: A Technology Policy for Canada*, 1980, p.46.

[5] Robert Kuttner, *The Economic Illusion*, Houghton Mifflin, 1984, p.136.
[6] This is a summary of the thesis put forward by Kerry Schott, one of the most careful and well-argued post-Keynesian expositions on incomes policy. See his *Policy, Power and Order, the Persistence of Economic Problems in Capitalist States*, Yale University Press, 1984.
[7] Peter Wiles, "Cost Inflation and the State of Economic Theory," *Economic Journal*, 1973.
[8] John C.P. McCallum, Clarence L. Barber, *Controlling Inflation: Learning from Experience*, Canadian Institute for Economic Policy, 1982, p.100.
[9] Robert Reich, *The Next American Frontier*, p.270.
[10] The fullest account of NDP industrial policy can be found in a discussion paper prepared for the 1981 party convention titled "A Democratic Socialist Economic Policy for the 1980's" and in "New Directions for Ontario's Politics" drawn up in 1979 by the Ontario NDP. The Ontario party has also published a series of detailed industry blueprints. The fullest account of CLC policy can be found in two convention documents, "The Battle of the Eighties: Trade Union Rights vs. Corporate Power" (1980) and "Economic Policy Statements" (1982) as well as in the Congress's submission to the Macdonald Royal Commission (1983).
[11] Donald Macdonald, Marcell Pepin, "Voluntary Guidelines," *Canadian Labour*, October 1969, p.4.
[12] A. Maslove and G. Swimmer, *Wage Controls in Canada: A Study in Public Decision-Making*, Institute for Research and Public Policy, p.5.
[13] For a discussion of the Manifesto and responses to it, see C. Gonick, "Labour's New Manifesto," *Canadian Dimension*, vol. II, no.5, June 1976; Cy Gonick, "Where Do We Go From Here?" *Canadian Dimension*, vol. II, no.8, November 1976; Cy Gonick, "On the Road to Tripartism," *Canadian Dimension*, vol. 12, no.1; Evert Hooger, "Report from the Convention," *Canadian Dimension*, vol. 13, no.3; J.C. Parrot, "Struggle, Unity and Leadership," *Canadian Dimension*, vol. 14, no.6; Cy Gonick, "State of the Unions," *Canadian Dimension*, vol. 14, no.7.

9:Incomes Policy

[1] L. Ulman, R. Flanagan, *Wage Restraint: A Study of Income Policies in Western Europe*, University of California Press, 1971, p.216.

[2] R. Flanagan, D. Soskice, L. Ulman, *Unionism, Economic Stabilization, and Income Policies: European Experience*, Brookings Institution, 1983, p.3.
[3] Ibid., p.83.
[4] Ibid., p.120.
[5] Ibid., p.329.
[6] Ibid., p.4.
[7] Ibid., p.4.
[8] Ibid., p.432.
[9] Roger Tarling and Frank Wilkinson, "The Social Contract: Post-war income policies and their inflationary impact," *Cambridge Economic Journal*, December 1977, pp.396, 412.
[10] R. Flanagan, et al., op cit., p.126.
[11] Ibid., pp.137-8.
[12] Ibid., p.333.
[13] Andrew Martin, "Trade Unions in Sweden: Strategic Responses to Change and Crisis," in P. Gourevitch, et al., *Unions and Economic Crisis: Britain, West Germany and Sweden*, George Allen, 1984.
[14] Cited in Leo Panitch, "The Tripartite Experience," p.63 in manuscript to be published in *State and Economic Interests*, vol. 32, University of Toronto Press.
[15] Ibid., p.64.
[16] Ibid., p.58.
[17] R. Flanagan, et al., op cit., p.285.
[18] Ibid., pp.241-2.
[19] Ibid., p.294.
[20] P. Schelk Anderson, P. Turner, "Incomes Policy in Theory and Practice," OECD Occasional Studies, p.38.
[21] Quoted in R. Kuttner, *The Economic Illusion*, p.166.
[22] Kerry Schott, *Policy, Power and Order, The Persistence & Economic Problems in Capitalist States*, Yale University Press, 1984, pp.175-6.
[23] Conference Board of Canada, *Inflation and Incomes Policy in Canada*, 1979.
[24] Cy Gonick, *Inflation and Wage Controls*, Dimension Publications, 1976, p.143.
[25] A. Maslove, G. Swimmer, *Wage Controls in Canada 1975-78*, p.154.
[26] D.A.L. Auld, et al., *The Determinants of Negotiated Wage Settlements in Canada*, cited in ibid., p.245.
[27] G. Swimmer, "Six and Five" in A. Maslove (ed.), *How Ottawa Speaks, 1984: The New Agenda*, Methuen, 1984, p.248.
[28] Ibid., p.241.

10:Industrial Policy

1. Tom Naylor, *The History of Canadian Business*, James Lorimer, vol. I, p.87.
2. Alfred Maizels, *Industrial Growth and World Trade*, Cambridge University Press, 1963, p.62.
3. Robert Reich, *America's Next Frontier*, p.198.
4. Ibid., p.130.
5. Statistics Canada, *Canadian Imports by Domestic and Foreign Controlled Enterprises*, 1978, p.xvi.
6. D.P. Demelto, et al., "Innovation and Technological Change" in *Five Canadian Industries*, Economic Council of Canada, p.44.
7. Science Council of Canada, *The Role of World Product Mandates*, p.11.
8. Science Council of Canada, *The Weakest Link*, 1978, p.154.
9. Lawrence Klein, "In Defence of Industrial Policy," *Western Economic Review*, March 1984.
10. Science Council of Canada, *Uncertain Prospects: Canadian Manufacturing Industry, 1971-1977*, 1977.
11. Science Council of Canada, *The Weakest Link*, 1978, p.185.
12. Ibid., p.187.
13. Ibid., pp.45-7.
14. A. Rotstein, op cit., pp.33-5.
15. Science Council of Canada, op cit., p.61.
16. These examples are culled from Robert Kuttner, *The Economic Illusion*, pp.125-6.
17. Quoted in R.D. French, *How Ottawa Decides*, James Lorimer, 1980, p.20.
18. Ibid., p.110.
19. Ibid., p.111.
20. Ibid., p.114.
21. Department of Finance, *Economic Development for Canada in the 1980's*.
22. Quoted in R.D. French, op cit., p.152.
23. This of course represents a mighty leap of faith. The British Labour Party was elected to office in 1974 on a platform of nationalizing key firms and imposing planning agreements on a hundred others — a strategy very similar to the one advocated by the NDP. In charge of implementing the program was Tony Benn, a man whose "political convictions" and "political will" are unquestionable. Yet when the Industry Bill was finally presented it was totally emasculated and Benn shunted aside. In the end, the only planning agreement by the Labour government was with the bankrupt Chrysler corpora-

tion. For an account of these events see Tom Forester, "Neutralizing the Industrial Strategy" in Ken Coates (ed.), *What Went Wrong*, Spokesman, 1979.
[24] Their statement, "Ethical Reflections on the Economic Crisis," is reprinted in *Canadian Dimension*, May 1983.
[25] Ibid.

11:Industrial Democracy

[1] Maurice Lemelin, "Trade Unions and Work Organization Experiments," in *Adapting to a Changing World, A Reader in Quality of Work Life*, Labour Canada, 1981, p.118.
[2] S.A.C. Brown, *The Social Psychology of Industry*, Penguin, p.14.
[3] Maurice Bauvin, "Managing and Improving the Quality of Working Life: A Managerial Overview," in Labour Canada, op cit., p.148.
[4] Eric Trist, "The Quality of Working Life and Organizational Improvement," in ibid., p.54.
[5] M. Boisvert, "Managing and Improving Quality of Working Life: A Managerial Overview," in ibid., p.147.
[6] Donald Nightingale, *Workplace Democracy*, University of Toronto Press, 1982, p.145.
[7] Ibid.
[8] D. Nightingale, op cit., pp.174-89.
[9] Paul Bernstein, "Necessary Elements for Effective Worker Participation in Decision-Making," *Journal of Economic Issues*, vol. X, no.2, June 1976.
[10] Ibid., pp.502-4.
[11] See NFB film *Temiscaming*, and D. Nightingale, *Profit Sharing and Employee Ownership: A Review and Appraisal*, Queen's University, 1980.
[12] Jean Remus, "Financial Participation of Employees: An Attempted Classification and Major Trends," *International Labour Review*, Jan.-Feb.1983.
[13] Nightingale, *Workplace Democracy*, op cit., p.160.
[14] Interview with Serge Lord, Director of Research and Communications, Canadian Paperworks Union, December 1985.
[15] International Labour Organisation, *World Labour Report*, 1985, p.26.
[16] D. Nightingale, op cit., pp.240-1.
[17] Wilfrid List, "A Plant Where Job Frustration Isn't Allowed on the Payroll," *Globe and Mail*, June 19, 1978.
[18] Andrew Wallace, "Labour-Management QWL Programs 'Work,' at a Shell Canada Chemical Plant," *World of Work Report*, February 1981.

[19] G.S. Walpole, *Management and Men*, quoted in K. Coates, T. Topham, *New Industrial Unionism*, pp.205-6.
[20] Ibid., p.218.
[21] *Toronto Star*, September 5, 1974.
[22] Don Wells, *Unions and "Quality of Work-Life" Programmes*, Centre for Labour Studies, Humber College, 1983, p.59.
[23] W.W. Daniel, N. McIntosh, *The Right to Manage?* MacDonald, 1972, p.49.
[24] QWL Focus, Spring 1984.
[25] CBC *Ideas*, 1986 "Labour At The Crossroads," no.2.
[26] Ibid.
[27] Ibid.
[28] See Don Wells, op cit.
[29] Ibid., p.26.
[30] Quotations are from ibid., pp.37-39, 48, 56, 62-64, 74-76, 79.
[31] Michael Poole, *Workers Participation in Industry*, Routledge & Kegan Paul, 1975, p.36.
[32] Quoted in Ken Coates, T. Topham, op cit., p.58.
[33] Quoted in B. Swerdling, "Beyond Boredom — A Look at What's New on the Assembly Line," *The Washington Monthly*, July-August 1973.

12: Income and Class

[1] A scholarly and thorough analysis of these changes in economic thought may be found in E.K. Hunt, *History of Economic Thought, A Critical Perspective*, Wadsworth, 1979.
[2] Quoted in Leo Panitch, "Corporatism in Canada," *Studies in Political Economy*, Spring 1979.
[3] Quoted in Ken Coates, Tony Topham, *The New Unionism*, Owen, 1972, p.86.
[4] I. Gillespie, "Taxes, Expenditure and the Redistribution of Income in Canada 1951-1977," *Reflections on Canadian Incomes, Economic Council of Canada*, 1979.
[5] *Globe and Mail, Report on Business*, August 25, 1984.
[6] Gary Becker, *Human Capital*, Columbia University Press, 1969.
[7] Kingsley Davis and Wilbert Moore, quoted in Charles Anderson, *The Political Economy of Social Class*, Prentice Hall, 1974, p.81.
[8] Frank Parkins, *Classes in Modern Society*, Vintage Books, 1967, p.11.
[9] Health and Welfare Canada, *Working Paper on Social Security of Canada*.

13:Where Do Profits Come From?

[1] Chan F. Aw, "Dual Labour Market Analysis: A Study of Canadian Manufacturing Industries," Labour Canada.
[2] Pat and Hugh Armstrong, *A Working Majority, What Women Must Do For Pay*, Canadian Advisory Council on the Status of Women, 1933, p.11.
[3] Erik Olin Wright, *Class Structure and Income Distributions*, Academic Press, 1979, p.89.
[4] Canadian Council on Social Development, *Not Enough, the Meaning and Measurement of Poverty in Canada*, 1984.
[5] National Council on Welfare, *The Working Poor: People and Programs*.
[6] National Council on Welfare, *Jobs and Poverty*, p.3.
[7] David M. Gordon, "Segmentation by Numbers," unpublished, New School for Social Research.
[8] Harry Braverman, *Labor and Monopoly Capital*, Monthly Review Press, 1974, p.407.
[9] H.C. Pentland, *A Study of the Social, Economic and Political Background of the Canadian System of Industrial Relations*, Task Force on Industrial Relations, 1968, p.2.
[10] Alfred Marshall, *Principles of Economics*, Macmillan, 1927, p.567.
[11] Ken Coates, Tony Topham, *The New Unionism*, Owen, 1972, p.76.
[12] Richard Hyman, *Industrial Relations, A Marxist Introduction*, Macmillan, 1975, p.64.
[13] Quotes from F.W. Taylor, *The Principles of Scientific Management*, Norton, 1967.
[14] Alan Fox, "The Myths of Pluralism and a Radical Alternative," in T. Clark, L. Clements (ed.), *Trade Unions under Capitalism*, Fontana, p.140.
[15] Richard Hyman, op. cit., pp.97-8.
[16] Vic Allen, *Militant Trade Unionism*, Merlin, 1966, p.27.
[17] C.W. Mills, *The New Men of Power*, Harcourt, Brace, 1948, p.9.
[18] R. Hyman, R. Fryer, "Trade Unions: Sociology and Political Economy," in Clark, Clements, op. cit., p.158.
[19] R. Hyman, *Strikes*, Fontana, 1972, p.93.
[20] A. Fox, op. cit., pp.145-6.
[21] A conventional measure of monopoly control is the level of industry concentration. Among industries where four or fewer enterprises supply at least 80 per cent of the output, the degree of monopoly control is considered "very high"; where four to eight enterprises account for 80 per cent or more of the output, the degree of monopoly control is considered "high"; where eight to twenty firms sell 80 per cent or more of the output it is considered "fairly high"; where it

takes fifty or more enterprises to account for 80 per cent of industry output, the degree of concentration is considered so low that active price competition is assumed to exist. Figures calculated from the Royal Commission on Corporate Concentration (study no. 17) provide the following breakdown in manufacturing for 1972: very high —25 per cent; high — 10 per cent; fairly high — 46 per cent; low — 19 per cent.

14:Business and the State

[1] James O'Connor, *The Fiscal Crisis of the State*, Saint Martin's Press, 1973.
[2] Richard Edwards, *Contested Terrain*, Basic Books, 1979, pp.91-7; Graham Lowe, "The Rise of Modern Management in Canada," *Canadian Dimension*, December 1979.
[3] C.B. Macpherson, "The Social Services" in J. Park (ed.), *The Culture of Contemporary Canada*, University of Toronto Press, 1957, p.20.
[4] The best discussion of this subject may be found in M. Dobb, *Studies in the Development of Capitalism*, Routledge, 1954.
[5] Donald Creighton, *The Empire of the St. Lawrence*, Macmillan, 1956.
[6] R. Whitaker, "Images of the State" in L. Panitch (ed.), *The Canadian State*, University of Toronto Press, 1977, p.42.
[7] Ibid., p.38.
[8] Goran Therborn, "The Role of Capital and the Rise of Bourgeois Democracy," *New Left Review*, no. 103, 1977.
[9] Vernon Fowke, "The National Policy — Old and New," *Canadian Journal of Economics and Political Science*, August 1952.
[10] Lithwick and Devlin, "Economic Development Policy: A Case Study in Underdeveloped Policy Making" in A. Maslove (ed.), *How Ottawa Spends, 1984: The New Agenda*, Methuen.
[11] M. Bliss, "Canadianizing American Business, The Route of the Branch Plant" in I. Lumsden (ed.), *Close the 49th Parallel*, University of Toronto Press, 1970; R.T. Naylor, *The History of Canadian Business*, vol. II, ch. 13, James Lorimer, 1975.
[12] O.J. McDairmid, *Commercial Policy in the Canadian Economy*, Harvard University Press, 1946, pp.192-3.
[13] Michael Ray, *Regional Aspects of Foreign Ownership of Manufacturing in Canada*, University of Waterloo, 1967.
[14] H. Binhammer, et al., *Government Grants to Private Sector Firms*, Economic Council of Canada, Discussion Paper 227, 1983.
[15] Phillip Mathias, *Forced Growth: Five Studies of Government Involvement in the Development of Canada*, James Lorimer.
[16] Herschel Hardin, *A Nation Unaware*, Douglas, 1974, p.240.

[17] H.V. Nelles, *The Politics of Development: Forests, Mines and Hydro-Electric Power in Ontario 1879-1941*, University of Toronto Press, 1974, pp.248-9.
[18] Ibid., p.47.
[19] Ibid., p.ix.
[20] R. Whitaker, op cit., p.60.
[21] Wallace Clement, *The Canadian Corporate Elite: An Analysis of Economic Power*, McClelland and Stewart, 1975, p.346.
[22] Quoted in C. Gonick, *Inflation or Depression*, James Lorimer, 1975, p.57.
[23] K. Marx, *Capital*, vol. I, Foreign Languages Publishing House, 1954, p.243.
[24] Quoted in Donald Swartz, "The Politics of Reform: Conflict and Accommodations in Canadian Health Policy" in L. Panitch, op cit., p.305.
[25] James Struthers, *No Fault of Their Own, Unemployment and the Canadian Welfare Sate 1914-1941*, University of Toronto Press, 1983, p.75.
[26] Ibid., p.147.
[27] Leo Panitch, "The Role and Nature of the Canadian State" in L. Panitch, op cit., p.20.
[28] Stuart Jamieson, *Times of Trouble: Labour Unionist and Industrial Conflict in Canada 1910-1966*, Task Force on Labour Relations, 1968.
[29] Paul Craven, *An Impartial Umpire: Industrial Relations and the Canadian State 1900-1911*, University of Toronto Press, 1980, p.306.
[30] Quoted in L. Panitch and D. Swartz, "Toward Permanent Exceptionalism: Coercion and Conduct in Canadian Industrial Relations" in *Labour/le Travais*, no. 13, p.137.
[31] See H.C. Pentland, *A Study of the Social, Economic and Political Background of the Canadian System of Industrial Relations*.
[32] Quoted in Stephen McBride, "Hard Times and the Rules of the Game: A Study of the Legislative Environment of Labour-Capital Conflict," unpublished, p.10.
[33] Eugene Swimmer, "Labour Canada: A Department 'of' Labour 'for' Labour" in B. Doern (ed.), *How Ottawa Spends Your Tax Dollars, 1981*, James Lorimer, p.159.
[34] McBride, op cit., p.17.

15:The Economic Roller Coaster

[1] For expositions of Marx's theories of the crisis see: Thomas Weiskopf, "Marxism Crisis Theory and the Rate of Profit in the Post-

War US Economy," *Cambridge Journal of Economics*, December 1979, and "Marxist Perspectives on Cyclical Crisis" in *US Capitalism in Crisis*, Union for Radical Political Economics, 1978; E.O. Wright," Alternative Perspectives in Marxist Theory of Accumulation and Crisis," *Insurgent Sociologist*, Fall 1975; A. Shaikh, "An Introduction to the History of Crisis Themes," *US Capitalism in Crisis*, op cit.
[2] K. Marx, *Capital*, vol. I, Foreign Languages Publishing House, p.639.
[3] Ibid., p.595.
[4] K. Marx, *Grundrisse*, Vintage, p.748.
[5] K. Marx, *Capital*, vol. III, p.233.
[6] See J. Holloway, S. Picciotto (eds.), *State and Capital*, Arnold, 1978, and in particular, Joachim Hirsch therein, pp.57-107.
[7] Quoted in Jim Campen, "Economic Crisis and Conservative Economic Policies," *Radical America*, Spring 1981, p.40.

16: From Depression to Prosperity and Back

[1] Mike Davis, "The Political Economy of Late Imperial America," *New Left Review*, Jan.-Feb. 1984.
[2] Cited in Noam Chomsky, *Turning the Tide: U.S. Intervention in Central America and the Struggle for Peace*, South End Press, 1985.
[3] Quotes below from P. Armstrong, et al., *Capitalism Since World War II*, Fontana, 1984, pp.72-96, 111-2.
[4] Cited in Glen Williams, *Not for Export*, McClelland and Stewart, 1983, p.121.
[5] P. Armstrong, et al., op cit., p.236-7.
[6] Employment in Canada more than doubled between 1946 and 1971 (from 3.7 million to 8.6 million). A major source of paid labour had been the dramatic decline of self-employed proprietors, from nearly a million in 1946 to barely half a million in 1971. Unpaid family workers dropped from 400,000 to 186,000. Most of this transfer resulted from the movement from rural employment. Immigrant labour supplied fully 75 per cent of the new jobs created in the 1950s and a third of the new jobs created in the 1960s. Nearly half of the new jobs over the period 1946 to 1961 was filled by women whose participation rate rose from 23 per cent in 1946 to 39 per cent in 1971. Women comprised 35 per cent of the unpaid labour force in 1971 compared to 26 per cent in 1946. Finally, massive capital investment with increased mechanization permitted large increases in output in the goods-producing sector without proportional increases in labour. Between 1948 and 1971 agricultural output doubled while

employment halved; mining output increased five-fold and manufacturing four-fold with only a 60 per cent increase in labour. Labour saved in these sectors was released for the more labour-intensive service and clerical employment. (Sources: Labour Force Survey; Census Canada; Economic Council of Canada, tenth *Annual Review*.)

[7] Ibid., pp.139-40.
[8] Ibid., p.153.
[9] U.N. *Yearbook of International Trade*.
[10] According to the Marxian hypothesis, the favourable relationship between real wages and productivity would have produced a rate of exploitation sufficiently great to affect any rise in the organic composition of capital. The latter, in turn, would have been held down by low material costs and by technologically induced productivity advances in capital-goods industries.
[11] In Canada productivity gains exceeded wage and benefit gains for most years between 1950 and 1965 in the goods-producing sector of the economy. In fact labour costs per unit of output were lower in 1965 than they were in 1950, sufficiently so to offset increasing labour costs in the service sector of the economy (Statistics Canada, *Historical Statistics of Canada*, Series F250-258).
[12] Bert Hickman, *Growth and Stability in the Post-War Economy*, Brookings Institution, 1960.
[13] P. Armstrong, et al., op cit., p.271.
[14] Department of Finance, *Economic Review*, April 1982, p.163.
[15] These so-called "supply shocks" are examined more thoroughly in Cy Gonick, *Inflation and Wage Controls*, Canadian Dimension Publications, 1976.
[16] Armstrong, et al., op cit., p.313.
[17] Mike Davis, op cit., p.14.
[18] Cy Gonick, *Inflation or Depression*, James Lorimer, 1975, p.214.
[19] Armstrong, et al., op cit., p.219.
[20] A much more detailed analysis of this process may be found in Cy Gonick, op cit., pp.208-39.
[21] Jacob Morris, "Inflation," *Monthly Review*, September 1973.
[22] Ernest Mandel, *Late Capitalism*, New Left Books, 1975, p.453.
[23] Morris, op cit.
[24] Armstrong, et al., op cit., p.317.

17:The Road to Recovery?

[1] *Business Week Magazine*, December 23, 1985.
[2] *Business Week*, March 16, 1983.

[3] Industrial Relations Centre, Queen's University, *Current Industrial Relations Scene in Canada*, 1984, p.317; 1985, p.307.
[4] James A. Craft, et al., "Concession Bargaining and Unions: Impacts and Implications," *Journal of Labour Research*, Spring 1985, p.168.
[5] Ibid., p.173.
[6] *US News and World Report*, December 23, 1985.
[7] Industrial Relations Centre, op cit., 1985, pp.303-4, 396.
[8] Ibid., p.417.
[9] Judy Steed, *Globe and Mail*, October 4, 1986.
[10] Jim Turk, "Workers Fight Shut-Down," *Our Times*, April 1985.
[11] Legislative Assembly of Ontario, November 20, 1984, p.4296, and *Business Week*, August 26, 1985.
[12] *Our Times*, op cit., p.38.
[13] Thomas E. Maher, "Lifetime Employment in Japan: Exploding the Myth," *Business Horizons*, Nov.-Dec. 1985, p.24.
[14] *Business Week*, November 28, 1984, p.86.
[15] Wallace Peterson, "The US 'Welfare State' and the Conservative Counter-Revolution," *Journal of Economic Issues*, September 1985, p.630; *Business Week*, Sept. 1, 1986.
[16] Peterson, ibid., p.637.
[17] Ibid., p.629.
[18] Armstrong, et al., op cit., p.414.
[19] *Manchester Guardian Weekly*, January 5, 1986.
[20] *The Economist*, "Europe's Withering Welfare States," October 16-22, 1982.
[21] The editors, "The Strange Recovery of 1983-4," *Monthly Review*, October 1985.
[22] P. Armstrong, et al., op cit., p.393.
[23] Ibid., p.358.
[24] *Financial Times*, January 6, 1986.
[25] By passing the Gramm-Rudman Act in December 1985, the American Congress has in fact accepted this latter alternative, but with spending cuts of $70 billion or more scheduled for 1987, which would soon be followed by a major recession, many observers doubt whether policy-makers will stay the courses (*Business Week*, Feb. 10, 1986).
[26] *Financial Times*, op cit.
[27] *Business Week*, March 3, 1986, p.56.
[28] Ibid., p.62.
[29] Ibid., p.59.
[30] Ibid., p.79.
[31] Ibid., p.72.
[32] *Financial Post*, June 29, 1985, p.c7
[33] Sources cited in Fred Block, "The Myth of Re-Industrialization," *Socialist Review*, Jan.-Feb. 1984.

[34] Sunder Magun, "The Effects of Technological Changes on the Labour Market in Canada," paper presented to the Canadian Economics Association, Guelph, May 1984.

[35] W. Leontieff, et al., *The Future Impact of Automation on Workers*, Oxford University Press, 1986, p.84.

[36] Heather Menzies, *Computers on the Job*, p.56.

[37] Heather Menzies, *Women and the Chip*, Institute for Research and Public Policy, 1981, pp.65-74.

[38] J. Rada, *The Impact of Micro-Electronics*, International Labour Office, 1980, p.80.

[39] I. Barron, R. Curnnow, *The Future With Microelectronics: Forecasting the Effects of Information Technology, 1980*, p.199.

[40] Richard M. Bird, "Is Increasing Employment in 'High Tech' Industry a Sensible Policy Goal for Ontario?" Policy and Economic Analysis Program, Institute for Policy Analysis, University of Toronto, pp.15-6

[41] The most elaborate and detailed study for the U.S. up to the year 2000 shows that technology will have a devastating impact on clerical workers and managers but that overall it will not add to unemployment — the new jobs it will create in the production of investment goods will offset labour displacement. There are at least four important caveats to this conclusion, however. The first is that while computer automation may not add to overall unemployment, there will be massive dislocation. For example, as the principle author of this study, Wassily Leontieff, has quipped, auto workers have as much of a chance finding jobs building robots as horses did building automobiles. Second, the study takes into account only computer-related technological change. Other technological changes, for example, material substitution and changes in the organization of work, will have their own impact on future employment. Third, the study excludes "any major break-throughs in computer technology that might effect significant numbers of workers before the year 2000." Fourth, the study presumes that the increased supply of computer equipment will be produced in the U.S., whereas the hollowing trend indicates that much of the finished equipment and parts will be produced offshore. Wassily Leontief and Faye Duchin, *The Future Impact of Automation on Workers*, Oxford University Press, 1986.

[42] See, for example, Andre Gorz, *Farewell to the Working Class*, South End Press.

[43] Gatt-fly, *Debt Bondage or Self Reliance*, 1985, p.3.

[44] Ibid., p.1.

[45] Ibid., p.18.

[46] Economic Council of Canada, Annual Report, *Steering the Course*, p.62.

[47] Gatt-fly, op cit., p.21.
[48] Ibid., pp. 58-9.
[49] The Editors, "Two Faces of World Debt," *Monthly Review*, January 1984, p.7.
[50] Gatt-fly, op cit., p.69.
[51] Ibid., p. 76.
[52] Ibid., p. 43.
[53] *Business Week*, October 29, 1984, p.103.
[54] *In These Times*, December 12-18, 1984.
[55] *Business Week*, July 1, 1985.
[56] J.S. McCallum, "Canada's Weak Industrial Balance Sheet: An Impartial Public Policy Issue," *Western Economic Review*, Winter 1985, p.34.
[57] Economic Council of Canada, op cit., pp.52-6.
[58] *Financial Post*, February 1986, p.4.
[59] J. McCallum, op cit., pp.37-8.
[60] Cited in "Reagan II," *Progressive*, January 1985, p.22.

Index

Abbott, D.C., 92
Afghanistan, 335
Air Canada, 285, 350
Alberta, 281, 296, 298
Allende, Salvador, 335
Angola, 335
Anti-communism, 322
Anti-inflation Board (Canada), 164, 184-6, 203, 297
Arbenz, Jacobo, 335
Argentina, 329, 335, 370
 opposition to IMF, 373
Armstrong, Hugh, 252
Armstrong, Pat, 252
Australia, 329
Austria
 incomes policy, 175
 inflation rate, 183
 trade unions, 175
 unemployment rate, 183
 worker representation, 213
Automation, effects of, 361-9
 in Canada, 363
 on clerical work, 367
 on factory work, 365
 in France, 363
 in Japan, 363
 on management, 365-6
 on retail work, 366
 on service sector, 366
 on unemployment, 363-9 passim
 in U.S., 363
 in West Germany, 363
Auto Pact between Canada and U.S., 160, 195, 282

Baker, James, 359
Bank failures, 375
Bank of Canada, 115-6, 373
Bank of Montreal, 114, 372
Bankruptcy, corporate, 378
Barber, Clarence, 145, 184
B.C. Electric, 285
Beaudry Commission (Canada, 1985), 61
Becker, Gary, 240
Belgium, 353
Bell, Daniel, 101
Bell Canada, 121
Bell Company (Saskatchewan), 285
Benlux countries, 320
Bennett, Bill, 137, 138
Bennett, R.B., 289, 290, 291
Bennett, W.A.C., 285
Beveridge, William, 86
Bird, Richard, 136
Black, Conrad, 239
Black & Decker, 350
Blair, Bob, 204
Blue Cross, 360
Board of Economic Development Ministers (Canada), 204
Bolivia, 335
Bouey, Gerald, 115-6
Brazil, 192, 335, 370,
 effects of loan default, 373
 labour unrest, 373
Bretton Woods agreement, 317, 334
British Columbia, 285, 296, 298
 Social Credit policies, 137-41

Royal Commission on Industrial Disputes (1903), 293
unemployment, 140
British Gas, 349
British Petroleum, 349
British Telecom, 349
Brookings report on incomes policy and wage restraint, 171
Bronfman, Edgar, 234, 239
Bronfman, Edward, 239
Bronfman, Peter, 239
Budget deficits. *See* public debt
Business cycles, 301-8 passim
  absence of, between WWII and early 60s, 325
  the Great Depression, 52-3
  and liquidity, 306
  Marx on, 302, 307-8
Business magazine, 317
Business Week, 346, 360, 375

Cabinet Committee in Priorities and Planning (Canada), 203
Cambridge Policy Institute, 145
Canada Assistance Plan, 299
Canadair, 284, 349
Canada Pension, 299
Canada Post, 223, 296, 350
Canadian Automobile Workers, 348, 388
Canadian Bank of Commerce, 284
Canadian Broadcasting Corporation, 286
Canadian Commercial Bank, 378
Canadian Conference of Catholic Bishops, 208, 388
Canadian Council on Social Development, 239, 254
Canadian economy, *see also* economic policy; free trade; incomes policy; inflation; monetarism; monopoly; public debt; supply-side economics; taxation; trade unions; wages; welfare state.
  capital inflows, 196-7
  compared to other countries, 190
  competitive position, 191-2, 195-7
  concentration of wealth, 236
  corporate-political linkages, 286-8
  dependency on exports, 193, 319-20
  economic crisis after 1974, 342-3
  effects of automation, 363
  effects of Auto Pact, 195
  foreign borrowing, 336
  foreign ownership, 193-7 passim, 198-9
  high manufacturing costs, 194
  investment, 344
  mercantilism, 279-80
  merchant capital, 189
  multinationals, 194-5, 319
  nature of, 189
  and new technologies, 197-9
  procurement policies, 198
  standard of living, 254-5, 259
  state role in industrial strategy, 197-9
  as strike prone, 209, 220
  stunted industrialization, 189, 193
  trade balance, 324, 336-7
Canadian General Electric, 350
Canadian Institute for Economic Policy, 145, 160
Canadian International Paper Ltd., 214
Canadian Labour Congress, 145, 160, 162, 187, 299
  on incomes policy, 163-6

"Labour's Manifesto for
  Canada", 164-5
and wage restraint, 184
Canadian Labour Market and
  Productivity Centre, 205,
Canadian National, 348
Canadian National Railroad, 284,
  350
Canadian Northern railway, 284
Canadian Pacific, 348
Canadian Pacific Railway
  Company, 277
Canadian Paper Workers Union,
  214
Canadian Trade Unions Act, 293
Canadian Union of Postal
  Workers, 223, 387
Canadian Union of Public
  Employees, 388
Capitalism, *see also* economic
  theory; Marx, Karl; profits.
  accumulation in, 323-4, 326
  business cycles, 301-8 passim
  circuit of, 302-3
  crises of, 304-13 passim, 331-2,
    326, 340-2
  and democracy, 16-7, 106
  as economy of unpaid costs, 63
  and environmentalists, 59-60
  Marx on, 307-10
  overproduction, 304, 307
  post-war boom, 317-26
  primitive accumulation, 278
  in radical economic theory,
    231-2
  rate of exploitation, 309-10
  restructuring of, 345-54
  treatment of labour, 60-63
Carlisle, C.H., 88
Carr, Shirley, 204
CCF, 89
  converted to Keynesianism,
    158

history of economic outlook,
  158-9
Liberals borrow program of,
  100
Regina Manifesto, 158
C.D. Howe Institute, 124
Central Intelligence Agency, 335
Chase Manhattan Bank, 330,
  371-2
Chile, 130, 335
Chrétien, Jean, 203
Chrysler Corporation, 284, 362
Churchill, Winston, 86
CIO, 322
Clement, Wallace, 287
Cold war, 334
Cominco, 348
Commoner, Barry, 60
Communist Party
  of France, 318
  of Italy, 318
  of U.S., 322
Confédération Générale La
  Travail (France), 321
Consumer sovereignty doctrine,
  56
Cornwall, John, 145
Corporations
  bankruptcy, 378
  and corporate welfarism, 283-4
  hollowing of, 359-61
  and incomes policy, 179
  and industrial policy, 206-7
  political influence of, 34-5
  protective of autonomy, 168
  takeovers, 377
Courchene, Thomas, 107
CP Air, 285
Crosbie, John, 107
Crosland, Anthony, 97
Cuba, 335
Czechoslovakia, 320

Davidson, Paul, 145
De Beauvoir, Simone, 388
Defence Production Sharing
 Agreement, 282
De Havilland, 284, 349
Denmark, 213, 353
Deregulation, 351, 375-6
Desmarais, Paul, 239
Devlin, 282
Disabled Persons Act (Canada), 299
Distant Early Warning Line, 282
Distribution of income, 234-43, 248
 in Canada, 234-6
 effect of taxation, 236
 in Marxist theory, 241-3
 in orthodox theory, 240
 and welfare system, 242-3
Dome Petroleum, 284
Dominican Republic, 335
 unrest over price hikes, 373
Dominion Stores, 251
Drury, Bud, 286
Durable goods, market saturation of, 330
Dye, Kenneth, 123

East Germany, 320
Economic Council of Canada, 25
Economic Development,
 Canadian Ministry of State for, 204
Economic policy, see also
 Canadian economy; economic theory; employment; incomes policy; state, role of; taxation; unemployment.
 in British Columbia, 138-41
 in Canada, 32, 87-9, 90-3, 116, 117
 on Canadian money supply, 115-6
 and exchange rates, 181-2
 and full employment, 32, 325
 and private enterprise, 32
 and the state, 31-2
 and unemployment, 24-7
 in U.S., 32
Economic recovery, prospects for, 356-7, 379
Economic Recovery Act (U.S., 1981), 352
Economic theory,
 class divisions in, 233-4
 critique of socialism, 46
 on depressions, 52-3
 and the environment, 59-60
 and the free market, 46-7, 56-8, 106, 233
 function of, 20
 and ideology, 19-20
 and monetarism, 105
 nature of, 19-20
 and the poor, 51
 profits in, 21-4
 symmetry of capital and labour, 22
 tenets of orthodox, 46
 treatment of capital, 21-4
 view of the state, 47
 and the worker, 20-1
Eldorado Nuclear, 349
Employment, see also full
 employment; unemployment
 guaranteed, 383-4
 job consultation, 221
 job enlargement, 216, 221-2
 job enrichment, 216-221
 job redesign, 215-8
 job rotation, 216, 221
 and labour force participation, 133-4
 and profit-sharing, 214-5, 226-7
 and public debt, 150

and worker alienation, 209-10
and worker participation, 212-3
and worker representation, 213-4
Employment and Income, Canadian White Paper on (1945), 32, 87
Engels, Friedrich, 233
Environmental conservation and renewal, 384-5
Ethiopia, 335

Fairweather, Gordon, 139
Federal Reserve Bank (U.S.), 136, 373
Feldstein, Martin, 135
Finance, Canadian Department of, 123-5, 136, 202-6 passim
Financial Post, 88
Flannagan, R., 168
Fleming, D.M., 92
Flyer Industries bus company, 284
Ford Automobile Co., 223
Foreign Investment Review Agency (FIRA), 118, 198, 350
Fortune Magazine, 26
Fowke, Vernon, 282
France, 193, 206, 213, 214-5, 318, 320, 353
  car ownership in, 330
  effects of automation, 363
  Mitterrand government, 206, 326, 350, 381
  strikes in, 327
  trade unions in, 321
France, Anatole, 14
Fraser Institute, 137, 138
Free trade
  affect on Canadian imports, 199-200
  battle against in Canada, 30
  J.M. Keynes on, 29

managed trade as alternative, 200-1
and the NDP, 30
problems with theory of, 28-30
with U.S. pursued by Canada, 117
French, Richard, 203, 205, 206
Friedberg, Albert, 374
Friedman, Milton, 25, 99, 105-6, 108, 130
Fryer, Richard, 266
Full employment
  commitment to, 316
  consequences of sustained, 179
  and economic policy, 32
  legislation, 85-6
  as a policy, 325
  and strength of working class, 154
Full Employment Bill (1946, U.S.), 32, 85

Galbraith, John Kenneth, 4, 56, 80, 145
Gallagher, John, 235
Garcia, Alan, 373
General Electric Co., 359
General Foods, 217
General Motors Co., 245, 268, 360
General Workers Confederation (Dominican Republic), 373
Ghana, 335
Gilder, George, 119
Gillespie, Alistair, 203
Gillispie, Irwin, 92-3, 125
Gladstone, William Ewart, 288
Godwin, William, 50
Goodwin, Ginder, 293
Gordon, Myron, 145
Gordon, H. Scott, 92
Gordon, Walter, 92, 145, 203, 320
Goulart, Joav, 335

Index 415

Gramm-Rudman Bill (1985, U.S.)
Gramsci, Antonio, 16, 313
Granatstein, Jack, 89
Grand Trunk railway company, 284
Gray, Herb, 203, 204
Great Britain, 351, 354
  and destruction of Indian textile industry, 28
  employment policies under Churchill, 86
  and free trade, 28
  inflation rate, 183
  Labour government, 170-1, 172
  strikes in, 327
  Thatcher government, 15, 172, 344, 346, 349, 353, 379, 380
  trade unions in, 170-1, 172, 321-2
Greater London Council, 387
Grenada, U.S. invasion of, 15
Guaranteed Income Supplement (Canada), 299
Guatemala, 335
Guineau-Bissau, 335
Gulf Canada, 121

Halliday, Fred, 335
Hanisch, Ted, 181
Hanson, Alvin, 94
Hardin, Herschel, 284
Harrington, Michael, 102
Harris, Walter, 92
Harrison, George Allen, 134
Harrod, Roy, 145
Hayek, F.A., 99, 112, 130, 131
Hedborg, Anna, 137
Heilbroner, Robert, 30
Heinrichs, H.W., 62
Hitachi, 359
Hitler, Adolf, 79
Honduras, 380

Hong King, 191
Horner, Jack, 203
Howe, C.D., 285, 286, 287, 319, 320
Hudson Bay Company, 279, 280
Hudson Bay Mining and Smelting, 348
Hunter, H.T., 88
Hussein, King, 335
Hyde Park Agreement, 281-2
Hydro-Quebec, 285
Hyman, Richard, 266

Ibn Khaldun, 119
Ideology, *see also* social consent
  capitalist, 15-7
  and class structure, 6-10 passim
  and distribution of income, 234
  and economic theory, 19-20
  and education, 13
  Heilbroner on, 30
  and the media, 13-4
  and nationalism, 15
  nature of, 3
  in political discourse, 3-4
  proletarian, 17-8
  role of family in, 13
  shifts with policy changes, 312
Ilsley, J.L., 92
Imperial Oil, 121, 161
Inco, 348
Income maintenance programs and unemployment, 133-4
Incomes policy, 311, *see also* by country name.
  Austria, 175
  breakdown of, in latter half of 60s, 171
  in Canada, 163-6, 184-8 passim
  and corporations, 179
  effectiveness of, 168, 188
  history of, in Europe, 169-77
  in Netherlands, 169-70, 173

and Post-Keynesians, 178-9
and problem of social
consensus, 179, 180-1
results of, in Europe, 183
from 70s to early 80s, 171
and trade unions, 180-1 passim
in West Germany, 176
India, 28, 191
Industrial Disputes and
Investigations Act (1902,
Canada), 293
Industrial policy and corporate
power, 206-297
Industrial strategy needed for
Canada, 189
Industry, Trade and Commerce,
Canadian Department of, 202,
204
Inflation, 338-40, 354, *see also*
by country name.
and arms race, 128
blamed on worker demands,
98
and budget deficits, 151
in Canada, 186
and Canadian interest rates,
116
causes of, 97, 126-7
effects of government policy
on, 129-30
factors in, 127
inversely related to
unemployment, 97-8
and Korean War, 169
and money supply, 128-30
and monopoly, 127-8
nature of, in past 30 years,
126
in Post-Keynesian theory, 147-
8, 155-7
and trade unions, 179-80
and unemployment, 154-56
passim

Interest rates
and budget deficits, 148-50
effects on Canadian economy,
116
International Labour
Organization, 367
International Monetary Fund,
172, 369, 372-4 passim
International trade, 324, 330, *see
also* by country name.
Investment, 324, 342, 344, 355-6
Iran, 335
Iraq, 335
Israel, 335
Italy, 318, 337
Communist Party, 318
growth of exports, 332
Mitterrand government, 206,
326, 350, 381
Socialist Party, 318
strikes in, 327
trade unions in, 321

Jaguar, 349
Jamaica, 335
James Bay Project, 282
Jamieson, Don, 203
Japan, 133, 192-3, 200, 319, 320,
336, 337, 348, 351, 358
economic competition from,
332-3
effects of automation, 363
against free trade, 29
importance of exports, 168
Japanese League of Employers,
321
Johnson, Harry, 21
Johnson, Lyndon B., 102, 333,
337
Johnston, Donald, 4, 5, 6, 186
Johnston, William, 9
Jordan, 335
*Journal of Post-Keynesian
Economics*, 145

Kahn, Lord, 79
Kaiser Aluminum, 348
Kaldor, Nicholas, 131, 145
Kalecki, Michael, 81-2, 85, 93-4, 134, 145
Kapp, K. William, 63
Kaufmann, Henry, 376
Kennan, George, 317
Kennedy, John F., 102, 335
Kent, Tom, 203
Kerr, Clark, 101
Keynes, John Maynard, 24, 56, 73-84 passim, *see also* Keynesianism.
  and authoritarian state, 79
  breaks with orthodoxy, 73-4
  contradictions in, 81-2
  criticism of his theories, 81-4
  dislike of capitalism, 80
  effect of Depression on, 73-4
  on free trade, 29
  his *General Theory of Employment, Interest and Money*, 53, 74, 79, 81, 326
  and inflation, 77-8
  and interest rates, 76
  paraphrased, 374
  and private investment, 76
  and savings, 75
  and Say's law, 39
  and state intervention, 74, 76-7
  supports Lloyd George, 74
  on trade unions, 74, 78-9
  on unemployment, 79
  view of economic theory, 31
  vision of full employment capitalism, 78-80, 81
  and wage controls, 78-9
Keynesianism, *see also* Post-Keynesians
  becomes new orthodoxy, 94-7
  common point with monetarism, 205
  as distortion of Keyne's vision, 94-6
  as dominant theory, 45
  in economic policy, 93-4
  end of, 99-100
  not put to test, 325
King, Mackenzie, 89, 281, 286, 290-1, 292
Klein, Lawrence, 196
Kondratieff, Nicolai, 301
Kondratieff wave, 301
Korea, 191, 192
Kuhn, Thomas, 44, 45
Kuttner, Robert, 27, 145

Labour, Canadian Department of, 298
Laffer, Arthur, 119
Laidlaw Lumber Company, 216, 217
Lamontagne, Maurice, 203
Laxer, James, 145, 162
Lebanon, 335
Less Developed Countries, 356
Lévesque, René, 285
Liberalism in its heyday in early 60s, 100-1
Liberal Party (Canada), 286
  borrows from CCF program, 100
  on incomes policy, 163-4
Libya, 335, 380
Light, W.F., 234
Lindblom, Charles, 11, 34
List, Frederick, 28
List, Wilfred, 217
Lithwick, 282
LTV Steel Company, 346

McBride, Stephen, 299
McCallum, John, 145, 184
McDermott, Dennis, 299
Macdonald, Donald S., 37
Macdonald, John A., 281

Macdonald Royal Commission on
  the Economic Union, 37-43,
  42-3, 184, 354, 387
Machinery
  and profits, 245-6, 305,
  role in capitalism, 308-10
Maclean-Hunter, 138
MacMillan Bloedel, 121
McNaughton, Andrew, 290
Macpherson, C.B., 278
Maizels, Alfred, 190
Major Capital Projects to the
  Year 2000, Task Force on,
  204-5
Malaysia, 191
Malthus, Thomas, 50
Managed trade, see free trade.
Management rights, 261-2
Mandel, Ernest, 339
Manitoba, 284, 285, 286, 296, 298
  health and safety inspection
    in, 62
  NDP government, 122
Manitoba Political Economy
  Group, 387
Manoil, 286
Marketing boards, 283
Marshall, Alfred, 262
Marshall Plan, 321
Marx, Karl, 63-70 passim, 233,
  307-10
  analysis of capitalism, 65, 67-9
  on capitalist circuit, 302-3
  his *Communist Manifesto*, 65,
    67
  on currency values, 338
  early career, 63
  impact of, 69-70
  mode of analysis, 64-6
  on monopoly, 268
  and survival of capitalism, 15-
    6
  theory of consent, 10-1

Marxism
  history of in 20th century, 69-
    70
  and working class gains under
    capitalism, 36
Maslow, Abraham, 210
Massey-Ferguson, 284
Media and social consensus, 13-4
Medicare (Canada), 299
Mellon, Andrew, 119
Menzies, Heather, 366
Merritt, William Hamilton, 284
Mexico, 192, 200, 370
  effects of loan default, 373
Michelin Bill (Nova Scotia), 297
Miliband, Ralph, 287
Mill, John Stuart
  on distribution of wealth, 54
  his *Principles of Political
    Economy*, 53-6
  reformer of capitalism, 54-6
  on state intervention, 54-5
Mills, C. Wright, 266
Mills, Edwin, 227
Mitterrand, François, 206, 326,
  350, 381
Monetarism
  and budget deficits, 110
  in Canada, 107, 114-8
  in Chile, 130
  common point with
    Keynesianism, 205
  criticism of, 131-2
  defenses of, 131
  and effects of demand
    management, 111-2
  and finance capital, 132
  and free market, 130
  on inflation, 106, 107, 109-113
    passim
  and interest rates, 132
  and money supply, 109-13, 131
  and optimal use of resources,
    109

and productions costs, 133
and productive capacity, 133
and profits, 132-3
and public sector, 113-4
side-effects of, 132-3
and social justice, 130
strengthens state power, 114
in Third World countries, 372-4
on trade unions, 106, 111-2
on unemployment, 111-3
view of equality, 106
view of government, 108-9
and wages, 133
Monopoly, 267-74
in Canada, 267-8, 271
and pricing process, 273
and profits, 246
Monthly Review
Montreal, 279
Morgan Guaranty Trust, 358
Moritu, Akio, 359
Morris, Jacob, 339
Mozambique, 335
Mulholland, W.D., 132
Mulroney government
deregulation, 351
divestment, 349, 350
electoral base, 379
elite links, 287
free trade, 27
meshes legitimacy and accumulation, 299
reduces social welfare outlays, 354
taxes rich, 17
Multinationals, *see also* Canadian economy.
world products, 352
Murdoch, Rupert, 345

National Association of Manufacturers (U.S.), 85

National Council on Welfare (Canada) 255
National Energy Program (NEP), 388
National Film Board, 286
Nationalization, 349, 382, *see also* state, role of.
National Labour Relations Board (U.S.), 347, 351
National Pension Fund (Sweden), 137
National Policy, 280-1
National Research Council, 283
National savings rate, 137
NCR Corporation of Canada, 214
Nelles, H.V., 285, 286
Neo-conservatives, *see* New Right.
Netherlands, 213, 353-4
incomes policy, 173
inflation rate, 183
strikes in, 327
unemployment rate, 183
New Democratic Party, see also by province.
on bank nationalization, 161
on FIRA, 161
on free trade, 30
on grants to corporations, 161
on incomes policy, 163
on job security, 161
on job training, 161
on Petro-Canada, 161
Post-Keynesian outlook, 160, 162
on production agreements, 160-1
proposals for Crown corporations, 161-2
Waffle movement, 159-60
New Right, 126, 137, 141-2, 379
Post-Keynesian criticisms of, 153-4
New York *Times*, 380

Nicaragua, 192, 335, 380
Nielsen, Frank, 283
Nielson, Robert, 220
Nightingale, Donald, 211, 212
Nixon, Richard M., 334
NORAD Agreement, 282
Northern Transportation, 349
Northland Bank, 378
North-South Institute, 375
Norway, 213, 217
 inflation rate, 183
 unemployment rate, 183
Nova Scotia, 284, 296, 297

O'Connor, James, 275
Occupational Safety and Health Administration (U.S.), 351
Oil
 crisis, 329-30, 334
 prices, 330, 334
Oil, Chemical and Atomic Workers Union, 217
Old-Age Pension Act (Canada), 289
Old-Age Security (Canada), 299
Ontario, 281, 282, 286, 296, 298
 employment in high-tech industries 368
 Labour Ministry, 213
Ontario Development Corporation, 350
Ontario Hydro, 286
Ontario Public Service Employees Union, 387
OPEC, 330, 335, 336, 338, 370
Organization for Economic Cooperation and Development (OECD), 180
Ornstein, Michael, 9
Ouellet, André, 298

Pacific Great Eastern, 285

Palestine Liberation Organization, 335
Panitch, Leo, 291
Parrot, Jean Claude, 5, 6, 222
Pépin, Jean-Luc, 203
Peru, 335, 373
Petro-Canada, 161, 286, 350
Philippines, 191
Phillips, A.W., 25, 98
Phillip's curve, 98
Plant closures
 in Canada, 350
 legislation, 384
Pocklington, Peter, 239
Poland, 320
Popper, Karl, 19
Porter, John, 6
Portugal, 28, 335
Post-capitalism, theories of, 101
Post-Keynesians
 acknowledge need for monetarist policies, 178
 and Canada-U.S. free trade
 on capitalist crises, 177
 criticism of monetarism, 147-8
 criticism of New Right, 153-4
 and demand management, 177, 178
 divide industry into two sectors, 155
 and European experience, 177-83
 and full employment, 177
 on incomes policy, 178-9
 and industrial policy, 207
 and inflation, 147-8, 155-7, 177-8
 liberal model of, 162
 "misery rate", 154
 on nature of government deficits, 148-51, 152
 need for new system of industrial relations, 209

and NDP, 160, 162
problems in theories of, 177-83
rejection of Keynesian fine-
   tuning, 152
on relations of labour and
   capital, 153, 381
on relations of unemployment
   and inflation, 155-6
social democratic model of, 162
and state intervention, 145-6
and trade unions, 146-7, 156-7
views of modern capitalism,
   146-7
Poverty discovered in 60s, 102
Prince Edward Island, 296
Private debt, 338, 377-8
Privy Council Office (PCO), 202-
   5 passim
Productivity in Canada, 220
Profits,
   decline of, 305-6, 338-9
   factors in, 246-8
   in Marxist theory, 244, 246
   nature of, 244-5
   of oil companies, 330
   rate of, 323-4, 341-2, 354
   risk-taking and, 246
   tendency for the rate of, to
      fall, 309-10
Program Review, Canadian Task
   Force on, 354
Public debt
   and arms spending, 150
   in Canada compared to other
      countries, 148
   causes of, 148-51
   "crowds out" private sector,
      134-5
Public expenditures, *see also*
   state, role of.
   efforts to limit, 33
   role of, 134-5

Quality of Working Life, 210-228,
   see also employment; trade
   unions; worker.
Quebec, 215, 281, 285, 296, 298
Quebec Solidarity Fund, 215

Radio Corporation of America
   (RCA), 359
Rand, Justice, 294-5
Rand Corporation, 363
Raw materials, price boom of,
   329-30
Ray, Michael, 283
Reagan, Ronald, 344, 359, 379,
   380
   economic policies, 377
   effect of tax cuts, 135
   revises tax system, 352-3
Regional Economic Expansion,
   Canadian Department of, 202
Reich, Robert, 145, 147, 157,
   192
Reimer, Neil, 222
Ricardo, David, 64, 232
   on free trade, 28
Richard, William, 235
Richardson, 286
Robbins, Lionel, 29, 53
Roberts, Wayne, 222
Robertson, Gideon, 289
Robinson, Jean, 23, 84, 145
Rockefeller, John, 286
Roosevelt, Franklin D., 79
Rotstein, Abraham, 145, 147-8
Rupert's Land, 280

Safeway Stores, 251, 268
St. Laurent, Louis, 160, 286, 319
St. Lawrence water system,
   279, 282
Samuelson, Paul, 98-9
Saskatchewan, 285, 286, 290, 296
Saskatchewan Potash
   Corporation, 387

Sask Oil, 286
Sass, Bob, 62
Saturday Night Magazine, 87, 89
Say, J.B., 52
Say's law, 39
Schmidt, Helmut, 176
Schott, Kerry, 145
Schumpeter, Joseph, 19, 53
Science Council of Canada, 145, 152, 190, 192, 195, 197, 198, 199, 205, 388
Science and Technology, Canadian Ministry of State for, 363
Self-sufficiency, economic, 385
Senior, Nassau, 50-1
Sharp, Mitchell, 287
Shell Canada, 121
Shell Chemical, 217
Shonfield, Andrew, 205
Singapore, 191
Skalbania, Nelson, 239
Smith, Adam
  according to Milton Friedman, 105-6
  on acquisitiveness, 49
  on conflict of capital and labour, 48-9
  and free market, 47-8
  and free trade, 278
  on the state, 32-3, 48
  his *Wealth of Nations*, 47-50 passim
Social consent
  and belief in equality, 14-5
  and the Macdonald Report, 43
  mobilization of, 12-4
  and pragmatic acceptance, 10-2
  theories of, 10-7
Socialism, 381, 383

Socialist Party
  of France, 318
  of Italy, 318
Social ownership, 383
Social Planning Council of Metro Toronto, 254
Soviet Union, 336, 380
Spain, 387
Spinney, G.W., 88
Stagflation, 99
Stanfield, Robert, 185
Stapleton, Richard G., 113
State, role of
  according to Adam Smith, 32-3
  in capital accumulation, 282-4
  under capitalism, 275-300 passim
  conflicts over, under capitalism, 312-3
  as contemporary quandry, 382
  effect of, on profits, 331
  governed by "logic of capitalism", 310-3
  in incomes policy, 311
  in industrial strategy, 201
  interventionism, 54-8 passim, 97, 146
  in Macdonald Report, 38
  in market regulation, 311
  in Marxist theory, 34
  in mercantilism, 278-9
  in monetarist theory, 106
  in planning of aggregates, 385
  post-Keynesian views on, 152
  and private enterprise, 32-3
  in profit restoration, 344
  in public ownership in Canada, 284-6
  in recent history, 324-5
  in reproducing labour power, 311
  in social expenditures, 275-7, 311-2, 331, 353-4
  in social welfare, 288-92

and state-owned enterprises, 270-1, 349-50
for supply-siders, 141-2
views on, in economic life, 166-7
Statistics Canada, 254
Stelco, 121
Supply-side economics, 105, 118-20, 135-7, *see also* taxation.
in Canada, 120-25 passim
contrasted with monetarism, 120
Supreme Court (U.S.), 347
Surplus value, 67, 302, 309, 310, *see also* profits.
Sweden, 79, 137, 200, 213, 215, 216, 387
inflation rate, 183
its labour-market policy, 155
Meidner plan, 174-5, 215
Social Democrats, 174-5
stance of corporations, 174, 181
unemployment rate, 183
Switzerland, 320
Sydney Steel Co., 284
Syncrude, 198
Syria, 335

Taiwan, 191, 192
Tarling, Roger, 172-3
Taxation
of Canadian corporations, 120-5 passim
of Canadian personal income, 122-5 passim
effect on economy, 135-7
Reagan tax cuts, 135
restructuring of, 353
role of, in supply-side economics, 118-20
Tax Reform Act (1986, U.S.), 352

Taylor, Fredrich Winslow, 210, 263-4
Taylor, Harriet, 54
Technology, *see also* automation.
and labour discipline, 263
and productivity, 323
and profits, 246-7
revolution in, 355
stagnation in American, 328-9
state as promoter of, 310-1
Teleglobe, 349
Thatcher, Margaret, 172, 344, 346, 349, 353, 379, 380
and Falklands War, 15
Thayer, Paul, 380
Third World,
capital flight from, 371
debt problems, 334, 369-75
rebellion in, 335
Thurow, Lester, 145
Timbec Forest Products, 214
Time Magazine, 370
Times (London), 82-3
Toronto Stock Exchange, 237-8
Towers, Graham, 89-90
Trade unions, 251, 261-3, 321-2, 345-9 passim, *see also* by country.
in Austria, 175
in Canada, 89, 118, 219-20, 293-300, 348
and concentration of capital, 311
concessions to, 168-9
demand new social contract, 171-2
in Great Britain, 170-1, 172
growth of, 328
on incomes policy, 164, 180-1 passim
and industrial democracy, 211-2
and inflation, 156-7, 179-80
influence of, 187-8

in Macdonald Report, 38
　　in monetarist theory, 111-2
　　in Netherlands, 169-70, 173
　　in orthodox economic theory, 53
　　power position of, 264-7
　　and profit-sharing, 215
　　and quality of working life, 211-3, 225, 227-8
　　and strikes, 219-20
　　in Sweden, 170, 173-5
　　in U.S., 295-6, 322
　　in West Germany, 176
　　and worker representation, 222-8
　　after WWII, 218-9
Tripartism, 182, 187, *see also* state, role of.
Trist, Eric, 210-1
Trudeau, Pierre Elliot, 102, 185, 202, 233-4
Tucker, Robert, 380
Turk, Jim, 350
Turner, John, 122, 124, 163, 287

Ulman, L., 168
Unemployment, 79, 289, 290-1, 301-2, 320, 341, 354, *see also* by country.
　　and automation, 363-9 passim
　　in British Columbia, 140
　　and economic policy, 24-7
　　in economic theory, 24-7
　　and full employment, 24
　　and Great Depression, 316
　　and inflation, 97-8, 154-6 passim
　　insurance, 133-4
　　and Macdonald Report, 39-40
　　in monetarist theory, 111-3
Unemployment Insurance Program (Canada), 299
United Auto Workers, 348
United Farm Workers, 251

– United Fruit Co., 335
United States
　　currency revaluation, 334
　　Department of Health, Education and Welfare, 209
　　economic hegemony, 317-8 passim, 332-6
　　interest rates, 357, 358
　　interventionism, 380
　　Johnson Administration, 102, 333, 337
　　Kennedy Administration, 102, 335
　　military expenditures, 333, 357
　　Nixon Administration, 334
　　public debt, 357
　　Reagan Administration, 135, 344, 352-3, 359, 377, 379, 380
　　trade deficit, 358-9
　　value of dollar, 357-9 passim
United Steel Workers, 346, 348
Uruguay, 335

VIA Rail, 350
Vietnam, 333, 335, 337, 380
Volvo, 216

Wages, *see also* incomes policy.
　　in Canada, 110, 185
　　and class, 259-61
　　controls on, 297
　　determination of, 248-61
　　and discriminating factors, 251-3
　　and economic breakdown, 304-5
　　and inflation, 156
　　and labour market, 249-51
　　low, 320
　　and productivity, 328
　　Marx on, 308
　　and profits, 246-8, 305, 306

in service sector, 331, 361
and skills, 253
squeezed in crisis, 346-7
wage-price spiral, 156, 328
and women, 251-2
after WWII, 322-3
Wagner Act (1936, U.S.), 85
Walker, Michael, 137, 138
Welfare state, 97, see also state, role of.
in Canada, 88, 89, 100, 299-300, 331
Macdonald Report, 38-40 passim
and Marxism, 59
Weintraub, Sidney, 145, 156
Welland Canal Co., 284
Wells, Don, 224
Westell, Dan, 238
West Germany, 151, 193, 213, 318, 337, 354, 357
automation, 363
economic miracle, 176
export growth, 324, 332
incomes policy, 176
inflation rate, 183
strikes in, 327
trade unions in, 176, 218-9, 321
tripartism, 176
unemployment rate, 183
Wheat Board (Canada), 283
Wheat production, 329
Whitaker, Reg, 279
Wilhelm I, Kaiser, 288
Wilkinson, Bruce, 145
Wilkinson, Frank, 172-3
Wilson, Charles, 119
Wilson, Michael, 4, 124
Windmuller, John, 175
Winnipeg City Hydro, 285
Winnipeg Free Press, 87
Winnipeg General Strike (1919), 219, 288, 293

Winters, Robert, 286
Workers
alienation, 209-10
control, 383
health hazards of, 61-3
their labour as commodity, 302
and labour contract, 244
and labour costs, 327, 355
and power, 262-3
and profits, 245-8 passim
in public sector, 331
representation, 213
and scientific management, 263-4
sources of, after WWII, 320
supervision of, 327
unrest among, 318, 327
and worker effort, 261-6
Workers Unity League, 290
World Bank, 369, 372
Wright, Erik Olin, 7, 8, 9

Zuckerman, Mortimer, 348